1001 days out
with your
kids

1001 days out
with your kids

p

This is a Parragon Book
First Published in 2005

Parragon
Queen Street House
4 Queen Street
Bath BA1 1HE, UK

All the information given in this book has come directly
from the attractions included and was correct at the time
of going to press. The Publishers will be grateful for any
information that will assist in keeping future editions up
to date. While every care has been taken in the preparation
of this book, neither the Compilers nor the Publishers
can accept any liability for any consequences arising from
the use thereof, or the information contained therein.
The prices, times and facilities given should be used as
a guide only as they will vary with time.

ISBN 1-40544-412-6

Designed by Butler and Tanner
Printed in China

Front cover
Cover images courtesy of Britain on View, © brand x pictures,
Colliford Lake Park
Frontispiece
The London Eye
Right
Durdle Door, Dorset

IMPORTANT NOTE FOR THE READER

We have made every effort to ensure the information in this
guide is accurate and up to date, but things do change very
quickly. Prices and opening times are sometimes altered at
short notice, and sadly some venues close unexpectedly. We
would therefore urge readers to TELEPHONE THE VENUE
BEFORE SETTING OUT ON A VISIT. This will ensure that you
are aware of any changes in ticket prices or opening times,
and will avoid unexpected disappointments or problems.

The contents of this book are believed correct at the time of
printing. The Publisher cannot be held responsible for any errors,
omissions or changes in the information in this guide or for the
consequences of any reliance on the information provided.

Contents

Introduction

Welcome to the third edition of *1001 Days Out with Your Kids*. Revised, with updated information and a wealth of brand new entries, this book will give you fresh ideas for places to visit throughout the year and no matter what the weather, as well as giving you up-to-date information on famous attractions.

There is an amazing variety of places in Britain that can capture a child's imagination. They can be educational, inspirational, or just plain fun!

Attractions range from crumbling castles surrounded by magnificent moats to wildlife parks teeming with fabulous creatures; from exciting river journeys and railway trips to fascinating collections of old vehicles; from beautiful country parks with children's nature trails to theme and adventure parks packed with breathtaking rides for even the biggest 'kids'. We have also included a range of museums where you will find displays on everything from children's writers to Viking warriors.

Children's imaginations are captured by the most unexpected things at times so in order to provide ideas and inspiration for even the most difficult to please we have tried to present the widest possible selection of attractions.

Whatever day out you choose, don't forget to phone the venue and check the details before setting out.

Most of all, enjoy your days out with the kids!

About this guide

This guide covers England, Scotland (including the Northern and Western Islands) and Wales and is arranged in regions, shown on the national map on page viii. The counties within each region, the towns within each county and the attractions within each town are all, where possible, arranged alphabetically (we have taken the occassional licence with the running order to enable us to include the best images). Each attraction also has a reference number and this is used on the regional map at the beginning of each section.

Understanding the entries

Coloured bands at the top of each page indicate regions; the numbers in the top corners next to the regional name refer to the numbered range of attractions on the page. The nearest major town or village to the attraction is indicated above the name of the attraction.

Quick reference icons

an all-weather attraction

an attraction for sunny days only

1 hr + the expected duration of your visit

Apr–Oct when the attraction is open

Description

Each entry has a brief description of the attraction and a flavour of what visitors may expect to find. Additional features are also highlighted beneath the description.

Facilities

WC toilet facilities available

 space available for you to eat your own food

restaurant, café or kiosk facilities available

good access for wheelchairs   restricted access

dogs allowed, but they may have to be kept on a lead

Disabled visitors

Visitors with mobility difficulties should look for the wheelchair symbol showing where all or most of the attraction is accessible to wheelchair bound visitors. We strongly recommend that visitors telephone in advance of a visit to check exact details, including access to toilets and refreshment facilities. Assistance dogs are usually accepted unless stated otherwise. For the hard of hearing, please check that hearing induction loops are available by contacting the attraction itself.

Location

These are simple directions, usually for motorists (although directions are given for those using the Underground in London) and have been provided by the attraction itself.

Opening times

These times are inclusive, e.g. Apr–Oct indicates that the attraction will be open from the beginning of April to the end of October. Where an attraction has varied opening times, these are indicated; and if it is open seven days a week, this is simply referred to as 'Daily'. Bank Holiday opening is indicated where provided by the attraction. If you are travelling a long way please check with the attraction itself to ensure any unexpected circumstances are not going to prevent your entry.

Admission

Wherever possible the charges quoted are for the 2004–5 season, but please note that prices are subject to change and are only correct at the time of going to print. If no price is quoted, it does not mean that a charge will not be made. Many places that do not charge admission may ask for a voluntary donation. In some instances discounts may be available to families, groups, local residents or members of certain organisations such as English Heritage and the National Trust.

Contact details

We have given details of the administrative address and telephone number for each attraction. While this is usually the details of the attraction itself, some properties are administered by an area office, in which case these details are given (several English Heritage properties fall into this category).

Telephone numbers, email and website addresses are also included wherever possible.

colour bar indicating region

nearest town to the attraction

quick reference icons

general description

additional features

reference number on regional map

facilities available

detailed information: location, opening times, admission prices, contact details

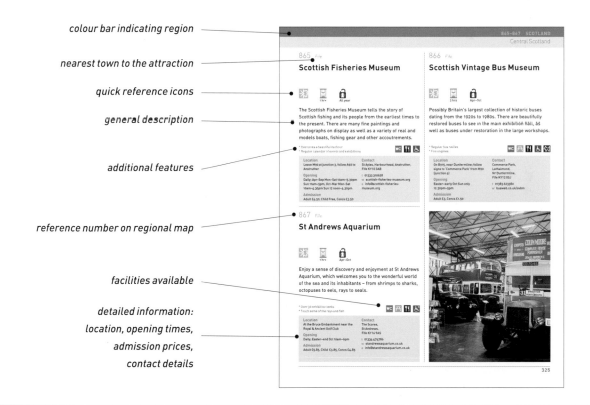

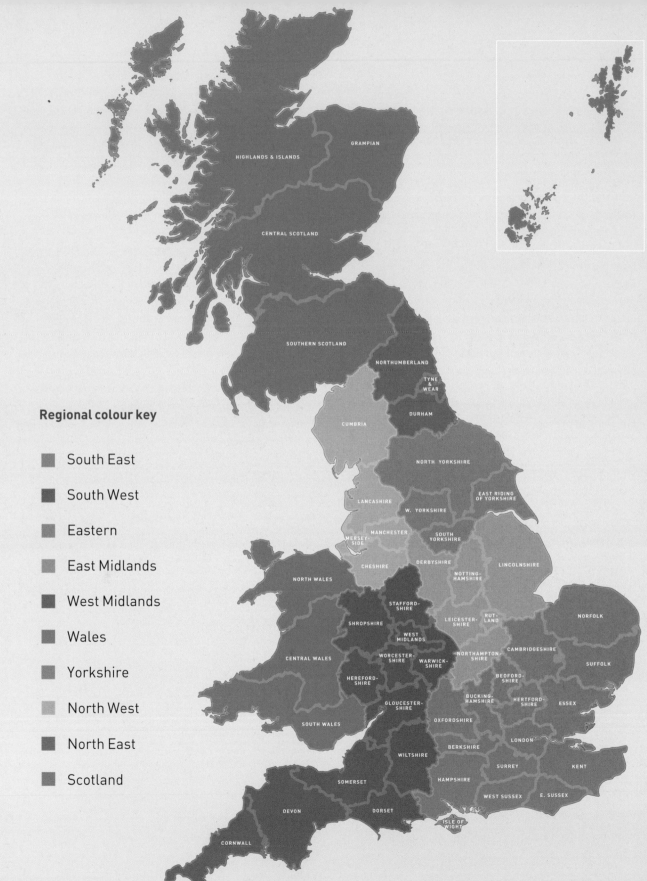

Regional colour key

- South East
- South West
- Eastern
- East Midlands
- West Midlands
- Wales
- Yorkshire
- North West
- North East
- Scotland

Brighton, East Sussex

South East

Berkshire Buckinghamshire East Sussex
Hampshire and Isle of Wight Kent London
Oxfordshire Surrey West Sussex

001 Newbury

The Living Rainforest

1 hr+   All year

Experience the sights, sounds and smells of a rainforest under glass at this unique conservation area. There is something for everyone here including special children's activities and art workshops.

* Adopt an animal
* Events for all ages

Location
Clearly signed from junction 13 of the M4

Opening
Daily 10am–5.15pm
(last admission 4.30pm)

Admission
Phone for details or check website

Contact
Hampstead Norreys RG18 0TN

t 01635 202444
w livingrainforest.org
e enquiries@livingrainforest.org

002 Reading

Beale Park

4 hrs   Easter–Oct

Beale Park is dedicated to the conservation of rare birds. There is something for everyone, ranging from gentle walks to madcap adventure play areas.

* Meerkat & wallaby enclosures and pets' corner
* Splash pool & miniature golf for children

Location
6 miles from Reading on the A329 between Pangbourne & Streatley

Opening
Daily; Easter–Oct 10am–6pm

Admission
Adult £6, Child £4, Concs £5

Contact
Lower Basildon,
Reading RG8 9NH

t 0118 984 5172
w bealepark.co.uk
e administration@bealepark.co.uk

003 Windsor

Legoland Windsor

4 hrs+   Mar–Nov

A land where creativity meets fun, Legoland Windsor has more than 50 rides and attractions based around exhilarating activity areas and surrounded by extensive gardens and parkland.

* Spectactular lego models
* Daily shows

Location
2 miles from Windsor town centre on the B3022 Bracknell–Windsor road

Opening
Please phone or visit the website for details

Admission
Please phone or visit the website

Contact
Winkfield Road
Windsor SL4 4AY
t 0870 504 0404
w legoland.co.uk

004 Windsor

Windsor Castle

2 hrs+   All year

This is an official residence of the Queen and the largest occupied castle in the world. It has been a royal palace and fortress for over 900 years. The castle and grounds cover 13 acres and include a magnificent castle.

* Changing programme of events, including concerts
* Visit Queen Mary's dolls' house, a miniature mansion

Location
Follow brown signs to central Windsor

Opening
Daily; Mar–Oct 9.45am–5.15pm
Nov–Feb 9.45am–4.15pm
Closed 25, 26 Dec

Admission
Please phone for details

Contact
Ticket Sales and Information Office,
The Official Residences of The Queen,
London SW1A 1AA
t 0207 766 7304
w royal.gov.uk
e information@royalcollection.org.uk

005 Wokingham

California Country Park

1 hr+   All year

This park offers fishing and walks around a scenic lake. It contains an area of heathland and an ancient bog, which is a Site of Special Scientific Interest.
A countryside events programme runs all year.

* Conservation Award for management of SSSI 2002
* New café, toy shop & paddling pool

Location
Join Nine Mile Ride from the A321, B3016 or A3095

Opening
Daily; Please phone for details

Admission
Free, Car park £1
(weekends & holidays)

Contact
Nine Mile Ride, Finchampstead,
Wokingham RG40 4HT
t 0118 934 2016
w wokingham.gov.uk
e countryside@wokingham.gov.uk

006 Wokingham

Dinton Pastures Country Park

2 hrs+   All year

Dinton Pastures Country Park is a 400-acre mosaic of rivers, lakes, meadows and wooded areas for visitors to explore. Countryside events are organised throughout the year, including butterfly and bird walks, pond dips for children and activity days.

Location
Off the A329, Reading–Wokingham road. 15 mins' walk from Winnersh station

Opening
Daily; summer opening at 8am (closing times vary); winter opening 8am (main car park closes 6pm)

Admission
£1. Free car park (summer, weekends & Christmas)

Contact
Davis Street, Hurst RG10 0TH
t 0118 934 2016
w wokingham.gov.uk
e countryside@wokingham.gov.uk

007 Aylesbury

Buckinghamshire Railway Centre

2 hrs+   Apr–Oct

A working steam centre where you can ride behind full-size steam engines and on the extensive miniature railway. The museum houses a large collection of locomotives, carriages and wagons.

* Steam train driving courses
* 'Day out with Thomas' events

Location
Signed from A41 nr Waddesdon & A413 at Whitchurch

Opening
Apr–Oct Wed–Sun 10.30am–4.30pm

Admission
Adult £6, Child £4, Concs £2

Contact
Quainton Road Station, Quainton, Aylesbury HP22 4BY

t 01296 655720
w bucksrailcentre.org.uk
e abaker@bucksrailcentre.
   btopenworld.com

008 Aylesbury

Bucks Goat Centre

3 hrs+   All year

A centre with examples of all the British breeds of goat as well as donkeys, pets, reptiles, llamas, wallabies, pigs and poultry. There is also a play barn with facilities for talks and seminars.

* Petting pen
* Trampoline & play centre

Location
½ mile S of Stoke Mandeville on the A4010

Opening
Daily; summer 10am–5pm, winter 10am–4pm

Admission
Adult £3.50, Child £2.50, Concs £3

Contact
Layby Farm, Old Risborough Road, Stoke Mandeville, Aylesbury HP22 5XJ

t 01296 612983
w bucksgoatcentre.co.uk
e bucksgoat@ccn.go-free.co.uk

009 Aylesbury

Tiggywinkles, The Wildlife Hospital Trust

1½ hrs+   All year

Did you know bread and milk is bad for hedgehogs? Come to the vistor centre to find out why and learn about the hundreds of sick animals the hospital cares for. Visit the gardens and wild areas to see some other permanent disabled residents (birds and badgers).

* Learn how to help wild birds in your garden
* See animals in their natural habitat

Location
Signed off the A418 from Aylesbury

Opening
Easter–Sep, Mon–Sun 10am–4pm
Oct–Easter, Mon–Fri 10am–4pm

Admission
Adult £3.80, Concs £2.80

Contact
Aston Road, Haddenham, Aylesbury HP17 8AF

t 01844 292292
w sttiggywinkles.com
e mail@sttiggywinkles.org.uk

010 Aylesbury

Oak Farm Rare Breeds Park

2 hrs   Apr–Oct

This is a small, traditional working farm with friendly farmyard animals and pets. The animals all have names and many are rare breeds.

* Play area & farm walk
* Exhibition area & hand-feeding

Location
Just off the A41, signed to Broughton. Follow brown tourist signs

Opening
Please phone for details

Admission
Adult £3, Child £2

Contact
Broughton,
Aylesbury HP22 5AW

t 01296 415709
w pebblesculpt.co.uk/oakfarm
e original@oakfarm13.freeserve.co.uk

011 Aylesbury

Roald Dahl Children's Gallery

1 hr   All year

Awaken your senses at this award-winning museum, with its innovative touchable displays and exciting programme of events. Come along and let your imagination run wild!

Location
In the old part of Aylesbury, nr town centre

Opening
Mon–Sat 10am–5pm; Sun 2pm–5pm; in term time opens 3pm
Please phone for details

Admission
Dahl Gallery: Adult £3.50, Child £2.75
Main museum: free

Contact
Church Street,
Aylesbury HP20 2QP

t 01296 331441
w buckscc.gov.uk/museum
e museum@buckscc.gov.uk

012 High Wycombe

Wycombe Museum

1 hr+   All year

Explore the history of the Wycombe district in the lively modern displays in this museum. There are hands-on activities for children and special events throughout the year.

* Superb collection of Windsor chairs
* Gardens include a Norman 'castle' mound

Location
Off A404 towards Amersham

Opening
Mon–Sat 10am–5pm; Sun 2pm–5pm
Closed Bank Hols

Admission
Free, donations appreciated

Contact
Priory Avenue,
High Wycombe HP13 6PX

t 01494 421895
w wycombe.gov.uk/museum
e museum@wycombe.gov.uk

013 Beaconsfield

Bekonscot Model Village

2 hrs   Feb–Oct

The oldest model village in the world, Bekonscot is a miniature wonderland depicting rural England in the 1930s. A gauge 1 model railway winds its way through the mini-landscape among castles, thatched cottages and a cricket match on the green.

* Sit-on railway available weekends & school holidays
* Children's play area & parties in the new log cabin

Location
Junction 2 off the M40 (near junction 16 of the M25). Follow signs to the Model Village from the A355

Opening
Daily; Feb–Oct 10am–5pm

Admission
Family (2+) £15

Contact
Warwick Road,
Beaconsfield HP9 2PL

t 01494 672919
w bekonscot.com
e info@bekonscot.co.uk

014 High Wycombe

Wycombe Summit Ski & Snowboard Centre

2 hrs   All year

The longest ski slope in England and a world-class ski and snowboard centre for all ages and abilities. Wycombe Summit has seven nursery-slope areas.

* Holiday activities
* Orienteering

Location
Between junctions 3 & 4 of the M40, just ½ hour from London

Opening
Summer Mon–Fri 10am–10pm;
Sat & Sun 10am–6pm.
Winter 10am–10pm; please phone to confirm opening dates & times

Admission
Please phone for details

Contact
Abbey Barn Lane,
High Wycombe HP10 9QQ

t 01494 474711/439099
w wycombesummit.com
e info@wycombesummit.com

East Sussex

015 Milton Keynes

Milton Keynes Museum

2 hrs   All year

Housed in a beautiful Victorian farmstead, attractions include room settings depicting Victorian and Edwardian domestic life, plus live demonstrations of cooking and printing from a bygone age.

*Jessie the shire-horse & historical shopping street
* Special events throughout the year

Location
Off McConnell Drive in Wolverton, just off the A5 & A422

Opening
Apr–Oct Wed–Sun 11am–4.30pm
Nov–Mar Sat & Sun 11am–4.30pm
Christmas opening times vary
(please phone for details)

Admission
Adult £3.50, Concs £2.50

Contact
McConnell Drive, Wolverton,
Milton Keynes MK12 5EL

t 01908 316222
w mkmuseum.org.uk
e enquiries@mkmuseum.org.uk

017 Olney

Emberton Country Park

4 hrs+   All year

A country park with 200 acres of beautiful parkland including five lakes and various children's activities, all bordered by the River Ouse. The park also includes many picnic areas.

* 2 children's play areas
* Junior fishing

Location
On the A509, 10 miles N of junction 14 off the M1, nr Milton Keynes

Opening
Daily 24 hrs
Café Apr–Oct open weekends
10am–5pm

Admission
Free. Car Park Apr–Oct £3
Nov–Mar £1.80

Contact
Emberton, Nr Olney MK46 5DB

t 01234 711575
w mkweb.co.uk/embertonpark
keynes.gov.uk

016 Battle

Battle Abbey & Battlefield

1 hr+   All year

The site of the Battle of Hastings (1066) is now home to the Discovery Centre: a fun, activity-based exhibition open to families on weekends and during school holidays. There's also a children's themed outdoor play area, a battlefield and an audio tour of the abbey.

* Site of the most famous battle in English history
* Free interactive audio tour recreates the battle

Location
In Battle, at S end of High Street.
Battle is reached by turning off A21 onto A2100 10 mins from Battle Station

Opening
Daily; Apr–Sep 10am–6pm
Oct–Oct 10am–5pm
Nov–Mar 10am–4pm;

Admission
Adult £5, Child £2.50, Concs £3.80
Phone for events prices

Contact
High St, Battle TN3 30AD

t 01424 773792
w english-heritage.org.uk

018 Brighton

Brighton Sea Life Centre

2 hrs+   All year

For a fun and educational day out visit Brighton Sea Life Centre. Walk through the Underwater Tunnel, be amazed by the fantastic Ocean Tank and get close up to sharks, rays, giant sea turtles and tropical fish. Children under 14 must be accompanied.

Location
Take the M23/A23 from London or the A27 from Portsmouth & Lewes

Opening
Daily from 10am. Please phone for details of winter opening

Admission
Adult £8.50, Child £5.50, Concs £7.50

Contact
Marine Parade,
Brighton BN2 1TB

t 01273 604234
w sealifeeurope.com
e slcbrighton@merlinentertainment.biz

019 Etchingham

Bateman's

2 hrs+   Mar–Oct

If you enjoyed *The Jungle Book* or the *Just So Stories*, then take a trip to the home of Rudyard Kipling. See original drawings of Mowgli and Shere Khan, and Kipling's study – just as he left it.

* Children's quiz
* Gardens & watermill

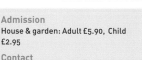

Location
Off the A265 or B2096, ½ mile S of Burwash

Opening
House: 19 Mar–30 Oct Sat–Wed
11am–5pm
Wild garden: 5–19 Mar Sat–Sun
11am–4pm; 29 Mar–30 Oct 11am–5pm

Admission
House & garden: Adult £5.90, Child £2.95

Contact
Burwash,
Etchingham TN19 7D
t 01435 882302
w nationaltrust.org.uk
e batemans@nationaltrust.org.uk

020 Bodiam

Bodiam Castle

3 hrs+   All year

Bodiam Castle is one of the most famous and atmospheric castles. Explore the spiral staircases, visit the medieval lavatories and watch out for the enemy from the battlements. You can even try on some medieval armour (please call in advance).

* Bat Pack Discovery fun pack for young children
* Walk the battlements

Location
Off the B2244, 3 miles S of Hawkhurst & 3 miles E of the A21 nr Hurst Green

Opening
1 Nov–6 Feb, Sat & Sun 10am–4pm; 7 Feb–31 Oct, daily 10am–6pm

Admission
Adult £4.20, Child £2.10

Contact
Bodiam, nr Robertsbridge,
TN32 5UA
t 01580 830436
w nationaltrust.org.uk
e bodiamcastle@nationaltrust.org.uk

021 Ditchling

Stoneywish Nature Reserve

4 hrs+   All year

Stoneywish Nature Reserve is set in 52 acres of meadows and ponds. A wildlife walk enables visitors to pass through fields to a play and picnic area.

* Pets' corner with pigs & goats

Location
Take the A23 from Brighton or London, then the B2116. Located ¼ mile E of Ditchling

Opening
Daily; summer 9.30am–5pm (last admission 4.30pm); winter 9.30am–4pm (last admission 3.30pm); closed 25, 26 Dec & 1 Jan

Admission
Adult £3.50, Child £2.50, Concs £2.50

Contact
Spatham Lane
Ditchling, Hassocks

t 01273 843498

022 Eastbourne

Drusillas Park

5 hrs   All year

Drusillas Park has more than 100 animal species in naturalistic environments including meerkats, otters, monkeys, penguins, bats and lemurs. The excellent children's play areas includes climbing, sliding and swinging fun with the penguin slide.

* Mokomos Jungle Rock & Jungle Adventure Golf
* Gold panning & Explorer's Lagoon

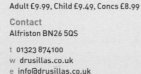

Location
Off the A27 between Lewes & Eastbourne

Opening
Daily; summer 10am–6pm; winter 10am–5pm
closed 24–26 Dec

Admission
Adult £9.99, Child £9.49, Concs £8.99

Contact
Alfriston BN26 5QS

t 01323 874100
w drusillas.co.uk
e info@drusillas.co.uk

023 Eastbourne

'How We Lived Then' Museum of Shops

1 hr+   All year

More than 100,000 exhibits of old shops, displays, and room sets depicting 100 years of shopping and social history. Stroll through Victorian-styled streets and pay a visit to the grocer, chemist and many more.

Location
Take the A22 from London or the A27 from Brighton

Opening
Daily; 10am–5.30pm; winter closing time subject to change;
closed 24–26 Dec
Please phone before visiting

Admission
Adult £3.50, Child £2.50, Concs £3

Contact
20 Cornfield Terrace
Eastbourne BN21 4NS

t 01323 737143
w how-we-lived-then.co.uk
e howwelivedthen@btconnect.com

024 Eastbourne

Treasure Island

4–6 hrs   All year

This is a children's adventure playground filled with climbing apparatus and *Treasure Island* characters. There are also trampolines, inflatable slides and remote control boats, cars and bikes.

* Paddling pools & sandpits
* 18-hole golf & indoor play area

Location
Take the A27 from Brighton or the A22 from London. Follow signs for seafront E

Opening
Park: Easter–Sep daily 10am–6pm
Golf: Daily 10am– 10pm

Admission
Park: Adult £2, Child £4
Golf: Adult £4, Child £3.50

Contact
Royal Parade,
Eastbourne BN22 7AA
t 01323 411077
w treasure-island.info
e fun@treasure–island.info

025 Exceat

Seven Sisters Country Park

4 hrs+   All year

A great location for outdoor activities, including family cycle routes, guided bike tours and canoe tuition for all abilities. Sussex Wildlife Trust offers exciting programmes for all age groups. Visit in spring to see newborn lambs on the working farm.

* Bicycle & canoe hire
* Shop selling leaflets, maps & souvenirs

Location	Contact
Off the A259 between Eastbourne and Seaford or bus 712, 713 or 714 from Eastbourne	Exceat, Seaford BN25 4AD
Opening	t 01323 870280
Daily	w www.sevensisters.org.uk
Admission	e sevensisters@southdowns-aonb.gov.uk
Free	

026 Hastings

A Smuggler's Adventure

1 hr   All year

A hands-on opportunity to learn more about the secrets of smugglers in a series of spooky caverns and passages. Find out what happened when the smugglers got caught and how they were punished!

Location	Admission
Junction 5 off the M25 & follow the A21 to Hastings. Take the A259 from Eastbourne or Rye	Adult £5.95, Child £3.95, Concs £4.95
	Contact
Opening	West Hill, Hastings TN34 3HY
Daily; Easter–Sep 10am–5.30pm; in winter 11am–4.30pm;	t 01424 444412 (bookings)
	w discoverhastings.co.uk

027 Hastings

Hastings Castle & 1066 Story

1 hr+   All year

Come to the first Norman castle in Britain. At Hastings you can enjoy a spectacular audio-visual show, The 1066 Story, in a medieval siege tent.

* ⅓ off entry to A Smuggler's Adventure when a ticket for the castle is purchased

Location	Admission
Leave the M25 at junction 5 & follow the A21 to Hastings. Take the A259 from Eastbourne or Rye	Adult £3.40, Child £2.20, Concs £2.75
	Contact
Opening	Castle Hill Road, West Hill, Hastings
Daily; Jan–Mar 11am–3.30pm; Apr–Sep 10am–5pm; Oct–Dec 10am–3.30pm; closed 24, 25 Dec	t 01424 781112
	w hastings.gov.uk
	e bookings@discoverhastings.co.uk

028 Lewes

Mohair Centre

2 hrs · All year

A children's farm with Angora goats and other farm animals. Come along and watch the lambing and kidding in the spring.

* Pre-booked holiday activity days for children
* Play area

Location
Just off the A22 between Eastbourne & East Grinstead; take the B2124 from Lewes

Opening
Sun only 11am–dusk

Admission
Adult free, Child £2.50

Contact
Lewes Road, Whitesmith, Lewes BN8 6JG

t 01825 872457
e mohaircentre@hotmail.com

029 Newhaven

Newhaven Fort

2 hrs+ · Mar–Nov

The massive ramparts, gun emplacements and tunnels fire the imagination with exciting glimpses into England's wartime past.

* Quality Assured Visitor Attraction
English Tourism Council

Location
M23/A23 from London to Brighton then follow the A27 towards Eastbourne. At Lewes follow the A26 to Newhaven. It is signed from there

Opening
Daily; Mar–early Nov 10.30am– 6pm (last admission 5pm); Nov open weekends only

Admission
Adult £5, Child £3.50, Concs £4.45

Contact
Fort Road, Newhaven BN9 9DL

t 01273 517622
w newhavenfort.org.uk
e enquiries@newhavenfort.org.uk

030 Newhaven

Paradise Park

3–6 hrs · All year

Discover 'Planet Earth' for an unforgettable experience. A unique Museum of Life, Dinosaur Safari, beautiful Water Gardens with fish and wildfowl, planthouses, themed gardens, Heritage Trail. Playzone includes crazy golf and adventure play areas.

* Fantasy Golf & Voyage of Discovery exhibition
* Children's rides & miniature railway

Location
Take the A27 Brighton/Lewes bypass, then the A26; or take the A259

Opening
Daily; 9am–6pm; closed 25, 26 Dec

Admission
Phone for details

Contact
Avis Road, Newhaven BN9 0DH

t 01273 616006 (24-hr info line)
  01273 512123
w paradisepark.co.uk
e promotions@paradisepark.co.uk

031 Sheffield Park

Bluebell Railway

1 hr+ · All year

The Bluebell Railway operates standard-gauge steam trains through nine miles of scenic Sussex countryside between Sheffield Park, Horsted Keynes and Kingscote.

* Famous Terrier-class engines, Stepney & Fenchurch
* Featured in the film *The Railway Children*

Location
Sheffield Park Station

Opening
Daily; May–Sep 11am–4pm; Oct–Apr Sat & Sun 11am–4pm

Admission
Adult £8.50, Child £4.20

Contact
Sheffield Park Station TN22 3QL

t 01825 720800
w bluebell-railway.co.uk
e info@bluebell-railway.co.uk

032 Andover

The Hawk Conservancy Trust

 4 hrs **Feb–Nov**

A bird of prey park and hawk conservation centre set in 22 acres of woodland. It has more than 250 birds of prey including hawks, eagles, vultures and owls. There is also the chance to hold and fly a bird of prey. The eagles and vultures flying display is daily at 2pm.

* Flying displays & feeding times
* Duck racing

Location
4 miles W of Andover, off the A303

Opening
Daily; 12 Feb–31 Oct 10.30am–5.30pm

Admission
Adult £7.25, Child £4.65, Concs £6.70

Contact
Andover SP11 8DY
t 01264 772252
w hawk-conservancy.org
e info@hawk.conservancy.org

033 Brockenhurst

Beaulieu Abbey and National Motor Museum

 3 hrs+ **All year**

Home of the National Motor Museum, Beaulieu has more than 250 vehicles on display. Visitors can also tour the abbey and Lord Montagu's home, as well as enjoy the many rides and drives.

* James Bond Experience
* 800th anniversary of abbey

Location
Going W on M27 take A326. Signed Beaulieu or National Motor Museum

Opening
Daily; May–Sep 10am– 6pm,
Oct–April 10am–5pm
closed 25 Dec

Admission
Adult £13.50, Child £7.50, Concs £12.50

Contact
Brockenhurst SO42 7ZN
t 01590 612345
w beaulieu.co.uk
e info@beaulieu.co.uk

034 East Cowes

Osborne House

3 hrs+   Apr–Sep

Osborne House was bought by Queen Victoria and Prince Albert in 1845 and used as a retreat from the stresses and strains of court life. Today it is one of the most important memorials to Britain's monarchy. Enjoy a horse and carriage ride through the grounds.

* Children's play area & interactive displays
* Glorious gardens and Swiss cottage

Location
1 mile SE of East Cowes

Opening
Apr–Sep, 10am–5pm

Admission
Prices vary, phone for details

Contact
East Cowes PO32 6JY

t 01983 200022
w english-heritage.org.uk

035 Eastleigh

Space Ace

1 hr+   All year

An indoor adventure play area with giant slides, ball pools, rope nets, bouncy castles and much more.

Location
Off the M3 at junction 13

Opening
Daily; 10am–6pm (7pm in winter)

Admission
Mon–Fri £2.75
Sat, Sun & school holidays £3.75,
Adults free

Contact
5 Renown Close, School Lane
Chandlers Ford, Eastleigh SO53 4HZ

t 023 8025 5777

036 Fareham

The Royal Armouries – Fort Nelson

2 hrs   All year

Fort Nelson is a Victorian fortress overlooking Portsmouth Harbour, home to the Royal Armouries' collection of over 350 historic big guns. Children can explore the massive fort with its secret underground chambers, tunnels and grass ramparts.

* Big-gun salutes every day & historical performances
* Professional guided tours for the family

Location
Leave the M27 at junction 11, taking the A27 towards Portchester from the Delme Arms roundabout. Left at the second traffic lights

Opening
Daily; Apr–Oct 10am–5pm; Nov–Mar 10.30am–4pm; salutes in summer at noon & 3pm; in winter at 1pm only

Admission
Free

Contact
Down End Road, Fareham PO17 6AN

t 01329 233734
w armouries.org.uk
e fnenquiries@armouries.org.uk

037 Freshwater

The Needles Park

4 hrs+   All year

Overlooking the Needles, the park has attractions and rides for all the family. The chairlift boasts the most famous view on the island of the uniquely coloured sand cliffs.

* Magic in the Skies firework finale
* Boat trips

Location
Reached via the B3322

Opening
Easter–early Nov open daily 10am–5pm; 28 Jul–25 Aug late-night opening on Thurs; Nov–Mar open partially (please phone for details)

Admission
Free (plus paying attractions/rides)
Car park: £3 per vehicle

Contact
Alum Bay
Isle of Wight PO39 0JD
t 08704580022
w theneedles.co.uk
e info@theneedles.co.uk

038 Gosport

Explosion! The Museum of Naval Firepower

2 hrs+   All year

Everything you've ever wanted to know about naval firepower is here: from gunpowder, cannons, guns, shells and munitions to mines, torpedoes, modern missiles, even an atom bomb. Learn too about the 2500 women who worked here during World War II.

* Gift shop with books & souvenirs
* Café with great views of Portsmouth Harbour

Location
M27 to junction 11. Follow A32 to Gosport and brown tourist signs

Opening
Daily; Apr–Oct 10am–5.30pm;
Nov–Mar Thu, Sat & Sun
10am–4.30pm

Admission
Adult £5.50, Child £3.50, Concs £4.50

Contact
Priddy's Hard, Gosport PO12 4LE
t 023 9250 5600
w explosion.org.uk
e info@explosion.org.uk

039 Havant

Staunton Country Park

3-4 hrs   All year

Set in 1000 acres of parkland with huge glasshouses, walled gardens and folly. This park also has the only remaining ornamental farm in England, with horses, pigs, sheep, llamas, peacocks and waterfowl.

* 1-hour walks on Sundays (book at visitor centre)
* Black Cat trail, play area & special events

Location
On the B2149 between Havant & Horndean, easily accessible by the A27 & A3. Follow the brown tourist signs

Opening
Daily; 10am–5pm (4pm closing in winter)

Admission
Adult £4.50, Child £3.30, Concs £4

Contact
Middle Park Way,
Havant PO9 5HB

t 023 9245 3405
w hants.gov.uk/staunton

040 Newport

Classic Boat Museum

2 hrs +   Mar-Nov

A great indoor collection of lovingly restored sailing and motorised classic boats, dating back to C19. Highlights include the ultimate sailing classic, a Dragon, WW2 airborne lifeboats, and a fragile folding canoe. Also on display are engines, equipment and memorabilia.

* Displays and boats change annually

Location
On the harbour, free parking

Opening
29 Mar–2 Nov, daily, 10am-4.30pm

Admission
Adult £3, Child £1, Concs £2

Contact
The Quay, Newport Harbour,
Newport, Isle of Wight PO30 2EF

t 01983 533493
w netguides.co.uk/wight/boatmus
e cbmiow@fsmail.net

041 Romsey

Paultons Park

5 hrs+   All year

A family leisure park with over 40 attractions for all ages, including big rides, little rides, play areas, museums and entertainment.

* Voted best family theme park in 2003

Location
Off the M27 at junction 2

Opening
Daily; 13 Mar–31 Oct 10am–6.30pm (last admission 4.30pm); earlier closing in spring, autumn & winter

Admission
Adults £13.50, Child £12.50

Contact
Ower, Romsey SO51 6AL

t 023 8081 4442
w paultonspark.co.uk
e bookings@paultons.co.uk

042 Ryde

Isle of Wight Steam Railway

2 hrs+   Apr-Oct

A 5-mile steam railway that uses Victorian and Edwardian locomotives and carriages.

* Children's playground
* Woodland walks

Location
3 miles south-west of Ryde by road

Opening
Apr–Oct open selected days; Jun–mid Sep open daily
Please phone for details of opening dates & times

Admission
Adult £8.00–£11.00 Child (4–15) £4–£7

Contact
Railway Station, Havenstreet
Ryde PO33 4DS

t 01983 882204
w iwsteamrailway.co.uk
e havenstreet@iwsteamrailway.co.uk

043 Sandown

Isle of Wight Zoo

2 hrs+   Apr–Oct

Situated on Sandown's beautiful seafront, this zoo is renowned for its collection of magnificent tigers and big cats. There are also rare lemurs and the Nightmares of Nature exhibit.

Location
On the B3395

Opening
Apr–Oct open daily 10am–5pm
Please phone to confirm

Admission
Adult £5.95, Child £4.95, Concs £4.95

Contact
Granite Fort, Yaverland Seafront
Sandown PO36 8QB

t 01983 403883
w isleofwightzoo.com
e enquiries@iow-zoo.freeserve.co.uk

044 Seaview

Flamingo Park Wildlife Encounter

3-4 hrs   Mar–Oct

Set in acres of landscaped gardens overlooking the Solent, this wildlife park has penguins, pelicans, flamingos, parrots, beavers and fish, and a Discovery Zone where guests can learn about animal conservation.

Location
Off the B3330 between Ryde &
Seaview. Well signposted from Ryde

Opening
Mar–Oct open daily 10am–5pm (last
admission 4pm)

Admission
Adult £6.75, Child £4.75, Concs £5.75

Contact
Springvale
Seaview, Isle of Wight PO34 5AP

t 01983 612153
w flamingoparkiw.com
e flamingo.park@virgin.net

045 Shanklin

Shanklin Chine

1 hr   Apr–Oct

A natural scenic gorge with a 45-foot waterfall and stream leading to a beach. Shanklin Chine was once a site for shipwrecks and smuggling. It was later used for training Commandos during World War II.

 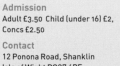

Location
Enter via the old village, off the A3055
or through the Western end of
Shanklin Esplanade, off Chine Hill

Opening
1 Apr–20 May & 27 Sep–31 Oct open
daily 10am–5pm;
21 May–26 Sep open daily 10am–10pm

Admission
Adult £3.50 Child (under 16) £2,
Concs £2.50

Contact
12 Ponona Road, Shanklin
Isle of Wight PO37 6PF

t 01983 866432
w shanklinchine.co.uk
e jill@shanklinchine.co.uk

046 Southampton

Calshot Castle

2 hrs   Apr–Oct

Calshot Castle formed part of the chain of coastal forts built by Henry VIII in 1539. Its strategic importance, alongside the deep-water channel between Southampton and Portsmouth, led to it being manned throughout the centuries.

* Best known as a flying boat & RAF base in C20
* Played a key support role in WWII

Location
From M27 (junction 2) take the A326 to Fawley & Calshot

Opening
Daily; Apr–Oct 10am–4pm

Admission
Adult £2.50, Child £1.50, Conc £1.80

Contact
Calshot Spit, Fawley,
Southampton SO45 1BR

t 023 8089 2023
w calshot.com
e calshot.ac@hants.gov.uk

047 Southampton

Longdown Activity Farm

3 hrs+   Feb–Dec

A modern commercial farm with cows and calves, goats, sheep and different kinds of pigs, including the unusual Kune Kunes. Children particularly enjoy the den, where they can stroke and feed the rabbits, chicks, ducklings, piglets and lambs. Free guided tours for school groups.

* Bottle-feeding & hand-feeding calves and goat kids
* National Dairy Council Museum Collection on show

Location
Just off the A35 from Southampton to Lyndhurst

Opening
Daily; Feb–Dec 10am–5pm

Admission
Adult £5, Child £4.25, Concs £4.25

Contact
Deerleap Lane, Longdown
Ashurst, Southampton SO40 4UH

t 023 8029 3326
w longdownfarm.co.uk
e enquiries@longdownfarm.co.uk

---

048 Southampton

Royal Victoria Country Park

5 hrs+   All year

There are over 240 acres of parkland, woodland and foreshore to be explored. The park is in the grounds of an old military hospital which now houses a fascinating exhibition depicting its history, a tower with superb views and a shop.

* Miniature railway & activity sheets
* Programme of events, play area & sensory garden

Location
Take junction 8 off the M27 & follow the tourist signs

Opening
Park: Daily; Apr–Oct 8am–9pm;
Nov–Mar 8am–5pm
Exhibition, tower & shop: Daily;
Apr–Sep 12pm–4.30pm

Admission
Adult 80p, Child 40p, Concs 40p

Contact
Netley Abbey,
Southampton SO31 5GA

t 023 8045 5157
w hants.gov.uk/rvcp
e rvcp@hants.gov.uk

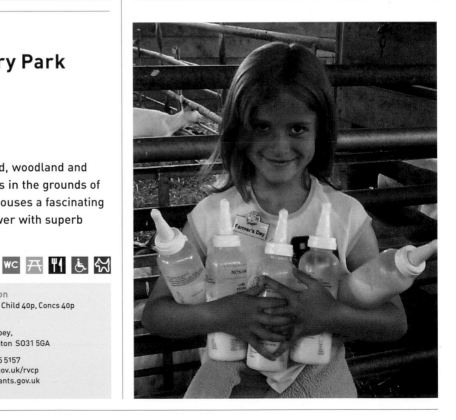

049 Southampton

Southampton Maritime Museum

1 ½ hrs   All year

The museum is a medieval stone warehouse containing exhibitions on the port of Southampton and the *Titanic*. There are ship models and 'All Hands on Deck', an interactive exhibition.

Location
On waterfront (Town Quay) opposite the old Royal Pier

Opening
Tue–Sat 10am–5pm (4pm closing on Sat), Sun 2pm–5pm; closed daily 1pm–2pm

Admission
Free

Contact
Wool House, Town Quay
Southampton SO14 2AR

t 023 8022 3941
w southampton.gov.uk/leisure/heritage

050 Stockbridge

Museum of Army Flying

2 hrs+   All year

This museum traces the development of army flying, from balloons and kites through both World Wars up to the present day. Aircraft include a Sopwith Pup, a Miles Magister and a collection of World War II gliders.

* Children's science & education centre
* Viewing gallery overlooking airfield

Location
A343 6 miles from Andover & 12 miles from Salisbury. Accessible from A30, A303 & M3

Opening
Daily 10am–4.30pm; closed 19 Dec–1 Jan

Admission
Adult £5, Child £3.50, Concs £4

Contact
Middle Wallop,
Stockbridge SO20 8DY

t 01980 674421
w flying-museum.org.uk
e enquiries@flying-museum.org.uk

051 Ventnor

Blackgang Chine Fantasy Park

 4 hrs   Mar–Oct

This park, originally Victorian gardens, has been developed into a family-friendly theme park. The fun themed areas include Frontierland, Smugglerland, Fantasyland and Nurseryland.

* Water gardens & Maze
* High-speed family water coaster

Location
On the A3005 Chale–Ventnor road

Opening
End Mar–end Oct open daily
10am–5pm; Jul & Aug open daily
10am–10pm (floodlit until 10pm)

Admission
Please phone for details

Contact
Chale, Ventnor
Isle of Wight PO38 2HN
t 01983 730330
w blackgangchine.com
e info@blackgangchine.com

052 Winchester

Marwell Zoological Park

 2 hrs+   All year

A 100-acre park with over 200 species of animals in large paddocks and thoughtfully designed enclosures. Come face-to-face with an Amur tiger and hear the jungle call of the gibbons.

Location
On the B2177 Winchester–Bishops
Waltham road. Signed from the M27 &
M3

Opening
Daily; summer 10am–6pm;
winter 10am–4pm;
closed 25 Dec

Admission
Please phone for details

Contact
Colden Common,
Winchester SO21 1JH

t 01962 777407
w marwell.org.uk
e marwell@marwell.org.uk

053 Winchester

INTECH–Hands–on Science & Technology Centre

2 hrs+   All year

This centre houses an interactive technology exhibition set up to bring the worlds of science, technology, engineering and mathematics to life. There is something for every age group.

Location
Junction 9 off the M3, take the B3404 towards Alton

Opening
Daily; 10am–4pm; closed 25,26,Dec & 1 Jan

Admission
Adult £5.95, Child £3.75, Concs £4

Contact
INTECH, Telegraph Way
Morn Hill, Winchester SO21 1HX

t 01962 86379
w intech-uk.com
e htct@intech-uk.com

054 Yarmouth

Fort Victoria Model Railway

1 hr+   Apr–Sep

This is the largest and most technically advanced model railway in Britain. It is entirely computer controlled and has over 400 model buildings, 800 model people and 180 vehicles.

Location
Take the Alum Bay/Freshwater road out of Yarmouth. Take the 1st turning right at the brown tourist sign, then follow Westhill Lane to the end

Opening
Easter – Sep open daily 10am–5pm
Oct weekends & half–term 10am–5pm

Admission
Adult £4.00 Child £3.00 Concs £3.00

Contact
Westhill Lane, Yarmouth
Isle of Wight PO41 0RR

t 01983 761553
w wight-attractions.co.uk

055 Yarmouth

Fort Victoria Marine Aquarium

1 hr+   Apr–Oct

See poisonous weever fish, graceful rays, beautiful anemones and amazing cuttlefish that change colour before your eyes. Extraordinary tropical fish and much more can be seen at this aquarium.

Location
West from Yarmouth on the A3054

Opening
Easter–31 Oct open daily 10am–6pm

Admission
Adult £1.90 Child (5–16) 95p Family £5 Concession £1.70

Contact
Fort Victoria Country Park
off Westhill Lane
Yarmouth PO41 0RR

t 01983 760283
w fortvictoria.co.uk
e pfblake@tiscali.co.uk

056 Canterbury

The Canterbury Tales

1 hr+   Mar–Jan

This fascinating audio-visual experience, sited in the centre of Canterbury, is one of the town's most popular visitor attractions. Step back in time to experience the sights, sounds and smells of the Middle Ages in this stunning reconstruction of C14 England.

* Uses headsets with earphones
* Recreates the pilgrimages of Chaucerian England

Location	Contact
City centre, off the High Street	23 St Margaret's Street, Canterbury CT1 2TG
Opening	
Daily; Mar–Jun 10am–5pm; Jul to Aug 9.30am–5.30pm; Sep–Oct 10am–5pm; Nov–Jan 10am–4.30pm	t 01227 479227
	w canterburytales.org.uk
	e info@canterburytales.org.uk
Admission	
Adults £6.95, Child £5.25, Concs £5.75	

057 Canterbury

Druidstone Park & Art Park

3 hrs   Mar–Nov

Set in attractive gardens and woodland, Druidstone caters for the imaginations of all ages. Go on a discovery trail through the enchanted woodland, explore the Art Park sculpture in many forms and enjoy hands-on experiences in the farmyard.

* Farm animals
* Play areas for all ages

Location	Contact
On the A290, between Canterbury & Whitstable	Honey Hill, Blean, Canterbury CT2 9JR
Opening	
Daily; Feb–Nov 10am–5.30pm	t 01227 765168
	w druidstone.net
Admission	
Adult £4.10, Child £3, Concs £3.60	

058 Canterbury

Howletts Wild Animal Park

2 hrs   All year

Howletts Wild Animal park is set in mature parkland and contains John Aspinall's collection of animals. See one of the largest collections of tigers in the world and the largest breeding colony of gorillas in captivity.

* Animals include deer, leopards & elephants
* Jurassic Mine & dinosaur & fossil shop

Location	Contact
On the A2, 3 miles S of Canterbury	Bekesbourne, Canterbury CT4 5EL
Opening	
Daily; 10am–dusk closed 25 Dec	t 01303 264647
	w howletts.net
	e info@howletts.net
Admission	
Adult £11.95, Child £8.95, Concs £8.95	

059 Canterbury

Museum of Canterbury with Rupert Bear Museum

1 hr   All year

This museum offers new and exciting interactive displays including a medieval discovery gallery, the Blitz Gallery and the Rupert Bear Museum. They're all set in one of the city's finest medieval buildings.

Location	Admission
Follow the M2/A2 from London; take the A28 from Ashford. Located in the city centre, on Stour Street	Adult £3.10, Child £2.10, Concs £2.10
Opening	**Contact**
Mon–Sat 10.30am–5pm, except Jun–Sep 1.30pm–5pm (last admission 4pm) closed Good Friday & Christmas	Stour Street, Canterbury CT1 2NZ
	t 01227 475202
	w canterbury-museum.co.uk

060 Canterbury

Roman Museum

1 hr | All year

This underground museum of the Roman town is an exciting mix of excavated real objects, authentic reconstructions, and remains of a Roman town house with mosaics. Reconstructions also include a Roman market place, with a shoemaker, fruit and vegetable stall.

* Computer reconstruction shows the Roman house
* Touch-screen computer game on Roman technology

Location
Butchery Lane, close to cathedral

Opening
Mon–Sat 10am–5pm (last admission 4pm); Jun–Oct; daily 1.30pm–5pm (last admission 4pm).

Admission
Adult £2.70, Child £1.70, Concs £1.70

Contact
Longmarket, Butchery Lane, Canterbury CT1 2JE
t 01227 785575
w canterbury.gov.uk
e museums@canterbury.gov.uk

061 Chislehurst

Chislehurst Caves

1 hr | All year

Experienced guides take visitors on a lamp-lit tour through some of the 20 miles of caverns and passageways, telling tales of druids, Romans and Saxons. See the tunnels, which were used as an air-raid shelter during WWII, a church, a druid altar and a haunted pool.

* Facilities for children's parties
* Private tours of the caves

Location
Take the A222 between the A20 & A21. At the railway bridge turn into Station Road then right again to Caveside Close

Opening
School hols daily 10am–4pm (except Christmas). Rest of the year Wed–Sun 10am–4pm

Admission
Adults £4, Child £2, Concs £2

Contact
Old Hill, Chislehurst BR7 5NB
t 020 8467 3264
w chislehurstcaves.co.uk
e enquiries@chislehurstcaves.co.uk

062 Chatham

The Historic Dockyard Chatham

4 hrs+ | Feb–Nov

Visitors can enjoy 400 years of exciting naval history and architecture set in an 80-acre site. Visitors can see *HMS Cavalier*, Britain's last World War II destroyer, the submarine *Ocelot* and the Victorian sloop *Gannet*, now fully restored.

* Wooden Walls exhibit with animatronic adventure
* Riverfront museum

Location
Leave the M2 at junction 1, 3 or 4 & follow the signs

Opening
Daily; Feb–Nov 10am–6pm (last admission 4pm);
closed Jan 2005
Weekends only in Nov 10am–6pm

Admission
Adult £10, Child £6.50, Concs £7.50

Contact
Chatham ME4 4TZ
t 01634 823800
w chdt.org.uk
e info@chdt.org.uk

063 Dover

Bridledown Children's Farm

3 hrs | All year

A large agricultural barn containing a variety of animals including rabbits, guinea pigs, ferrets, goats, reptiles and birds of prey.

* Rabbit City & play area
* Pony rides & woodland walks

Location
From Dover or Folkestone follow the A20 then turn onto the B2011 then follow signs

Opening
Daily 10am–5pm

Admission
Adult £4, Child £2

Contact
West Hougham, Dover CT15 7AG
t 01304 201382

064 Dover

Crabble Corn Mill

1 hr+   All year

A restored watermill dating from 1812 and in full working order with devices not seen elsewhere. Demonstrations of flour milling take place and there is a programme of craft and art exhibitions.

Location	Admission
M2/A2 from London–Canterbury then the A256 to River. From Folkestone follow the B2060	Adult £3, Child £2.50, Concs £2.50 Guided tour: Adult £4, Child £3, Concs £3
Opening	**Contact**
Daily; Easter–Sep 11am–5pm; winter open weekends only 11am–5pm	Lower Road, River, Dover CT17 0UY t 01304 823292

066 Eynsford

Eagle Heights
Bird of Prey Centre

4 hrs+   All year

Home to birds of prey (eagles, falcons and vultures) and reptiles (pythons, crocodiles and iguanas), the centre offers daily flying displays, indoor demonstrations of owls and reptiles, falconry courses, and bird of prey experience days. It also operates as a sanctuary.

* Facilities for birthday parties
* A range of courses offering hands-on experience

Location	Contact
Off M25 at junction 3 onto A20, or M20 at junction 1	Lullingstone Lane, Eynsford DA4 0JB
Opening	t 01322 866466
Daily Mar–Oct 10.30am–5pm, Nov–Feb weekends 11am–4pm	w eagleheights.co.uk e office@eagleheights.co.uk
Admission	
Adult £6.60, Child £4.60, Concs £5.60	

065 Dover

Dover Castle

3 hrs+   All year

Commanding the shortest English sea crossing, this site has been the UK's most important defence against invasion since the Iron Age. It was built in the C12 and reinforced by Henry VIII in the 1530s. Underneath the nearby white cliffs are a series of underground tunnels.

* Reconstruction of Henry VIII's visit in 1539
* Visit the Dunkirk command room

Location	Admission
Clearly signed to the E of the city, on the white cliffs	Adults £8, Child £4, Concs £6
Opening	**Contact**
Daily; Mar–Sep 10am–6pm, Oct 10am–5pm, Nov–Mar 10am–4pm	Dover CT16 1HU t 01304 201628 w english-heritage.org.uk

067 Faversham

Farming World

4 hrs   Mar–Nov

There are more than 100 traditional breeds of farm animals to meet in this safe environment. In the Hawking Centre visitors can see many indigenous birds of prey in spectacular displays. There is also indoor play and crafts.

* Just indoor play, crafts & animal barn open in winter
* Tourism for All award

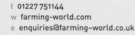

Location
Off the A299, ¼ mile E of the M2 at junction 7

Opening
Daily; Mar–Oct 9.30am–5.30pm

Admission
Adult £5.50, Child £4.50, Concs £5

Contact
Nash Court, Boughton, Faversham ME13 9SW

t 01227 751144
w farming-world.com
e enquiries@farming-world.co.uk

068 Hamstreet

South of England Rare Breeds Centre

3 hrs   All year

Here's a chance to meet and pet all your favourite friendly farm animals as you wander around a farm trail. The centre is also home to many endangered and rare British animals. Set in acres of beautiful woodland there are plenty of places to picnic while the kids play.

* Mysterious Marsh woodland adventure
* Piglet racing in season & trailer rides all year

Location
Leave M20 at junction 10, follow signs to Brenzett and Hamstreet. Situated between Hamstreet & Woodchurch

Opening
Daily; Apr–Sep 10.30am–5.30pm; Oct–Mar, Tue–Sun 10.30am–4.30pm

Admission
Adult £5.50, Child £5.50, Concs £4.50

Contact
Woodchurch, Ashford TN26 3RJ

t 01233 861493
w rarebreeds.org.uk
e visit@rarebreeds.org.uk

069 Herne Bay

Wildwood

2 hrs   All year

Set in 40 acres of ancient woodland, this unique discovery park is home to more than 300 animals from over 50 species. See owls and otters, bees and beavers, wild boar and wolves – plus many more.

* Quality Assured Visitor Attraction
* Conservation programmes & woodland play area

Location
Close to Canterbury, just off the A291, near Herne Bay

Opening
Daily; 10am–5pm (last admission 4pm)

Admission
Adult £8, Child £6, Concs £6.50

Contact
Herne Common, Herne Bay CT6 7LQ

t 01227 712111
w wildwoodtrust.org
e info@wildwoodtrust.org

070 Hythe

Port Lympne Wild Animal Park

4 hrs   All year

A 400-acre wild animal park situated in the gardens of historic Port Lympne Mansion. The collection includes the largest herd of captive-bred black rhino outside Africa, plus elephants, tigers and many more.

Location
Leave the M20 at junction 11 & follow the signs to Lympne

Opening
Daily; summer 10am-6pm (last admission 4.30pm); winter 10am-dusk (last admission 3pm)

Admission
Adult £11.95, Child £8.95, Concs £8.95

Contact
Lympne, Hythe CT21 4PD

t 01303 264647
w howletts.net
e info@howletts.net

071 Maidstone

Leeds Castle

3 hrs   All year

This medieval castle, situated on two islands in a lake set in 500 acres of parkland is a popular attraction. Once a Norman stronghold, the castle has since been a residence for six of England's medieval queens, a palace for Henry VIII, and a retreat for the powerful.

* Open-air concert programme
* Grand firework spectacular

Location
Leave M20 at junction 8, castle is 7 miles E of Maidstone

Opening
Daily; Mar-Oct 10am-5.30pm
Nov-Mar 10am-3pm

Admission
Adult £13.50, Child £9, Concs £11
Gardens & attractions Adult £10, Child £7, Concs £9

Contact
Maidstone ME17 1PL

t 01622 765400
w leeds-castle.com
e enquiries@leeds-castle.co.uk

072 Maidstone

Museum of Kent Life

2 hrs+   Feb-Nov

A unique open-air living museum that celebrates 300 years of Kentish history. Traditional crafts are demonstrated in a working farm. This is one of the only places in England where hops are grown, harvested, dried and packed using time-honoured techniques.

* Calendar of events throughout the year
* Hop-picking festival in September

Location
Off M20 at junction 6, follow road signs

Opening
Daily; Feb-Nov 10am-5.30pm daily

Admission
Adult £6.50, Child £4.50, Concs £5

Contact
Cobtree, Lock Lane, Sandling, Maidstone ME14 3AU

t 01622 763936
w museum-kentlife.co.uk
e enquiries@museum-kentlife.co.uk

073 New Romney

Romney, Hythe & Dymchurch Railway

2 hrs+   All year

This was the world's smallest public railway when it opened in July 1927. It now runs regular passenger services covering a distance of 13½ miles from the picturesque Cinque Port of Hythe, near the channel tunnel, to the fishermen's cottages and lighthouses at Dungeness.

* Thomas the Tank Engine & Santa specials
* Dining-train specials

Location
The stations at New Romney, Dungeness and Hythe are all on or near the A259 trunk road

Opening
Trains run daily Apr-Sep, & weekends Oct-Mar. Please phone or see website for timetable

Admission
Adult £5.80-£9.60, Child half fare
Price dependent on journey length

Contact
New Romney TN28 8PL

t 01797 362353
w rhdr.org.uk
e info@rhdr.org.uk

074 Sittingbourne

Bredgar & Wormshill Light Railway

2 hrs+   May–Oct

One of the best narrow-gauge railways in the UK, this steam-train service runs along the line between Warren Wood and Stony Shaw, through attractive Kent countryside. There are 11 restored steam locomotives, plus steam traction engines.

* Woodland walks
* Vintage cars, a beam engine & a model railway

Location
4½ miles N of the M20 (junction 8/Leeds Castle exit) on the B2163. 1 mile S of Bredgar

Opening
1 May–2 Oct open 1st Sun in the month 11am–5pm

Admission
Adult £6, Child £3

Contact
The Warren, Bredgar, Sittingbourne ME9 8AT

t 01622 884254
w bwlr.co.uk
e thewarren@prquis.net

075 Strood

Diggerland

4 hrs+   All year

A unique adventure park based on the world of construction machinery, where children and adults can ride and drive real diggers and dumpers in safety.

* ROSPA Award for saftey
* Suitable for adults & children

Location
Exit the M2 at junction 2 onto the A228; follow signs to Strood; turn right at roundabout & park is on right

Opening
Feb–Nov open weekends, Bank holidays & school holidays 10am–5pm; Dec–Jan daily 10am–5pm; closed 25, 26 Dec & Jan 1

Admission
Adult £2.50, Child £2.50, Concs £1.25

Contact
Medway Valley Leisure Park, Strood ME2 2NU

t 08700 344437
w diggerland.com
e mail@diggerland.com

076 Tenterden

Kent & East Sussex Railway

2 hrs   Mar–Oct

Take a nostalgic trip behind a full-size steam engine on Britain's first light railway. Journey through 10½ miles of unspoilt countryside between Tenterden and the Sussex village of Bodiam and experience the sights and sounds of steam engines.

* Video theatre, children's play area & museum
* Quality Assured Visitor Attraction

Location
Follow the A28 from Ashford or Hastings

Opening
Mar–April & Oct open weekends;
May–Sep open Mon & Fri, daily in Jul

Admission
Adult £10, Child £5, Concs £9

Contact
Tenterden Town Station, Tenterden TN30 6HE

t 01580 765155
w kesr.org.uk
e enquiries@kesr.org.uk

077 Tunbridge Wells

Groombridge Place Gardens & The Enchanted Forest

4 hrs+   Apr–Nov

In addition to the formal gardens, visit the enchanted forest and enjoy exciting playgrounds, huge swings, strange plants, giant rabbits and shy deer. Other attractions include a raised wooden adventure boardwalk, a dinosaur and dragon valley and a serpent's lair.

* Home to 1 of only 2 zeedonks (zebra-donkey) in the UK
* Largest centre for birds of prey in the south-east

Location
A26 towards Tunbridge Wells, turn right onto B2176 towards Penshurst. 3 miles past Penshurst village, turn left at T junction with A264. Follow signposts

Opening
Daily; Apr–Nov 9.30am–6pm

Admission
Adult £8.50, Child £7, Concs £7.20

Contact
The Estate Office, Groombridge Place, Groombridge,
Royal Tunbridge Wells TN3 9UG

t 01892 863999 / 861444
w groombridge.co.uk
e office@groombridge.co.uk

078 Whitstable

Snappy's Adventure Play Centre

2 hrs+   All year

Snappy's is a large indoor adventure play centre with an extensive range of approved play equipment all set within an exciting dinosaur theme. There is a dedicated area for under-fours, a twin wavy-board slide, and a Game Zone for older children.

Location
From Whitstable take the A290 up Borstal Hill & turn left onto the A2990. At the next roundabout turn right then right again

Opening
Daily; 10am–6.30pm; closed 25 Dec–1 Jan

Admission
Adults free, Child £3.80

Contact
45b Joseph Wilson Estate, Millstrood Road
Whitstable CT5 3PS

t 01227 282100
w mwadventureplay.co.uk

079 Baker Street

London Planetarium

1 hr+   All year

A virtual reality trip through space! Before the star show, wander through the interactive Space Zones, see Stephen Hawking, Einstein and Armstrong and learn about black holes and the search for extra-terrestrial intelligence.

WC | &

Location	Contact
Underground **Baker Street**	Marylebone Rd, London NW1 5LR
Opening	t 0870 400 3000
Daily; please phone for show times	w london-planetarium.com
Admission	
Family tickets available (include entry to Madame Tussaud's) please phone for details (not suitable for under 5s)	

080 Baker Street

Madame Tussaud's

2 hrs+   All year

You can see all your favourite stars here in the world's most famous waxworks collection but did you know you can also try out as a Pop Idol, be photographed by the paparazzi, have your DNA checked and explore the galaxy?

* Gift shop with great souvenirs
* In the same building as the Planetarium

WC | ⚫ | &

Location	Admission
Underground **Baker Street**	9am–3pm: Adult £21.99, Child £16.99, Concs £17.99; 3pm–5pm: £17.99, £13.99, £14.99, 5pm–6pm: £13, £8; £11
Opening	
Weekdays 9.30am–5.30pm	**Contact**
Weekends 9.00am–6.00pm	Marylebone Road, London NW1 5LR
	t 0870 400 3000
	w madame-tussauds.com
	e csc@madame-tussauds.com

081 Bloomsbury

The British Museum

2 hrs+   All year

Far more than a collection of arts and antiquities, the British Museum offers virtual tours for children of all ages, family activities and events, plus exhibitions of games and toys – a great cultural day out for the whole family.

* Spectacular new covered courtyard

WC | ⚫ | &

Location	Contact
Underground **Tottenham Court Road**	Great Russell Street, London WC1B 3DG
Opening	t 020 7323 8299
Daily; Sat–Wed 10am–5.30pm, Thu–Fri 10am–8.30pm (selected galleries 5.30pm–8.30pm)	w thebritishmuseum.ac.uk
	e information@ thebritishmuseum.ac.uk
Admission	
Free, exhibitions may charge	

082 Brentford

Kew Gardens

2 hrs+   All year

Set in 120 hectares, Kew Gardens is home to over 30,000 plant varieties. Enjoy exhibitions, tropical and temperate glasshouses, a trip on the *Kew Explorer*, daily walking tours and self-guided trails.

* World Heritage Site – UNESCO

Location	Contact
Underground **Kew Gardens**	Richmond, Surrey TW9 3AB
Opening	t 020 8332 5655
Daily from 9.30am	w kew.org
Please phone for details	e info@kew.org
Admission	
Adult £8.50, Child free, Concs £6	

083 Brentford

London Butterfly House

1 hr+   **All year**

See hundreds of butterflies flying free in a tropical greenhouse garden. Watch the butterflies feeding, courting and laying their eggs. The insect gallery has giant spiders, locusts, lizards, scorpions and stick insects and there is a walk-through aviary.

Location
Underground Gunnersbury ,then bus 237 or 267 to Brent Lea Gate
Opening
Daily; Jan–27 Mar & 25 Oct–Dec 10am–3.30pm; 28 Mar–24 Oct daily 10am–5pm;

Admission
Adult £4.95, Child £3.95, Concs £4.25
Contact
Syon Park, Brentford, London TW8 8JF
t 020 8560 7272
w butterflies.org.uk

084 City

Museum of London

2 hrs   **All year**

Experience London as you've never seen it before. Visit the Romans, take a walk down a Victorian street, or hear a cockney tale of London life.

* Covers the history of the city since it began
* Regular calendar of exhibitions & special events

Location
Underground Barbican, St Paul's
Opening
Mon-Sat 10am–5.50pm
Sun 12 noon–5.50pm
Admission
Free

Contact
London Wall, London EC2Y 5HN
t 0870 444 3852
w museumoflondon.org.uk
e info@museumoflondon.org.uk

085 Camberwell

Livesey Museum for Children

1 hr+   **All year**

The Livesey Museum runs a changing programme of lively, unusual, fully hands-on exhibitions for children up to the age of 12. An all-new interactive exhibition is shown every year.

Location
Underground Elephant & Castle, then the 21, 53, 172 or 453 bus
Opening
During exhibitions only open Tue–Sat 10am–5pm; closed Bank holidays

Admission
Free
Contact
682 Old Kent Road, London SE15 1JF
t 020 7639 5604
w liveseymuseum.org.uk
e livesey.museum@southwark.gov.uk

086 County Hall

London Aquarium

2 hrs   All year

London Aquarium offers more than 350 species from oceans, lakes, rivers and streams around the world. Visitors can stand face-to-face with spectacular sharks in a two-storey tank, get hands-on with a ray at the touchpool or spot animals in the coral reef.

* Late-night opening times in summer
* Themed activity weeks

WC ♿

Location
Inside County Hall on the south bank of the Thames by Westminster Bridge
Underground Westminster

Opening
10am–6pm (7pm on selected summer evenings)

Admission
Please phone for details

Contact
County Hall, Westminster Bridge Road, London SE1 7PB
t 020 7967 8000
w londonaquarium.co.uk
e info@londonaquarium.co.uk

087 County Hall

London Eye

½ hr   All year

The London Eye is the tallest observation wheel in the world. It takes guests on a gradual 30-minute flight high above London and offers fantastic views of the capital's celebrated landmarks.

* Over 15,000 people a day travel on the Eye
* Views are spectacular in all conditions

WC ⛼ 🍴 ♿

Location
On the south bank in front of County Hall
Underground Waterloo

Opening
Daily 9.30am–8pm
Please phone for details

Admission
Adult £11.50, Child £5.75 Concs £10

Contact
BA London Eye, Riverside Building, County Hall, London SE1 7PB
t 0870 5000 600
w ba-londoneye.com
e customer.services@ba-londoneye.com

088 Green Park

Buckingham Palace

2 hrs+   Aug–Sep

Do you fancy being Queen for a day? Take a trip around the official residence of the Royal Family with audio tours introduced by HRH Prince Charles. Enjoy a walk in the palace grounds or take part in an activity trail and catch the changing of the guard.

* The State Rooms form the heart of the working palace
* Furnished with treasures from the Royal Collection

Location
Mainline Victoria
Underground Victoria, Green Park & Hyde Park Corner

Opening
Daily; Aug–Sep 9.30am–6pm

Admission
Please phone for details

Contact
Ticket Sales and Information Office, The Official Residences of The Queen, London SW1A 1AA

t 020 7766 7300
w royal.gov.uk
e buckinghampalace@royalcollection.org.uk

089 Hendon

Royal Air Force Museum

4 hrs   All year

Soar through the history of aviation for an aerodynamic day of fun. With a brand new interactive gallery, film shows and more than 80 legendary aircraft on display, this is the place to land for a great family day out.

Location
Easy access from the M25. Signed from the M1, A41, A5 & A406.
Underground Colindale
Mainline Mill Hill Broadway

Opening
Daily 10am–6pm;

Admission
Free; under-16s must be accompanied by an adult

Contact
Grahame Park Way, London NW9 5LL

t 020 8358 4849
w rafmuseum.org
e wotson@rafmuseum.org

090 Liverpool Street

Bank of England Museum

1 hr+   All year

This museum housed within the Bank of England traces the history of the bank. Visitors can view gold bars dating from ancient to modern times, as well as coins, a unique collection of banknotes and more.

* Try to lift a real gold bar
* Special events & activities

Location
Underground Bank & Liverpool Street

Opening
Weekdays 10am–5pm; closed Sat, Sun & Bank holidays

Admission
Free

Contact
Threadneedle Street, London EC2R 8AH

t 020 7601 5491
w bankofengland.co.uk
e museum@bankofengland.co.uk

091 London Bridge

London Dungeon

1 hr+   All year

The London Dungeon is an interactive historic horror attraction which dispenses fear and fun in equal doses. Visitors encounter The Great Fire of London, Jack The Ripper and the Judgement Day Boat Ride.

* Great Plague exhibition
* The terrible truth about Jack the Ripper

Location
Underground **London Bridge**

Opening
Daily; Jul–Sep 9.30am–7.30pm
Some late night summer opening
Oct–Mar 10.30am–5.30pm

Admission
Adult £13.95, Child £9.95, Concs £11.25

Contact
28–34 Tooley Street,
London SE1 2SZ

t 020 7403 7221
w thedungeons.com
e londondungeon@
    merlinentertainments.biz

---

092 Kensington

Science Museum

3 hrs+   All year

Come and see more than 40 galleries and 2000 hands-on imaginative exhibits at this amazing museum. You can step into the future in the Wellcome Wing, change your sex, age 30 years in 30 seconds and create your own identity profile – all in a day!

* Interactive exhibits, including new energy gallery
* IMAX cinema

Location
Underground **South Kensington**

Opening
Daily 10am–6pm

Admission
Free; donations welcome, exhibitions may charge

Contact
Exhibition Road, South Kensington,
London SW7 2DD

t 0870 870 4868
w sciencemuseum.org.uk
e sciencemuseum@nmsi.ac.uk

---

093 Marylebone

Sherlock Holmes Museum

1 hr   All year

The museum consists of Holmes' apartment on the first floor, plus the entire second, third and fourth floors which contain the new exhibition area. Features several life-size wax figures from the best–known Sherlock Holmes adventures.

Location
Underground **Baker Street**

Opening
Daily 9.30am–6.30pm; closed 25 Dec

Admission
Adult £6, Child £4

Contact
221B Baker Street
London NW1 6XE

t 020 7935 8866
w sherlock-holmes.co.uk

094   Regent's Park

London Zoo

4 hrs   All year

Set in the leafy surroundings of Regent's Park, London Zoo houses more than 650 species of animals and hosts a daily programme of events.

* Regular programme of feeding times & special shows
* New Komodo dragon

Location
At the NE corner of Regent's Park on the Outer Circle
Underground Camden Town

Opening
Daily; Mar–Oct 10am–5.30pm
Oct–Mar 10am–4pm

Admission
Adult £13, Child £9.75, Concs £11

Contact
Regent's Park, London NW1 4RY

t 020 7722 3333
w londonzoo.co.uk

095   Shepherd's Bush

BBC Television Centre Tours

2 hrs   All year

On this tour you will see behind the scenes of the BBC TV Centre. You may visit areas such as the News Centre, dressing rooms and studios. No two tours are ever the same. All tours must be pre-booked and visitors must be ten years and over.

* The 2003 Group Travel Awards 2003
* Best sightseeing tour in London 2002

Location
Underground White City

Opening
Tours run 6 times a day Mon–Sat.
Booking essential

Admission
Adult £7.95, Child £5.95

Contact
BBC Television Centre
Wood Lane
London W12 7RJ

t 0870 603 0304 (bookings)
w bbc.co.uk/tours
e bbctours@bbc.co.uk

096   South Kensington

Natural History Museum

2 hrs+   All year

The Natural History Museum has hundreds of exciting, interactive exhibits. Highlights include Dinosaurs, Creepy-Crawlies, Human Biology, the must-see exhibition about ourselves, and Mammals, with its unforgettable huge blue whale.

Location
Underground South Kensington

Opening
Mon–Sat, Bank holidays
10am–5.50pm, Sun 11am–5.50pm
(last admission 5.30pm);
closed 24, 25, 26 Dec

Admission
Free

Contact
Cromwell Road, London SW7 5BD

t 020 7942 5000
w nhm.ac.uk

097   Stepney

Stepping Stones Farm

2 hrs+   All year

This is an urban working farm with a full range of livestock. Educational sessions and structured demonstrations, such as sheep shearing, can be arranged for groups, according to season.

* Play area & activity room
* Farm trail

Location
Corner of Stepney Way & Stepney High Street,
Underground Stepney Green

Opening
Tue–Sun 9.30am–6pm; closed Mon except Bank holidays; open Easter, Christmas period & New Year

Admission
Free;
small charges for special events

Contact
Stepney Way, London E1 3DG

t 020 7790 8204
e lynne.rosie@btconnect.com

098 Stepney

Ragged School Museum

1 hr   All year

This museum is dedicated to London's East End.
On the old site of Barnardo's ragged school, the
museum has a reconstructed Victorian classroom, along
with exhibits on housing, education and work in the East
End from the 1880s to 1900.

Location
Underground **Mile End**
Mainline **Limehouse**

Opening
Wed & Thu 10am–5pm; 1st Sun of each
month open 2pm–5pm

Admission
Free

Contact
46–50 Copperfield Road,
London E3 4RR

t 020 8980 6405
w raggedschoolmuseum.org.uk
e enquiries@raggedschoolmuseum.
org.uk

099 South Bank

Globe Theatre

1–3 hrs   All year

This museum is an exciting, engaging introduction to
the life, works and theatre of Shakespeare's time.
Experience a performance in a replica Elizabethan
theatre, or enjoy the interactive exhibits about
Shakespeare's life.

* Annual programme of Shakespeare's plays
* Permanent exhibition & theatre tours

Location
Main line **London Bridge, Waterloo**
Underground **Southwark & St Pauls**

Opening
Daily; May–Sep, *Theatre* 10am–7.30pm
Exhibition 9am–5pm. Oct–Apr
10am–5pm
Theatre 10am–5pm

Admission
Exhibition Adult £8.50, Child £6,
Concs £7

Contact
21 New Globe Walk, London SE1 9DT

t *Enquiries* 020 7902 1400
   Box office 020 7401 9919
w shakespeares-globe.org
e info@shakespearesglobe.com

100 Tower Bridge

Tower Bridge Exhibition

1 hr   All year

Inside the Tower Bridge Exhibition you will learn how
the world's most famous bridge works and the history
of its construction. Enjoy panoramic views from the
walkways situated high above the Thames and visit the
original Victorian engines.

* New interactive computer displays
* Special ticket rate for Tower Bridge & Monument

Location
Underground **Tower Hill and London
Bridge** *Riverboat* **Tower Pier**

Opening
Daily 9.30am–6pm

Admission
Adult £5.50, Child £3 Concs £4.25

Contact
Tower Bridge, London SE1 2UP

t 020 7403 3761
w towerbridge.org.uk
e enquiries@towerbridge.org.uk

101 Tower Hill

Tower of London

3 hrs   All year

A visit to the Tower of London's 11 towers encompasses
1000 years of history – some of it bloody. Far more than
just a trip to see the Crown Jewels, there are talks,
tours, holiday events and family trails, all included in
the basic ticket price.

* Ceremony of the keys (please apply in writing)
* Constant calendar of special events

Location
Underground **Tower Hill, Fenchurch
Street, London Bridge**

Opening
Mar–Oct Tues–Sat 9am–5pm
Mon–Sun 10am–5pm
Nov–Feb Tue–Sat 9am–4pm
Sun–Mon 10am–4pm

Admission
Adult £13.50, Child £9 Concs £10.50

Contact
Tower Hill, London EC3N 4AB

t 0870 756 6060
w tower-of-london.org.uk

102 Trafalgar Square

National Gallery

1 hr+   All year

The National Gallery holds one of the finest permanent collections of western European art. It includes all the greats, and is sure to please even the most reluctant gallery-goer.

* Selection of courses & lectures available
* Weekend & school holiday family events

Location
Trafalgar Square
Underground Leicester Square,
Charing Cross

Opening
Daily 10am–6pm (Wed 10am–9pm)

Admission
Free; donations welcome, exhibitions
may charge

Contact
Trafalgar Square, London WC2N 5DN

t 020 7747 2885
w nationalgallery.org.uk
e information@ng–london.org.uk

103 Tower Bridge

Winston Churchill's Britain at War Experience

1 hr+   All year

An educational adventure about the home front of World War II Britain. Special effects and original artefacts recreate everyday life for ordinary people–the Blitz, rationing, blackouts and evacuation.

Location
Underground London Bridge

Opening
Daily; Oct–Mar 10am–4pm, Apr–Sep
10am–5pm;
closed 24–26 Dec

Admission
Adult £8.50, Child £4.50, Concs £5.50

Contact
64–66 Tooley Street, London SE1 2TF

t 020 7403 3171
w britainatwar.co.uk
e britainatwar@dial.pipex.com

104 Westminster

Houses of Parliament

2 hrs   July–Oct

Take a trip through the history and politics of our country – sit on the backbenches, or become a Lord. This is an invaluable introduction to politics and a great insight into citizenship.

* See & hear debates
* Tours of the clock tower available on request

Location
Underground Westminster

Opening
Tours available during summer
recess end Jul–early Oct

Admission
Please telephone for details

Contact
House of Commons Information
Office, Westminster, London
SW1A 0AA

t 0870 906 3773
w parliament.uk
e hcinfo@parliament.uk

105 Waterloo

Imperial War Museum

3 hrs+   All year

Come and relive life during World Wars I and II. Walk through the trenches and share the dramatic Blitz experience, complete with the sounds and smells of London during an air raid. Find out about spies in the Secret War Exhibition.

* London Family Attraction of the Year 2003

Location
Main line Waterloo, Elephant and
Castle.
Underground Lambeth North 5 min
walk.

Opening
Daily 10am–6pm

Admission
Free; exhibitions may charge

Contact
Lambeth Road, London SE1 6HZ

t 020 7416 5320
w iwm.org.uk
e mail@iwm.org.uk

106 Wimbledon

Polka Theatre

2 hrs   Oct–Aug

Polka is the only theatre building in Britain producing and presenting work just for children. Shows range from classic and contemporary book adaptations to new work for the stage.

* Playground
* Exhibits of costumes & props

Location
Underground Wimbledon, turn left down the Broadway & the theatre is on left

Opening
Oct–Aug Tues–Sat 9.30am–4.30pm
Please phone for performance times

Admission
Please phone for details

Contact
240 The Broadway, London SW19 1SB

t 020 8543 4888
w polkatheatre.com

107 Woolwich

Thames Barrier Learning Centre

1 hr+   All year

The £500 million Thames Barrier spans the river at Woolwich Reach. There is an exhibition with a video and a working model. Please phone or check the website for dates of the monthly test gate closures. There are also riverside walkways and a play area.

Location
On the A206. On the S side of the Thames between the S exit of the Blackwall Tunnel & the Woolwich Ferry

Opening
Daily; Apr–Sep 10.30am–4.30pm;
Oct–Mar 11.30am–3.30pm

Admission
Adult £1.50 Child 50p Concs £1

Contact
1 Unity Way, London SE18 5NJ

t 020 8305 4188
w environment-agency.gov.uk
e learning.centre@environment-agency.gov.uk

108 Burford

Cotswold Wildlife Park & Gardens

3 hrs+   All year

The park, which is set in 160 acres of parkland and gardens around a listed Victorian manor house, has been open to the public since 1970. It's home to a collection of mammals, birds, reptiles and invertebrates, from ants to white rhinos and bats to big cats.

* Insect & reptile houses
* Tikki the 7-year-old, 19¾ ft python

Location
On A361, 2 miles S of Burford

Opening
Daily; Mar–Sep 10am–4.30pm
Oct–Feb 10am–3.30pm

Admission
Adult £8, Child £5.50, Concs £5.50

Contact
Burford OX18 4JW

t 01993 823006
w cotswoldwildlifepark.co.uk

109 Chinnor

Chinnor & Princes Risborough Railway

1 hr   Mar–Dec

Hop aboard a steam or heritage diesel train at Chinnor, then sit back and enjoy the seven-mile round trip as it heads into the country, past a stud farm, the former site of a Roman villa and the local cricket grounds.

* Learn how to drive a train on special training days
* Travel on Thomas the Tank Engine. Phone for details

Location
Station Road just off the B4009

Opening
Weekends Mar–Dec 10am–5.30pm, phone for timetable details

Admission
Adult £4–£6, Child £2–£3

Contact
Chinnor Station, Station Road, Chinnor OX39 4ER

t 01844 353535/354117
w cprra.co.uk
e samuel@cprra.co.uk

110 Didcot

Didcot Railway Centre

2 hrs+   All year

A living museum of the Great Western Railway, based around the original depot, and now housing a collection of steam locomotives, carriages and wagons. On steam days the locomotives come to life and visitors can ride in the 1930s trains.

Location
Signed from the M4 (junction 13) & the A34

Opening
Weekends 10am–5pm; May–5 Sep & school holidays open daily 10am–4pm; please phone or visit website

Admission
Adult £4–£8.50 Child £3–£7.50
Concs £3.50–£8

Contact
Great Western Society, Didcot OX11 7NJ

t 01235 817200
w didcotrailwaycentre.org.uk
e didrlwc@globalnet.co.uk

111 Oxford

The Oxford Story

1 hr+   All year

Climb aboard this amazing ride and travel through 900 years of history, complete with sights, sounds and smells of the Middle Ages. Discover the link between *Alice in Wonderland* and the University.

Location
By road via the A44. Follow the city centre signs. A Park & Ride service is available

Opening
Jul–Aug open daily 9.30am–5pm; Jan–Jun & Sep–Dec open Mon–Sat 10am–4.30pm & Sun 11am–4.30pm; closed 25 Dec

Admission
Adult £6.95 Child £5.25 Concs £5.75

Contact
6 Broad Street Oxford OX1 3AJ

t 01865 728822
w oxfordstory.co.uk
e info@oxfordstory.co.uk

112 Wallingford

Wellplace Zoo

4 hr+   All year

A small zoo designed for children, with a museum and garden centre. The zoo houses exotic animals and farmland animals. Residents include rabbits, lemurs, donkeys, meerkats, penguins, otters, tortoises, flamingos, monkeys and many more.

* Children's play area
* Bird feeding

Location
On the A4074

Opening
Jan–Mar open Sat & Sun 10am–4pm; Apr–Sep open daily 10am–5pm; Oct–Dec open Sat & Sun 10am–4pm; last admission 1 hr before closing

Admission
Adult £2.50 Child £1

Contact
Ipsden, Wallingford OX10 6QZ

t 01491 680473
w wellplacezoo.fsnet.co.uk

113 Witney

Cogges Manor Farm Museum

2 hrs   Apr–Oct

Find out what life was like for the Victorians of rural Oxfordshire. The manor house includes a new Victorian schoolroom display, and the farm has original Cotswold buildings, traditional animal breeds, a walled garden and a riverside walk.

* Programme of special events

Location
½ mile south-east of Witney, off the A40

Opening
Apr–Oct open Tue–Fri & Bank holidays 10.30am–5.30pm, Sat & Sun 12pm–5.50pm

Admission
2004: Adult £4.40 Child £2.30 Concs £2.85 Please phone for 2005 prices

Contact
Church Lane, Witney OX28 3LA

t 01993 772602
w westoxon.gov.uk

114 Woodstock

The Oxfordshire Museum

2–3 hrs   All year

This award-winning redevelopment of Fletcher's House provides a home for the new county museum celebrating Oxfordshire. It features local history, art and archaeology, as well as innovative industries.

* Interactive exhibits offer new learning experiences

Location
On the A44

Opening
All year open Tue–Sat 10am–5pm; Sun & Bank holidays 2pm–5pm; last admission 4.30pm

Admission
Free

Contact
Fletcher's House, Park Street Woodstock OX20 1SN

t 01993 811456
w oxfordshire.gov.uk/the_oxfordshire_museum
e oxon.museum@oxfordshire.gov.uk

115 Chertsey

Thorpe Park

8 hrs   Mar–Nov

A park with thrilling roller-coasters and water rides, including the new Nemesis Inferno, the Rumba Rapids, a white-water ride that twists and turns, tosses and twirls riders through a river, and Colossus, the world's first 10-looping coaster.

* New Samurai ride

Location
Leave the M25 at junction 11 or 13 & follow the signs via the A320 to Thorpe Park

Opening
Please phone or visit website

Admission
Please phone or visit website

Contact
Staines Road,
Chertsey KT16 8PN

t 01932 569393
   0870 444 4466 (tickets)
w thorpepark.com

116 Cobham

Painshill Park

2 hrs+   All year

The Hon. Charles Hamilton created one of the great C18 landscape parks before running out of money in 1773. After years of neglect, the garden won a 'Europa Nostra Award for Exemplary Restoration' with its impressive plant collection being painstakingly reassembled.

* Historic vineyard now replanted for production
* 14-acre lake fed by a spectacular waterwheel

Location
Off A3 and A245 at Cobham

Opening
Mar–Oct 10.30am–6pm closed Mon; Nov–Feb 11am–4pm or dusk closed Mon & Tue

Admission
Adults £6, Child £3.50, Concs £5.25

Contact
Portsmouth Road, Cobham KT11 1JE

t 01932 868 113
w painshill.co.uk
e info@painshill.co.uk

117 Edenbridge

British Wildlife Centre

2 hrs+   Easter–Oct

The British Wildlife Centre is home to one of the finest collections of native mammals in the country, with more than 25 species set in 30 acres.

Location
Leave the M25 at junction 6, then follow the A22 S to Newchapel

Opening
Easter–Oct open Sat, Sun, Bank holidays & daily during school holidays 10am–5pm

Admission
Adult £6 Child £4

Contact
Newchapel
Lingfield RH7 6LF

t 01342 834658
w britishwildlifecentre.co.uk
e info@britishwildlifecentre.co.uk

118 East Molesey

Hampton Court Palace

3 hrs+   All year

Embark on a magical journey back through 500 years of royal history. Discover the magnificent State Apartments of Henry VIII and William III, explore 60 acres of immaculate riverside gardens and enjoy the free tours and presentations.

* Tours with costumed guides
* World-famous maze

Location
From M25, junction 10 to A307 or junction 12 to A308

Opening
Mar–Oct Tue–Sat 9.30am–6pm Mon 10.15–6pm Nov–Feb shuts at 4.30pm; closed 24–26 Dec

Admission
Adult £11.80, Child £7.70, Concs £8.70

Contact
East Molesey KT8 9AU

t 0870 752 7777
w hrp.org.uk

119 Epsom

Horton Park Children's Farm

4 hrs+   All year

A friendly children's farm set up for the under-nines. There are lots of different farm animals including cows, sheep, pigs, goats, ponies, a donkey, a llama, poultry, rabbits, guinea pigs, gerbils, mice, birds – and even a friendly snake! There is also a play barn.

Location
Leave the M25 at junction 9 & follow the A243 north

Opening
Daily; summer 10am–6pm; winter 10am–5pm; closed 25, 26 Dec

Admission
Adult £4.95, Child £4.95
1 adult free with each paying child

Contact
Horton Lane
Epsom KT19 8PT

t 01372 743984
w hortonpark.co.uk
e childrensfarm@hortonpark.co.uk

120 Epsom

Chessington World of Adventures

8 hrs   Mar–Oct

An exciting range of themed attractions, games, rides and adventures. Halloween events. Rides and attractions include Beanoland, Trail of the Kings, Toytown & Vampire.

* New Land of the Dragons
* Toadie's Crazy Cars

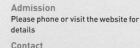

Location
Just 12 miles from London on the A243, 2 miles from the A3 & M25 (junction 9 or 10)

Opening
Mar–Oct; opening times vary Please phone or visit the website for details

Admission
Please phone or visit the website for details

Contact
Leatherhead Road
Chessington KT9 2NE

t 01372 729560
w chessington.com

121 Farnham

Rural Life Centre

2 hrs+   All year

The Rural Life Centre is a museum of past village life covering the years from 1750 to 1960. It is set in over ten acres of garden and woodland and housed in purpose-built and reconstructed buildings including a chapel, village hall and cricket pavilion.

* Displays show village crafts & trades
* Arboretum with over 100 species of trees

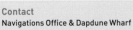

Location
Off A287, 3 miles S of Farnham

Opening
Mar 21–Oct 5 Wed–Sun & Bank Hol Mons 10am–5pm
Oct–Mar Wed–Sun 11am–4pm

Admission
Adult £5, Child £3, Concs £4

Contact
Old Kiln Museum, Reeds Road, Tilford, Farnham GU10 2DL

t 01252 795 571
w rural-life.org.uk
e rural.life@lineone.net

122 Guildford

Burpham Court Farm Park

2 hrs   All year

A 76-acre conservation centre for endangered breeds of farm livestock including cattle, sheep, pigs, goats and llamas. There is also a nature trail and many opportunities for hands-on contact with the animals including collecting eggs with the farmer.

*Angling available for people with a rod licence

Location
From the A3 southbound, take Burpham & Merrow exit; signed from the A3100, or from A320 at Jacobs Well

Opening
Daily 10am–6pm (or dusk if earlier); feeding time 4pm in summer & 3pm in winter

Admission
Adult £4.25 Child £3.95 Concs £3.50

Contact
Clay Lane, Jacobswell Guildford GU4 7NA

t 01483 576089
w burphamcourtfarm.org

123 Guildford

River Wey & Godalming Navigations

2 hrs+   Mar–Oct

Discover the story of Surrey's oldest waterway and the people who lived and worked on it. Climb aboard a Wey barge and enjoy the interactive exhibits or take a boat trip.

* Surrey Industrial History Group Conservation Award
* Guildford Borough Council Access Award

Location
On Wharf Road, off Woodbridge Road (A322), ½ mile N of Guildford town centre

Opening
Mar–Oct Thu–Mon 11am–5pm

Admission
Adult £3, Child £1.50

Contact
Navigations Office & Dapdune Wharf Wharf Road, Guildford GU1 4RR

t 01483 561389
w nationaltrust.org.uk/riverwey
e riverwey@nationaltrust.org.uk

124 Leatherhead

Bocketts Farm Park

2 hrs+   All year

This is a working family farm set in beautiful downland countryside with many friendly farm animals who enjoy being fed and handled. The farm boasts tractor & pony rides, a 70ft slide and daily pig races.

* Surrey Farm Diversification Award 2002
* Play barn

Location
Just off the A246 Epsom–Guildford road, south of Leatherhead

Opening
Daily 10am–6pm; closed 25, 26 Dec & 1 Jan

Admission
2004: Adult £4.75, Child £4.25 Please phone for 2005 prices

Contact
Young Street, Fetcham Leatherhead KT22 9BF

t 01372 363764
w bockettsfarm.co.uk
e jane@bockettsfarm.co.uk

125 Redhill

Godstone Farm

6 hrs+   All year

Set in 40 acres of wooded farmland, Godstone Farm is home to cows, sheep, pigs, horses, ponies, goats, llamas, ducks, chickens, rabbits and more. Children can hold the smaller animals.

* Large indoor soft play area & outdoor play barn
* Toboggan run

Location
From the M25 (junction 6) follow the road to Godstone. Signposted from the village

Opening
Daily 10am–6pm; closed 25, 26 Dec

Admission
Adult & Child £4.80 1 adult free with each paying child

Contact
Tilburstow Hill Road
Godstone RH9 8LX

t 01883 742546
w godstonefarm.co.uk
e havefun@godstonefarm.co.uk

126 Weybridge

Brooklands Museum

3 hrs+   All year

A family-friendly motorsport and aviation museum with walk-on exhibits, a hands-on discovery centre and regular family activities. There are motorsport events and fly-ins throughout the year. Parts of Concorde also now ready to assemble for show.

* Extensive programme of motoring events
* Large display of cars, bikes and aircraft

Location
Off B374. A3 to A245, follow signs

Opening
Tue–Sun & Bank Hols
Summer 10am–5pm
Winter 10am–4pm
Closed Dec 24–31 & Good Friday

Admission
Adults £7, Children £5, Concs £6

Contact
Brooklands Rd, Weybridge KT13 0QN

t 01932 857381
w brooklandsmuseum.com
e info@brooklandsmuseum.com

127 Arundel

Amberley Working Museum

3 hrs+   Mar–Nov

Amberley is a 36-acre open–air museum set on the South Downs. With its historic buildings, working exhibits and demonstrations the museum aims to show how science, technology and industry have affected people's lives. New railway exhibition hall open.

* Variety of crafts demonstrated daily
* Trips on vintage bus & narrow gauge railway

Location
Off B2139 between Arundel & Storrington

Opening
Mar–Nov Wed–Sun 10am–5.30pm
Open daily in school time & Bank Hols

Admission
Adult £7.50, Child £4.30, Concs £6.50

Contact
Amberley,
Arundel BN18 9LT

t 01798 831370
w amberleymuseum.co.uk
e office@amberleymuseum.co.uk

128 Arundel

WWT Arundel

2 hrs+   All year

The new visitor centre at Arundel is surrounded by ancient woodland and overlooked by the town's historic castle. The wetlands are home to many rare species of wetland wildlife. Learn more about them in the new Eye-of-the-Wind wildlife art gallery.

* Programme of educational activities & events

Location
Close to A27 & A29 follow brown duck signs on approaching Arundel

Opening
Daily 9.30–5.30pm (4–30pm in winter); closed 25 Dec

Admission
Adult £5.75, Child £3.50, Concs £4.75

Contact
Mill Road, Arundel BN18 9PB

t 01903 883355
w wwt.org.uk/visit/arundel
e enquiries@wwt.org.uk

129 Billingshurst

Fishers Farm Park

5–7 hrs   All year

A mixture of rural farmyard and dynamic adventure playground, Fishers Farm Park has a combine-harvester ride and tractor, pony and horse rides. There are also quad bikes, bumper boats, a mega bouncy slide, theatre and shows.

* Quality Assured Visitor Attraction

Location
Near the village of Wisborough Green. Follow the signs on the A272 & B2133

Opening
Daily 10am–5pm;

Admission
High season: Adult £9.25 Child £8.75; Mid-season £7.25, £6.75; Low season £6.25, £5.75

Contact
Newpound Lane, Wisborough Green RH14 0EG

t 01403 700063
w fishersfarmpark.co.uk
e ffp@aol.com

130 Chichester

Earnley Butterflies & Gardens

3 hrs+   Mar–Nov

At Earnley Gardens, visitors can see the ornamental butterfly house and covered theme gardens from around the world. The gardens also house Noah's Ark, a rescue centre for small animals, including reptiles. There is a shipwreck museum and exotic bird gardens.

* Noah's Ark educational talks
* 15-hole crazy golf course & animal handling

Location
Follow the A286 from Chichester to the Witterings. After 3 miles turn left & follow the signs

Opening
End Mar–early Nov open daily 10am–6pm

Admission
Adult £7, Child £4, Concs £6

Contact
133 Almodington Lane, Earnley, Chichester PO20 7JR

t 01243 512637
e william.priddle@ntlworld.com

131 Chichester

Military Aviation Museum

4 hrs+   Feb–Nov

Learn about 70 years of military aviation in Sussex, in particular the air war over southern England from 1939 to 1945. Meet the friendly volunteers, many of whom were wartime RAF pilots, navigators and groundcrew. On display are planes, uniforms and other memorabilia.

* Houses two world-speed record holders

Location
3 miles E of Chichester off A27

Opening
Feb–Nov daily 10am–4.30pm
Mar–Oct daily 10am–5.30pm

Admission
Adult £5 Child £1.50 Concs £4

Contact
Military Aviation Museum, Tangmere, Chichester PO20 6ES

t 01243 775 223
w tangmere–museum.org.uk
e admin@tangmere–museum.org.uk

132 Chichester

Royal Military Police Museum

1 hr   Feb–Nov

Charting the role of the military police from Tudor times to the present day. See life-size models of military policemen dressed in uniforms from camouflage gear to dress uniform. Visitors can try on some of the uniforms and have their fingerprints taken.

* Armoured reconnaissance vehicle
* Display of weapons used in crimes

Location
Off A286 Chichester–Midhurst Road

Opening
Tues–Fri 10am–4.30pm
Sat & Sun 2pm–4.30pm;
not open weekends in winter

Admission
Free, donations appreciated
Group visits by appointment only

Contact
Broyl Road, Roussillon Barracks
Chichester PO19 6BL

t 01243 534225

---

133 Chichester

Weald & Downland Open Air Museum

2 hrs+   All year

This museum set in 50 acres of beautiful Sussex countryside offers a chance to wander through a collection of nearly 50 historic buildings dating from the C13 to the C19. Many with period gardens and farm animals. There are also woodland walks and a lake.

* Leading museum of historic buildings in England
* See food prepared in the working Tudor kitchen

Location
Situated 7 miles N of Chichester
on the A286

Opening
Mar–Oct 10.30am–6pm
Nov–Feb Sat & Sun only
10.30am–4pm

Admission
Adult £7.50, Child £4, Concs £6.50

Contact
Singleton, Chichester PO18 0EU

t 01243 811348
w wealddown.co.uk
e office@wealddown.co.uk

---

134 Crawley

Tulleys Farm

3 hrs+   All year

A farm with pick-your-own soft fruit and vegetables and a seven-acre maize maze to entertain all the family. At the farm there are also special events, including the Halloween Spooktacular festival. Animals include goats, pigs, chipmunks, rabbits and guinea pigs.

* Play area & pets' corner

Location
Take the B2110 from East Grinstead to
Turners Hill. Signed from there

Opening
Tearoom: 10am–5pm;
Farm shop: 9am–6pm; 5pm in winter;
Maize Maze: Daily; Jul–early Sep
10am–6pm

Admission
Maze: Adult £6 Child £5

Contact
Turners Hill, Crawley RH10 4PE

t 01342 718472
w tulleysfarm.com

135 Haywards Heath

Borde Hill Gardens

2 hrs+   All year

Borde Hill is set in 200 acres of traditional country estate. The garden was established from 1900 plants gathered from the Himalayas, China, Burma and Tasmania. Today Borde Hill has one of the most comprehensive collections of trees and shrubs in England.

* Magnificent rhododendrons, azaleas & camellias
* Largest private collection of 'champion' trees

Location
1½ miles N of Haywards Heath

Opening
Daily 10am–6pm

Admission
Summer Adult £6, Child £3.50, Concs £5
Winter £4, £2.50, £4

Contact
Balcombe Road,
Haywards Heath RH16 1XP

t 01444 450326
w bordehill.co.uk
e info@bordehill.co.uk

136 Littlehampton

Harbour Park

3 hrs+   All year

A family amusement park right by the beach, with traditional attractions – dodgems, waltzer, arcade, plus a host of other rides and activities for all ages.

Location
The A27, then follow the A280 or A284 to Littlehampton

Opening
Arcade, play area & food bar: open 10am–6pm (later in summer); outside attractions: Easter–Oct open from 12pm; limited opening in winter (please phone for details)

Admission
Free
Charges for individual rides

Contact
Sea Front Littlehampton BN17 5LL
t 01903 721200
w harbourpark.com
e fun@harbourpark.com

137 Pulborough

Bignor Roman Villa

1 hr+   Mar-Oct

Discovered in 1811, this C2 AD site is one of the largest Roman villas in Britain and boasts amazing mosaics of gladiators in combat. It has 65 rooms in the main complex and nine outbuildings, including a bathhouse and a summer and winter dining room.

* Spectacular mosaics of Venus and Medusa
* Bathing complex with baths & plunge pool

Location
6 miles N of Arundel, signed from the A29 (Bignor-Billingshurst) and the A285 (Chichester-Petworth)

Opening
Mar-Apr, Tues-Sun and bank hols 10am-5pm
May & Oct, daily 10am-5pm
Jun-Sep, daily 10am-6pm

Admission
Adult £4, Child £1.70, Concs £2.85

Contact
Bignor Lane
Pulborough RH20 1PH

t 01798 869259
w pyrrha.demon.co.uk
e bignorromanvilla@care4free.net

Eden Project, Cornwall

Fishguard
St David's
PEMBROKESHIRE
CARMARTHEN
Carmarthen
Narberth
537
St Clears
532
Haverfordwest
Kidwelly
Milford
Haven
Neyland
Pembroke
Dock
541
Burry
Port
Llanelli
M4
Pembroke
Tenby
Swans
SWANSEA
*Caldey
Island*
SWANSEA
Port
Einon
*St Govan's
Head*
*Mumble
Head*

Ilfracombe
177
*Hartland
Point*
Barns
179–180
182
Bideford
181
*Great
Torrington*
DE
150
Bude
Holsworthy
Okehampton
Tintagel
Launceston
158
Dar
Trevose Head
146
Wadebridge
*Bodmin
Moor*
Tavistock
Padstow
CORNWALL
Buckfa
PLYMOUTH
Bodmin
147–149
Liskeard
PLYMOUTH
NEWQUAY
173–174
159–160
Plympt
Newquay
Saltash
162–165
St Austell
Fowey
Looe
Torpoint
199–203
170–172
161
175
Sa
Truro
151
176
St Ives
Camborne
*Dodman
Point*
169
Redruth
153
St Mawes
St Just
Penzance
157
152
Falmouth
Sennen
166–168
Helston
Land's End
154–155
156

212
Lizard
*Lizard
Point*
Isles of Scilly

138 City Centre

@Bristol

3 hrs+   All year

At EXPLORE, you can play virtual volleyball, test your memory and run in a giant hamster wheel. WILDWALK takes you on a journey through life on earth using botanical houses, animals and multimedia. The IMAX Theatre is the biggest cinema screen in the region.

* Tropical forest with free flying birds & butterflies
* Imaginarium – Bristol's very own planetarium

Location
Off Anchor Road in central Bristol

Opening
Daily; 10am–6pm, closed 25 Dec

Admission
Explore Adult £7.50, Child £4.95, Concs £5.95
Wildwalk & IMAX £6.50,£4.50,£5.50

Contact
Harbourside, Bristol BS1 5DB

t 0845 345 1235
w at-bristol.org.uk
e information@at-bristol.org.uk

139 City Centre

Bristol Ice Rink

2 hrs   All year

Bristol Ice Rink offers a variety of family and disco skating sessions every day. Learn-to-ice-skate courses are available throughout the year.

* Birthday parties
* Refreshments available

Location
In Bristol city centre

Opening
Daily from 10am–10.30pm

Admission
Adults from £4, Child £2.40, please phone for details

Contact
Frogmore Street, Bristol BS1 5NA

t 0117 929 2148
w jnll.co.uk
e jnlbristol@nikegroup.co.uk

140 City Centre

Bristol Zoo Gardens

3 hrs   All year

Award-winning seal and penguin coasts with fantastic underwater viewing is a must for all visitors. Other favourites include Zona Brazil, Bug World, Twilight World and Gorilla Island.

Location
From the M5 (junction 17 or 18), follow the brown elephant signs

Opening
Daily; 9am–5.30pm (Animal Houses close at 4.30pm in winter); closed 25 Dec

Admission
Adult £9.50, Child £6, Concs £8.50

Contact
Clifton,
Bristol BS8 3HA

t   0117 973 8951
w bristolzoo.org.uk
e information@ bristolzoo.org.uk

141 City Centre

City Museum & Art Gallery

2 hrs+   All year

The museum and gallery house a wide range of objects, from real Egyptian mummies, fossils and Alfred the gorilla to art, pottery and clothing. Activities include workshops, children's holiday activities, family Sunday Fundays, walks, and arts and crafts sessions.

* Awarded designated status by the Government

Location
In Clifton, follow brown signs from town centre

Opening
Daily 10am–5pm; closed 25,26 Dec

Admission
Free

Contact
Queen's Road, Bristol BS8 1RL

t   0117 922 3571
w bristol-city.gov.uk/museums
e general_museum@
    bristol-city.gov.uk

142 City Centre

SS *Great Britain*

2 hrs   All year

Visit the world's first great ocean liner, the pinnacle of Victorian engineering and luxury. Take a hard-hat tour and witness the conservation of this historically important iron ship.

* Designed by Isambard Kingdom Brunel
* The largest ship of her day

Location
Follow anchor signs within Bristol Historic Dockyard

Opening
Daily; Apr–Oct 10am–5.30pm
Nov–Mar 10am–4.30pm.
Closed 24,25 Dec

Admission
Adult £6.25, Child £3.75, Concs £5.25

Contact
Great Western Dockyard,
Gas Ferry Road, Bristol BS1 6TY

t   0117 926 0680
w ss-great-britain.com
e enquiries@ss-great-britain.com

143 Tockington

Oldown Country Park

3 hrs+   Feb–Oct

A great place to let off steam, use up energy or just have a quiet woodland walk. It has an open farm, tractor and trailer rides, ancient woodland, a miniature steam train and challenge equipment for all ages. There are also go-karts and forest challenges.

* Animal interaction

Location
Near the M4/M5 interchange N of Bristol & junction 16 off the M5. Go N on the A38 towards Thornbury & follow the brown Oldown signs

Opening
Feb half-term to autumn half-term; school holidays open daily 10am–5pm; Jun–Jul open Tue–Sun 10am–5pm

Admission
Adult £5.50, Child, £4.50, Concs £4.50

Contact
Foxholes Lane, Tockington, Bristol BS32 4PG

t 01454 413605
w oldown.co.uk
e info@oldown.co.uk

144 Whitchurch

HorseWorld

3 hrs+   All year

HorseWorld Visitor Centre is a great day out for all the family. Support the equine welfare work of this registered charity and meet the rescued horses, ponies and donkeys. There are interactive museums and a nature trail as well as pony rides and pet handling.

* Twice-daily presentations
* Indoor & outdoor play areas

Location
Take A37 from Bristol. Through Whitchurch – Horseworld is on left

Opening
Mar–Sep 10am–5pm, Oct–Feb 10am–4pm. Closed Mon Sep–Mar

Admission
Please phone for details

Contact
Staunton Manor Farm, Staunton Lane, Whitchurch, Bristol BS14 0QJ

t 01275 540173
w horseworld.org.uk
e visitorcentre@horseworld.org.uk

145 Wraxall

Noah's Ark Zoo Farm

3 hrs+   Feb–Oct

This centre has plenty to entertain children – water buffalo, yaks, monkeys, reptiles and 80 other species. There are indoor and outdoor adventure play areas and tractor rides; plus the chance to bottle-feed lambs, handle baby chicks and milk a bionic cow!

* Quality Assured Visitor Attraction
* World's longest hedge maze

Location
On the B3128 Bristol to Clevedon road

Opening
Feb half-term to Oct, Tues–Sat 10.30am–5pm.
School hols open Mon–Sat

Admission
Adult £7, Child £5, Concs £6

Contact
Failand Rd, Wraxall, Bristol BS48 1PG

t 01275 852606
w noahsarkzoofarm.co.uk
e info@noahsarkzoofarm.co.uk

146 Bolventor

Colliford Lake Park

4 hrs+   Easter–Oct

Spectacularly set on Bodmin Moor, overlooking Colliford Lake, this 40-acre park combines natural beauty with an action-packed day out. There are pedal-karts, challenging agility trails and a target range.

* Extensive indoor & outdoor play areas
* Nature trail & animal centre

Location
500 yards off A30 between Launceston & Bodmin

Opening
Daily; Easter–Oct 11am–6pm

Admission
Adult £5.50, Child £4.50, Concs £4

Contact
Bolventor,
Bodmin Moor PL14 6PZ

t 01208 821469
w collifordlakepark.com
e info@collifordlakepark.com

147 Bodmin

Bodmin & Wenford Railway

2 hrs+   Mar–Oct

A trip on this standard-gauge railway, operating mainly steam engines, lasts for 6½ miles from Bodmin town to Bodmin Parkway. You'll pass through the beautiful River Fowey valley, and stop at Boscarne Junction for the Camel Trail.

Location
On the B3268 in central Bodmin

Opening
Please phone for details

Admission
Adult £9, Child £5

Contact
Bodmin General Station,
Lostwithiel Road,
Bodmin PL31 1AQ

t 01208 73666
w bodminandwenfordrailway.co.uk
e enquiries@bodminandwenfordrailway. co.uk

148 Bodmin

Camel Trail

All day   All year

Take a whole day to explore this way-marked path, which runs along 17 miles of the Camel Estuary and Camel Valley from Padstow to Poley's Bridge. The route is suitable for pedestrians, cyclists and horses.

Location
Accessible from Wadebridge town, or the A389 from Bodmin or the main car park in Padstow

Opening
All year

Admission
Free

Contact
3–5 Barn Lane,
Bodmin PL31 1LZ

t 01208 265644
w ncdc.gov.uk

149 Bodmin

Lanhydrock House

3 hrs+   Apr–Oct

One of the finest houses in Cornwall, built in the late nineteenth century. It is set in wooded parkland and surrounded by a garden with rare shrubs and trees.

* Children's guide & quizzes
* Organized activities in school holidays

Location
2 miles E of Bodmin, follow signs off either A30 or A38

Opening
Apr–Oct, Tue–Sun & Bank Hol Mons 11am–5.30pm (5pm in Oct)

Admission
House Adult £7.50, Child £3.75
Garden £4.20, £2.10

Contact
Lanhydrock, Bodmin PL30 5AD

t 01208 265950
w nationaltrust.org.uk
e lanhydrock@nationaltrust.org.uk

150 Bude

Brocklands Adventure Park

4 hrs+   All year

Younger children will enjoy the sandpit, swings and slides at this activity-packed park. For older kids there is a mini assault course and Aqua Blaster, pony rides, bumper boats, two-seater Supakarts, a new tenpin bowling centre and much more.

* Quality Assured Visitor Attraction

Location	Contact
On the A39 Atlantic Highway between Bude & Bideford	West Street, Kilkhampton, Bude EX23 9QW
Opening	t 01288 321920
Please phone for details	w brocklands.com
Admission	
Standard £7.50, Child £6.50, Concs £5.95	

151 Cambourne

Tehidy Country Park

4 hrs+   All year

Enjoy an active day at this country park in 345 acres of woodland, lakes and ponds, with nine miles of footpaths to explore. There is the opportunity to follow horse, bike and woodland trails.

* Sensory trail for visually impaired visitors

Location	Contact
Access on the B3301 from Portneath to North Cliffs	Tehidy, Cambourne TR14 0HA
Opening	t 01209 714494
All year	w cornwall.gov.uk
Admission	e enquiries@cornwall.gov.uk
Free	

152 Falmouth

Glendurgan Gardens

2 hrs   Feb–Nov

These delightful subtropical gardens include an extensive laurel maze, the Giant's Stride swing and a reconstructed nineteenth-century schoolroom. The gardens run down to the sandy beach of Durgan, with good swimming and rock pools.

Location	Admission
4 miles SW of Falmouth, ½ mile SW of Mawnan Smith on the road to Helford Passage	Adult £4.20, Child £2.10, Concs £3.60
Opening	**Contact**
Feb–Nov Tue–Sat 10.30am–5.30pm; (last admission 4.30pm); open Bank Hol Mons	Mawnan Smith Nr Falmouth TR11 5JZ
	t 01326 250906
	e glendurgan@nationaltrust.org.uk

153 Falmouth

National Maritime Museum Cornwall

2 hrs   All year

This multi award-winning new generation of museum, located on the water, is a hands-on attraction inspired by the sea. With famous boats, access to the water and the opportunity to go under the sea, this museum has something for everyone.

* Cimb to the top of the tower for views over harbour
* Display of Cornish maritime heritage

Location	Contact
SE end of harbourside. Or follow signs from A39 for Park & Float	Discovery Quay, Falmouth TR11 3QY
Opening	t 01326 313388
Daily 10am–5pm	w nmmc.co.uk
Admission	e enquiries@nmmc.co.uk
Adult £6.50, Child £4.30, Concs £4.30	

154 Helston

Flambards Theme Park

4 hrs+   Easter–Nov

Set in glorious gardens, this Cornish theme park combines internationally acclaimed exhibitions such as Britain in the Blitz with thrilling playground rides and family shows.

Location
On the A3083 Lizard road. Signed from the A394 Truro to Helston road & the A394 Penzance to Helston road

Opening
Easter–Nov 10.30am–5pm.
Peak season open 10am–5.30pm.

Admission
Super Family Saver tickets available

Contact
Helston TR13 0QA

t 0845 6018684 (24-hr info)
w flambards.co.uk
e info@flambards.co.uk

155 Helston

Poldark Mine & Heritage Complex

3 hrs   All year

A guided tour of a genuine eighteenth-century Cornish tin mine, with a museum, gardens, children's play areas and craft demonstrations.

Location
2 miles from Helston on B3297

Opening
Please phone for details

Admission
Underground tour Adult £5.95, Child £3.75

Contact
Wendron,
Helston TR13 0ES

t 01326 573173
w poldark-mine.co.uk
e info@poldark-mine.co.uk

156 Goonhilly

Goonhilly Satellite Earth Station

2 hrs+   Feb–Dec

Visit Goonhilly, the largest satellite station on Earth, to learn about space and modern communications. There are interactive exhibits, film shows and high-speed touch-screen internet terminals, plus a multimedia visitor centre.

* 3D virtual head creation display
* Guided tours

Location
Follow B3293 Helston to St Keverne Rd

Opening
Daily; opens 10am–4pm and 10am–6pm. Please phone for details. Closed Mon in Feb, Mar, Nov & Dec

Admission
Adult £5, Child £3.50, Concs £4

Contact
Goonhilly TR12 6LQ

t 0800 679593
w goonhilly.bt.com
e goonhilly.visitorscentre@bt.com

157 Helston

National Seal Sanctuary

2 hrs   All year

Get to know the seals at this leading marine mammal rescue centre. Watch them at feeding time and learn about their characteristics from informative staff. The centre also has other rescued animals such as ponies and goats.

* Barbecues in summer
* See the otters in Otter Creek

Location
Follow the A3083 from Helston towards the Lizard. Turn left onto the B3291 & into Gweek

Opening
Daily from 10am
Please phone for last admissions

Admission
Adult £8.50, Child £5.50, Concs £6.50

Contact
Gweek, Helston TR12 6UG

t 01326 221361
w sealsanctuary.co.uk

158 Launceston

Trethorne Leisure Farm

4–7 hrs   All year

This farm and leisure park offers over 45,000 square feet of indoor attractions. They include virtual climbing wall, Jolly Roger Ball Blaster, ball pools, assault course and pony rides. Visitors can also pet and hold the animals.

* Ride-on electric cars
* Crazy golf & tenpin bowling

Location
On the A395, 3 miles west of Launceston, just off the A30

Opening
Daily
Leisure park 10am–6pm
Tenpin bowling 10am–11pm

Admission
Adult £5.95, Child £5.50, Concs £4.50

Contact
Kennards House,
Launceston PL15 8QE

t 01566 86324
w cornwall-online.co.uk/trethorne
e trethorneleisure@eclipse.co.uk

159 Liskeard

Porfell Animal Land Wildlife Park

2 hrs+   Apr–Oct

A place where families can enjoy close contact with domestic, exotic and wild animals. Discovery and surprise are all part of the fun as you feed the ducks, chickens, goats and deer. There are also zebras, lemurs, raccoons, wallabies and many more.

* New children's farm opened June 2004
* Small children's play area

Location
Take the A38 from Liskeard to Dobwalls. Turn onto the A390 & at East Taphouse turn left onto the B3359. First turning on right

Opening
1 Apr–31 Oct open daily 10am–6pm

Admission
Adult £5 Child (3–13) £4
Concs £4.50

Contact
Trecangate, Nr Lanreath
Liskeard PL14 4RE

t 01503 220211
w porfellanimalland.co.uk

160 Liskeard

The Yarg Cheese Farm

1 hr+   Mar–Oct

A working farmyard with animals, milking, calf-rearing and cheese-making where children can watch and learn about these activities. There is also a farm shop and a picnic orchard.

* Park with nature walk
* Museum of memorabilia

Location
From Launceston follow the A30 west, then the B3257; from Callington follow the B3257; from Liskeard follow the B3254

Opening
Mar–Oct open Mon–Fri 10am–5pm (last admission 2.45pm); Sat 10am–2pm (last admission 1pm)

Admission
Adult £3 Child (5–16) £1.50 Under-5s Free Concs £2

Contact
Netherton Farm, Upton Cross
Liskeard PL14 5BD

t 01579 362244
w cornishyarg.co.uk
e mhorrell@lynherdairies.co.uk

161 Looe

The Monkey Sanctuary

2 hrs   Easter–Sep

See Amazon woolly monkeys in their own spacious territory at this environmentally aware centre. Talks are given throughout the day about the monkeys and their threatened rainforest habitat. There is also an opportunity to see a colony of lesser horseshoe bats.

* Wildlife gardens
* Children's activity rooms & play area

Location
Signed on the B3253 Looe–Plymouth road at No Man's Land. 4 miles from Looe; 18 miles from Plymouth

Opening
1st Sun before Easter–Sep; plus autumn half-term; Sun–Thu 11am–4.30pm

Admission
Adult £5, Child £3, Concs £4

Contact
Looe PL13 1NZ

t 01503 262532
w monkeysanctuary.org
e info@monkeysanctuary.org

162 Newquay

Dairyland Farm World

5 hrs   Easter–Oct

One of the UK's leading working farm attractions, Dairyland has a wealth of animals that children love to pet. Among the menagerie are kittens, kids, lambs, rabbits, donkeys, chipmunks and chinchillas. You can even have a go at milking Clarabelle, the cyber cow.

* Pony rides
* Daily events

Location
On the A3058, 4 miles from Newquay

Opening
Daily; Easter–Oct 10am–5pm

Admission
Adult £6.95, Child £5.95, Concs £4.95.

Contact
Tresillian Barton, Summercourt, Newquay TR8 5AA

t 01872 510246
w dairylandfarmworld.com
e farmworld@yahoo.com

163 Newquay

Holywell Bay Fun Park

3 hrs   Easter–Oct

Great rides, go-karts, crazy golf and a maze are just a few of the attractions at this fun park. Others include bumper boats, children's fun rides, a climbing wall and a beach nearby.

* Quality Assured Visitor Attraction

Location
Follow the A3075 Newquay to Perranporth road, turn right to Cubert. Located on the right-hand side, 1 mile past Cubert

Opening
Daily; Easter–Oct from 10.30am

Admission
'Pay as you play' token system

Contact
Holywell Bay, Newquay TR8 5PW

t 01637 830531
w holywellbay.co.uk
e info@trevornick.co.uk

164 Newquay

Lappa Valley Steam Railway

2 hrs+   Apr–Oct

Enjoy a two-mile steam train journey, paddle boats, crazy golf, a maze and woodland walks in scenic countryside. Included in the admission price is entry to the viewing platform of the largest mine-engine house in Cornwall.

Location
Follow the A3075 to Newquay. Just past Newquay turn E to St Newlyn East & follow the tourist signs to the railway

Opening
Mid Apr–Oct. Please phone for details.

Admission
Please phone for details

Contact
St Newlyn East,
Newquay TR8 5HZ

t 01872 510317
w lappavalley.co.uk

166 Penzance

Isles of Scilly Steamship Company

10 hrs   Easter–Nov

Cruise to the Isles of Scilly on a ship. During the journey you can see an interesting exhibition about the islands and enjoy a commentary by the ship's captain.

Location
On the A30, A394 to Penzance

Opening
Easter–early Nov Mon–Fri 8am–5pm
Sat 8am–4pm

Admission
2004: Day trip: Adult £32 Child (2–15)
£16

Contact
Steamship House, Quay Street
Penzance TR18 4BZ

t 01736 334220
w ios-travel.co.uk
e sales@islesofscilly-travel.co.uk

165 Newquay

Newquay Zoo

2 hrs+   All year

Home to many of the world's endangered species, Newquay Zoo is set in beautiful subtropical gardens. Explore the rainforest and its fascinating wildlife in the Tropical Zone and learn about farmyards from around the world in the Village Farm.

* Quality Assured Visitor Attraction
* Winner of many awards

Location
Off the A3075 Edgcumbe Avenue in Trenance Park, Newquay

Opening
Apr–Oct open daily 9.30am–6pm
(last admission 5pm);
Nov–Mar open daily 10am–dusk;
closed 25 Dec

Admission
Phone or check website for details.

Contact
Trenance Park, Newquay TR7 2LZ

t 01637 873342
w newquayzoo.org.uk
e info@newquayzoo.org.uk

167   Penzance

Land's End Visitor Centre

2 hrs+   All year

This heritage centre is set amid the breathtaking scenery of Land's Ends, one of the UK's most famous sites. The centre has exhibitions and shows including the Air Sea Rescue theatre experience. There is also a playground.

* New Land's End sweet factory
* Stunning scenery

Location
At the end of the A30, 12 miles from Penzance

Opening
Daily; summer 10am–4pm; winter 10am–3pm; closed 25, 26 Dec

Admission
Adult £12, Child £6, Concs £5

Contact
Land's End, Sennen, Penzance TR19 7AA

t 01736 871501
w landsend-landmark.co.uk
e info@landsendlandmark.fsnet.co.uk

168   Penzance

The Pilchard Works

1 hr+   Easter–Oct

A working factory museum that produces salt fish. Learn about Cornwall's fishing heritage over the last 400 years, including the trades of salting, pressing and stencilling. Children can use the pulleys and presses and make their own stencil prints.

Location
From Penzance follow the promenade for 1 mile to Newlyn. From the A30 follow signs on the Penzance bypass

Opening
Easter–Oct Mon–Fri 10am–6pm (last admission 5pm)

Admission
Adult £3.25, Child, £1.95, Concs £2.95

Contact
Tolcarne, Newlyn, Penzance TR18 5QH

t 01736 332112
w pilchardworks.co.uk
e nick@pilchardworks.co.uk

169   Redruth

Cornish Mines & Engines

2 hrs   Mar–Oct

Discover the story of Cornwall's industrial heritage, and find out what it was like for the miners of tin, copper and china clay. You can also see the enormous working beam engine and find out about the fascinating geology of the area.

* National Trust property

Location
At Pool, 2 miles W of Redruth on either side of A3047. Midway between Redruth and Camborne.

Opening
31 Mar–30 Jul 11am–5pm closed Sat
Aug daily 11am–5pm
Sep–Oct 11am–5pm closed Sat

Admission
Adult £5.25, Child £3.25, Concs £4.85

Contact
Pool, Nr Redruth TR15 3NP
t 01209 315027
t 01209 210900 (booking)
w nationaltrust.org.uk
e trevithicktrust@aol.com

170   St Austell

Charlestown Shipwreck & Heritage Centre

2 hrs   Mar–Oct

Learn about diving, rescues and shipwrecks in this major display of maritime history, the largest shipwreck artefact collection in the British Isles. There is also an exhibition about the *Titanic*.

Location
Reached via the A390

Opening
Daily; Mar–Oct 10am–5pm

Admission
Adult £4.95, Child £2.50, Under-10s free, Concs £3.45

Contact
Quay Road, Charlestown, St Austell PL25 3NJ

t 01726 69897
w shipwreckcharlestown.com
e admin@shipwreckcharlestown.com

171 St Austell

Polkyth Leisure Centre

2 hrs+ All year

Well-equipped sports hall with badminton courts, squash courts, tennis courts and swimming pools. Hoist available for disabled visitors.

* Hydrotherapy pool
* Fitness room

Location
Accessible via the A390 & A391. Follow the brown tourist signs

Opening
Daily; Mon–Fri 9am–10pm,
Sat & Sun 9am–5pm

Admission
Please phone for details

Contact
Carlyon Road,
St Austell PL25 4DB

t 01726 223344
w restormel.gov.uk/polkyth
e polkythmanagement@restormel.
   gov.uk

172 St Austell

The Eden Project

3 hrs+ All year

Visit the largest greenhouses in the world with plants from many diverse habitats such as the tropical rainforest, Mediterranean fruit groves and fields of California. There are also free events throughout the year

* Project has two million visitors a year
* See coffee plants, palm trees and pineapples

Location
Follow signs from A390 at St Austell and A30 Bodmin bypass

Opening
Daily; summer 9.30am–6pm,
winter 10am–4.30pm

Admission
Adult £12, Child £5, Concs £9

Contact
Bodelva,
St Austell PL24 2SG

t 01726 811900
w edenproject.com
e info@edenproject.com

173 St Columb

Spirit of the West Theme Park

 3 hrs+   May–Sep

A theme park dedicated to the Wild West with Native American artefacts and live street-action shows. Set in 100 acres, there are two themed towns. Pan for gold, fish at Retallack and visit the museums. There's also a Western store and a photographic parlour.

* Westworld auto raceway
* Shooting gallery & pony trail rides

Location
On the A39 St Columb–Wadebridge road, just off Winnards Perch round-about on the B3274

Opening
Theme Park May–Sep Sun–Fri 10.30am (last admissions 4pm)
Fishery Open all year

Admission
Adult £6, Child, £4, Concs £4

Contact
Retallack Park, Winnards Perch, Nr St Columb TR9 6DE

t 01637 881160
w wildwestthemepark.co.uk
e sheriffjaybee@aol.com

174 St Columb

Springfields Fun Park & Pony Centre

 5 hrs+   Easter–Oct

This is a large undercover complex with indoor water gardens, free-fall slides, trampolines and more. There is also a nature walk, pond dipping, plus indoor and outdoor play zones.

* Farm animals & bottle feeding
* Pony cart & train rides

Location
From the A30 follow signs for the airport for 2 miles. Signed from the St Columb roundabout bypass on the A39

Opening
Daily; Easter–Sep 10am–6pm (last admission 4pm);
Oct weekends & half-term only

Admission
Adult £6.50, Child £5.50, Concs £4.50.

Contact
Ruthvoes,
St Columb TR9 6HU

t 01637 881224
w springfieldsponycentre.co.uk
e info@springfieldsponycentre.co.uk

175 Torpoint

Mount Edgcumbe House & Park

 2 hrs+   All year

For 400 years this was home to the Earls of Mount Edgcumbe. Its landscaped park overlooking Plymouth Sound has fallow deer, woodland and coastal walks.

* Children's interest sheets
* Ferry cruise on River Tamar

Location
Take Torpoint ferry or Cremyll foot ferry from Plymouth, then A374 & B3247

Opening
House 27 Mar–29 Sep, Sun–Thu 11am–4.30pm *Park* All year; daily

Admission
House & Earl's Garden Adult £4.50, Child £2.25, Concs £3.50
Combined ticket Adult £7, Child £4.50

Contact
Cremyll, Torpoint, PL10 1HZ

t 01752 822236
w mountedgcumbe.gov.uk
e mt.edgcumbe@plymouth.gov.uk

176 Truro

Royal Cornwall Museum

 2 hrs   All year

A fascinating museum for older children interested in history and archaeology. It has displays on the history and natural history of Cornwall, a magnificent collection of minerals and crystals and antiquities from ancient Egypt, Rome and Greece.

* Diverse range of children's activities
* Open summer & winter

Location
Truro town centre

Opening
Mon–Sat 10am–5pm;
closed Bank Hols

Admission
Free

Contact
River Street, Truro TR1 2SJ

t 01872 272205
w royalcornwallmuseum.org.uk
e enquiries@royalcornwallmuseum.org.uk

177 Barnstaple

Arlington Court

3 hrs+   Easter–Oct

The Victorian home of Miss Rosalie Chichester, Arlington Hall is full of fascinating artefacts that she collected. In the basement, from May to September, visitors can follow the activities of Devon's largest colony of lesser horseshoe bats.

* National Trust property
* Carriage rides around the grounds

Location
Follow signs off A39, 8 miles N of Barnstaple

Opening
House Easter–Oct 10.30am–5.30pm, closed Sat
Garden Jul–Aug daily

Admission
Adult £6.50, Child £3.25

Contact
Arlington, Barnstaple EX31 4LP

t 01271 850296
w nationaltrust.org.uk
e arlingtoncourt@nationaltrust.org.uk

178 Beer

Beer Quarry Caves

1 hr+   Easter–Oct

Take an eerie tour of this vast underground quarry with a long and eventful history, from the Romans to the Victorians. Beer Quarry stone was used in 24 cathedrals, plus Hampton Court, Windsor Castle and the Tower of London.

* Used for secret Catholic worship in the past
* Used to hide contraband

Location
Take the B3174 to Beer; follow the brown tourist signs from there

Opening
Daily; Mon before Easter–30 Sep 10am–5pm; Oct 11am–4pm

Admission
Adult £4.75, Child, £3.50, Concs £3.50

Contact
Quarry Lane, Beer, Seaton EX12 3AS

t 01297 625830
w beerquarrycaves.fsnet.co.uk
e john@beerquarrycaves.fsnet.co.uk

179 Barnstaple

Barnstaple Heritage Centre

1 hr+   All year

Over 1000 years of Barnstaple's history is on show here, with hands-on visual and audio displays and life-size models and reconstructions.

Location
In the centre of Barnstaple, on the quayside

Opening
Apr–Oct Mon–Sat 10am–5pm;
Nov–Mar Mon–Fri 10am–4.30pm &
Sat 10am–3.30pm

Admission
Adult £2.50, Child £1.50, Concs £2

Contact
Queen Anne's Walk, The Strand,
Barnstaple EX31 1EU

t 01271 373003
w devonmuseums.net/barnstable heritage
e dteague@barumheritage.fsnet.co.uk

180 Barnstaple

North Devon Farm Park

3 hrs+   Apr–Oct

A visit to this farm park gives children a chance to meet and feed animals in their natural environment, as well as enjoy a choice of beautiful woodland walks.

* Indoor & outdoor play areas
* Tractor & pony rides & ferret racing

Location
Signed from the A361

Opening
Daily; Apr–Oct 10am–5pm;
closed Wed in term time.
Phone for winter opening details

Admission
Adult £5.99, Child £4.99, Concs £4.99

Contact
Marsh Farm, Landkey,
Barnstaple EX32 0NN

t 01271 830255 (Gate)
  01271 830111 (Café)
w farmpark.co.uk

181 Bideford

Lundy Island

4 hrs+   All year

Enjoy a day walking on this beautiful island. Three miles long and only 24 miles out in the Bristol Channel, it has a lighthouse and castle and is ideal for bird-watching. It is a great place to take children, not least because there are no roads or cars.

Location
Take the A361 to Ilfracombe
& the A386 to Bideford for the MS
Oldenburg to Lundy Island

Opening
Please phone for details

Admission
Adult £28, Child £14, Concs £25
(included in MS *Oldenburg* fare)

Contact
Bideford EX39 2LY

t 01271 863636
w lundyisland.co.uk
e info@lundyisland.co.uk

182 Bideford

The Milky Way Adventure Park

4 hrs   All year

Set in 18 acres of landscaped grounds, this is an all-weather attraction with games and slides for all age groups. The North Devon Bird of Prey Centre is also located here.

* Clone Zone Alien Encounter
* Dodgems

Location
On the A39 Bideford–Bude road, 2 miles from Clovelly

Opening
Daily; Apr–Oct 10.30am–6pm;
Nov–Mar weekends & school holidays
11am–5pm

Admission
Adult £7.50, Child £6.50, Concs £5.50

Contact
Downland Farm, Clovelly,
Bideford EX39 5RY

t 01237 431255
w themilkyway.co.uk
e info@themilkyway.co.uk

183 Bovey Tracey

Wonderland & The Cardew Tea Pottery

4 hrs   Feb–Dec

This venue includes 10 acres of woodland filled with activities, plus the Tea Pottery, where visitors can paint their own pottery to take home. There is also the Cheshire Cat's aerial walkway, duck feeding, an adventure play area and tour of a working pottery.

* Tour of working pottery
* Adventure play area

Location
On the A382 Bovey Tracey to Newton Abbot road, just off the A38

Opening
Daily 10am–5.30pm

Admission
Please phone for details

Contact
Newton Road,
Bovey Tracey TQ13 9DX

t 01626 832172

184 Buckfastleigh

Buckfast Butterfly Farm & Dartmoor Otter Sanctuary

2 hrs   Easter–Oct

Walk among some of the most beautiful butterflies in the world, flying free in a tropical garden with waterfalls, ponds and bridges. At the otter sanctuary visitors can see the playful otters from above and below the water, and at feeding time.

* Butterfly habitat constructed to maximise viewing
* British, Asian & North American otters on show

Location
Follow signs from A38 at A384 to Buckfastleigh

Opening
Good Friday–Oct 10am–5.30pm

Admission
Adult £5.95, Child £4.50, Concs £5.50

Contact
Buckfastleigh TQ11 0DZ

t 01364 642916
w ottersandbutterflies.co.uk
e info@ottersandbutterflies.co.uk

185 Buckfastleigh

Pennywell Farm & Wildlife Centre

4 hrs+   Feb–Oct

With a different hands-on activity, show or display every 30 minutes, children won't get bored at this fun farm. From feeding the animals to egg-collecting, this is also a great educational experience.

* Visitor Attraction of the year 2002
* Pony & donkey rides & go-karts

Location
Follow the A38 from Exeter or Plymouth–Buckfastleigh

Opening
Daily; Feb half-term to Oct 10am–5pm

Admission
Adult £7.25, Child £6.25, Concs £6.25

Contact
Buckfastleigh TQ11 0LT

t 01364 642023
w pennywellfarmcentre.co.uk
e info@pennywellfarmcentre.co.uk

186 Buckfastleigh

South Devon Railway

2 hrs   Apr–Oct

Enjoy a traditional steam-train journey through a beautiful stretch of Devon countryside. There is a free vintage bus service around town in summer.

* Play area
* Small museum

Location
Between Exeter & Plymouth on the A38 Expressway

Opening
Daily; Apr–Oct 10am–5pm

Admission
Adult £8 return ticket
Child £4.80 return ticket

Contact
The Station,
Buckfastleigh TQ11 0DZ

t 0845 3451420
w southdevonrailway.org
e info@southdevonrailway.org

187 Budleigh Salterton

Bicton Park Botanical Gardens

3 hrs+   All year

Gardeners, young or old, will be interested in this historic garden with its nineteenth-century palmhouse, glasshouses and Italian garden. There are also indoor and outdoor play areas and train rides on offer.

* Indoor play area & guided tours
* Railway, museum & nature trail

Location
Off M5 at junction 30, follow signs via Newton Poppleford

Opening
Daily; summer 10am–6pm; winter 10am–5pm. Closed 25,26 Dec

Admission
Adult £4.95, Child £3.95, Concs £3.95

Contact
East Budleigh,
Budleigh Salterton EX9 7BJ

t 01395 568465
w bictongardens.co.uk
e info@bictongardens.co.uk

188 Chulmleigh

Eggesford Country Centre

1 hr   All year

A heritage centre depicting local social history, set in the beautiful Taw Valley.

* Cycle trails & guided tours
* Large rural garden centre

Location
Take the A377 from Barnstaple or Exeter

Opening
Daily 9am–5pm

Admission
Free

Contact
Eggesford Gardens,
Chulmleigh EX18 7QU

t 01769 580250

189 Cullompton

Diggerland

3 hrs+   Feb–Nov

Based on the world of construction machinery, this is a unique adventure park where children and adults can experience the thrill of riding and driving real diggers and dumpers in safety.

Location
Exit the M5 (junction 27), head E on the A38, turn right at the roundabout onto the B3181 & the park is 3 miles on the left

Opening
Feb–Nov weekends, Bank hols & school hols 10am–5pm

Admission
Adult £2.50, Child £2.50, Concs £1.25

Contact
Verbeer Manor,
Cullompton EX15 2PE

t 08700 344437
w diggerland.com
e mail@diggerland.com

190 Dartmouth

Blackpool Sands

1hr+   Apr–Oct

Blackpool Sands is an award-winning beach in an unspoilt sheltered bay among evergreens and pines. There is also a watersports centre for kayaking, surfing, snorkelling and more.

* Quality Assured Visitor Attraction
* Dogs allowed Nov–Mar only

Location
On the A379, 3 miles from Dartmouth

Opening
Daily; Apr–Oct 9am–7pm;
closed 3–25 Dec

Admission
Free
Car park charges apply Apr–Oct

Contact
Blackpool,
Dartmouth TQ6 0RG

t 01803 770606
w blackpoolsands.co.uk
e info@blackpoolsands.co.uk

191 Exeter

Killerton House

2 hrs+   Mar–Oct

Built in the C18, Killerton House offers a display of costumes and has period room sets, laundry, stable yard and chapel. It is set in delightful gardens and parkland, filled with many exotic plants and trees. Children can find the ice house and rustic Bear's Hut.

* Discovery centre
* Family events & extensive woodland walk

Location
6 miles from Exeter off B3181

Opening
16 Mar–31Oct 11am–5pm closed Tue
Open daily in Aug
Closed Mon & Tues in Oct

Admission
Adult £6.50, Child £3

Contact
Broadclyst, Exeter EX5 3LE

t 01392 881345
w nationaltrust.org.uk
e killerton@smtp.ntrust.org.uk

192 Exeter

Crealy Adventure Park

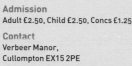

4 hrs+   All year

Visit Crealy to share its legendary magic and adventures, where maximum fun is guaranteed!

* Special events throughout the year

Location
Take junction 30 on the M5 onto the A3052. Follow signs to Crealy

Opening
Daily; summer 10am–6pm;
winter 10am–5pm;
closed 24–26 Dec & 1 Jan

Admission
Please phone for details

Contact
Clyst St Mary, Sidmouth Road,
Exeter EX5 1DR

t 0870 1163333
w crealy.co.uk
e fun@crealy.co.uk

193 Exmouth

Exmouth Model Railway

1 hr   Apr–Sep

With over 7500 feet of track, this is one of the world's largest scenic 00-gauge model railways. It runs through villages and towns, all exquisitely modelled in great detail.

* Model railway accessories for sale

Location
On Exmouth seafront, via the A376

Opening
Daily; Easter–Sep 10am–5pm

Admission
Adult £2.25, Child £1.75, Concs £1.75

Contact
Seafront,
Exmouth EX8 2AY

t 01395 278383

194 Kingsbridge

Sorley Tunnel Adventure Worlds

4 hrs   All year

A working organic dairy farm with animals, riding stables and pony rides. There's also a children's nature trail which runs through an eerie, reputedly haunted, railway tunnel. Other attractions include trampolines, slides, quad bikes, mini quads & grass track karts.

* Green Tourism Gold Award
* Four-storey indoor play area

Location
Off the A381 Totnes–Plymouth road

Opening
Daily; Jan–Mar 10am–5pm; Apr–Oct 10am–6pm; Nov–Dec 10am–5pm

Admission
Adult £5.50, Child £3.50, Concs £4

Contact
Loddiswell Road,
Kingsbridge TQ7 4BP

t 01548 854078
w sorleytunnel.com
e info@sorleytunnel.co.uk

195 Exmouth

Stuart Line Cruises & Boat Trips

1 hr+ All year

Enjoy a pleasureboat cruise along the beautiful River Exe or a sea trip along the East Devon coast (known for the fossils exposed in its rocks and now an official World Heritage Site). There are also day trips to Torquay and evening barbecue cruises.

* Guided tours for individuals
* Mackerel & evening deep-sea fishing trips

Location
Exmouth Marina on the seafront

Opening
Daily; please phone for details

Admission
Adult from £4.50, Child from £2.50
Fares depend on trip

Contact
Exmouth Marina, Exmouth Docks,
Exmouth EX8 1DU

t 01395 279693/222144
w stuartlinecruises.co.uk
e info@stuartlinecruises.co.uk

196 Newton Abbot

House of Marbles

1 hr All year

A working glass-blowing factory which also has a museum of glass artefacts, including toys and marbles. See the largest marble runs in the world! Visitors can watch glass-blowing when work is in progress.

Location
On the A382 from Newton Abbot to
Bovey Tracey & the A38 from Exeter

Opening
Daily; Mon–Sat 9am–5pm,
Sun 11am–5pm

Admission
Free

Contact
The Old Pottery, Pottery Road,
Bovey Tracey,
Newton Abbot TQ13 9DS

t 01626 835358
w houseofmarbles.com
e uk@houseofmarbles.com

197 Newton Abbot

Tuckers Maltings

 **2 hrs+** **Easter–Oct**

Take a unique guided tour of England's only working malthouse. Visitors can watch Victorian machinery producing malt from barley. Suitable for all ages to see, touch, smell and taste.

* Guided tours last one hour
* Video & hands-on discovery centre

Location
3 mins walk from Newton Abbot railway station

Opening
Good Friday–Oct, closed Sun except Jul & Aug

Admission
Adult £5.25, Child £3.25, Concs £4.75

Contact
Teign Road,
Newton Abbot TQ12 4AA

t 01626 334734
w tuckersmaltings.com
e info@www.tuckersmaltings.com

198 Paignton

Paignton & Dartmouth Steam Railway

 **2 hrs+** **Apr–Oct**

Travel Torbay's spectacular coast and the beautiful River Dart by steam train from Paignton to Kingswear. The trip can be combined with river excursions to picturesque Dartmouth.

* Thomas the Tank Engine weekends
* Santa Specials in December

Location
Follow the brown tourist signs to the centre of Paignton. Situated next to mainline trains

Opening
Daily Jun–Sep;
Apr, May & Oct open on selected dates. Please phone for details

Admission
Please phone for details

Contact
Queens Park Station, Torbay Road,
Paignton TQ4 6AF

t 01803 555872
w paignton-steamrailway.co.uk

199 Plymouth

Crownhill Fort

 **2 hrs** **Apr–Oct**

The largest of Plymouth's great Victorian forts, visitors can discover the underground tunnels, explore the ramparts, marvel at Victorian architecture and view the guns, including the 'disappearing' Moncrieff.

Location
Just off the A386 Plymouth to Tavistock road

Opening
Daily; Apr–Oct 10am–5pm
Open all year to pre-booked groups

Admission
Adult £5, Child £3, Concs £4

Contact
Crownhill Fort Road,
Plymouth PL6 5BX

t 01752 793754
w crownhillfort.co.uk
e info@crownhillfort.co.uk

200 Plymouth

Dartmoor Wildlife Park

 **2 hrs+** **All year**

At this wildlife park, visitors can mingle with the friendly animals in a two-acre walk-in enclosure. There are falconry displays at 12pm and 4pm, Big Cat talk at 3.30pm and close encounters of the Animal Kind at 2pm.

* Adventure playground

Location
6 miles from Plymouth on the A38.
Follow the brown tourist signs

Opening
Daily 10am–5pm

Admission
Adult £7.95, Child £4.95, Concs £5.95

Contact
Sparkwell,
Plymouth PL7 5DG

t 01752 837209
w dartmoorwildife.co.uk
e ellisdaw@wildlifepark.freeserve.co.uk

201 Plymouth

The Green House Visitor Centre

3 hrs · All year

The Green House is the UK's first leisure-based sustainable waste exhibition. Suitable for all the family, its imaginative interactive exhibits are designed to intrigue and challenge children.

* Green Apple Award for Education & Innovation
* Hands-on interactive exhibits & craft area

Location
2 miles east of Plymouth, off the A379 Kingsbridge Road. Follow the signs for Chelson Meadow

Opening
Tue–Sat 10am–5pm (last admission 4pm); open Mon by appointment; closed Christmas & Bank holidays

Admission
£3 per person

Contact
The Ride, Chelson Meadow, Plymouth PL9 7JA
t 01752 482392
w thegreenhouseplymouth.org.uk
e info@thegreenhouseplymouth.org.uk

202 Plymouth

Plymouth Boat Cruises

1 hr+ · Feb–Nov

Plymouth Boat Cruises offer daily cruises around the naval harbour, as well as regular cruises to Calstock on the River Tamar.

Location
Follow signs to Plymouth city centre, via Plymouth Hoe, then through the Barbican to Phoenix Wharf

Opening
Daily; Feb–Nov 10am–3pm

Admission
Please phone for details

Contact
Phoenix Wharf, Barbican, Plymouth PL10 1A
t 01752 671166
e pbc@pbc.onyxnet.co.uk

203 Plymouth

Plymouth Dome

2 hrs · All year

Learn about the famous explorers who left the shores of Plymouth and travelled the world. These great tales of adventure are accompanied by sight, sound and smell. Walk through an Elizabethan Street, and relive the devastation of the port during World War II.

* Walk the gun deck of a galleon
* See the devastation of the Blitz

Location
Follow signs from city centre for Hoe

Opening
Apr–Oct daily 10am–5pm; Nov–Mar Tues–Sat 10am–4pm

Admission
Adult £4.75, Child £3.25, Concs £3.75

Contact
The Hoe, Plymouth PL1 2NZ
t 01752 603300
w plymouthdome.info
e plymouthdome@plymouth.gov.uk

204 Seaton

Pecorama Pleasure Gardens & Exhibition

3 hrs All year

At a visit to these pleasure gardens visitors can enjoy a gentle stroll around the Peco Millennium Celebration Garden, which has five linked and themed gardens, and a one-mile miniature steam locomotive journey on the Beer Heights Light Railway.

* Daily children's entertainment
* Children's activity areas & crazy golf

Location
Follow the A3052 W from Lyme Regis or E from Exeter then the B3174 to Beer

Opening
Model exhibition & shop **All year daily**
Outdoor facilities **Easter–Oct Mon–Fri**
10am–5.30pm; Sat 10am–5.30pm

Admission
Please phone for details

Contact
Underleys, Beer,
Seaton EX12 3NA

t 01297 21542
w peco-uk.com
e pecorama@btconnect.com

205 Seaton

Seaton Tramway

2 hrs Feb–Oct

Take a leisurely journey through the glorious Axe Valley in a unique narrow-gauge tramcar. Enjoy panoramic views of the estuary's wading birds and the beautiful countryside from an open-topper. In poorer weather, take shelter in the elegant, enclosed saloon cars.

* Small Visitor Attraction of the Year
* Quality Assured Visitor Attraction

Location
Follow the brown tourist signs on the A3052 Exeter–Lyme Regis road, or the A358 from Taunton, Chard & Axminster

Opening
12–20 Feb & 19Mar–30 Oct daily;
26 Feb–13 Mar & 6 Nov–24 Dec Sat & Sun only

Admission
Adult £5.50, Child £3.85, Concs £5

Contact
Harbour Road, Seaton EX12 2NQ

t 01297 20375
w tram.co.uk
e info@tram.co.uk

206 Sidmouth

The Donkey Sanctuary

2 hrs   All year

The donkey sanctuary is home to over 400 rescued donkeys. Set in beautiful surroundings, it has five walks and a donkey quiz for children.

WC

Location
On the A3052 just outside Sidford, towards Lyme Regis. Follow the brown tourist signs

Opening
Daily 9am–dusk

Admission
Free

Contact
Sidmouth EX10 0NU

t 01395 578222
w thedonkeysanctuary.org.uk
e enquiries@thedonkeysanctuary.com

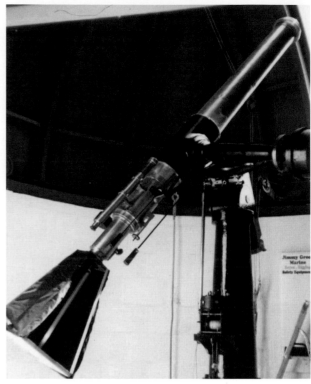

207 Sidmouth

Norman Lockyer Observatory & James Lockyer Planetarium

2 hrs   All year

The solar system, space travel, communications and the weather are all explained and explored in fascinating exhibitions, models and hands-on activities. Radio room where visitors can talk to people all over the world.

* Exhibition hall with models of the solar system
* Satellite station producing weather pictures

WC

Location
Take the A3052 Exeter–Seaton road, turn right after the Blue Ball Inn at Sidford & follow the signs

Opening
Please phone for details

Admission
Adult £4, Child £2

Contact
Salcombe Hill Road,
Sidmouth EX10 0NY

t 01395 579941
w ex.ac.uk/nlo/
e g.e.white@exeter.ac.uk

208 Teignmouth

Grand Pier

1 hr+ All year

Enjoy a few hours of fun on this traditional pier, with many family amusements and games, including the thrills and spills of a roller-coaster.

* Mini-railway
* Pirate ship

Location	Admission
Via the A379	Free, Charges for individual attractions
Opening	**Contact**
Daily; Easter–Sep 10am–9pm; Nov–Mar 11am–5pm	The Seafront, Teignmouth TQ14 8BB
	t 01626 774367

209 Tiverton

Knightshayes Court

3 hrs Mar–Oct

This lavish house was built around 1870 by William Burges. Its much-admired garden features a water-lily pond, topiary and a newly restored walled garden.

* National Trust property
* Woodland walks & children's quizzes

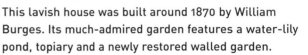

Location	Admission
2 miles N of Tiverton, turn off the A396 (Bampton Road) at Bolham	*House & garden* Adult £6.50, Child £3.20 *Garden* £5, £2.50
Opening	**Contact**
House Mar–Oct Sat–Thu 11am–5.30pm (Oct closes 4pm)	Bolham, Tiverton EX16 7RQ
Garden Mar Sat & Sun 11am–5.30pm; mid Mar–Oct daily 11am–5.30pm	t 01884 254665 w nationaltrust.org.uk e knightshayes@nationaltrust.org.uk

210 Tiverton

Tiverton Museum of Mid Devon Life

2 hrs Feb–Dec

This is a comprehensive regional museum. The railway gallery contains a Great Western Railway locomotive and there is a Heathcote lace machine gallery. Also on show are agricultural and domestic implements and a collection of Devon farm wagons.

Location	Contact
Via the A396, A373 or A361	Beck's Square, Tiverton EX16 6PJ
Opening	
Feb–Dec Mon–Fri 10.30am–4.30pm, Sat 10am–1pm; closed 22 Dec–end Jan	t 01884 256295 w tivertonmuseum.org.uk e curator@tivertonmuseum.org.uk
Admission	
Adult £3.50, Child £1, Concs £2.50	

211 Torquay

Babbacombe Model Village

2 hrs All year

There are hundreds of 1:12 scale models set in award-winning gardens at this model village. There are villages, farms and rural areas, beautiful lakes and waterfalls, railways and details of everyday life.

* Illuminations & Aquaviva laser show in summer
* Summer evening opening

Location	Contact
Take the A380 to Torquay, then follow the brown tourists signs	Hampton Avenue, Babbacombe, Torquay TQ1 3LA
Opening	
Daily; from 10am; also open summer evenings, please phone for details	t 01803 315315 w babbacombemodelvillage.co.uk e sw@babbacombemodelvillage. co. uk
Admission	
Adult £6.70, Child £4.20	

212 Torquay

Bygones

2 hrs+   All year

Bygones has a life-size Victorian street with period rooms. Children will enjoy the large Hornby railway layouts, medals and militaria and the illuminated 'fantasyland'.

* Housed in a former cinema
* Christmas winter wonderland in a Victorian setting

Location
Town centre, direction St Mary Church

Opening
Jul–Aug Mon–Thu 10am–9.30pm,
Fri–Sun 10am–6pm;
Apr–May & Sep–Oct 10am–6pm,
Nov–Feb 10am–4pm

Admission
Adults £4.50, Child £3, Concs £3.95

Contact
Fore Street, St Marychurch,
Torquay TQ1 4PR

t 01803 326108
w bygones.co.uk
e info@bygones.co.uk

213 Torquay

The Riviera International Centre & Leisure Pool

2 hrs   All year

There is something for children of all ages at this leisure complex. It has a health and fitness centre, a choice of leisure pool, restaurants and cafés.

* Children's water spray area
* Leisure pool, flume & wave machine

Location
2 min walk from Torquay seafront

Opening
Please phone for details

Admission
Family swim £10.50.
Please phone for details

Contact
Chestnut Avenue,
Torquay TQ2 5LZ

t 01803 299992
w rivieracentre.co.uk
e enquiries@rivieracentre.co.uk

214 Totnes

Totnes Elizabethan Museum

1 hr   Mar–Oct

This Elizabethan house, built in 1575, features an Elizabethan herb garden, a Tudor bedroom, kitchen and a Victorian nursery. Displays cover 5000 years of local history, and there is a special exhibition on Charles Babbage, father of the modern computer.

Location
On the main street in front of East Gate Arch in Totnes

Opening
Mid Mar–Oct Mon–Fri 10.30–5pm (last admission 4.30pm)

Admission
Adult £1.50, Child 50p, Concs £1

Contact
70 Fore Street,
Totnes TQ9 5RU

t 01803 863821
w devonmuseums.net/totnes
e totnesmuseum@btconnect.com

215 Totnes

Woodlands Leisure Park

3 hrs+   Mar–Oct

An excellent combination of indoor and outdoor attractions for all ages. Some of the attractions include 3 water-coasters, toboggan run, 15 play zones, massive indoor centres and animals.

* UK's biggest indoor venture centre
* Falconry centre with flying displays

Location
On A3122 between Totnes & Dartmouth

Opening
Daily; 26 Mar–Oct & school hols

Admission
Please phone for details

Contact
Blackawton,
Totnes TQ9 7DQ

t 01803 712598
w woodlandspark.com
e fun@woodlandspark.com

216 Bournemouth

Oceanarium Bournemouth

 2 hrs   All year

Explore the secrets of the ocean in some of the world's most amazing waters. Come face-to-face with a vast array of colourful creatures from green turtles, stingrays, sharks and exotic fish to piranhas, chameleons and tortoises.

* Gift shop
* Great café

Location
Follow signs to Bournemouth beaches & piers

Opening
Daily 10am–5pm; closed 25 Dec

Admission
Adult £6.95, Child £3.95
Concs £4.95/£3.95

Contact
Pier Approach,
Bournemouth BH2 5AA

t 01202 311993
w oceanarium.co.uk
e info@oceanarium.co.uk

217 Bovington

Tank Museum

 3 hrs+   All year

The Tank Museum houses the world's finest indoor collection of Armoured Fighting Vehicles. Tanks in Action displays are held throughout the summer.

* Indoor collection of 150 vehicles from 26 countries
* Vehicle rides and live demonstrations

Location
Off the A352, between Dorchester & Wareham, near Wool. Follow signs from Bere Regis

Opening
Daily 10am–5pm, closed 25, 26 Dec

Admission
Please phone for details

Contact
Bovington BH20 6HG

t 01929 405096
w tankmuseum.co.uk
e info@tankmuseum.co.uk

218 Bournemouth

Dorset Belle Cruises

1 hr+   All year

Take a cruise from Bournemouth around the Purbeck coast, visit the Isle of Wight for a day or explore Brownsea Island.

* Boats available for charter & evening cruises
* Fireworks & magnificent sunset cruises

Location
Boats depart from Bournemouth pier, Swanage or Poole

Opening
Seasonal timetable available, check website or phone for details

Admission
Please phone for details

Contact
Pier Approach,
Bournemouth BH2 5AA

t 01202 558550
w dorsetbelles.co.uk
e info@dorsetbelles.co.uk

220 Dorchester

The Dorset Teddy Bear Museum

1 hr   All year

An unusual museum where the teddy bears are life-size. See the teddy bear family at work, rest and play. A large selection of teddy bears is available at the period shop.

Location
In the town centre

Opening
Daily 9.30am–5pm;
closed 25, 26 Dec

Admission
Adult £3.95, Child, £2.50

Contact
Antelope Walk
Dorchester DT1 1BE

t 01305 263200
w teddybearhouse.co.uk
e info@teddybearhouse.co.uk

219 Dorchester

The Dinosaur Museum

1 hr+   All year

The award-winning Dinosaur Museum combines fossils, skeletons and life-size dinosaur reconstructions with video, hands-on and computer displays. This is fascinating fun for all the family.

* Winner of the Dorset 'Family Attraction' award
* Top 10 'Hands-on Museum in Britain'

Location
Centre of Dorchester

Opening
Easter–Oct 9.30am–5.30pm;
Nov–Mar 10am–4.30pm

Admission
Adults £5.50, Child £3.95

Contact
Icen Way,
Dorchester DT1 1EW

t 01305 269880
w thedinosaurmuseum.com
e info@thedinosaurmuseum.com

221 Dorchester

Dorset County Museum

1 hr+   All year

Explore Dorset wildlife, geology and social history in interactive exhibitions and audio-visual displays. Visit the gallery of Dorset writers including Thomas Hardy, and archaeology gallery.

* Interactive audio guide
* Film on Roman invasion of Maiden Castle

Location
Town centre, follow museum signs

Opening
Oct–Jun Mon–Sat 10am–5pm
Jul–Sep daily 10am–5pm

Admission
Adults £4.20, Child free, Conc £3.20

Contact
High West Street,
Dorchester DT1 1XA

t 01305 262735
w dorsetcountymuseum.org
e nicky@dor-mus.demon.co.uk

222 Dorchester

Kingston Maurward Gardens

2 hrs+   All year

A formal Edwardian garden with a stunning ornamental lake in front of the eighteenth-century mansion house. The animal park has a collection of miniature Shetland ponies, as well as donkeys, rabbits and guinea pigs.

* National Collections of penstemons and salvias
* Edwardian formal & walled demonstration gardens

Location
1 mile E of Dorchester off the A35

Opening
Daily; 5 Jan–19 Dec 10am–5.30pm or dusk if earlier.
Closed over Christmas

Admission
Adult £4, Child £2.50

Contact
Dorchester DT2 8PY

t 01305 215003
w www.kmc.ac.uk
e administration@kmc.ac.uk

223 Poole

Farmer Palmer's Farm Park

4 hrs   Feb–Dec

A delightful farm designed for children up to eight years old, where they can enjoy lots of hands-on fun with animals and ride a tractor trailer. There is also an undercover straw mountain, bouncy castles and pedal tractors. New indoor soft play area for 2005.

* Maize maze (in summer)
* Large play area

Location
Off A35 Poole–Dorchester road

Opening
Daily; 12 Feb–30 Oct 10am–5.30pm;
31 Oct–18 Dec Thurs & Fri 10am–7pm,
Sat & Sun 10am–4pm

Admission
Adult £4.50, Child, £4.25, Concs £4

Contact
Organford, Poole BH16 6EU

t 01202 622022
w farmerpalmer.co.uk
e farmerpalmers@bigfoot.com

224 Poole

Upton Country Park

2 hrs   All year

Upton House has pretty, formal gardens which lead into woodland, meadow, and a saltmarsh teeming with wildlife on the edge of Poole harbour.

* Nature trails
* Cycling allowed on way-marked cycle route

| WC | 🏕 | 🍴 | ♿ | 🐾 |

Location
On the S side of the A35/A3409,
4 miles west of Poole town centre

Opening
Daily 9am–dusk

Admission
Free

Contact
Upton Road, Upton
Poole BH17 7BJ

t 01202 672625

226 St Leonards

Avon Heath Country Park

2 hrs+   All year

Enjoy a day at Dorset's largest country park, walking or cycling in the beautiful heathland and woods. There are activities and events at the visitor centre.

* Barbecue hire available
* Nature activity trails

| WC | 🏕 | 🍴 | ♿ | 🐾 |

Location
On the A31, 2 miles W of Ringwood

Opening
Park: Daily; Apr–Sep 8am–7.30pm;
Oct–Mar 8.30am–5.30pm
Visitor centre: Daily 11am–4pm

Admission
Free; Car park charge

Contact
Brocks Pine, St Leonards,
Ringwood BH24 2DA

t 01425 478470
e sdavies@dorsetcc.gov.uk

225 Poole

Brownsea Island National Trust

3 hrs+   Mar–Oct

Once a haunt of smugglers, Brownsea Island is now a haven for wildlife. It offers a rich variety of sea birds, plus peacocks and red squirrels. Children can take the Smuggler, Young Historian and Explorer trails.

* Family events throughout the year
* Guided walk in nature reserve (summer only)

| WC | ♿ | 🍴 |

Location
By boat from Poole, Bournemouth,
Swanage or Sandbanks

Opening
27 Mar–Oct from 10am

Admission
Adult £3.70, Child £1.60

Contact
Poole Harbour BH13 7EE

t 01202 707744
w nationaltrust.org.uk/brownsea
e office@brownseaisland.fsnet.co.uk

227 Studland

Studland Beach & Nature Reserve

  3 hrs+   All year

There are miles of golden sands at Studland. The shallow waters are perfect for bathing, and the heathland behind the beach is a National Nature Reserve. This haven for birds and wildlife can be enjoyed from several public paths and two nature trails, plus bird hides at Little Sea.

* Guided discovery walks & storytelling (summer)
* Dogs allowed on beach Sep–Jun only

Location
Across B'mth & Swanage motor road ferry or via Corfe Castle on the B3351

Opening
Daily

Admission
Parking charges vary through seasons, please telephone for details

Contact
Countryside Office, Studland, Swanage BH19 3AX

t 01929 450259
w nationaltrust.org.uk
e studlandbeach@nationaltrust.org.uk

228 Swanage

Swanage Railway

 2 hrs+   All year

Enjoy a nostalgic steam-train journey through magnificent countryside and the village of Corfe Castle, offering good views of the historic ruins. Eastern gateway to World Heritage Jurassic Coast.

* Special events programme
* Train-driving lessons

Location
Station in centre of Swanage, a few mins walk from the beach

Opening
Trains daily Apr–Oct and 26–31 Dec. Weekends only rest of year.

Admission
Adult £7, Child £5, Concs £5

Contact
Station House, Swanage BH19 1HB

t 01929 425800
w swanagerailway.co.uk
e general@swanrail.freeserve.co.uk

229 Swanage

Durlston Country Park

3 hrs+   All year

A country park with wildflower meadows, downland, cliffs, sea and a wealth of wildlife. There is also a visitor centre for local information.

* Theme trails & ranger-guided walks
* Education service

Location
Take the A351 to Swanage & follow the brown tourist signs

Opening
Park Daily, dawn–dusk
Visitor centre Apr–Oct daily 10am–5pm, Nov–Mar weekends & holidays 10.30am–4pm

Admission
Free; car park charge

Contact
Durlston
Swanage BH19 2JL

t 01929 424443
w durlston.co.uk
e info@durlston.co.uk

230 Wareham

Corfe Castle

1 hr+   All year

Explore this ruined castle with a long and fascinating history as a fortress, prison and home. The Castle View Visitor Centre has hands-on displays and children are encouraged to touch castle artefacts and try on replica medieval clothing.

* Special events including historical re-enactments
* Guided tours available

Location
On the A352 Wareham to Swanage road

Opening
Daily; closed 25,26 Dec

Admission
Adult £4.70, Child £2.30

Contact
The National Trust, The Square, Corfe Castle, Wareham BH20 5EZ

t 01929 481294
w nationaltrust.org.uk
e corfecastle@nationaltrust.org.uk

231 Wareham

Lulworth Castle

3 hrs+   All year

There's plenty to entertain children at this historic building. After viewing the house, take a woodland walk and feed the animals at a nearby farm. There are plenty of new exhibitions in the castle.

* Adventure playground & indoor activity room
* August jousting shows Monday to Friday

Location
3 miles SW of Wareham, follow signs

Opening
Summer 10.30am–6pm; winter 10.30am–4pm. Closed Sat & 24 Dec to early Jan

Admission
Adults £7, Child £4, Concs £5

Contact
East Lulworth,
Wareham BH20 5QS

t 01929 400 352
w www.lulworth.com
e estate.office@lulworth.com

232 Wareham

Monkey World

2 hrs+   All year

A sanctuary for over 150 primates including chimpanzees, orangutans and gibbons. Learn how they are looked after and live in social groups. Other attractions include a bird pond, a pet's corner with donkeys, and an adventure play area.

* Largest group of chimpanzees outside Africa
* Featured in many TV shows, including *Animal Hospital*

Location
Located between Bere Regis and Wool, 1 mile from Wool station

Opening
Daily 10am–5pm (6pm Jul & Aug)

Admission
Adult £8, Child £6, Concs £6

Contact
Longthorns,
Wareham BH20 6HH

t 01929 462537
w www.monkeyworld.org
e apes@monkeyworld.org

233 Weymouth

Abbotsbury Swannery

2 hrs   Mar–Oct

Visitors can walk among the free-flying mute swans that live here and, during the hatching period (end May to end June), watch the eggs hatch.

* Feeding of up to 600 swans daily at 12pm & 4pm
* Audio-visual show

Location
On the B3157 between Bridport and Weymouth

Opening
Daily; Mid Mar–Oct 10am–6pm (last admission 5pm)

Admission
Adult £6.50, Child £3.80, Concs £5.80

Contact
New Barn Road, Abbotsbury
Weymouth DT3 4JG
t 01305 871858
w abbotsbury-tourism.co.uk
e info@abbotsbury-tourism.co.uk

234 Weymouth

Brewers Quay

3 hrs+   All year

Visit this redeveloped Victorian brewery in the Old Harbour to enjoy the shops and café, and to see an award-winning exhibition that takes you on a voyage with Miss Paws, the brewery cat, through 19 life-size scenes, recreating 600 years of local history.

Location
On harbour, 5 mins from town centre

Opening
Daily 10am–5.30pm

Admission
Free entry to complex.
Timewalk attraction Adult £4.50, Child £3.25, Concs £4.00

Contact
Hope Square, Weymouth DT4 8TR
t 01305 777 622
w brewers-quay.co.uk
e brewersquay@yahoo.co.uk

235 Weymouth

Pirate Adventure Golf

½ hr   All year

This is a serious test of putting skill within an exciting and dramatic setting. A swashbuckling golf game for all the family. The holes themselves have top quality astro-turf surfaces, wide undulating greens and each has its own unique challenges.

*Sound effects

Location	Contact
On the A353 Preston Beach Road	Lodmoor Country Park Weymouth DT4 7SX
Opening	
All year open daily 10am–5pm (later in Jul & Aug); closed Christmas & New Year	t 01305 781797
Admission	
Adult £4.95 Child (4–16) £3.95	

236 Wimborne

Stapehill Abbey, Crafts & Gardens

3 hrs   All year

Award-winning gardens and woodland surround this C19 Cistercian Abbey. It has a craft centre, countryside museum, Japanese garden and home farm, where a range of domestic animals can be seen at close quarters.

Location	Admission
8 miles from Ringwood on A31	Adult £7.50, Child £4.50, Concs £7 Please phone for winter rates
Opening	
Apr–Sep daily 10am–5pm; Oct–Mar Wed–Sun 10am–4pm. Closed 23 Dec–early Feb	**Contact** Wimborne Road West, Stapehill, Wimborne BH21 2EB
	t 01202 861686

237 Wimborne

Wimborne Model Town & Gardens

2 hrs   Mar–Oct

Set in award-winning gardens, the models are exact 1:10 scale replicas of the town of Wimborne Minster as it was in the 1950s. Children will enjoy the play houses in Wendy Street.

Location	Contact
Accessible via the A31	16 King Street Wimborne Minster BH21 1DY
Opening	
Daily; 26 Mar–3 Oct 10am–5pm; Aug & Sep open evenings 6pm–9pm	t 01202 881924 w wimborne-modeltown.com e wimbornemodeltown@hotmail.com
Admission	
Adult £3, Child £2, Concs £2.50	

238 Berkeley

Berkeley Castle

 ⏳ 4 hrs 🔓 Apr–Oct

This stunning medieval castle, stately home of the Berkeley family for 900 years, was the scene of Edward II's murder. It is filled with treasures and is set in beautiful Elizabethan terraced gardens. There is a programme of events, with lots of fun activities for children.

WC ⛱ 🍴

Location
On the A38 (M5, exit 13 or 14)
W of Dursley

Opening
1 Apr–2 Oct Tues–Sat & Bank Hol
Mons 11am–4pm; Sun 2pm–5pm;
3–31 Oct Sun only

Admission
Adult £7, Child £4, Concs £5.50

Contact
Berkeley GL13 9BQ

t 01453 810332
w berkeley-castle.com
e info@berkeley-castle.com

239 Berkeley

Cattle Country Adventure Park

 ⏳ 3 hrs 🔓 Mar–Oct

A farm park specializing in exotic cattle such as American bison. It also has Gloucester Old Spot pigs and a large adventure playground with big slides and an outdoor paddling pool (in summer).

* Zip wire ride
* Ideal for private parties

WC ⛱ 🍴 ♿

Location
On the B4066, near Berkeley

Opening
School holidays (except Christmas)
open daily 10am–5pm;
Please phone for other opening hours.
Closed Nov–Feb.

Admission
Summer: £5.50; *Winter:* £4.90

Contact
Berkeley Heath Farm, Berkeley Heath
Berkeley GL13 9EW

t 01453 810510
w cattlecountry.co.uk
e info@cattlecountry.co.uk

240 Bourton-on-the-Water

Cotswold Motor Museum & Toy Collection

⏳ ½ hr 🔓 Feb–Nov

Alhough the main focus is on motoring, the museum has a toy collection which includes teddy bears, aeroplanes and rare pedal cars. It's also home to Brum, the little yellow car, from the hit children's BBC TV series which was filmed here.

* Largest collection of historic motoring signs

WC ♿ 🐕

Location
Bourton town centre at junction with
Sherborne Street

Opening
Daily; Feb–Nov 10am–6pm

Admission
Adult £2.75, Child £1.95, Family £8.60

Contact
The Old Mill, Sherbourne Street,
Bourton-on-the-Water,
Cheltenham GL54 2BY

t 01451 821255
w cotswold-motor-museum.com
e motormuseum@csma-netlink.co.uk

241 Cheltenham

Birdland Park

 ½ Day · All year

Visit the penguins, flamingos, storks, cranes, parrots, ibis, hornbills and many other birds at this centre, set in woodland and gardens.

* Children's play area

Location
Follow the A436 to Bourton-on-the-Water

Opening
Daily; 1 Apr–31 Oct open 10am–6pm; 1 Nov–31 Mar open 10am–4pm (last admission 1 hr before closing time); closed 25 Dec

Admission
Adult £4.75 Child (4–14) £2.65
Concs £3.75

Contact
Rissington Road
Bourton-on-the-Water
Cheltenham GL54 2BN
t 01451 820480
e sb.birdland@virgin.net

242 Cheltenham

Chedworth Roman Villa

 2 hrs · Mar–Nov

See the remains of one of the largest Romano-British villas in the country. The site comprises over a mile of walls, several fine mosaics, two bath houses, hypocausts, a water shrine and a latrine. The museum houses objects from the villa.

* National Trust property
* Audio-visual presentation

Location
3 miles NW of Fossebridge on the Cirencester to Northleach road (A429); from A429 via Yanworth or from the A436 via Withington

Opening
Mar–mid Nov Tue–Sun 10am–5pm
Mar & Nov 11am–4pm

Admission
Adult £4.30, Child £2.10

Contact
Yanworth
Nr Cheltenham GL54 3LJ
t 01242 890256
w nationaltrust.org.uk
e chedworth@nationaltrust.org.uk

243 Cheltenham

Cotswold Farm Park

 3 hrs · Mar–Oct

Meet over 50 flocks and herds of British rare breeds. Enjoy seasonal demonstrations and children's activities, including adventure playgrounds, an indoor tractor school, farm safari rides and a pets' corner.

Location
Follow the B4077 from Stow for 5 miles. Signed

Opening
Daily; Mar–Sep 10.30am–5pm;
Oct weekends & autumn half-term open 10.30am–4pm

Admission
Adult £4.95, Child £3.50, Concs £4.65

Contact
Guiting Power,
Cheltenham GL54 5UG
t 01451 850307
w cotswoldfarmpark.co.uk
e info@cotswoldfarmpark.co.uk

244 Cheltenham

Sandford Parks Lido

 2 hrs+ · Apr–Oct

Set in beautiful grounds, the whole family can enjoy swimming in the 50-metre heated outdoor pool.

* Playground
* Children's pool

Location
Off the A40, near the centre of Cheltenham

Opening
Daily; 20 Apr–4 Oct 11am–7.30pm.
Early morning swims, please phone for details

Admission
Adult £3, Child £1.70, Concs £1.70

Contact
Keynsham Road
Cheltenham GL53 7PU
t 01242 524430
w sandfordparkslido.org.uk
e swim@sandfordlido.freeserve.co.uk

245 Coleford

Puzzle Wood

1 hr+   Feb–Oct

This pre-Roman open-cast iron-ore mine is set in 14 acres of spectacular scenery. Pathways take you through deep ravines and passageways through moss-covered rocks, forming a very unusual maze. There is also an opportunity to meet the farm animals.

* Quality Assured Visitor Attraction
* Indoor wood puzzle with secret doorways

Location
Take the B4228 from Coleford to Chepstow. Puzzle Wood is ½ mile from Coleford

Opening
Easter–Sep Tues–Sun 11am–5.30pm (last admission 4.30pm); Oct & Feb half-term 11am–4pm (last admission 3pm)

Admission
Adult £3.90, Child £2.60

Contact
Lower Perrygrove Farm, Coleford GL16 8RB

246 Chipping Sodbury

Dyrham Park

2 hrs   All year

Dyrham Park was built between 1691 & 1702 for William Blathwayt, and its rooms have changed little since they were first furnished. There are restored Victorian domestic rooms, including kitchen, bells passsage, the bakehouse, larders, tenants' hall and a Delft-tiled dairy.

* National Trust property
* Peacocks & fallow deer in the park

Location
8 miles N of Bath & 12 miles E of Bristol, off the A46

Opening
House Mar–Oct Fri–Tue 12pm–4.45pm (Last admission 4pm)
Gardens Mar–Oct Fri–Tue 11am–5.30pm
Park All year daily 11am–5.30pm

Admission
Adult £7.90, Child £3.90,
Garden & park only: £3, £1.50

Contact
Dyrham
Nr Bath SN14 8ER

t 01179 372501
e dyrhampark@nationaltrust.org.uk

247 Gloucester

Beatrix Potter's House of *The Tailor of Gloucester*

½ hr   All year

The attraction and shop are in the house used by Beatrix Potter for her story of a mouse, *The Tailor of Gloucester*. Displays and models bring this classic English tale to life.

Location
In the city centre, off Westgate Street (pedestrian area). Easily reached from the M5 (junction 11, 11A or 12)

Opening
Apr–Oct Mon–Sat 10am–5pm;
Nov–Mar 10am–4pm;
closed Bank holidays

Admission
Adult £1, Child free, Concs 50p

Contact
9 College Court
Gloucester GL1 2NJ

t 01452 422856
w hop-skip-jump.com
e hop-skip-jump.com

248 Gloucester

National Waterways Museum

2 hrs — All year

Take a journey through Britain in this award-winning museum, telling the 200-year story of inland waterways. Investigate interactive displays, historic craft, a traditional blacksmith's and an activities room. Boat trips are available Easter to October.

* See Gloucester's role as an important dock
* For Boat trips please phone for availability

Location
Follow signs for 'Historic Docks'

Opening
Daily 10am–5pm. Closed Christmas Day

Admission
Adult £5, Child £4, Concs £4

Contact
Llanthony Warehouse,
Gloucester Docks GL1 2EH

t 01452 318200
w nwm.org.uk
e bookingsnwm|@ thewaterwaystrust
.org

249 Gloucester

Prinknash Bird & Deer Park

1 hr — All year

Enjoy a wildlife experience walking in this bird park with fallow deer and pygmy goats, peacocks and cranes. There are bird pavilions and a reputedly haunted fish pond teeming with large trout!

* Tame deer
* Tudor-style wendy house

Location
Exit the M5 at junction 11a & then take the A46 towards Stroud

Opening
Daily; summer 10am–5pm;
winter 10am–4pm

Admission
Adult £4, Child £2.50, Concs £3.50

Contact
Prinknash Abbey, Cranham
Gloucester GL4 8EX

t 01452 812727
w prinknash-bird-and-deerpark.com

250 Gloucester

Robinswood Hill Country Park

1 hr+ — All year

Enjoy 250 acres of open countryside with way-marked nature trails and a visitor centre. Pay a free visit to the new rare breeds farm and see traditional breeds of farm animals.

Location
Take the Gloucester outer ring road, S of the city road

Opening
Daily dawn–dusk

Admission
Free

Contact
Reservoir Road
Gloucester GL4 6SX

t 01452 303206

251 Gloucester

Soldiers of Gloucestershire Museum

1 hr+ — All year

The story of Gloucestershire's soldiers and their families in peacetime and war over the last 300 years is told in this award-winning museum.

* Archive film & computer animations
* Life-size displays & sound effects

Location
Follow signs to 'Historic Docks'

Opening
10am–5pm; closed winter Mondays & Christmas. (last entry 4.30pm)

Admission
Adult £4.25, Child £2.25, Concs £3.25
Family £13, under fives free

Contact
Gloucester Docks GL1 2HE

t 01452 522682
w glosters.org.uk
e rhqrgbw@milnet.uk

252 Nympsfield

Woodchester Park & Mansion

2 hrs+   All year

Known as 'The Secret Valley', this park was formerly an eighteenth-century park with five lakes and is now virtually covered with trees. It contains an unfinished Victorian gothic mansion. There are way-marked walks and trails through the woods.

Location
1 mile north-west of Nailsworth; 4 miles south-west of Stroud

Opening
Mansion: Easter–Oct weekends 11am–4pm
Park: Daily

Admission
Mansion: Adult £5 Child Free Concs £4
Park: Free

Contact
Nympsfield
Stonehouse GL10 3TS
t 01453 750455
w woodchestermansion.org.uk
e visitor@woodchestermansion.org.uk

253 Nympsfield

WWT Slimbridge Wildfowl & Wetlands Centre

3 hrs+   All year

Visit a large collection of exotic, rare and endangered ducks, geese and swans in this reserve. The Discovery Centre has hands-on displays.

* Face-painting & badge-making
* Special activities during school holidays

Location
Between Bristol & Gloucester, just off the A38, signed from the M5 (junction 13 or 14)

Opening
Daily 9.30am–5pm; Nov–Mar 4pm; closed 25 Dec

Admission
Adult £6.75, Child £4, Concs £5.50

Contact
Slimbridge GL2 7BT
t 01453 891900
w wwt.org.uk/visit/slimbridge
e info.slimbridge@wwt.org.uk

254 Stroud

Museum in the Park

2 hrs+   All year
1 hr+   All year

An innovative museum set in a park, it has imaginative displays including dinosaur bones, a Roman temple and the world's first lawnmower. There are also family activity packs, special events and exhibitions.

* Guided tours
* Quiz trails

Location
From junction 13 of the M5, take the A419 Ebley bypass towards Stroud

Opening
Apr–Sep Tue–Fri 10am–5pm,
Sat & Sun 11am–5pm;
Oct–Mar Tue–Fri 10am–4pm,
Sat & Sun 11am–4.30pm

Admission
Free

Contact
Stratford Park, Stratford Road,
Stroud GL5 4AF
t 01453 763394
w stroud.gov.uk
e museum@stroud.gov.uk

255 Bath

Bath Balloon Flights

1 hr   Apr–Oct

Ever wanted to fly over rooftops? You can in a hot-air balloon! You'll ascend as high as 3000 feet and travel up to 10 miles during the one-hour flight, depending on the weather conditions. Good stout shoes are recommended in case the balloon lands in a field.

* Fantastic views of the city
* No two trips are the same

Location
Royal Victoria Park is 5 mins walk from the city centre

Opening
Apr–Oct (office open all year)

Admission
Please phone for details

Contact
8 Lambridge, London Road, Bath BA1 6BJ

t 01225 466888
w bathballoons.co.uk
e flights@bathballoons.co.uk

256 Bath

The Jane Austen Centre

1 hr   All year

Jane Austen lived on this street from 1801 to 1806. This exciting and informative centre tells the story of her time in Bath and of the influence the city had on her novels *Northanger Abbey* and *Persuasion*.

Location
City centre N of Queen Square

Opening
Daily; Mon–Sat 10am–5.30pm
Sun 10.30am–5.30pm

Admission
Adults £4.65, Child £2.50, Concs £3.95

Contact
40 Gay Street,
Bath BA1 2NT

t 01225 443000
w janeausten.co.uk
e info@janeausten.co.uk

257 Bath

Roman Baths & Pump Rooms

2 hrs   All year

The Roman Baths are one of the best-preserved Roman sites north of the Alps. Below the streets of Bath are the Sacred Spring, a Roman temple and the Roman bath house, while the Georgian pump house stands at street level.

* Taste the water in C18 Pump Room above the Temple
* Displays include sculpture, coins & jewellery

Location
City centre near Abbey

Opening
Daily; Jan–Feb, Nov–Dec
9.30am–4.30pm
Mar–June, Sep–Oct 9am–5pm
July–Aug 9am–9pm
Closed 25,26 Dec
(exit 1 hr after close)

Admission
Adult £9, Child £5, Concs £8

Contact
Abbey Church Yard, Bath BA1 1LZ

t 01225 477785
w romanbaths.co.uk
e romanbath_bookings@bathsnes.
gov.uk

258 Bath

Prior Park Landscape Garden

1 hr+   All year

Enjoy an exhilarating walk through this stunning garden set in a sweeping valley with magnificent views of the City of Bath. This unique eighteenth-century garden is in the final stages of restoration and includes the Gothic Temple, Serpentine Lake, Cascades and Palladian Bridge.

* National Trust property

Location
There is no parking (except pre-booked disabled) at the gardens. Please phone for details of public transport connections

Opening
Feb–Nov Wed–Mon 11am–5.30pm;
Dec–Jan Fri–Sun 11am–dusk

Admission
Adult £4, Child £2, NT Free

Contact
Ralph Allen Drive
Bath BA2 5AH

t 01225 833422
w nationaltrust.org.uk
e priorpark@nationaltrust.org.uk

259 Barrington

Barrington Court

2 hrs+   Mar–Oct

An enchanting garden laid out in a sequence of walled rooms, with a working kitchen garden. The Tudor manor house is an antique furniture showroom.

* Children's activities
• Nature trail

Location
5 miles NE of Ilminster on A358

Opening
Mar & Oct Thu–Sun 11am–4.30pm
Apr–Sep daily (closed Wed)
11am–5.30pm

Admission
Adult £6, Child £3

Contact
Barrington TA19 0NQ

t 01460 241938
w nationaltrust.org.uk
e barringtoncourt@
    nationaltrust.org.uk

261 Chard

The Wildlife Park at Cricket St Thomas

1 hr+   All year

This park is home to over 600 animals, including lemur, monkeys, leopards, oryx, zebra, bison, wallabies, birds and wildfowl. Through its captive breeding programmes, the park plays an important part in the conservation of rare and endangered species.

* Licensed for civil marriages
* Safari train, crazy golf & mini car ride

Location
3 miles from Chard on A30. Signed
from M5 junction 25 and A303

Opening
Mon–Sun 10am–6pm in summer;
10am–dusk in winter

Admission
Adults £6.95, Child £4.95, Concs £5.95

Contact
Chard, TA20 4DB

t 01460 30111
w www.wild.org.uk

260 Berrow

Animal Farm Adventure Park

4 hrs+   All year

Children can pet and feed many of the friendly animals at this farm. There is a playbarn with big indoor slides and a large play park to enjoy.

* Phone for details of special events
* Delightful walks

Location
10 mins from junction 22 on the M5.
Head for Berrow & follow the signs

Opening
Daily; summer 10am–5.30pm;
winter 10am–4.30pm

Admission
Adult £5, Child £5, Concs £4.50

Contact
Red Roan, Berrow TA8 2RW

t 01278 751628
w animal-farm.co.uk
e mike@afap.fsnet.co.uk

262 Chard

Ferne Animal Sanctuary

3 hrs   All year

Take your time to stroll around the 51 acres of tranquil surroundings for 300 rescued and retired animals, ranging from horses to chipmunks.

* Quality Assured Visitor Attraction

WC 🏕 🍴 🐾

Location
3 miles W of Chard in Somerset, signed from the A30

Opening
Daily 10am–5pm; closed 25 Dec & 1 Jan

Admission
Free (donations welcome)

Contact
Chard TA20 3DH

t 01460 65214
w ferneanimalsanctuary.org
e info@ferneanimalsanctuary.org

263 Cheddar

Cheddar Gorge & Caves

3 hrs+   All year

The fascinating caves at Cheddar Gorge have long been popular attractions. Wonder at the mysterious stalagmites and stalactites in Gough's Cave and enjoy the Crystal Quest Challenge in the underground fantasy adventure game. There are explorer audio-guide tours.

* Open-top scenic bus tours in summer
* Cheddar Man

WC 🏕 🍴 ♿ᴿ 🐾

Location
Follow signs from junction 22 on M5 & A38 or take B3135 from A37 and the east

Opening
Jul–Aug 10am–5pm
Sep–Jun 10.30am–4.30pm

Admission
Adult £9.50, Child £6.50

Contact
Cheddar BS27 3QF

t 01934 742343
w cheddarcaves.co.uk
e info@cheddarcaves.co.uk

264 Dunster

Dunster Castle

2 hrs   Mar–Nov

The fortified home of the Luttrels for 600 years, this castle is set in beautiful parkland and has a terraced garden of rare shrubs. Attic and basement tours with below-stairs exhibition are popular, plus children's guide, trail and activity sheets are available.

* Guided tours available for groups
* Dogs allowed in park only

Location
Off A39, 3 miles SE from Minehead

Opening
Castle 19 Mar–30 Oct 11am–5pm;
31 Oct–6 Nov 11am–4pm,
closed Thur & Fri
Garden & Park Daily; closed 25,26 Dec

Admission
Castle Adult £7.20, Child £3.60
Garden & Park £3.90, £1.70

Contact
Dunster, Nr Minehead TA24 6SL

t 01643 821314
w nationaltrust.org.uk
e dunstercastle@nationaltrust.org.uk

265 Farleigh Hungerford

Farleigh Hungerford Castle

2 hrs   All year

In 1370, Sir Thomas Hungerford began the fortification of the original Farleigh Manor, into what became Farleigh Hungerford Castle. The two south towers still remain, as do parts of the curtain wall, the outer gatehouse, and the C14 chapel and crypt.

* Important collection of lead coffins in chapel crypt
* Programme of living history throughout the year

Location
8 miles SE of Bath off A36

Opening
Daily; Apr–Jun 10am–5pm
Jul–Aug 10am–6pm
Sep 10am–5pm;
Oct –Mar Sat & Sun 10am–4pm

Admission
Adult £2.80, Child £1.40, Concs £2.10

Contact
Farleigh Hungerford,
Nr Trowbridge BA2 7RS

t 01225 754026
w english-heritage.org.uk/southwest
e customers@english-heritage.org.uk

266 Glastonbury

Glastonbury Abbey

2 hrs   All year

Steeped in history and legend, this ancient abbey, though now ruined, is still a Christian sanctuary and an oasis of peace and quiet. Set in parkland with ponds and wildlife areas, the whole family can relax in its tranquil surroundings.

* Visitor centre with award-winning museum
* Period-dressed guides in summer months

Location
Take A39 from junction 23 of M5, follow signs from Glastonbury

Opening
Daily; Jun-Aug 9am–6pm (or dusk if earlier); Mar–May & Sep–Nov, 9.30am–6pm; Dec–Feb 10am–dusk

Admission
Adults £4, Child £1.50, Concs £3.50

Contact
Abbey Gatehouse, Magdalene Street, Glastonbury BA6 9EL

t 01458 832267
w glastonburyabbey.com
e info@glastonburyabbey.com

267 Highbridge

Alstone Wildlife Park

1 hr+   All year

A small, non-commercial family-run park and licensed zoo with camels, pigs, deer, ponies, emu, owls and llama. Special features include Theodore, the friendly camel, tame red deer, and a pets' corner.

Location
A38 Highbridge to Bridgwater road, signed turning on the right half a mile from Highbridge

Opening
Daily; 10am–5.30pm

Admission
Adults £4, Child £3, Concs £3.50

Contact
Alstone Road, Highbridge, Somerset TA9 3DT

t 01278 782405

268 Minehead

West Somerset Railway

3 hrs   Feb–Dec

This preserved steam railway operates between Minehead and Bishop's Lydeard, near Taunton. It is the longest independent railway in Britain.

* Visitor centres & museums
* Model railway

Location
Reached via the A39 & A358

Opening
Feb–Dec (daily late May–late Sep). Please phone for details

Admission
Adult £11, Child £5, Concs £10

Contact
The Station, Minehead TA24 5BG

t 01643 700384
w west-somerset-railway.co.uk
e info@west-somerset-railway.co.uk

269 Minehead

West Somerset Rural Life Museum

1 hr+   Easter–Oct

Visit the schools of the past in this museum, housed in an old school building, with a thatched roof and riverside garden. Children can dress up in Victorian clothes, write on slates and play with traditional toys.

Location
On the A39 from Minehead

Opening
Easter & 6 May–mid Oct Mon–Fri 10.30am–1pm & 2pm–4.30pm; Sun during school summer holidays 2pm–4.30pm

Admission
Adult £1.50, Child 50p

Contact
The Old School, Allerford, Minehead TA24 8HN

t 01643 862529
w allerfordwebsite.ic24.net

Radstock Museum

1 hr   Feb–Nov

This award-winning museum depicts the social and industrial heritage of the former North Somerset coalfield. It offers a unique insight into life in the region since the C19.

* Interactive & hands-on displays
* Heritage trail

Location	Admission
10 miles S of Bath	Adult £3, Child £2, Concs £2
Opening	**Contact**
Feb–Nov Tue–Fri & Sun 2pm–5pm, Sat 11am–5pm; open Bank Holidays 2pm–5pm	The Market Hall, Waterloo Road, Radstock BA3 3ER
	t 01761 437722
	w radstockmuseum.co.uk

Haynes Motor Museum

3 hrs   All year

Travel through 100 years of motoring history with Britain's most spectacular collection of historic cars from around the world.

* Fabulous collection of American sports cars
* 70-seater video theatre

Location	Contact
½ mile N of Sparkford on A359	Sparkford BA22 7LH
Opening	t 01963 440804
Daily; Mar–Oct 9.30am–5.30pm; Nov–Feb 10am–4pm; closed 25,26 Dec & 1 Jan	w haynesmotormuseum.co.uk
	e info@haynesmotormuseum.co.uk
Admission	
Adult £6.50, Child £3.50, Concs £5	

272 Street

Viaduct Fishery

5 hrs   All year

Set in the beautiful Cary Valley, this fishery offers six coarse lakes spread out over a peaceful 25-acre site. Tuition is available for beginners.

* Tackle shop

Location
On the northern outskirts of Somerton

Opening
Open dawn–dusk

Admission
Adult £6, Child £4, Concs £4

Contact
Cary Valley,
Somerton TA11 6LJ

t 01458 274022

273 Taunton

Somerset County Museum

2–3 hrs   All year

An interesting museum housed in Taunton Castle, it has costumes, silver and a C16 almshouse on display. Recent additions include the shipwreck coin hoard – the largest hoard of Roman silver coins found in Britain.

Location
Reached via the A38, M5

Opening
Tue–Sat 10am–5pm,
closed 29 Mar, 25, 26 Dec & 1 Jan

Admission
Free

Contact
Taunton Castle, Castle Green,
Taunton TA1 4AA

t 01823 320201
w somerset.gov.uk
e countymuseums@somerset.gov.uk

274 Weston–super–Mare

The Helicopter Museum

2 hrs   All year

Over 70 helicopters dating from 1931 to the present day are displayed here in hangars. There are open cockpit days and helicopter experience flights available.

* Guided tours for groups of 12 or more

Location
On the A371, off M5 (junction 21)

Opening
Apr–Oct Wed–Sun 10am–5.30pm;
Nov–Mar 10am–4.30pm;
school summer & Easter holidays daily
10am–5.30pm

Admission
Adult £4.95, Child £2.95

Contact
The Heliport, Locking Moor Road,
Weston-super-Mare BS24 8PP

t 01931 635227
w helicoptermuseum.co.uk

275 Weston–super–Mare

Seaquarium, Weston-super-Mare

2 hrs   All year

Walk through the underwater tunnel to view hundreds of fascinating fish, including sharks and rays, in 30 naturally themed marine habitats.

* Discovery trail

Location
On the seafront; take junction 21 or 22
off the M5. Follow brown tourist signs

Opening
Daily 10am–5pm, 4pm in winter (last
admissions 4pm)

Admission
Adult £5.25, Child £4.25, Concs £4.25

Contact
Marine Parade,
Weston-super-Mare BS23 1BE

t 01934 641603
w seaquarium.co.uk
e weston@seaquarium.co.uk

Somerset

276 Weston-super-Mare

Weston-super-Mare Heritage Centre

1 hr — **All year**

The heritage centre is an exhibition of what it was really like to be rich or poor in a Victorian town, and highlights the main features that can still be visited today. A working model gives children a good idea of all the fun of the Edwardian seaside.

Location
Turn onto the A370 from the M5. Follow signs to seafront N & turn right at traffic lights at the High Street

Opening
Mon–Sat 10am–4.30pm; closed Bank Holidays

Admission
Adult £1, Child free (accompanied)

Contact
3–6 Wadham Street,
Weston-super-Mare BS23 1JY

t 01934 412144

277 Wookey Hole

Wookey Hole Caves & Papermill

4 hrs — **All year**

It is said that the infamous Witch of Wookey lived in these spectacular caves. Guided tours of the caves are amazing. Visitors can also watch demonstrations of traditional paper-making at a 400-year-old papermill. There are numerous activities for children.

* Magical mirror maze & penny arcade
* New Haunted Witches Ghost Train

Location
Junction 22 of M5 & follow signs
A39 from Bath to Wells

Opening
Daily; Mar–Oct 10am–5pm, Nov–Feb 10.30am–4.30pm, closed 17–25 Dec

Admission
Adults £8.80, Child £5.50, Concs £5.50

Contact
Wookey Hole, nr Wells BA5 1BB

t 01749 672243
w wookey.co.uk
e witch@wookey.co.uk

278 Yeovil

Fleet Air Arm Museum

3 hrs+ — **All year**

Take off for a fabulous day out at the Fleet Air Arm Museum. Experience the exciting development of Britain's Flying Navy in highly imaginative exhibitions. Walk through the first British Concorde and find out how it feels to be on board an aircraft carrier.

* Interactive touch-screen displays
* Tour of an aircraft carrier's nerve centre

Location
1 mile off A303/A37 roundabout

Opening
Daily; Apr–Oct 10am–5.30pm,
Nov–Mar 10am–4.30pm;
closed 24,25,26 Dec

Admission
Adult £8.50, Child £5.75, Concs £6.75

Contact
PO Box D6, RNAS, Yeovilton,
Illchester BA22 8HT

t 01935 840565
w fleetairarm.com
e info@fleetairarm.com

279 Amesbury

Stonehenge

1 hr   All year

Now a World Heritage Site, Stonehenge is a powerful witness to the Stone and Bronze Ages. These monolithic stones – whether they were part of a sun-worshipping religion or formed a giant astronomical calendar – are a tribute to their architects and builders.

* World Heritage site
* Audio tours in nine languages

Location	Admission
2 miles W of Amesbury on junction of A303 & A360	Adult £5.20, Child £2.50, Concs £3.90
Opening	**Contact**
Daily; 16 Mar–31 May 9.30am–6pm, Jun–Aug 9am–7pm, Sep–15 Oct 9.30am–6pm, 16 Oct–15 Mar 9.30am–4pm; closed 24–26 Dec & 1 Jan	Stonehenge Information Line t 01980 624715 w english-heritage.org.uk/stonehenge

280 Avebury

Avebury

1 hr   All year

This great stone circle, encompassing part of the village of Avebury, is roughly ¼ mile across. It encloses an area of about 28 acres and contains two smaller circles within. It is believed to be an ancient religious and ceremonial centre.

* World Heritage site
* World's biggest megalithic monument

Location	Contact
6 miles W of Marlborough, 1 mile N of the Bath road (A4) on A4361 and B4003	nr Marlborough SN8 1RF t 01672 539250 w www.nationaltrust.org.uk e avebury@nationaltrust.org.uk
Opening	
Daily	
Admission	
Free	

281 Avebury

Silbury Hill

½ hr   All year

Silbury Hill is the largest human-built mound in Europe. In sheer volume of material it rivals the great pyramids of Egypt. It has been estimated that it would have taken a team of 500 men about 15 years to complete Silbury Hill, and then only if they worked round the clock!

* The largest purpose-built structure in Europe

Location	Admission
N of the A4 between Marlborough and Beckhampton	Free
Opening	**Contact**
Daily, dawn–dusk	Kennet District Council, Devizes w kennet.gov.uk

282 Calne

Bowood House

3 hrs   Mar–Nov

Fun, beauty and history are all on offer at the magnificent family home of the Marquis and Marchioness of Lansdowne. The house is set in beautiful Capability Brown parkland, and there is an adventure playground, plus the Soft Play Palace, to entertain children.

Location	Contact
Off the A4 Chippenham–Calne road in Derry Hill village	Derry Hill, Calne SN11 0LZ
Opening	t 01249 812102
Daily; 19 Mar–1 Nov 11am–6pm (last admission 5pm)	w bowood.org
Admission	e houseandgardens@bowood.org
Adult £6.60, Child from £3.40, Concs £5.50	

283 Chippenham

Lacock Abbey & Fox Talbot Museum

2 hrs+   Mar–Nov

This fine medieval abbey and house, set in gardens and woodland, is home to a museum dedicated to former resident William Henry Fox Talbot, inventor of the positive/negative photographic process.

* National Trust property
* The Abbey is a location in the Harry Potter films

Location	Admission
3 miles S of Chippenham, just E of the A350	Adult £6.50, Child £3.60
Opening	**Contact**
Abbey Daily; end Mar–early Nov 11am–5.30pm	w nationaltrust.org.uk
Museum Early Mar–early Nov 11am–5.30pm; Winter open weekends only	

284 Malmesbury

Athelstan Museum

½ hr   All year

This museum has local history exhibits such as costumes, an early fire engine, photographs of the town and an educational hands-on activity called the Mini Museum Detective. There is also an activity corner for younger children.

Location	Admission
Off the A429, 5 miles from the M4 (junction 17)	Free
Opening	**Contact**
April–Sep Tue–Sat 10am–2pm Oct–Mar Thu 10am–2pm Sat 10am–12pm; Please phone to confirm	Town Hall, Cross Hayes, Malmesbury SN16 9BZ
	t 01666 829258
	w northwilts.com
	e athelstanmuseum@northwilts.gov.uk

285 Stourhead

Stourhead Gardens

3 hrs+   All year

Stourhead's magnificent landscaped gardens offer space to let off steam and there's plenty to discover and explore. Discover the mini temples, a spooky grotto and climb Alfred's Tower to enjoy the spectacular views. The house has fine interiors, paintings and furnishings.

* Children's guide & quiz
* Hands-on activities

Location	Contact
Just off A303 at Mere	Stourhead Gardens, nr Warminster BA12 6QD
Opening	t 01747 842020
Gardens Daily	w national-trust.org.uk
House Apr–Oct, closed Wed & Thu	e stourhead@nationaltrust.org.uk
Admission	
Gardens or House Adult £5.40, Child £3	
Both Adult £9.40, Child £4.50	

286 Salisbury

Cholderton Rare Breeds Centre

  2 hrs+ Mar–Oct

This park for rare farm animals has a wealth of things to see and do, and is home to one of Britain's largest collections of rabbit breeds. There is also a replica iron-age roundhouse farm & nature trail

* Toddlers' play area & adventure playground
* Pig-racing & Tractor rides (in season)

Location
Reached by the A303 from Andover or the A338 from Salisbury or Marlborough

Opening
Feb 15–Mar 2 open daily 10am–5pm
Mar 3–19 Sat & Sun 11am–4pm
Mar 20–Oct 31 open daily 10am–6pm

Admission
Adult £5.50 Child (2–16) £3.95
Concs £4.50

Contact
Amesbury Road, Cholderton
Salisbury SP4 0EW
t 01980 629438
w rabbitworld.co.uk
e group@rabbitworld.co.uk

287 Swindon

Link Centre

 2 hrs+ All year

This multi-purpose sports centre offers an ice rink, swimming pool, badminton and squash courts, a climbing wall, and snooker.

Location
In west Swindon, 1½ miles from the town centre. Follow the brown tourist signs from the M4 (junction 16)

Opening
Please phone or visit website for details

Admission
Please phone or visit website for details

Contact
Whitehill Way, Westlea
Swindon SN5 7DL
t 01793 445566
w swindon.gov.uk/link

288 Swindon

STEAM – Museum of the Great Western Railway

2 hrs+ Daily

STEAM tells the story of workers of the Great Western Railway. Housed in beautiful railway buildings, this award-winning museum has hands-on exhibits and famous locomotives and is a great day out for all the family.

* Day out with Thomas the Tank Engine
* Featuring world famous GWR locomotives

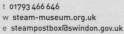

Location
Follow signs from Swindon town centre

Opening
Open all year round
except Dec 25/26 & Jan 1

Admission
Adult £5.95, Child £3.80, Concs £3.90

Contact
Kemble Drive, Swindon SN2 2TA
t 01793 466 646
w steam-museum.org.uk
e steampostbox@swindon.gov.uk

289 Swindon

Oasis Leisure Centre

2 hrs+   All year

This leisure centre has activities for all age groups including an under-fives' play area, giant water slides and lagoon pool wave machine.

* Outdoor multi-play pitches
* Soft play centre

Location
Follow the brown tourist signs on all major roads to Swindon

Opening
Please phone for details

Admission
Please phone for details

Contact
North Star Avenue, Swindon SN2 1EP

t 01793 445401
w swindon.gov.uk/oasis

---

291 Westbury

Westbury White Horse & Bratton Camp

3 hrs+   All year

The 300-year-old Westbury white horse is the oldest in Witshire. It is in a great location on a very steep slope, which is ideal for kite-flying and hang-gliding, just below the Iron-Age hill fort of Bratton camp. Spectacular views for miles around.

*Neolithic barrow or burial mound

Location
Between Westbury and B3098

Opening
All year, any reasonable time

Admission
Free

Contact
Westbury Tourist Information Centre

t 01373 827158
w english-heritage.org.uk

290 Warminster

Longleat

4 hrs+   Feb–Nov

From safari to stately home and from miniature trains to mazes and safari boat rides, there is always something to discover at Longleat. Visitors can enjoy close encounters with some of the world's most exotic animals, King Arthur's mirror maze & pets' corner.

*Longleat hedge maze
* Featured in TV's *Lion Country* and *Animal Park*

Location
Off the A36 between Bath & Salisbury (A362 Warminster to Frome road)

Opening
Daily; 12 Feb –6 Nov.
Please phone for details

Admission
Please phone for details

Contact
The Estate Office, Longleat, Warminster BA12 7NW

t 01985 844400
w longleat.co.uk
e enquiries@longleat.co.uk

Cromer, Norfolk

Eastern

Bedfordshire Cambridgeshire Essex
Hertfordshire Norfolk Suffolk

Gainsborough

The Wolds

Market Rasen
Louth
413
Mablethorpe

410–411 Lincoln
Washingborough
Horncastle
408–409 Ingoldmells
Skegness
419
415–417
428
Newark-on-Trent
420 Coningsby
414

LINCOLNSHIRE

406–407
Grantham
399
Sleaford
Boston

Wells-next-the-Sea
350 **338**
Sheringham
Cromer
351 **362**
339
349
North Walsham
342
363–364 **344**
356

Spalding **418**
Holbeach
412
King's Lynn **354** **310**
Fakenham
Aylsham
Bourne
353
Dereham
359–361
357
355
Caister-on-Sea
347 The **348**
343
Broads
Great Yarmouth

RUTLAND
440
Stamford
The Fens
Wisbech
Swaffham
340
NORFOLK
Oakham
Uppingham
Peterborough
Downham Market
Watton
Wymondham
345–346
439–440
303–306
March
Attleborough
Lowestoft
421
Corby
Oundle
A1(M)
Chatteris
Littleport
Brandon
337
358 **336**
366–368
Bungay
Beccles **373**
Kettering
Sawtry
311
CAMBRIDGESHIRE
Ely
365
Thetford
341
Diss
Halesworth
376
375 Southwold
422–423
427
Huntingdon
Mildenhall
Eye
Rushden
Brampton
St Ives
383
Saxmundham
Leiston
Northampton
309
Waterbeach
369–371
Bury St Edmunds
426
St Neots
Newmarket
377–380
Stowmarket
SUFFOLK
Aldeburgh
292
302 **374**
312
017
Bedford
Cambridge
384–385
Orford Ness
Newport Pagnell
Biggleswade
Haverhill
377
382 Woodbridge
Milton Keynes
294
330 **307**
Royston
Sudbury
Ipswich
015
300 **301**
293
Letchworth
Baldock
321
Saffron Walden
381
372
295
Hitchin
297
A1(M)
331–332
ESSEX
Halstead
322
317–319
Felixstowe
Harwich
Leighton Buzzard
Luton
327
Stevenage
STANSTED
Braintree
Colch
320
Manningtree
The Naze
298 **299**
Welwyn Garden City
Bishop's Stortford
314
Witham
007–011
Tring
324
Hemel Hempstead
St Albans
329 Ware
Hertford
Harlow
Chelmsford
Maldon
West Mersea
Clacton-on-Sea
Wendover
Berkhamsted
334 **328**
Hatfield
Hoddesdon
325
316 **296**
Amersham
High Wycombe
012
Watford
326
Barnet
Enfield
Chigwell
Brentwood
313
Rayleigh
315
Burnham-on-Crouch
Foulness Island
014 **013**
Beaconsfield
Uxbridge
335
M1
Harrow
Basildon
Southend-on-Sea
Marlow
Maidenhead
Slough
LONDON
079–107
Woolwich
Tilbury
Canvey Island
Sheerness
Herne Bay
Margate
Windsor
Bracknell
HEATHROW
Richmond
Kingston upon Thames
Dartford
Gravesend
Rochester
Isle of Sheppey
Whitstable
069
Ramsgate
005–006
118
Staines
Sutton
061
Swanley
075
Gillingham
Sittingbourne
078
Faversham
115 **126**
Woking
119–120
Croydon
066
Chatham
062
074
116

292 Bedford

Bedford Butterfly Park

2 hrs+   Jan–Dec

Set in a landscape of wildflower hay meadows, this fascinating conservation park features a tropical glasshouse. Visitors walk through a wonderful scene of waterfalls, ponds and lush foliage, with spectacular butterflies flying around.

* Quality Assured Visitor Attraction
* Nature trails & mini-farm

Location
Off the A421, near Bedford. From Bedford town centre follow signs for Cambridge. As you leave Bedford turn left for Renhold & Wilden & follow the signs for Wilden

Opening
8 Jan–10 Feb Thur–Sun 10am–4pm
11 Feb–31 Oct daily 10am–5pm
1 Nov–18 Dec Thur–Sun 10am–4pm

Admission
Adult £4.50, Child £2.75, Concs £3.50

Contact
Renhold Road, Wilden,
Bedford MK44 2PX

t 01234 772770
w bedford-butterflies.co.uk
e enquiries@bedford-butterflies.co.uk

293 Dunstable

Leighton Buzzard Railway

2 hrs   Mar–Oct

Take a journey into the world of the English light railway – experience sharp curves, steep gradients and level crossings.

* Children's play area
* Explore the Guntry terminus

Location
Off the A4146 on the edge of Leighton Buzzard, close to the junction with the A505, Dunstable–Aylesbury road

Opening
Sundays & other holiday services early Mar–end Oct;
Please phone for details

Admission
2004; Adult £5.50, Child £2.50, Concs £4.50

Contact
Billington Road,
Leighton Buzzard LU7 4TN

t 01525 373888
w buzzrail.co.uk
e info@buzzrail.co.uk

294 Biggleswade

The English School of Falconry

3 hrs+   All year

Located in woodland, this family-run centre has recreated an environment close to the birds' natural habitat. Here you can see over 300 birds, including falcons, hawks, eagles, vultures and owls, some of which you can handle or watch fly during the daily displays.

* Three flying displays daily
* Hands-on experience

Location
Old Warden is 2 miles W of A1 where it bypasses Biggleswade

Opening
Daily; Nov–Mar 10am–4pm
Apr–Oct 10am–5pm

Admission
Adult £6, Child £4

Contact
Old Warden Park, Biggleswade
SG18 9EA

t 01767 627527
w shuttleworth.org
e falconry.centre@virgin.net

295 Dunstable

Whipsnade Wild Animal Park

3–5 hrs   All year

You can't fail to have fun at Whipsnade. With more than 2500 wild animals, it is one of the largest wildlife conservation centres in Europe. The park includes 600 acres of beautiful parkland, Safari Tour bus & herds of Asian animals.

* Children's farm & adventure playground
* Free-flying bird display & penguin feeding

Location
Follow the brown elephant signs from the M1 (junction 9 or 12). Just 20 mins from the M25 (junction 21)

Opening
Daily; from 10am.
Please see website for details

Admission
2004: Adult £13.50, Child (3–15) £10, Concs £11.50, Car park £3
Please phone for 2005 prices

Contact
Dunstable LU6 2LF

t 01582 872171
w whipsnade.co.uk

296 Henlow

Stondon Motor Museum

2 hrs   All year

Travel back in time to discover vehicles from the beginning of the century up to modern-day classics–400 vehicles are housed in five halls and include Rolls Royce and Bentley cars. Outside the museum is an exact replica of Captain Cook's ship, HM Bark *Endeavour*.

* Full size replica of Captain Cook's HM Bark *Endeavour*
* Large free car park

Location
At Lower Stondon nr Henlow off the A600

Opening
Daily; 10am–5pm

Admission
Adult £6, Child £3, Concs £5

Contact
Station Road, Lower Stondon, Henlow SG16 6JN

t 01462 850339
w transportmuseum.co.uk
e info@transportmuseum.co.uk

297 Luton

John Dony Field Centre

1 hr+   All year

The Field Centre is located close to a number of important sites of natural historical interest in north-east Luton. There are displays featuring local and natural history, conservation and archaeology.

* Wildlife garden

Location
In the Bushmead Estate, nr A6, in north Luton. Signed from the round-about at Barnfield College on A6

Opening
Please phone for opening times

Admission
Free

Contact
Hancock Drive, Bushmead, Luton LU2 7SF

t 01582 486983
w luton.gov.uk
e russells@luton.gov.uk

298 Kensworth

Dunstable Downs Countryside Centre & Whipsnade Estate

2 hrs+   All year

A great place to learn all about flora and fauna, walk, cycle along designated routes, fly kites or watch paragliders. Visit in July to see spectacular displays during the annual kite-flying festival. The centre has exhibitions and a wide range of kites for sale.

* Annual kite festival
* Designated area of outstanding natural beauty

Location
4miles NE of Ashridge between B4540 & B4541

Opening
Downs Daily
Centre Daily; Apr-Oct 10am-5pm
Nov-Apr Sat-Sun 10am-4pm

Admission
Free

Contact
Whipsnade Road, Kensworth, Dunstable LU6 2TA

t 01582 608489
w www.nationaltrust.org.uk
e dunstabledowns@nationaltrust.org.uk

299 Luton

Stockwood Craft Museum & Gardens

1 hr+   All year

This award-winning museum covers nine centuries of garden history and rural life. Its collection of vehicles, which vistors can ride on, illustrates the development of horse-drawn road transport in Britain from Roman times to the 1930s. Events and activities all year round.

* Sculpture garden with work by Hamilton Finlay
* Largest display of horse-drawn carriages in the UK

Location
2 miles S of Luton town centre, close to junction 10 of M1

Opening
Apr-Oct Tues-Sun 10am-5pm
Nov-Mar Sat-Sun 10am-4pm

Admission
Free

Contact
Farley Hill, Luton LU1 4BH

t 01582 738714
w www.lutonline.org.uk
e museum.gallery@luton.gov.uk

300 Milton Keynes

HULA Animal Rescue: South Midlands Animal Sanctuary

1 hr+   All year

HULA Animal Rescue is the headquarters of the charity founded in 1972. It houses rescued and abandoned animals. Ponies, donkeys, cattle, chickens, ducks, sheep and pigs are residents, and dogs, cats, rabbits, small rodents and birds await adoption into new homes.

* Café & shop open on monthly open days
* Animal houses

Location
From the village square in Aspley Guise turn into Church Road, then into Salford Road & the entrance to Glebe Farm is on the right

Opening
Sat & Sun 1pm–3pm
Please phone for details of monthly open days & Bank holiday opening

Admission
Adult £1, Child 50p

Contact
Glebe Farm, Salford Road, Aspley Guise, Milton Keynes MK17 8HZ
t 01908 584000
w hularescue.org
e hularescue@yahoo.co.uk

301 Milton Keynes

Woburn Safari Park

6 hrs   All year

This famous safari drive-through also has an extensive leisure park. There are animal contact areas, a children's playground (indoor and outdoor), boats and a railway train. It's the only reserve with two species of carnivore, where wolves and bears roam together.

* Visitor Attraction of the Year 2000

Location
5 minutes off M1 (junction 13). Follow the signposts

Opening
Daily; Mar–Oct 10am–5pm (last admission); Nov–Feb open weekends 11am–3pm

Admission
Please phone for details

Contact
Woburn MK17 9QN
t 01525 290407
w woburnsafari.co.uk
e enquires@woburnsafari.co.uk

302 Duxford

Imperial War Museum Duxford

3 hrs+   All year

With its air shows, unique history and atmosphere, nowhere else combines the sights, sounds and power of aircraft quite like Duxford.

* 'D-Day Experience' complete with video story
* Flying displays held throughout the summer

Location
Off junction 10 of M11

Opening
Daily; summer Mar– Sep 10am–6pm; winter 10am–4pm

Admission
Adult £10, Child free, Concs £8

Contact
Duxford CB2 4QR

t 01223 835 000
w iwm.org.uk/duxford
e duxford@iwm.org.uk

303 Huntingdon

Houghton Mill

1 hrs   Mar–Nov

Discover how flour is made at this working watermill situated on an island in the Great Ouse. Have a go at turning the millstone and pull on a rope to lift the bags of flour. There has been a mill on this site since 974. The flour's for sale and there are family and children's guides.

* National Trust property
* Hands-on activities & children's quiz & trail

Location
In the village of Houghton, signed from A1123 Huntingdon–St Ives road

Opening
April & Oct open weekends 1pm–5pm ; May–Sep open Sat–Wed 1pm–5pm; Open to groups at other times by arrangement

Admission
Adult £3.20 Child £1.50

Contact
Houghton,
nr Huntingdon PE17 2AZ

t 01480 301494
w nationaltrust.org.uk
e sally.newton@nationaltrust.org.uk

Flag Fen Bronze Age Centre

4 hrs   All year

Travel back in time to the Bronze Age and visit a mock archaeological sand dig, a real Roman road and reconstructed Iron Age roundhouses. See artefacts discovered here, learn about sword-making or enjoy a guided tour of excavations (spring and summer only).

* Featured on Channel 4's *Time Team*
* The oldest wheel in England discovered here

Location	Contact
NE of Peterborough, off A1139 or A605	The Droveway, Northey Road, Peterborough PE6 7QJ
Opening	
Daily; 10am–5pm except Christmas day	t 01733 313414
	w flagfen.com
Admission	e office@flagfen.freeserve.co.uk
Adults £4, Child £3, Concs £3/£3.50	

Nene Valley Railway

3 hrs+   All year

Home to a real 'Thomas' the Tank Engine, Nene Valley railway provides an exciting day out for train enthusiasts both young and old. Travel on a 15-mile round trip through the beautiful Nene Park and enjoy one of Britain's leading collection of engines and carriages, both steam and diesel.

* Train galas in March, June and September
* Talking Timetable 01780 784404

Location	Contact
Off the southbound A1 at Stibbington between the A47 & A605 junctions	Wansford Station, Stibbington, Peterborough PE8 6LR
Opening	t 01780 784444
Daily; 9am–4.30pm	w nvr.org.uk
closed 24 Dec–1 Jan	e nvrorg@aol.com
Admission	
Adults £10, Child £5, Concs £7.50	

Peterborough Museum & Art Gallery

2 hrs   All year

This former hospital houses over 220,000 objects, including Jurassic fossils of marine reptiles (underwater dinosaurs), remains from Anglo-Saxon burials and finds from Roman times. Lively programme of workshops, talks and informal, hands-on activities.

* Changing exhibitions, talks and workshops
* Gift shop with a range of books and souvenirs

Location	Contact
Peterborough town centre	Priestgate, Peterborough PE1 1LF
Opening	t 01733 343329
Tue–Fri 12noon–5pm, Sat 10am–5pm, Sun 12noon–4pm	w peterboroughheritage.org.uk
	e museum@peterborough.gov.uk
Admission	
Free	

307 Royston

Wimpole Home Farm

 2-4 hrs   All year

Built in 1794, Wimpole is a working farm and home to a number of rare farmyard breeds. Children can feed and handle many of the animals, and can enjoy the adventure playground with pedal tractors.

* National Trust property

Location
6 miles N of Royston,
8 miles SW of Cambridge

Opening
Tue-Thu & Sat-Sun 10.30am-5pm
(11am-4pm in winter); open Bank hol-iday Mon; open extra days in school holidays (please phone for details)

Admission
Adult £6.90, Child £3.40,
Discounts for NT members

Contact
Arrington,
Royston SG8 0BW
t 01223 206000
e wimpolefarm@nationaltrust.org.uk

308 Royston

Shepreth Wildlife Park

 2-4 hrs   All year

Shepreth offers a fun and interactive day out for the family. It's home to animals, including tigers, meerkats, wolves, deer and farmyard animals. Children can visit Bug City and Waterworld, where they'll come face-to-face with scorpions, giant spiders and a dwarf alligator.

* Pirate ship adventure area
* Play area & sandpit for toddlers & children's playroom

Location
Easily reached from A10
Cambridge-Royston road & A1198
Royston-Huntingdon road. Good access by train from London King's Cross to Shepreth station

Opening
Daily; Apr-Sep 10am-6pm; Oct-Mar 10am-dusk

Admission
Adult £6, Child £4.50, Concs £5
Bug City/Waterworld £1.75, £1.10, £1.45

Contact
Willersmill, Station Road, Shepreth, nr Royston SB8 6PZ
t 09066 800031 (info line – 25p/min)
   01763 262226 (group bookings)
w sheprethwildlifepark.co.uk

309 Waterbeach

Denny Abbey & The Farmland Museum

 1 hr+   Apr-Oct

Explore local rural life at the Farmland Museum with hands-on displays and interactive exhibits. Visit a traditional farmer's cottage and discover the story of the Benedictine monks, Knights Templar and Franciscan nuns who lived in Denny Abbey.

* English Heritage property

Location
6 miles N of Cambridge on A10

Opening
Daily; 1 Apr-31 Oct 12noon-5pm

Admission
Adult £3.70, Child £1.50, Concs £2.80

Contact
Ely Road,
Waterbeach CB5 9PQ
t 01223 860489
w dennyfarmlandmuseum.org.uk

310 Wisbech

Fenland & West Norfolk Aviation Museum

 1-2 hrs   Mar-Oct

Visitors have the chance to sit in the cockpit of a Jet Provost, a Vampire T.11 or a Lightning T.5. Inside the museum is a Jumbo Jet 747 cockpit, a Jet Provost systems trainer and a fine collection of aviation artefacts.

* Aircraft park
* Café & souvenir shop

Location
Follow the brown tourist signs from A47 Wisbech bypass; or take the old B198 to King's Lynn from Wisbech and the museum is ½ mile from the bypass

Opening
Mar-Oct weekends & Bank Holidays
9.30am-5pm (4pm in Mar & Oct)

Admission
Adult £1.50, Child 75p, Concs 75p

Contact
Old Lynn Road, West Walton,
Wisbech PE14 7DA
t 01945 461771
w fawnaps.co.uk
e bill@wwelbourne.freeserve.co.uk

311 Sawtry

Hamerton Zoo Park

2 hrs+   All year

Do you know what a curassow, a seriema or a binturong is? Find out by visiting the zoo's fascinating array of beautiful creatures from around the world. There are special enclosures with low windows to give children unrivalled views of the most popular animals.

* Spacious indoor-outdoor enclosures for monkeys
* Opportunity to handle many different animals

Location
On A14, turn off to B660 at junction 15 onto A1M follow signs

Opening
Daily; 10.30am–6pm (4pm in winter)
Closed 25 Dec

Admission
Please ring for details

Contact
Hamerton, nr Sawtry PE28 5RE

t 01832 293362
w hamertonzoopark.com
e office@hamertonzoopark.com

312 Woodhurst

The Raptor Foundation

2 hrs+   All year

Home to over 300 birds of prey and more than 43 species, the Raptor Foundation is a unique and exciting place for children and adults alike. Pay a visit to meet and learn about owls, falcons, hawks and buzzards.

* Quality Assured Visitor Centre
* Junior Raptors Club

Location
Off A14 St Ives exit. Turn onto B1040 to Somersham & follow the brown tourist signs

Opening
Daily; 10am–5pm
Closed 25 Dec & 1 Jan

Admission
Adult £3.50, Child £2, Concs £2.50

Contact
The Heath, St Ives Road,
Woodhurst PE28 3BT

t 01487 741140
w raptorfoundation.org.uk
e heleowl@aol.com

313   Billericay

Barleylands Craft Village & Farm Centre

2 hrs   All year

A unique attraction with probably the largest collection of working crafts in East Anglia and an impressive farm museum. Children can meet and feed the friendly pigs, cows, goats and sheep in the animal centre. There is also an adventure play area.

* Indoor sand pit & trampolines

Location
Follow the brown tourist signs from A127 or A129

Opening
Craft Village: open all year
Farm Centre: 1 Mar–31 Oct
Daily; 10am–5pm

Admission
Craft Village: Free
Farm Centre: £3

Contact
Barleylands Road,
Billericay CM11 2UD
t 01268 290229
w barleylands.co.uk
e info@barleylands.co.uk

315   Billericay

Hanningfield Reservoir Visitor Centre

2–3 hrs   All year

The visitor centre is the gateway to the 100-acre nature reserve on the shores of Hanningfield Reservoir. On a Site of Special Scientific Interest for its breeding of over-wintering birds.

* Events throughout the year
* Children's activities in summer

Location
Turn off the B1007 onto Downham Road & turn left onto Hawkswood Road. The centre is just beyond the causeway, opposite Crowsheath

Opening
Mon-Fri & Bank holidays 9am–5pm

Admission
Free (donations requested)

Contact
Hawkswood Road, Downham,
Billericay CM11 1WT
t 01268 711001
w essexwt.org.uk
e hanningfield@essexwt.org.uk

314   Braintree

The Original Great Maze

3 hrs+   Jul–Sep

The Great Maze offers more than 5 miles of pathway cut from 10 acres of maize and sunflowers, which reach a height of almost 10 feet. A new maze is designed every year, so enthusiasts can return time and time again to try to beat the latest creation.

* Viewing platform & Lost Souls map available
* Shopping at Blake House Craft Centre

Location
On A120 between Great Dunmow & Braintree

Opening
Daily; 10 Jul–12 Sep 10am–5pm

Admission
Adult £4, Child £2.50, Concs £2.50

Contact
Blake House Craft Centre,
Braintree CM7 8SH
t 01376 553146
w maze.info
e david@rochesterfm.freeserve.co.uk

316 Brentwood

Old MacDonald's Educational Farm Park

3 hrs+   All year

This educational farm park was created to offer a greater understanding of British farm livestock, wildlife & country-side. There are 17 acres of pasture & woodland, with hard paths to ensure dry feet & access for wheelchairs, and opportunities to get close to the animals.

* Playground
* Otters, red squirrels, owls

WC · picnic · food · wheelchair · animals

Location
Off M25 at junction 28 onto A1023. Left at 1st lights into Wigley Bush Lane, left at the junction with Weald Road, 2 miles on Weald Road. Farm is on the left

Opening
Daily; in summer 10am–5pm; in winter 10am–dusk

Admission
Adult £3.25, Child (2–15) £2, Concs £2.75

Contact
Weald Road, South Weald, Brentwood CM14 5AY
t 01277 375177
w oldmacdonaldsfarm.org.uk
e info@oldmacdonaldsfarm.org.uk

317 Chelmsford

Chelmsford Museum & Essex Regiment Museum

1 hr+   All year

The museum houses three permanent exhibitions. One takes visitors on a journey from the Ice Age to the present day; a natural-history display shows living conditions and wildlife during the Ice Age, and domestic life and costume gallerys depict life in C19 and C20.

* Bright & colourful Victorian pottery from Hedingham
* Period dress and room settings

WC · picnic · wheelchair

Location
In Oaklands Park, off Moulsham Street

Opening
Daily; Mon–Sat 10am–5pm
Sun 2pm–5pm
Winter 1pm–4pm

Admission
Free

Contact
Oaklands Park, Chelmsford CM2 9AQ
t 01245 615100
w chelmsfordmuseums.co.uk
e oaklands@chelmsfordbc.gov.uk

318 Colchester

High Woods Country Park

2 hrs+   All year

This country park boasts areas of woodland, wetland, grassland and farmland. Numerous footpaths provide an opportunity to see a wide range of wildlife and a visitor centre houses displays on the natural history and history of the area.

* Quality Assured Visitor Attraction

WC · picnic · food · wheelchair · animals

Location
Accessible from Mile End Road & Ipswich Road, travelling N from Colchester

Opening
Visitor Centre: 1 Apr–30 Sep open Mon–Sat 10am–4.30pm, Sun & Bank holidays 11am–5.30pm; 1 Oct–31 Mar open weekends only 10am–4pm

Admission
Free

Contact
Turner Road, Colchester CO4 5JR
t 01206 853588

319 Colchester

Colchester Zoo

6 hrs   All year

A modern and exciting attraction with a programme of daily displays and interactive areas. Highlights include an African Zone with giraffes, elephants, rhinos, cheetahs, warthogs, zebra & hyenas in savannah-style enclosures, & Playa Patagonia, a new underwater sea lion experience.

* Children's jungle safari train
*Kalahari Capers soft play area & rope bridge

Location
Take A1124 exit from A12

Opening
Daily; summer 9.30am–5.30pm
winter 9.30am–1 hr before dusk

Admission
Adult £12.49, Child £7.49, Concs £9.49

Contact
Maldon Road, Stanway,
Colchester CO3 0SL
t 01206 331292
w colchester-zoo.co.uk
e enquiries@colchester-zoo.co.uk

320 Colchester

Quasar at Rollerworld

1 hr+   All year

In this futuristic laser game each player is armed with a laser gun and shoots the opposition to win points. Players get unlimited lives and the game marshal instructs you on how to play. Under 12s must be accompanied by a playing adult.

* Suitable for ages 8 to 80
* Supervised by Games Marshal

Location
From A12, take the turn off to Harwich & Colchester. Continue straight over the roundabouts & follow the brown tourist signs

Opening
Please phone for details

Admission
Please phone for details

Contact
Eastgates,
Colchester CO1 2TJ
t 01206 868868
w rollerworld.co.uk

321 Saffron Walden

Mole Hall Wildlife Park

2 hrs   Easter–Oct

The park is in gardens adjoining a fully moated manor (not open to the public) and has otters, chimps, guanaco, lemurs, wallabies, deer and owls.

* Butterfly pavilion & pets' corner
* Animal adoption scheme & play areas

Location
Signposted from B1383 & junction 8 of M11

Opening
Daily; Easter–Oct 10.30am–dusk

Admission
Adult £5, Child £3.50, Concs £4

Contact
Widdington, nr Saffron Walden
CB11 3SS
t 01799 540400
w molehall.co.uk
e enquiries@molehall.co.uk

322 Halstead

Hedingham Castle

½ hr+   Apr–Oct

Built in 1140 by the Earls of Oxford, this is one of the best-preserved Norman keeps in England. The castle is set in beautiful parkland and holds special events such as jousts throughout the summer.

* Jousting tournaments

Location
Situated in Castle Hedingham, ½ mile from A1017 between Cambridge & Colchester

Opening
Apr–Oct Thu, Fri & Sun 11am–4pm
Special school holiday opening 10am–5pm, phone for details

Admission
Adult £4, Child £3, Concs £3.50

Contact
Halstead CO9 3DJ

t 01787 460261
w hedinghamcastle.co.uk
e hedinghamcastle@aspects.net.co.uk

323 Waltham Abbey

Royal Gunpowder Mills

3 hrs+   All year

Royal Gunpowder Mills mixes fascinating history, exciting science and beautiful surroundings to produce a magical trip for both old and young.

* Muskets, rifles, pistols, machine guns
* Tours by tractor-trailer train

Location
1 mile from junction 26 of M25, A121

Opening
Apr 30–Sep 25 Sat, Sun & Bank hols
11am–5pm (last entry 3.30pm)

Admission
Adult £5.50, Child £3, Concs £4.70

Contact
Beaulieu Drive, Waltham Abbey
EN9 1JY

t 01992 707370
w royalgunpowdermills.com
e info@royalgunpowdermills.com

324 Berkhamsted

Ashridge Estate

 4 hrs+ All year

There's plenty to see and do at Ashridge, no matter what season it is. Enjoy the spring bluebells, a picnic on a sunny day, or a woodland walk in autumn. Make sure you keep your eyes peeled as Ashridge is a wildlife haven – if you are lucky you might spot a badger or a woodpecker.

* Guided walks & hands-on activities
* Family deer-watching sessions

Location
Between Northchurch & Ringshall just off B4506

Opening
Visitor Center: Daily; 1pm–5pm weekdays 12noon–5pm weekends

Admission
Estate free
Monument Adult £1.20, Child 60p

Contact
Ringshall, Berkhamsted HP4 1LT

t 01442 851 227
w nationaltrust.org.uk
e ashridge@nationaltrust.org.uk

325 Broxbourne

Paradise Wildlife Park

  2 hrs+ All year

A friendly, family-run leisure park which offers excitement and enjoyment for all the family. Visitors can touch and feed paddock animals, including zebras and camels, shadow a keeper, and meet wolves and meerkats. There are also play areas and a fun-fair.

* Brazilian tapirs and reptilemania
* Parrot olympic training

Location
Junction 25 of M25 onto A10, signposted from Broxbourne

Opening
Daily; Mar–Oct 9.30am–6pm; Nov–Feb 10am–5pm

Admission
Adult £10, Child £7, Concs £7

Contact
White Stubbs Lane, Broxbourne EN10 7QA

t 01992 470 490
w pwpark.com
e info@pwpark.com

326 Borehamwood

Aldenham Country Park

 7 hrs+ All year

With a 65-acre reservoir, circular footpath and 175 acres of woods and meadowland, Aldenham Country Park offers a range of activities and interests for the whole family, from nature trails to Winnie the Pooh features. There are also rare breeds, cattle, sheep and other animals.

* Adventure playground
* Angling (day tickets £4)

Location
Drive via A5, A41, A1(M) or MI (junction 5) & the park is just off the A5183, north of Elstree on Aldenham Road

Opening
Daily; Nov–Feb 9am–4pm; Mar–Apr & Sep–Oct 9am–5pm; May–Aug 9am–6pm

Admission
Free
Car park: £3 per vehicle

Contact
Park Office, Dagger Lane, Elstree, Borehamwood WD6 3AT

t 0208 953 9602
w hertsdirect.org/aldenham

327 Hitchin

Waterhall Farm & Craft Centre

2hrs+   All year

A small open farm featuring rare breeds and offering a hands-on experience for visitors. There is also a play area featuring a straw bale battlefield, sandpit, slide and an old tractor.

* Tea room & gardens

Location	Admission
Off the B651 Hitchin–St Albans road, in the village of Whitwell	Adult £2.75 Child (2–16) £1.75 Concs £1.75
Opening	**Contact**
Weekends & school holidays; in summer open 10am–5pm; in winter open 10am–4pm	Whitwell Hitchin SG4 8BN t 01438 871256

328 Hatfield

Mill Green Museum & Mill

1 hr+   All year

A visit to this fully restored eighteenth-century working watermill that is still producing flour, is interesting and educational. The adjacent miller's house is now the local history museum for the district. There are events throughout the year for all to enjoy.

* Waterwheel in action every day
* Watch milling of organic flour on Tue, Wed & Sun

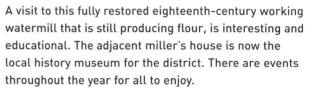

Location	Contact
Located in Mill Green, between Hatfield and Welwyn Garden City	Mill Green, Hatfield AL9 5PD t 01707 271362 w hertsmuseums.org.uk/millgreen e museum@welhat.gov.uk
Opening	
Tue–Fri 10am–5pm Sat, Sun & Bank Hols 2pm–5pm	
Admission	
Free	

329 Hertford

Hertford Museum

1–2 hrs   All year

A local history museum in an old town house with a recreated Jacobean knot garden. There are changing temporary exhibitions to cater for all ages, with related activities for children.

* Special events in school holidays, bookable in advance

Location	Admission
Just off the A414 in the centre of Hertford, a short walk from the multi-storey car park & within walking distance of the train station	Free
	Contact
	18 Bull Plain, Hertford SG14 1DT
Opening	t 01992 582686
Tue–Sat 10am–5pm	w hertfordmuseum.org
Please phone to confirm Bank holiday openings	e info@hertfordmuseum.org

330 Royston

Maple Street British Museum of Miniatures

2 hrs   All year

The Museum of Miniatures is a doll's house and miniatures museum. Its displays include the largest doll's house in the world, and the on-site shop is the largest doll's house shop in Europe.

* Full scale model of Wimpole Hall
* Collection of model railways

Location	Admission
Take A603 from Cambridge & A1198 to Royston	Adult £2.50, Child £1.50
Opening	**Contact**
Daily; Mon–Sat 9.30am–5pm & Sun 12noon–4pm; Please phone for Bank holiday opening times	Maple Street, Wendy, Royston SG8 0AB
	t 01223 207025
	w maplestreet.co.uk
	e info@maplestreet.co.uk

331 Stevenage

Stevenage Museum

1 hr+   All year

Learn all about Stevenage, from the Stone Age to the present day. Find your house or school in old photographs, try on Victorian costumes, see a Roman coin hoard, test your knowledge with computer quizzes, or travel back in time with Sam and his magic mirror.

* The Story of Stevenage – prehistory to 1700
* Varied programme of events

Location	Admission
Located underneath St.Andrew & St.Georges Church – signed from town centre	Free, exhibitions may charge
Opening	**Contact**
Daily; Mon–Sat 10am–5pm Sun 2pm–5pm. Closed Bank Hols	St George's Way, Stevenage SG1 1XX
	t 01438 218881
	w stevenage.gov.uk/museum
	e museum@stevenage.gov.uk

332 Stevenage

Fairlands Valley Park

4 hrs+   All year

This 120-acre park has a sailing centre offering water-sports, dinghy sailing, windsurfing and powerboat courses. There are crafts for hire during the summer months of May–Sep. Visitors can also go fishing in the bay.

* Children's play area
* Paddling pools

Location	Contact
Situated on Six Hills Way, 1 mile E of Stevenage	Six Hills Way, Stevenage SG2 0BL
Opening	t 01438 353241
Daily; 8am-dusk	w stevenage-leisure.co.uk/fairlands
Admission	e fairland@clara.net
Free	

333 St Albans

Willows Farm Village

3 hrs+   Apr–Oct

Children enjoy this farm village where they can get to know the farm animals in a countryside setting. Some attractions include bouncy haystack, Daft Duck trails, guinea pig village, children's theatre and a tractor trek.

* Falconry display
* Maze (summer holidays only)

Location	Contact
300 metres from junction 22 of M25	Coursers Road, London Colney, St Albans AL2 1BB
Opening	t 01727 822444
Daily; Apr–Oct 10am–5.30pm	w willowsfarmvillage.com
Admission	e info@willowsfarmvillage.com
Please phone for details	

334 St Albans

Verulamium Museum

 1–2 hrs   All year

Verulamium Museum is the museum of everyday life in Roman Britain. The award-winning displays include recreated Roman interiors, collections of glass, pottery, jewellery, coins, magnificent mosaics, wall paintings and reconstructions of Roman rooms.

* Quality Assured Visitor Attraction
* Hands-on discovery areas & playground

Location
Drive via M1 (junction 6) or M25 (junction 21A). The museum is just off the A4147, 1 mile from the centre of St Albans

Opening
Daily; Mon–Sat 10am–5.30pm & Sun 2pm–5.30pm;
Closed 25, 26 Dec

Admission
Adult £3.30, Child £2, Concs £2

Contact
St Michaels,
St Albans AL3 4SW

t 01727 751810
w stalbansmuseums.org.uk
e museum@stalbans.gov.uk

335 Watford

Activity World & Farmyard Fun

 3 hrs+   All year

This indoor and outdoor adventure playground has a separate area for toddlers and a baby play pool. Farmyard Fun allows close-up contact with a range of animals, from rabbits and sheep to cows and ponies.

Location
5 mins from M1 (junction 5) & 10 mins from M25 (junction 19) on Aldenham road.

Opening
Daily: *Activity World:* 10am–6pm
Farmyard Fun: 10am–5pm (or dusk, if earlier);

Admission
Adult £1, Child (over 5) £5,
Child (2–5) £4

Contact
Lincolnsfield Centre, Bushey Hall,
Drive, Bushey, Watford WD23 2ES

t 01923 219902
w lincolnsfields.co.uk
e info@lincolnsfields.co.uk

336 Banham

Banham Zoo

3-5 hrs   All year

Set in 35 acres of countryside and landscaped gardens, Banham Zoo is home to some of the world's most exotic and endangered animals, ranging from big cats to birds of prey, siamangs to Shire horses.

* Free safari roadtrain
* All-weather activity centre

Location
Between Attleborough & Diss; signed from A11 & A140

Opening
Daily; 10am (seasonal closing times, please phone for details)
Closed 25, 26 Dec

Admission
Vary according to season (please phone for details)

Contact
The Grove,
Banham NR16 2HE

t 01953 887771
w banhamzoo.co.uk

337 Brandon

Grimes Graves

1 hr   All year

At Grimes Graves there is a site exhibition with remarkable neolithic flint mines. The mines are 4000 years old and were first excavated in the 1870s, with over 300 pits and shafts. One pit is open to the public.

* No children under five allowed down shaft
* Site of Special Scientific Interest

Location
Located 7 miles NW of Thetford off A134

Opening
Daily; Apr–Sep 10am–6pm
Oct Thurs–Mon 10am–5pm
Nov–Mar Wed–Sun 10am–4pm

Admission
Adult £2.60, Child £1.30, Concs £2

Contact
Brandon, Lynford IP26 5DE

t 01842 810656
w english–heritage.org.uk

338 Blakeney

Blakeney Point

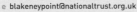

3 hrs   All year

One of Britain's foremost bird sanctuaries, the Point is noted for its colonies of breeding terns and for the rare migrants that pass through in spring and autumn. Common and grey seals can also be seen. Dogs are allowed April–August.

* Information centre at Morston Quay provides further details
* Restricted access during main bird breeding season

Location
Morston Quay, Blakeney and Cley are all off A149 Cromer to Hunstanton road ferrys run from Worston

Opening
Daily; all year, all times

Admission
Free

Contact
The Warden, 35 The Cornfield, Langham, Holt NR25 7DQ

t 01263 740480 (Apr–Sep)
   01263 740241 (Oct–Mar)
w nationaltrust.org.uk
e blakeneypoint@nationaltrust.org.uk

339 Cromer

Norfolk Shire Horse Centre

 2 hrs+   Apr-Oct

Children can see shire horses at work and learn about a bygone age when our tools were horse-powered. The centre also has a children's farm and riding school.

* Horse & cart rides
* Feed farmyard animals

Location
Off A148 & A149

Opening
Daily; 4 Apr-29 Oct 10am-5pm;
Closed Sat except Bank holiday weekends

Admission
Adult £5.50, Child £3.50, Concs £4.50

Contact
West Runton Stables, West Runton, Cromer NR27 9QH

t 01263 837339
w norfolk-shirehorse-centre.co.uk
e bakewell@norfolkshirehorse.fsnet.co.uk

340 Dereham

Roots of Norfolk

 4 hrs+   Mar-Nov

This is a remarkable museum housed in a former workhouse and in an idyllic rural setting. It has displays on village and rural life plus a farm worked with horses and stocked with rare breeds.

* Riverside trails
* Children's activities

Location
3 miles NW of East Dereham on A47

Opening
Daily; 8 Mar-31 Oct 10am-5pm (last admission 4.45pm); Nov open Sun 11am-4pm
Please phone for details

Admission
Adult £5.70, Child £4.40 Concs £5

Contact
Gressenhall,
Dereham NR20 4DR

t 01362 860563
w museums.norfolk.gov.uk
e greffenhall.museum@norfolk.gov.uk

341 Diss

Bressingham Steam Experience & Gardens

 4 hrs   Apr-Oct

A working steam experience in a nationally known garden setting with narrow-gauge railway rides, a Victorian steam roundabout, locomotive sheds, stationary engine displays, a royal coach, traction engines and gardens. There are miniature steam-hauled trains.

* Dad's Army National Collection
* Friends of Thomas the Tank Engine

Location
3 miles W of Diss on A1066
Diss-Thetford road

Opening
Daily; Easter-Oct 10.30am- 5.30pm
Please phone for details

Admission
Adult £6.50-£7.50, Child £4-£5,

Concs £5.50-£6.50, Rides £1.50
Unlimited rides tickets avalable

Contact
Bressingham,
Diss IP22 2AB

t 01379 686900
w bressingham.co.uk
e info@bressingham.co.uk

342 Fakenham

South Creake Maize Maze

 2 hrs+   Jul-Sep

Looking for excitement and adventure? Then take the challenge of a 7-acre maze in a maize field. Set in 18 acres of unspoilt Norfolk countryside, this is a chance to lose yourself in nature.

* Crazy golf
* Panning for gold

Location
Between Fakenham & Burnham Market on B1355, just off A148 King's Lynn- Fakenham road

Opening
Daily; 17 Jul-5 Sep 10am-6pm (last admission 5pm)

Admission
Adult £3.50, Child £2.50, Concs £2.50

Contact
Compton Hall, South Creake, Fakenham NR21 9JD

t 01328 823224

343 Great Yarmouth

Burgh Castle: Church Farm

1 hr   All year

The remains of a C3 Roman fort, Burgh Castle is one of a chain built to defend the coast against the Saxon raiders. It has impressive walls with projecting bastions.

* National Heritage Property

Location	Contact
Off A143. At the W end of Breydon Water on an unclassified road, 3 miles W of Great Yarmouth	Great Yarmouth NR31 9QG
	t 01493 780331
	w english-heritage.org.uk
Opening	
Daily; 9am-6pm	
Admission	
Free	

344 Great Yarmouth

Horsey Mere

2 hrs   Mar-Oct

This area of 1,900 acres on the edge of the Norfolk Broads is ideal for a few hours' walking. It has dunes, farmland and reedbeds and is teeming with wildlife. Nearby is the 90-year-old Horsey Windpump windmill, which still has sails and is open to visitors.

* National Trust property

Location	Admission
Off B1159, 15 miles N of Great Yarmouth, between Martham & Sea Palling	Adult £2, Child £1
	Contact
	Horsey,
Opening	Great Yarmouth NR29 4EF
Open March at weekends 10am-4.30pm; Apr-Oct open Wed-Sun & Bank Holidays	t 01493 393904
	w nationaltrust.org.uk
	e horseywindpump@nationaltrust.org.uk

345 Great Yarmouth

Great Yarmouth Sealife Centre

3 hrs   All year

Experience the spectacular eye-to-eye views of everything from shrimps and starfish to sharks and stingrays. The City of Atlantis has an underwater tunnel allowing visitors to walk on the seabed and encounter sharks and multi-coloured fish.

* Soft play area
* Lair of the Octopus exhibition

Location	Contact
Take A47 from Norwich, A143 from Beccles or A12 from Lowestoft	Marine Parade, Great Yarmouth NR30 3AH
Opening	t 01493 330631
Daily; from 10am	w sealifeeurope.com
Admission	e slcyarmouth@merlinentainment.biz
Please phone for details	

346 Great Yarmouth

Pleasure Beach, Great Yarmouth

2 hrs+   Mar–Oct

The Pleasure Beach is situated on the seafront at the southern end of Great Yarmouth's Golden Mile and covers 9 acres. As well as a main ride area with over 70 rides and the awe-inspiring Ejector Seat, there are two crazy golf courses and gardens.

* 70 rides & attractions
* Firework displays on Saturday nights

Location
Take A12 from Lowestoft or A47 from Norwich

Opening
Please phone for details

Admission
Free admission. Rides are paid for at reception or machines

Contact
Great Yarmouth NR30 3EH

t 01493 844585
w pleasure-beach.co.uk
e GYPBeach@aol.com

347 Great Yarmouth

Thrigby Hall Wildlife Gardens

3 hrs+   All year

Visit a wide selection of Asian mammals, birds and reptiles, including tigers, crocodiles and storks. There are superb willow pattern gardens and a play area. There is also a dramatic swamp house for crocodiles and other tropical swamp dwellers.

* Lime Tree Lookout
* Tiger Tree Walk

Location
Off A1064 Caister–Acle road

Opening
Daily; 10am–5pm

Admission
Adult £6.90, Child (4–14) £4.90, Concs £5.90

Contact
Filby,
Great Yarmouth NR29 3DR

t 01493 369477
w thrigbyhall.co.uk

348 Great Yarmouth

Tolhouse Museum

1 hr+   Apr–Oct

The Tolhouse Museum is one of the oldest prisons in the country. Explore the story of crime and punishment and discover what happened to smugglers, witches, pirates and murderers in Great Yarmouth.

* Audio guide brings to life the stories and characters
* Hands-on activities for all the family

Location
Great Yarmouth, near 'Historic South Quay'

Opening
Daily; Apr–Oct Mon–Fri 10am–5pm
Sat & Sun 1.15pm–5pm

Admission
Adult £2.70, Child £1.50, Concs £2.30

Contact
Tolhouse Street, Great Yarmouth NR30 2SH

t 01493 858900
w norfolkmuseumservice.org.uk
e yarmouth.museums@norfolk.gov.uk

349 Holt

Baconsthorpe Castle

1 hr+   All year

Baconsthorpe Castle is a C15 part-moated, semi-fortified house. The remains include the inner and outer gatehouse and curtain wall. The local post office sells guide books and postcards.

* English Heritage Property

Location
Off A148 & B1149, 3⁄4 mile N of the village of Baconsthorpe, off an unclassified road, 3 miles E of Holt

Opening
Daily; at any reasonable time

Admission
Free

Contact
Baconsthorpe, Holt

t 01604 730325
w english-heritage.org.uk

350 Holt

Bishop's Boats Seal Trips

1 hr+   Apr–Oct

On this boat trip you will be able to see the seals and birds on Blakeney Point. There are many species of birds and both grey and common seals from a colony of approximately 500.

* Optional landing trips
* Warm or waterproof clothing recommended

Location
Trips depart from Blakeney Point reached by A149

Opening
Please phone for details as times vary depending on the tides

Admission
Adult £6, Child £4

Contact
Blakeney Point,
Blakeney, Holt

t 01263 740753
w bishopsboats.co.uk
e bishopsboats@bigfoot.com

351 Holt

Langham Glass

3 hrs+   All year

Langham Glass is based in a large Norfolk barn complex that is pantiled and flint-faced. Teams of glass-makers can be seen working with molten glass using blowing irons and hand tools in a way that has been traditional for hundreds of years.

* Quality Assured Visitor Attraction
* Museum & video, play area & 7-acre maze

Location
Follow A148 from Holt to Fakenham for 3 miles, turn right onto the B1156 & follow brown tourist signs to Langham

Opening
Daily; 10am–5pm

Admission
Glassmaking: Adult £3.75, Child£2.75,
Concs £2.75

Contact
The Long Barn, North Street,
Langham, Holt NR25 7DG

t 01328 830511
w langhamglass.co.uk
e langhamglass@talk21.com

352 Hunstanton

Hunstanton Sea Life Centre

1 hr+   All year

Hunstanton has a breathtaking display of British marine life. Stroll around over 20 authentically recreated natural habitat settings as you view more than 2000 fish from 200 different species.

* Penguin sanctuary, home to rare Humboldt penguins
* Seal sanctuaries & hospital

Location
Take A140 from Kings Lynn to Hunstanton and follow the signs

Opening
Daily; 10am–4pm.
Times may vary during winter, phone for details

Admission
Adult £7.95, Child £4.95 concs £5.50

Contact
Southern Promenade, Hunstanton PE36 5BH

t 01485 533 576
w sealsanctuary.co.uk

353 Hoveton

Wroxham Barns

2–3 hrs   All year

Wroxham Barns will keep all the family happy. Watch traditional and contemporary craft workers at work, indulge in a spot of shopping, feed the friendly animals and have fun at the fair.

* Quality Assured Visitor Attraction
* Traditional farm, junior farm & country food shop

Location
Approximately 10 miles from Norwich. Follow A1151 towards Wroxham and then follow the brown tourist signs

Opening
Daily; 10am–5pm

Admission
Admission & car park Free
Junior farm £2.75

Contact
Tunstead Road, Hoveton NR12 8QU

t 01603 783762
w wroxham-barns.co.uk
e info@wroxham-barns.co.uk

354 Kings Lynn

Caithness Crystal Visitor Centre

2 hrs+   All year

Glass-making is a magical craft that can transform sand into exquisite glassware using only the heat of a furnace and the skill of hand and eye. Witness it for yourself at the visitor centre in King's Lynn and marvel at the demonstration of the skills of glass-making.

* Quality Assured Visitor Attraction

Location
Located off A149, A47 & A10.
Follow the brown tourist signs

Opening
Daily; Mon–Sat 9am–5pm, Sun 10.15am– 4.15pm; closed 31 Mar, 25, 26 Dec
Please phone for details of glassmaking demonstration times

Admission
Free

Contact
Paxman Road, Hardwick Industrial Estate, King's Lynn PE30 4NE

t 01553 765111
w caithnessglass.co.uk
e mdennis@caithnessglass.co.uk

355 Norwich

Barton House Railway

2 hrs   Apr–Oct

Barton House has a miniature steam passenger railway and a steam and battery-electric railway. There are full-size M and GN accessories, including signals and signal boxes.

Location
On A1151 from Norwich

Opening
Apr–Oct open 3rd Sun each month 2.30pm–5.30pm
Please phone for details

Admission
Adult 1.50p Child 75p
By boat from Wroxham Bridge:
Adult £2 Child £1

Contact
Hartwell Road, The Avenue, Wroxham, Norwich NR12 8TL

t 01603 782470

356 Norwich

Bank Boats

4 hrs+   All year

Hire all-weather dayboats and take a trip on the beautiful River Ant. Drift lazily past windmills and enjoy a picnic on the river bank. Canoes are also available.

* Electric dayboats
* Canoes

Location On the slip road off A149 between Stalham & Wroxham	**Contact** Staithe Cottage, Wayford Bridge, Stalham, Norwich NR12 9LN
Opening Daily; 9am–5pm	t 01692 582457
Admission From £24 for 2 hrs	

357 Norwich

Fairhaven Woodland & Water Garden

2–4 hrs   All year

These delightful woodland and water gardens have a fantastic combination of plants and flowers, together with a wildlife sanctuary for bird-watchers and picturesque waterways spanned by small bridges. There are special events on Sundays in summer.

* 180 acres of woodland
* Private broad

Location Follow the brown tourist signs off A147 at the junction with B1140 through South Walsham	**Admission** Adult £4, Child £1.50, Concs £3.50, Dogs 20p
Opening Daily; 10am–5pm; 2 May–31 Aug open Wed, Thu 10am–9pm	**Contact** School Road, South Walsham, Norwich NR13 6DZ t 01603 270449 w norfolkbroads.com/fairhaven e fairhavengardens@norfolkbroads.com

358 Norwich

ILPH Hall Farm

2-3 hrs   All year

Visit this centre to learn about the work of the International League for the Protection of Horses. Meet some of the horses and ponies in care, many of whom have been rescued from cruelty and neglect.

* Visitor centre, stabling & indoor riding area

Location
Off A11, signed between Attleborough & Thetford

Opening
Wed, Sat, Sun & Bank Holidays
11am–4pm;

Admission
Free

Contact
Snetterton,
Norwich NR16 2LR

t 01953 498898
w ilph.org
e info@ilph.org

---

359 Norwich

Dinosaur Adventure Park

4 hrs+   Apr–Oct

Come face-to-face with life-size dinosaurs on the ultimate family adventure. The park includes a secret animal garden, adventure play areas, Climb-a-saurus, the Lost World Amazing Adventure and Jurassic Putt.

* New Adventurer's Guide
* Country Capers & Raptor Races

Location
9 miles from Norwich. Follow the brown tourist signs from A47 or A1067 to Weston Park

Opening
Please phone or visit website for details

Admission
Adults £6.95, Child £5.95, Concs £5.95

Contact
Weston Park, Lenwade,
Norwich NR9 5JW

t 01603 876310
w dinosaurpark.co.uk
e info@dinosaurpark.co.uk

---

360 Norwich

Felbrigg Hall, Garden & Park

2 hrs+   Mar–Oct

One of the finest C17 houses in East Anglia, Felbrigg contains original C18 furniture, an outstanding library, and a beautifully restored walled garden with a working dovecote. The house is set in 500 acres of parkland and woodland.

* Many woodland walks
* Changing programme of exhibitions

Location
In Felbrigg, 2 miles SW of Cromer, off B1346. Signed from A140 & A148

Opening
Mar 19–Oct 30 Sat–Wed
Hall 1pm–5pm
Garden 11am–5pm

Admission
Hall, Garden & Park Adult £6.60, Child £3.10 *Garden only* £2.70, £1

Contact
Felbrigg, Norwich NR11 8PR

t 01263 837444
w nationaltrust.org.uk
e felbrigg@ntrust.org.uk

361 Sheringham

The Muckleburgh Collection

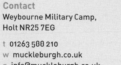

2 hrs   Apr–Nov

A collection of over 120 military vehicles, tanks and guns, plus items from Operation Desert Storm, militaria from C18, and scale models. Learn how to drive a tank, take a coastal ride on a US personnel carrier, or visit by air, landing on the adjoining airstrip.

* The Meteor is on loan from the Imperial War Museum.
* Gama Goat Rides – in a USA Personnel Carrier

Location
Signposted from A149 W of Cromer, 3 miles W of Sheringham

Opening
Please phone for details

Admission
Adult £5.50, Child £3, Concs £4.50

Contact
Weybourne Military Camp, Holt NR25 7EG

t 01263 588 210
w muckleburgh.co.uk
e info@muckleburgh.co.uk

362 Walsham

Elephant Playbarn

3 hrs   All year

A converted Norfolk flint barn filled with bouncy castles, ball pools and toys suitable for the under-eights. There is also a fully enclosed courtyard with an adventure play area and lots of pedal toys.

* Contact in advance for disabled accses

Location
Off A149, S of Cromer, on the B1145, ½ mile from Mundesley

Opening
Wed–Sun 10am–4pm; daily, school holidays

Admission
Adult free, Child £3.50

Contact
Mundesley Road, Knapton, North Walsham NR28 0RY

t 01263 721080

363 Walsham

Norfolk Motor Cycle Museum

3 hrs+   All year

Young bike enthusiasts will enjoy the displays covering a wide collection of motor cycles dating from 1920–60.

* Educational visits welcomed

Location
Near junction of B1150 Norwich road & A149 Great Yarmouth–Cromer road (the town bypass)

Opening
Please phone for details

Admission
Adult £3, Child £1.50, Concs £2.50

Contact
Railway Yard, North Walsham NR28 0DS

t 01692 406266

364 Brandon

High Lodge Forest Centre

6 hrs+   All year

Thetford Forest is Britain's largest lowland pine forest. High Lodge Forest Centre is in the heart of the forest with walks, cycle hire, an adventure playground, deer safaris and much more.

* Largest maze in Europe
* Bird walks & family fun walks

Location
Just off A11 on B1107 mid-way between Thetford & Brandon

Opening
Daily; 9am–dusk
Phone for details

Admission
£3.50 per car

Contact
Thetford Forest Park, Santon Downham, Brandon IP27 0TJ

t 01842 815434 (High Lodge Centre)
  01842 810271 (Forestry Commission)
w forestry.gov.uk

365 Bungay

Norfolk & Suffolk Aviation Museum

2 hrs   All year

This unique museum has 40 aircraft on display, from the early pioneers of flight and Luftwaffe crash planes up to the machines of the present day.

* 40 aircraft within 7 hangers
* Aircraft from pre WW1 to present day

Location
On B1062, off A143, 1 mile W of Bungay

Opening
Apr–Oct Sun–Thu 10am–5pm
Nov–Mar Tue Wed & Sun 10am–4pm
15 Dec–15 Jan closed

Admission
Free

Contact
The Street, Flixton NR35 1NZ

t 01986 896644
w aviationmuseum.net
e lcurtis@aviationmuseum.net

366 Bungay

Bungay Castle

1 hr   All year

The remains of this large Norman castle contain many interesting features. The massive gatehouse towers still stand, as do the bridge pit and curtain walls. A mine tunnel is exposed along with the forebuilding with its latrine chamber (garderobe).

* Visitor centre
* Café & Shop

Location
Off A143 & A144

Opening
Daily; 5 Jan–23 Dec 10am–4pm

Admission
Adult £1, Child 50p, Concs 50p

Contact
6 Cross Street
Bungay NR35 1AU

t 01986 893002 (tea rooms)
w bungay-suffolk.co.uk

367 Bungay

Otter Trust

2 hrs+   Apr–Sep

Children love to watch these beautiful animals and will enjoy a visit to the Trust, which promotes the cause of otters and encourages the public to see, enjoy and learn about them at its centres.

* Three lakes home to otters & wildfowl
* Information centre

Location
Located off A143, 1 mile W of Bungay

Opening
Daily; 1 Apr–30 Sep 10.30am–6pm

Admission
Adult £5, Child £3

Contact
Earsham,
Bungay NR35 2AF

t 01986 893470
w ottertrust.org.uk

368 Bury St Edmunds

Bury St Edmunds Abbey

2 hrs   All year

Visit the remains of a Benedictine abbey, church and precinct with Norman tower, set in beautifully kept gardens. The two fourteenth-century gateways are the best-preserved buildings. There is also a visitor centre with interactive displays.

* English Heritage property

Location
Off the A14, at the east end of Bury St Edmunds

Opening
Open at any reasonable time (please phone for details)

Admission
Free

Contact
Bury St Edmunds

t 01284 764667
w english-heritage.org.uk

369 Bury St Edmunds

Manor House Museum

1 hr+   All year

This magnificent Georgian town house displays some of the finest clocks and watches to be found in the world, costume and textiles from the C17 to the present day, and portrait paintings of national importance.

* Mixes art, science & history
* Three major collections

Location
Off A14, near Abbey ruins

Opening
Wed–Sun 11am–4pm

Admission
Adult £2.50, Child £2, Concs £2
Combined ticket available with Moyse's Hall Museum

Contact
Honey Hill,
Bury St Edmunds IP33 1RT

t 01284 757076
w stedmundsbury.gov.uk/ manorhse.htm
e manor.house@stedsbc.gov.uk

370 Bury St Edmunds

Moyse's Hall Museum

1 hr+   All year

Built in 1180, Moyse's Hall tells the story of West Suffolk from prehistoric times to the present day. Exhibits cover archaeology, the Suffolk Regiment, the notorious Red Barn murder, crime and punishment, coinage and witchcraft.

* Themed weekend events throughout the year
* Outstanding archaeology collection

Location
Off A14, in the centre of Bury St Edmunds

Opening
Daily; Mon–Fri 10.30am–4.30pm & Sat–Sun 11am–4pm

Admission
Adult £2.50, Child £ 2, Concs £2
Combined ticket available with Manor House Museum

Contact
Cornhill, Bury St Edmunds IP33 1DX
t 01284 706183
w stedmundsbury.gov.uk/moyses.htm
e moyses.hall@stedsbc.gov.uk

371 Ipswich

Ipswich Transport Museum

1 hr   Mar–Nov

The museum has the largest collection of transport items in Britain devoted to just one town. Everything was either made or used in and around Ipswich. The collection, started in 1965, consists of around 100 major exhibits, and numerous smaller transport related items.

* Timetables, photographs, maps, tickets and uniforms
* Varied programme of events as advertised

Location
SE of Ipswich near junction 57 of A14

Opening
Mar–Nov Sun and Bank Hols 11am–4pm, school hols Mon–Fri 1pm–4pm

Admission
Adult £3, Child £2, Concs £2.50

Contact
Old Trolleybus Depot, Cobham Road, Ipswich IP3 9JD

t 01473 715666
w ipswichtransportmuseum.co.uk
e enquiries@ipswichtransportmuseum.co.uk

372 Lowestoft

Lowestoft Maritime Museum

1 hr+   Easter–Oct

The museum houses models of fishing and commercial ships, shipwrights' tools, fishing gear, a lifeboat display, an art gallery and a drifter's cabin with models of fishermen.

* Hands-on exhibits
* School packs available

Location
Under the Lighthouse on Whaplode Road in Sparrow's Nest Park

Opening
Daily; May–Oct 10 & Easter hols 10am–5pm

Admission
Adult 75p, Child 25p, Concs 50p

Contact
Whapload Road, Lowestoft NR32 1XG

t 01502 561963

373 Newmarket

National Stud

1 hr+   Mar–Sep

Horse-crazy children will enjoy this stable tour, which takes in the superb stallion unit, along with the stallions in residence, nursery yards and mares and foals in their paddocks.

* Quality Assured Visitor Attraction

Location
Take A11, A1304 & A1303. The stud is 2 miles SW of Newmarket on A1304

Opening
1 Mar–30 Sep Mon–Sat;
Tours 11.15am, 2.30pm & Sun 2.30pm

Admission
Adult £5, Child £3.50, Concs £4

Contact
Newmarket CB8 0XE

t 01638 663464
w nationalstud.co.uk
e tours@nationalstud.co.uk

374 Southwold

Southwold Pier

2–4 hrs   All year

Visit this seaside pier and amusement centre. The new pier was completed in 2002 and is the first pier to be built in the UK for over 45 years. Additional attractions include a seaside holiday exhibition.

* Pier of the Year 2002
* Educational visits welcomed

Location
Off A145, follow signs for Southwold

Opening
Daily; 10.30am–sunset; Jun–Sep late closing at 10pm

Admission
Free

Contact
North Parade,
Southwold IP18 6BN

t 01502 722105
w southwoldpier.demon.co.uk
e admin@southwoldpier.demon.co.uk

375 Southwold

Coastal Voyager

1 hr+   All year

Coastal Voyager offers a variety of sea trips and river cruises. There is a half-hour high-speed blast trip and various tranquil river cruises along the beautiful River Blyth.

* 9-metre rigid inflatable
* Smooth, comfortable & safe rides

Location
Trips depart from Southwold Harbour

Opening
Please phone for details

Admission
1/2-hr high-speed blast:
Adult £16, Child £9

Contact
6 Strickland Place,
Southwold IP18 6HN

t 07887 525082
w blythweb.co.uk/sail-southwold
e thrills@southwold.ws

376 Stowmarket

Suffolk Owl Sanctuary

2 hrs+   All year

The Suffolk Owl Sanctuary is home to a variety of owls and birds of prey from all over the world, and has spectacular flying displays daily. There is also a woodland walk with a songbird hide and a red-squirrel enclosure.

* Kiddies play area
* Café & Shop

Location
On A1120, 8 miles from Ipswich & Stowmarket

Opening
Daily; summer 10am–5pm
winter 10am–4pm

Admission
Free (donations appreciated)

Contact
Stonham Barns, Pettaugh Road,
Stonham Aspal, Stowmarket IP14 6AT

t 01449 711425
w suffolk-owl-sanctuary.org.uk
e info@owl-help.org.uk

377 Stowmarket

Redwings Rescue Centre

2 hrs   May–Sep

Redwings Rescue Centre aims to relieve the suffering of horses, ponies and donkeys by providing them with a caring home for the rest of their days. See the animals in their peaceful retirement and learn more about their care and upkeep.

* 20-acre site
* Carriage horses

Location
Off A1120

Opening
Daily; May–Sep 10am–4pm

Admission
Adult £3.60, Child (3–15) £1.60,
Concs £2.60

Contact
Stonham Barns,
Stowmarket

t 0870 040 0033
w redwings.co.uk

378 Stowmarket

Mid-Suffolk Light Railway Museum

2 hrs   Apr–Sep

Dedicated to the Mid-Suffolk Light Railway, the museum shows restoration of the station and trackwork, plus artefacts and memorabilia.

* Check website & press for details of special events   WC 🏕 🍴 ♿ 🐕

Location
About 1 mile from A140 in the village of Brockford-cum-Wetheringsett

Opening
Good Fri–end Sep Sun & Bank holidays 11am–5pm; also open Weds in Aug 2pm–5pm

Admission
Adult £1.50, Child 50p
Rates vary for special events

Contact
Brockford Station, Wetheringsett, Stowmarket IP14 5PW

t 01449 766899
w mslr.org.uk

379 Stowmarket

Playworld Ocean Adventure

1 hr   All year

An indoor play area for children under 10 years old with ball ponds, scramble nets, slides, an aerial glide and a spooky room. There is also a toddlers' area.

* Large inflatable play area (May–Sep only)   WC 🏕 🍴 ♿

Location
Easy access from A14 into Stowmarket. Signed to the Leisure Centre from the town centre

Opening
Daily; Mon–Fri 9.30am–7pm, Sat & Sun 9am–6pm

Admission
Please phone for details

Contact
Mid-Suffolk Leisure Centre, Gainsborough Road, Stowmarket IP14 1LH

t 01449 674980

380 Sudbury

Clare Castle Country Park

3 hrs   All year

A 30-acre site fronting onto the river Stour, combining the remains of a Norman motte-and-bailey castle and a Victorian railway station with natural history interest.

* History & nature trail
* Visitor centre   WC 🏕 ♿ 🐕

Location
Signed off A1092 in the centre of Clare

Opening
Park Daily; dawn–dusk
Visitor centre Daily; (summer only) 10am–5pm

Admission
Free

Contact
Malting Lane, Clare, Sudbury CO10 8NW

t 01787 277491
e john.laws@et.suffolkcc.gov.uk

381 Woodbridge

Suffolk Horse Museum

2 hrs+   Apr–Sep

An indoor exhibition about the Suffolk Punch breed of heavy horse. This illustrates the history of the breed through paintings, photographs and exhibits and shows how the horse was used.

* Award winning museum
* The Life of the Horseman exhibition

Location
In the centre of Market Hill in Woodbridge, off A12 between Ipswich & Lowestoft

Opening
Apr–Sep Tue–Sun & Bank Holidays 2pm–5pm
Please phone for details

Admission
Adult £2, Child £1.50, Concs £1.50

Contact
The Market Hill, Woodbridge IP12 4LU

t 01394 380643
w suffolkhorsesociety.org.uk
e sec@suffolkhorsesociety.org.uk

382 West Stow

West Stow Country Park & Anglo-Saxon Village

  2 hrs+   All year

West Stow is a reconstructed Anglo-Saxon village, built on the site of an original settlement and set in a 125-acre country park. Finds from the site are displayed in an interpretation centre. This unique village is brought to life when authentic costume groups host special events.

* Nature trail & woodland walks
* River views & lake

Location
Off A1101, 6 miles NW of Bury St Edmunds

Opening
Daily; *Country park* summer 8am–8pm; *Village* 10am–5pm (last admission 4pm) *Country park* winter 9am–5pm, *Village* 10am–5pm (last admission 3.30pm)

Admission
Adult £5, Concs £4

Contact
Icklingham Road,
West Stow IP28 6HG
t 01284 728718
w stedmundsbury.gov.uk/weststow
e weststow@stedsbc.gov.uk

---

383 Woodbridge

Deben Cruises

  2 hrs+   May–Sep

The MV *Jahan* cruises through 10 miles of lovely countryside, departing from the quay at Waldringfield Boatyard and returning to Waldringfield. The cruises last two to three hours, depending on tides. Visit the picturesque port of Woodbridge or travel to Felixstowe.

* Lunches & afternoon teas
* Group deals by appointment

Location
From A12 at Orwell Bridge follow signs to Lowestoft. Take the sign at the roundabout to Waldringfield & it will take you straight to the village

Opening
Please phone for details

Admission
Adult £6 , Child £4

Contact
Waldringfield Boatyard Ltd, The Quay,
Waldringfield, Woodbridge IP12 4QZ
t 01473 736260

---

384 Woodbridge

Sutton Hoo

  2 hrs+   All year

Excavations here in 1939 revealed the burial chamber of a 90ft ship, filled with treasures including a warrior's helmet, weapons, armour, ornaments, tableware, and a purse with 37 gold coins from *c.* AD 620. The exhibition hall houses a full-size reconstruction of the chamber.

* The most important archaeological find in the UK
* Largest Anglo-Saxon ship ever discovered

Location
Off B1083 Woodbridge–Bawdsey road, signed from A12

Opening
Daily; Mar-Sep 11am-5pm
Oct Wed-Sun 11am-5pm
Nov-Dec Fri-Sun 11am-4pm

Admission
Adult £5, Child £2.50

Contact
Woodbridge IP12 3DJ
t 01394 389714
w www.nationaltrust.org.uk
e suttonhoo@nationaltrust.org.uk

Edale, Derbyshire

East Midlands

Derbyshire Leicestershire Lincolnshire
Northamptonshire Nottinghamshire Rutland

385 Bakewell

Haddon Hall

2 hrs+   Apr-Oct

A perfect example of a Tudor hall set in beautiful gardens. Guided tours are available and are adapted to suit different ages, abilities and interests. A costume room can be booked where the guide will give a talk illustrated with costumes.

* Annual children's weekend
* Film location for *Jane Eyre* and *Elizabeth*

Location
2 miles S of Bakewell on A6

Opening
Apr-Sep Daily; 10.30am-4.30pm
Oct, Thu-Sun, 10.30am-4.30pm

Admission
Adult £7.25, Child £3.75, Concs £6.25

Contact
Bakewell DE45 1LA

t 01629 812855
w haddonhall.co.uk
e info@haddonhall.co.uk

387 Buxton

Freshfields

3hrs+   All year

Freshfields is a farm deep in the Peak District of Derbyshire. It has twin aims – to provide a caring home for rescued donkeys and to cater for children with special needs.

* New riding ring
* Restricted access for dogs

Location
From the village of Peak Forest, take the road to Wormhill & Small Dale, then take the 5th entrance on the right. Watch out for a small sign & a long drive

Opening
Daily; 10am-4.30pm
Closed for 2 weeks at Christmas

Admission
Free (donations requested)

Contact
Peak Forest,
Buxton SK17 8EE

t 01298 79775

386 Bolsover

Bolsover Castle

1 hr+   All year

An enchanting early C17 castle, set on a hill with restored walled gardens, a magnificent indoor riding house and outstanding craftmanship everywhere. Visit the Discovery Centre and enjoy the interactive scale model of the castle and the audio tour.

* Regular living history events
* Visitor Attraction of the Year 2001

Location
Just off M1 at junction 29 or 30, 6 miles from Mansfield. Once in Bolsover the castle is 6 miles E of Chesterfield on A632

Opening
Apr-Sep Daily; 10am-6pm; Oct 10am-5pm; Nov-Mar Thu-Mon 10am-4pm

Admission
Adult £6.50, Child £3.30, Concs £4.90

Contact
Castle Street,
Bolsover S44 6PR

t 01246 822844
w english-heritage.org.uk
e bolsover.castle@english-heritage.org.uk

©English Heritage Photographic Library

388 Castle Donnington

Donington Grand Prix Collection

1 hr+   All year

Take a lap around the largest Grand Prix grid in the world, and prepare to be amazed as the exciting history of motorsport unfolds before you. Donington Park has the largest collection of McLaren racing cars on public display, along with numerous other unique racing cars.

* Ferraris, Lotus, Tyrells, Maseratis, Alfa Romeos
* Williams F1 cars from 1983–1999

Location
2 miles from M1 (junction 23a/24) & M42/A42, close to Nottingham, Derby & Leicester

Opening
Daily; 10am–5pm
(last admission 4pm)
Please phone for details of Christmas opening

Admission
Adult £7, Child £2.50,
Senior & Student £5

Contact
Donington Park, Castle Donington, Derby DE74 2RP
t 01332 811027
e enquiries@doningtoncollection.co.uk

389 Castleton

Peak Cavern

1 hr   All year

Set within a 250ft vertical cliff, and once home to a small village, there are various natural caverns within Peak Cavern, including the orchestra gallery which has amazing acoustic properties, Roger Rain's House with a perpetual waterfall and the devil's cellar.

* The biggest natural cavern in Derbyshire
* The largest entrance to a cave in the British Isles

Location
On A6187, between Haterssage and Whaley Bridge

Opening
Apr–Oct Daily; 10am–5pm
Nov–Mar Sat–Sun 10am–5pm

Admission
Adult £5.50, Child £3.50, Concs £4.50

Contact
Peak Cavern Road, Castleton,
Hope Valley S33 8WS
t 01433 620285
w devilsarse.com
e info@peakcavern.co.uk

390 Castleton

Peveril Castle

1 hr+   All year

There are breathtaking views of the Peak District from Peveril Castle, perched high above the pretty village of Castleton. Come and see the famous Great Square Tower of Henry II.

* Special events organised regularly

Location
On the south side of Castleton, 15 miles West of Sheffield on A6187

Opening
1 Apr–31 Oct Daily; 10am–6pm (5pm in Oct); 1 Nov–28 Mar Wed–Sun 10am–4pm

Admission
Adult £2.50, Child £1.30, Concs £1.90

Contact
Market Place, Castleton,
Hope Valley S33 8WQ
t 01433 620613
w english-heritage.org.uk

391 Derby

Derby Museum of Industry and History

1 hr   All year

Part of the Derwent Valley World Heritage Site, this museum introduces the history of Derby's industries. They include a major collection of Rolls Royce aero engines, railway engineering and research galleries and a Power for Industry gallery.

* Life-size replicas of engine driver's cabs
* Built on site of old silk mill

Location
Off the A6, near Derby Cathedral

Opening
All year open Mon 11am–5pm,
Tue–Sat 10am–5pm,
Sun & Bank holidays 2pm–5pm;
closed 25, 26 Dec & 1 Jan
Please phone to confirm holiday opening

Admission
Free

Contact
Silk Mill Lane, off Full Street
Derby DE1 3AF
t 01332 255308
w derby.gov.uk/museums

392 High Peak

Chestnut Centre Otter Haven & Owl Sanctuary

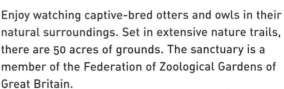

2 hrs+   All year

Enjoy watching captive-bred otters and owls in their natural surroundings. Set in extensive nature trails, there are 50 acres of grounds. The sanctuary is a member of the Federation of Zoological Gardens of Great Britain.

* Also see Scottish wild cats and foxes
* Wildlife gift shop

Location
Off A625. Follow the brown tourist signs

Opening
Daily; 10.30am-5.30pm
Jan-Feb open Sat & Sun only

Admission
Adult £5.75, Child £3.75

Contact
Castleton Road,
Chapel-en-le-Frith,
High Peak,
Derbyshire SK23 0QS

t 01298 814099
w ottersandowls.co.uk
e enquiries@ottersandowls.com

393 Ilkeston

The American Adventure

7 hrs   Mar–Oct

Visit The American Adventure and discover the epic story of the USA, from the Western Pioneers to the Pioneers of Space. With over 100 attractions, live shows and rides, The American Adventure is an enjoyable family day out for everyone.

* Events held throughout the year
* Quality Assured Visitor Attraction

Location
Take junction 26 off M1 & follow signposts along A610 to A608 & then A6007

Opening
Mar-Oct Daily; 10am-5pm

Admission
Adult (13+) £16.50, Child £13.50

Contact
Derbyshire DE7 5SX

t 0845 3302929
w www.americanadventure.co.uk
e sales@americanadventure.co.uk

394 Matlock Bath

Gulliver's Kingdom

6 hrs+   Apr–Sep

The park is designed for the younger family, where the adults can have as much fun as the children. It is set on a wooded hillside and includes over 40 attractions ranging from a log flume, roller coaster and chairlift to the Royal Mine Ride and family shows.

* Outdoor fantasy eating
* Disabled visitors are advised to phone prior to visit

Location
Easily reached from M1 or M6. Off A38 on the A6 between Matlock & Cromford

Opening
Apr-Sep
Please phone for details

Admission
Adult and Child £7.50, Child under 90cm tall Free, Concs £6.50

Contact
Temple Walk, Matlock Bath, Derbyshire DE4 3PG

t 01925 444888
w www.gulliversfun.co.uk

395 Ashby de la Zouch

Ashby de la Zouch Castle

1 hr   All year

Ashby de la Zouch Castle is a late medieval castle with impressive ruins which are dominated by the Hastings Tower. It offers panoramic views of the surrounding countryside and the chance to explore the secret tunnel used in the Siege of Ashby.

* Quality Assured Visitor Attraction
* Visit the secret tunnel from the kitchen

Location
In Ashby de la Zouch, 12 miles S of Derby, on A511

Opening
Please phone for details

Admission
Adult £3.20, Child £1.60, Concs £2.40

Contact
South Street, Ashby de la Zouch
LE65 1BR

t 01530 413343
w english-heritage.org.uk
e customers@english-heritage.org.uk

396 Ashby de La Zouch

Conkers

4 hrs+   All year

Conkers supplies hands-on fun for everyone at its 120-acre forest site. Inside the Discovery Centre you will find over 100 exhibits, from feeling a leaf breathe or touching a toad to dodging a diving kingfisher or travelling in a woodland time machine.

* Visitor Attraction of the Year Finalist
* Adventure playground & assault course

Location
3 miles from Ashby de la Zouch on B5003

Opening
Daily; in summer 10am–6pm in winter 10am–dusk

Admission
Adult £5.95, Child £3.95, Concs £4.95

Contact
Rawden Road, Moira, nr Ashby de la Zouch, Leicestershire DE12 6GA

t 01283 216633
w visitconkers.com
e info@visitconkers.com

397 Coalville

Snibston Discovery Park

7 hrs   All year

At this award-winning attraction, visitors of all ages can explore local industrial heritage and the wonders of technology with over 30 hands-on experiments.

* Colliery tours
* Science & water playgrounds

Location
West of Coalville & 10 mins from junction 22 of M1 or junction 13 of A42/M42

Opening
Daily; 10am–5pm

Admission
Adult £5.70, Child £3.60, Concs £3.90

Contact
Ashby Road, Coalville, Leicestershire LE67 3LN

t 01530 278444
e snibston@leics.gov.uk
w leics.gov.uk/museums

398 Desford

Tropical Birdland

2 hrs+   Easter–Oct

Come and see hundreds of beautiful and exotic birds, including macaws, parrots, parakeets, toucans and emus, wander around the walk-through aviary, see where chicks are hatched, or sit with friendly free-to-fly birds in the café. Some might even talk to you!

* Boarding service for pet birds when you go on holiday
* Hundreds of tropical birds from over 70 species

Location
Just off M1 at junction 22

Opening
Easter–Oct, Daily; 10am–5pm

Admission
Adult £4, Child £3, Concs £3.50

Contact
Lindridge Lane, Desford, Leicester LE9 9N

t 01455 824603
w www.tropicalbirdland.co.uk
e info@tropicalbirdland.co.uk

399 Grantham

Belvoir Castle

3 hrs+   Apr–Sep

Belvoir Castle is home to the Duke and Duchess of Rutland. This stunning castle has a hilltop position, breathtaking views and glorious gardens. Events are staged every weekend throughout the season.

* Hidden spring garden
* Calendar of events

Location
Off A52, 7 miles from Grantham & 9 miles from Melton Mowbray

Opening
Apr–Sep Daily; 11am–5pm
Please phone for details

Admission
Adult £8, Child £5, Senior £7

Contact
Grantham, Leicestershire NG32 1PD

t 01476 871002
w www.belvoircastle.com
e nwheeler@belvoircastle.com

400 Leicester

The National Space Centre

4–6 hrs   All year

Visit the UK's largest space attraction. Be amazed by rockets, forecast the weather, visit the Space Theatre or travel to a distant planet! Explore our understanding of space and how it might affect our future.

* Regular special events
* Some shows not suitable for under 4s

 WC ¶¶ &

Location
2 miles N of Leicester, off A6. Follow brown tourist signs from M1 (junction 21, 21a or 22)

Opening
School holidays Mon 12noon–6pm & Tue–Sun 10am–6pm; in term time Tue–Fri 10am–5pm & Sat–Sun 10am–6pm; Bank Holidays open 10am–6pm

Admission
Adult £8.95, Child £6.95
Please phone for 2005 prices

Contact
Exploration Drive, Leicester LE4 5NS

t 0870 607 7223
w www.spacecentre.co.uk
e info@spacecentre.co.uk

401 Loughborough

Great Central Railway

2 hrs+   All year

This is one of the few places in the world where you can see scheduled full-size steam trains in operation. Watch a demonstration of a freight or parcel train, jump aboard a classic corridor train or, for the adventurous, learn how to drive a steam or diesel train.

* Britain's only mainline steam railway
* Murder mysteries and Santa specials

  WC ⛫ ¶¶ &

Location
SE of Loughborough town centre

Opening
Trains run at weekends all year and midweek Jun–Aug, Please phone for details

Admission
Adult £11, Child & Concs £7.50

Contact
Great Central Road,
Loughborough LE11 1RW

t 01509 230 726
w gcrailway.co.uk
e booking_office@gcrailway.co.uk

402 Market Harborough

Foxton Canal Museum

3 hrs   All year

A canal museum featuring the story of the local canals and the unique boat lift, set in beautiful countryside with ten locks and all supporting facilities. The museum contains models of the lift, interactive displays, social history and a canal play boat for younger visitors.

* Guided tour and walks
* Calendar of events

Location
Follow the brown tourist signs from A6 Market Harborough–Leicester road or A4304 at Lubenham, or M1 junction 20 to the Market Harborough road

Opening
Daily; 10am–5pm, closed Thu & Fri in winter

Admission
Adult £2.50, Concs £2, Child free

Contact
Middle Lock, Gumley Road, Foxton, Market Harborough Leicestershire LE16 7RA

t 0116 279 2657
w fipt.org.uk
e foxton@realemail.com.co.uk

403 Market Harborough

Rockingham Castle

3 hrs   All year

Built by William the Conqueror over 900 years ago, the castle is set in beautiful grounds and has magnificent views across the Welland Valley. Apart from its role as a stronghold, it was also an important seat of government. Now home to the Saunders Watson family.

* Winner of awards for contributions to education
* Regular events including kite and Viking days

Location
Off A6003, 1 mile N of Corby

Opening
Please phone for details

Admission
Adult £7.50, Child £4.50, Concs £6.50

Contact
Rockingham, Market Harborough, Leicestershire LE16 8TH

t 01536 770240
w www.rockinghamcastle.com
e estateoffice@rockinghamcastle.com

404 Melton Mowbray

Twinlakes Park

7 hrs+   All year

A new family destination with a huge variety of activities for all ages, from climbing Black Knights Castle to shooting foam in the Master Blaster.

* Rowboats & pedal boats
* Falconry centre

Location
1 mile from Melton Mowbray & signed from A607 between Melton Mowbray & Grantham

Opening
Daily; 10am–5.30pm

Admission
Adult & Child £6.49, Under-3s Free

Contact
Melton Spinney Road, Melton Mowbray, Leicestershire LE14 4SB

t 01664 567777
w twinlakespsrk.co.uk
e fun@twinlakes.co.uk

405 Cleethorpes

Cleethorpes Humber Estuary Discovery Centre

1 hr   All year

Close to the beach and sand dunes, the centre has a great range of activities for all ages, including an interactive exhibition, guided walks and an observatory where you can enjoy the spectacular views across the estuary. Ideal for nature walks and boating.

* The centre is on the edge of an important habitat
* Site of special scientific interest

Location
From A180 & A16 follow signs for the lakeside

Opening
Daily; Jan–Jun , Sep & Oct 10am–5pm
Jul & Aug 10am–6pm,
Nov–Dec 10am–4pm

Admission
Adult £1.95, Child £1.30

Contact
Lakeside, Kings Road, Cleethorpes
DN35 0AG

t 01472 323232
w cleethorpesdiscoverycentre.co.uk
e lynne.emery@nelincs.gov.uk

---

406 Grantham

Grantham Museum

½ hr   All year

Learn about the great physicist, Isaac Newton, who was born and educated in Grantham; admire dolls by Madame Montanari, doll-maker to Queen Victoria's children; see part of a real bouncing bomb; learn about the famous Dambusters raid, partly planned in Grantham.

* Displays on Grantham-born Isaac Newton
* 1851 Great Exhibition gold medal winning doll

Location
Central Grantham

Opening
Mon–Sat 10am–5pm

Admission
Free

Contact
St Peter's Hill, Grantham NG31 6PY

t 01476 568783
w lincolnshire.gov.uk/
    granthammuseum
e grantham.museum@
    lincolnshire.gov.uk

---

407 Grantham

Woolsthorpe Manor

2 hrs   Mar–Oct

This small C17 manor house was the family home of Sir Isaac Newton. Its orchard includes descendants of the famous apple tree. Newton formulated some of his major works here during the plague years (1665–67).

* Science Discovery Centre & exhibition

Location
Leave A1 at the Colsterworth round-about, via B676 & follow the NT signs

Opening
Mar & Oct open Sat–Sun 1pm–5pm; Apr–Sep open Wed–Sun 1pm–5pm (6pm closing in Jul & Aug); Open Bank Holiday Mon

Admission
Adult £3.60, Child £1.80

Contact
23 Newton Way,
Woolsthorpe-by-Colsterworth,
Grantham, Lincolnshire NG33 5NR

t 01476 860338
e woolsthorpemanor@
    nationaltrust.org.uk

408 Ingoldmells

Hardy's Animal Farm

3 hrs   Apr–Oct

See commercial and rare breeds of cattle, sheep and goats. Visit the calf and pig units where you can see how the animals are cared for.

* Large adventure playground
* Horse & cart rides

Location
Take A52 north from Skegness to Ingoldmells. Go through Ingoldmells & take the 1st right down Anchor Lane

Opening
Easter–Oct Daily; 10am–5pm

Admission
Adult £3.50, Child £2.50

Contact
Grays Farm, Anchor Lane, Ingoldmells, Skegness

t 01754 872267

409 Ingoldmells

Magical World of Fantasy Island

3–5 hrs   Mar–Oct

This indoor theme park has rides and attractions to suit all ages, as well as live entertainment during the evenings throughout the main season. There are also outdoor rides and Europe's largest looping roller-coaster, The Millennium Coaster.

* Movie ride theatre
* Dazzling lightshows in the evenings

Location
Off A52, 4 miles north of Skegness

Opening
Daily; Easter–end Oct from 10am; Mar–Easter weekends Closing times vary - please phone for details

Admission
Free. Tokens available for rides

Contact
Ingoldmells, Skegness, Lincolnshire PE25 1RH

t 01754 872030
w www.fantasyisland.co.uk

410 Lincoln

Lincoln Medieval Bishop's Palace

1 hr+   All year

Set in the shadow of Lincoln Cathedral, the palace was the centre of the largest diocese in medieval England. Visit the superb new visitor facilities and the delightful contemporary heritage garden.

* Video and audio tour
* Vineyard

Location
On S of Lincoln Cathedral, in the centre of the city

Opening
1 Apr–31 Oct Daily; 10am–6pm (5pm in Oct); 1 Nov–31 Mar Sat & Sun 10am–4pm

Admission
Adult £3.20, Child £1.60, Concs £2.40

Contact
Bishop's Palace, Minster Yard, Lincoln LN2 1PU

t 01522 527468

411 Lincoln

Museum of Lincolnshire Life

2 hrs   All year

Experience the domestic, agricultural, industrial and social history of Lincolnshire with agricultural and industrial machinery built in the county. Also on show are Victorian room settings and a First World War tank. Special events are held throughout the year.

* Situated in Royal North Lincoln Militia barracks

Location
Take A15 & the B1398 & follow signs from A46

Opening
1 May–31 Oct Daily; 10am–5.30pm; 1 Nov–30 Apr Mon–Sat 10am–5.30pm, Sun 2pm–5.30pm

Admission
Adult £2, Child/Concs £1.20

Contact
Burton Road, Lincoln LN1 3LY

t 01522 528448
e lincolnshirelife_museum@lincolnshire.gov.uk

412 Long Sutton

The Butterfly & Wildlife Park

4 hrs   Mar–Oct

When you visit this park, you will see wallabies, llamas, ponies and lots more. Indoor attractions include tropical butterflies, snakes, crocodiles, an ant room and an insectarium.

* Quality Assured Visitor Attraction
* Lincolnshire Family Attraction of the Year 2003

Location
Signposted off A17 at Long Sutton

Opening
End Mar–end Oct from 10am
Please phone for details

Admission
Adult £5.50, Child (3–16) £3.80, Senior £4.80

Contact
Long Sutton, Spalding, Lincolnshire PE12 9LE

t 01406 363833
w butterflyandwildlifepark.co.uk
e butterflypark@hotmail.com

413 Mablethorpe

The Seal Sanctuary

1 hr+   Apr–Sep

The Seal Trust is a registered charity with the twin aims of caring for local wild creatures in distress (especially seals) and encouraging visitors to help wildlife themselves. It acts as a sanctuary for seals, owls and kestrels, as well as lynx, wildcats, snowy owls and harvest mice.

* New specially designed pools
* Educational natural history programmes

Location
Off A1031 via A1031, A104, A111 or A52

Opening
Easter–end Sept Daily; from 10am.
Please phone for details of winter opening

Admission
Adult £4.50, Child £2, Senior £3

Contact
North End
Mablethorpe
Lincolnshire LN12 1QG

t 01507 473346

414 Sibsey Boston

Sibsey Trader Windmill

1 hr   Apr–Oct

An impressive six-storey tower mill, Sibsey Trader Windmill was built in 1877 and restored in 2001. It contains its original machinery for grinding corn, with milling artefacts on show and flour for sale.

* Guided tours essential

Location
Half a mile west of Sibsey, off A16, 5 miles N of Boston

Opening
Apr–Oct Tue, Sat & Bank Holidays 10am–6pm (5pm in Oct) & Sun 11am–6pm (5pm in Oct). Please phone for exact dates

Admission
Adult £2, Child £1, Concs £1.50

Contact
Sibsey Boston, Lincolnshire PE22 0SY

t 01205 750036
w www.sibsey.fsnet.co.uk

415 Skegness

Butlins (Skegness)

6 hrs   Apr–Oct

Children can have great fun at Butlins, from Splash, an indoor sub-tropical waterworld, with its exciting water rides, to Hotshots, a terrific tenpin bowling centre and the amazing Skyline Pavilion. Younger children can meet Noddy, Big Ears and Mr Plod in Noddyland.

* Quality Assured Visitor Attraction
* Live shows

Location
3 miles N of Skegness, on A52
Ingoldmells, Chapel St Leonards,
Sutton-on-Sea & Mablethorpe Road

Opening
20 Apr–31 Oct Daily; 10am–late (last admission 4pm)

Admission
Please phone for details

Contact
Roman Bank, Ingoldmells,
Skegness, Lincolnshire PE25 1NJ

t 01754 765567 (day-visit hotline)
01754 762311
w www.butlins.co.uk

416 Skegness

Gibraltar Point Nature Reserve & Visitor Centre

2 hrs+   All year

This area of unspoilt coastline comprises sand-dunes, saltmarshes and freshwater habitats for rare plants and animals, including seals, water voles and pygmy shrews. There are two birdwatching hides, a nature trail, an interpretation centre, and various activities and events.

* Area of international scientific interest
* Home to many rare plants, insects and animals

Location
1½ miles S of Skegness, signed from town centre

Opening
May–Oct, Daily; 10.30am–4pm; Nov–Apr, Sat–Sun and Bank Holidays

Admission
Free

Contact
Skegness, Lincolnshire

t 01507 526667
w www.lincstrust.org.uk
e info@lincsrust.co.uk

417 Skegness

Natureland Seal Sanctuary

1 hr+   All year

Skegness Seal Sanctuary is well known for rescuing and rehabilitating orphaned and injured seal pups. The sanctuary also has crocodiles, penguins, reptiles, insects and tropical birds. There is also an aquarium, and from April to October you can view the tropical butterflies.

* Baby seal & penguin pools
* Underwater viewing pool

Location
At North Parade, Skegness,
at the N end of Skegness seafront

Opening
In summer open Daily; 10am–5pm;
In winter open daily 10am–4pm;

Admission
Adult £4.95, Child £2.25, Senior £3.95

Contact
North Parade, Skegness,
Lincolnshire PE25 1DB

t 01754 764345
w www.skegnessnatureland.co.uk
e natureland@fsbdial.co.uk

418 Spalding

Baytree Garden Centre (Owl Centre)

2 hrs+   All year

Baytree Garden Centre has 72 owls from around the world, and is set in a beautiful landscaped area. There are tame owls to hold or just to enjoy watching in flying displays.

* Unique interactive experience
* Visit tropical owls in the 'Hot House'

WC

Location
On the main A151 at Weston between Spalding & Holbeach

Opening
Daily; 10am–5pm

Admission
Adult £2, Child £1, Senior £1

Contact
High Road Weston, Spalding, Lincolnshire PE12 6JU

t 01406 372840
w www.baytree-gardencentre.com

419 Spilsby

Lincolnshire Aviation Heritage Centre

2 hrs+   All year

The Heritage Centre is part of a wartime bomber airfield under restoration, which includes the control tower and displays depicting the history of flying in Lincolnshire. There is also an exhibition by the Royal Air Force Escaping Society.

* Blast shelter & military vehicles
* A complete AVRO Lancaster NX611

WC

Location
Off A155

Opening
29 Mar–31 Oct Daily; Mon–Sat 10am–5pm; 1 Nov–28 Mar 10am–4pm

Admission
Adult £5, Child £1.50, Under-5s Free, Senior £4.50

Contact
The Airfield, East Kirkby, Spilsby, Lincolnshire PE23 4DE

t 01790 763207
w www.lincsaviation.co.uk

420 Tattershall

Tattershall Castle

1 hr+   Mar–Dec

Tattershall is a vast redbrick tower with a moat, built in medieval times for Ralph Cromwell, Lord Treasurer of England. There are grand tapestries and four great chambers, each with spectacular views across the Fens.

* Tower is over 100 feet high
* Huge Gothic fireplaces

WC

Location
Off the A153

Opening
Apr–Oct Sat–Wed 11am–5.30pm (4pm in Oct); Mar, Nov & Dec open weekends 12noon–4pm

Admission
Adult £3.50, Child £1.80

Contact
Tattershall, Lincoln LN4 4LR

t 01526 342543
w www.nationaltrust.org.uk

421   Corby

Kirby Hall

1–2 hrs   All year

Kirby Hall was one of the most outstanding Elizabethan mansions in the country. These peaceful ruins are home to peacocks, and the gardens now contain a fine parterre, with topiary.

* Elizabethan festivals
* Theatre productions

Location
On an unclassified road off A43, 4 miles NE of Corby

Opening
1 Apr–31 Oct Daily; 10am–6pm (5pm in Oct); 1 Nov–28 Mar Daily; Sat & Sun 10am–4pm

Admission
Adult £3.50, Child £1.80, Concs £2.60

Contact
Kirby Hall Deene, nr Corby, Northamptonshire NN17 5EN

t 01536 203230
w www.english-heritage.org.uk

---

422   Kettering

Rushton Triangular Lodge

½ hr   Apr–Oct

Probably the strangest building in Britain. Older children will enjoy this puzzling folly. Wander round the triangular rooms and try to decipher the mysterious quotations and numbers on the walls.

* Quality Assured Visitor Centre

Location
1 mile W of Rushton, on an unclassified road, 3 miles from Desborough on A6

Opening
Apr–Oct Daily; 10am–6pm (5pm in Oct)

Admission
Adult £2, Child £1, Concs £1.50

Contact
Rushton, Kettering, Northamptonshire NN14 1

t 01536 710761 (Apr–Oct)
  01604 735400 (Nov–Mar)
w 1001daysout.com

---

423   Kettering

Wicksteed Park

6 hrs+   seasonal

A large playground and an adventure park with over 30 different amusements including pirate ships, a water chute, the Rockin' Tug, roller-coasters and many more.

* UK's oldest theme park
* Regular calendar of events

Location
On A6, 1 mile S of Kettering town centre & 1½ miles from the A14 at junction 10. Follow the signposts

Opening
Grounds open all year; Rides are seasonal (please phone for details)

Admission
Please phone for details

Contact
Barton Road, Kettering, Northamptonshire NN15 6NJ

t 01536 512475
w www.wicksteedpark.co.uk
e information@wicksteedpark.co.uk

424 Northampton

Billing Aquadrome

3 hrs+ Mar–Nov

Billing Aquadrome is a leisure holiday park, set in 235 acres of parkland, woods and lakes. Facilities include an amusement centre, boating, coarse fishing and free children's play areas. There is also an outdoor swimming pool.

* Calendar of events and rallies

Location
Off A45, 3 miles from Northampton & 7 miles from M1 exit at junction 15

Opening
Mar–Nov Daily; until 8pm; 24-hr access for caravans & tents

Admission
Pedestrians £1, Cars Sat & Sun £10, weekdays £5

Contact
Crow Lane, Great Billing, Northampton NN3 9DA

t 01604 408181/01604 784948
w billingaquadrome.com

425 Northampton

Holdenby House, Gardens & Falconry Centre

2 hrs Apr–Sep

The house is based around the remaining kitchen wing of Holdenby Palace (1583), the largest house in Elizabethan England with 123 huge glass windows. Restored and expanded in the 1870s. The house is now a family home, set in 20 acres of gardens with a falconry centre.

* Winner of 4 Sandford awards for educational work
* Reed award for work with special needs children

Location
6 miles NW of Northhampton, off A5199 or A428

Opening
Easter–Sep 30 Sun & Bank Hols 1pm–5pm
Sep Sun 1pm–5pm

Admission
Gardens & Falconry Centre
Adult £4.50, Child £3, Concs £4

Contact
Holdenby, Northampton NN6 8DJ

t 01604 770074
w holdenby.com
e enquiries@holdenby.com

426 South Northampton

Abington Museum

3 hrs+ All year

The museum includes social and military history. Displays show Northamptonshire life, a Victorian cabinet of curiosities, the history of the building, Northamptonshire military history at home and abroad, and a C19 fashion gallery.

* C15 manor house
* Home of Shakespeare's granddaughter

Location
Approximately 1½ miles east of the town centre

Opening
Please phone for details of timings

Admission
Free

Contact
Abington Park,
Park Avenue
South Northampton
Northamptonshire NN1 5LW

t 01604 838110
w www.northampton.gov.uk/museums

427 Wellingborough

Irchester Country Park

4–6 hrs All year

Explore a network of trails running across 83 hectares of mixed woodland and observe the wealth of wildlife, including woodpeckers and sparrowhawks. A Forestry Centre of Excellence, the park balances conservation with timber production and recreation.

* Ironstone railway museum
* Accessible trails and orienteering trail

Location
2 miles S of Wellingborough, on B570, in the Nene Valley

Opening
Park Daily 24 hrs
Car park 9am–5pm

Admission
Free, £1.50 for car park

Contact
Gypsy Lane, Little Irchester,
Wellingborough NN29 7DL

t 01933 276866
w northamptonshire.gov.uk
e irchester@northamptonshire.gov.uk

428   Newark

Newark Air Museum

2 hrs   All year

An impressive collection of 65 aircraft and cockpit sections, including transport, training and reconnaissance aircraft, helicopters, jet fighters and bombers. Learn about the history of RAF Winthorpe, a Second World War bomber-training base.

* UK's largest volunteer-managed aviation museum

Location	Contact
Easily accessible from A1, A46, A17, A1133 and Newark bypass	Winthorpe Showground, Newark NG24 2NY
Opening	t 01636 707170
Daily; Mar–Oct 10am–5pm Nov–Feb 10am–4pm	w newarkairmuseum.co.uk e newarkair@lineone.net
Admission	
Adult £5.25, Child £3.50, Concs £4.50	

429   Nottingham

City of Caves

1 hr+   All year

Soak up the atmosphere of hundreds of years of local life in this ancient and mysterious labyrinth of sandstone caves buried deep beneath the city above. Descend into the depths of these original Anglo-Saxon tunnels, meeting the cave dwellers from its dramatic hidden past.

* Have a go at real archaeology
* Special events throughout the year

Location	Contact
Nottingham city centre. Inside the Broadmarsh shopping centre on the upper level	Drury Walk, Broadmarsh Centre, Nottingham NG1 7LS
Opening	t 0115 988 1955
Daily; 10.30am–4.30pm	w www.cityofcaves.com
Admission	
Adult £4.25 , Child/Concs £3.50	

430   Nottingham

Galleries of Justice

4 hrs   All year

Journey through 300 years of crime and punishment at this unique atmospheric site. Actors bring the experience to life as you discover first-hand what prison life was really like. Special family-based events are run throughout the school holidays.

* Visitor Attraction of the Year 2002
* Best Museum 2003

Location	Admission
Follow the brown tourist signs from Nottingham city centre	Adult £6.95, Child £5.25, Concs £5.95
Opening	**Contact**
Tue–Sun (Bank Holidays & Mon during school holidays); Peak times 10am–5pm; Off-peak 10am–4pm; closed at Christmas Please phone for details	Shire Hall, High Pavement, Lace Market, Nottingham NG1 1HN
	t 0115 952 0555
	w www.galleriesofjustice.org.uk

Nottingham Castle

3 hrs+   All year

Nottingham Castle is a C17 mansion with a range of historical and contemporary art exhibitions. Interactive displays feature museum collections of silver, ceramics and Nottinghamshire treasures. Children can also explore the hidden passageways under the building.

* Children's gallery
* Sit on the Queen's throne

Location
10-minute walk from Nottingham city centre, within easy reach of Nottingham train & bus stations

Opening
Daily; 10am–5pm (last admission 4.30pm)

Admission
Adult £2, Child £1, Concs £1

Contact
Off Friar Lane,
Nottingham NG1 6EL

t 0115 915 3700
e marketing@ncmg.demon.co.uk

Tales of Robin Hood

1 hr+   All year

Travel back in time as you discover the truth behind the legend of Robin Hood. Follow the Silver Arrow Trail and try your hand at archery and brass rubbing.

* Medieval banquets
* Events including falconry & weapons handling

Location
In Nottingham city centre, just 5 minutes' walk from Nottingham Castle

Opening
Daily; in summer 10am–6pm (last admission 4.30pm); in winter 10am–5.30pm (last admission 4pm)

Admission
Adult £6.95, Child £4.95, Concs £5.95

Contact
30–38 Maid Marion Way,
Nottingham NG1 6GF

t 0870 756 0440
e robinhoodcentre@mail.com

Wollaton Hall Museum

4 hrs   All year

Set in 500 acres of deer park, Wollaton Hall is one of the finest Elizabethan houses in England and is now home to Nottingham's Natural History Collection and Industrial Museum.

* See George the Gorilla
* Insect exhibition

Location
3 miles from Nottingham centre

Opening
Natural History Museum: Daily; Oct–Mar 11am–4pm; Apr–Sep 11am–5pm
Industrial Museum: Apr–Sep Daily; 11am–5pm

Admission
Each museum; Adult £1.50, Child £1 (Sat–Sun) Free (Mon–Fri), Concs 80p

Contact
Wollaton Park
Nottingham NG8 2AE

t 0115 915 3900
w www.nottinghamcity.gov.uk

434 Mansfield

Go Ape!

2 hrs+   All year

Discover the thrill of aerial trekking high above the forest floor. Go Ape! offers a high-wire assault course of extreme rope bridges, tarzan swings and zip slides. Full safety instruction is provided.

* Rural Visitor Attraction of the Year
* All under-18s must be accompanied

Location
Off B6030 near Old Clipstone

Opening
Apr–Oct Daily; Nov–Mar open weekends; selected opening days through Christmas period & spring half term. Please phone for details of opening times

Admission
Adult £15, Child (10–17) £10

Contact
Sherwood Pines Visitor Centre, Nottinghamshire

t 0870 444 5562
w www.goape.cc
e info@goape.cc

435 Mansfield

Making It! Discovery Centre

2 hrs+   All year

A fun, engaging, entertaining and educational interactive, hands-on day out. The galleries celebrate the inventiveness of a variety of industries including shoe manufacture, brewing, soft drinks, textiles, printing, engineering and electronics.

* Nottinghamshire Visitor Attraction of the Year

Location
Close to Mansfield town centre & Water Meadows leisure pool. Off A60 & A617

Opening
Daily; 10am–5pm

Admission
Adult £6.95, Child £6.25

Contact
Chadburn House, Weighbridge Road, Littleworth, Mansfield, Nottinghamshire NG18 1AH

t 01623 473297
e info@makingit.org.uk
w makingit.org.uk

436 Mansfield

Sherwood Forest Country Park & Visitor Centre

 2 hrs All year

Visit the home of Robin Hood and see the major oak, where he hid with his merry men, discover what life was like in the Middle Ages, learn about ecology in the Forests of the World exhibition or take a walk along one of many waymarked trails.

* See the Major Oak, Robin Hood's hiding place
* National nature reserve

Location In Edwinstowe village, off B6034	**Admission** Free, charges for car park
Opening *Visitor Centre* Daily; summer 10am–5pm, winter 10am–4.30pm *Park* dawn to dusk	**Contact** Edwinstowe, nr Mansfield NG21 9HN t 01623 823202 w sherwoodforest.org.uk e sherwood.forest@nott-cc.gov.uk

437 Southwell

Southwell Minster

 2 hrs All year

Southwell Minster, with its majestic Norman nave and glorious C13 chapter house, is one of the least-known jewels in the crown of Nottinghamshire. Nearby is the Minster Centre with an audio-visual theatre, a library, gallery and bookshop.

* Dedicated education officer
* Tours and talks for children

Location Southwell town centre	**Admission** Free but donations welcome
Opening *Minster* daily *Minster Centre* Mon-Fri, 9am-5pm; Sat, 10.30am-3.30pm, Sun 2.30-4.30pm	**Contact** Southwell, Nottinghamshire t 01636 812649 w www.southwellminster.org.uk e nikki-di@southwellminster.org.uk

438 Sneiton

Green's Mill

 2 hrs All year

One of the few working inner-city windmills in Britain, Green's Mill was once home to the C19 miller and mathematician George Green. Tour the mill and discover the fascinating process of turning grain into flour.

* Included in Best 50 Small Museums
* Hands-on experiments exploring magnetism, electricity & light

Location 1 mile outside Nottingham city centre	**Contact** Windmill Lane, Sneinton, Nottingham NG2 4QB
Opening Wed–Sun & Bank Holidays 10am–4pm	t 0115 915 6878 e www.greensmill.org.uk
Admission Free	

439   Empingham

Rutland Water

4hrs+   All year

The whole family can enjoy this award-winning attraction with a 3100-acre lake set in beautiful countryside and over 20 miles of off-road cycling or walking. Spend time at the butterfly and aquatic centre, then take in the nature reserve or have a go on the climbing wall.

* Cycle hire
* Watersports

Location	Admission
Close to A1 Grantham–Peterborough stretch & A47 Leicester–Peterborough. A606 Oakam–Stamford runs along the North Shore	Please phone for details
Opening	**Contact**
Opening times vary – please phone for details	Sykes Lane, Empingham, Rutland LE15 8PX
	t 01572 653026
	w rutlandwater.net
	e tic@anglianwater.co.uk

440   Lyddington

Lyddington Bede House

1 hr   Apr–Oct

Lyddington Bede House was the medieval palace of the bishops of Lincoln. The remaining building was converted into an almshouse in 1600. Discover the 'Bishop's Eye' and a mystery fire-fighting object!

* Free educational leaflet
* Free audio tour

Location	Admission
In Lyddington, 6 miles N of Corby, 1 mile E of A6003. Next to the church in Lyddington	Please phone for details
	Contact
Opening	Blue Coat Lane, Lyddington nr Uppingham, Rutland LE15 9LZ
1 Apr–30 Sept Daily 10am–6pm; Daily 10am–5pm	t 01572 822438
	w english-heritage.org.uk

441   Oakham

Rutland County Museum

1 hr+   All year

Learn about England's smallest county through the museum's displays of archaeology, architecture, agriculture, and domestic life. See the tools and equipment used by tradesmen – the wheelwright, carpenter, blacksmith, farrier, cooper, and shoemaker.

* A rare Saunderson tractor
* Tools and equipment of village tradesmen

Location	Admission
Off A603, near Oakham town centre	Free
Opening	**Contact**
Daily; Mon–Sat 10.30am–5pm Sun 2pm–4pm	Catmose Street, Oakham LE15 6HW
	t 01572 758440
	e museum@rutland.gov.uk

West Midlands

Herefordshire Shropshire Staffordshire
Warwickshire West Midlands Worcestershire

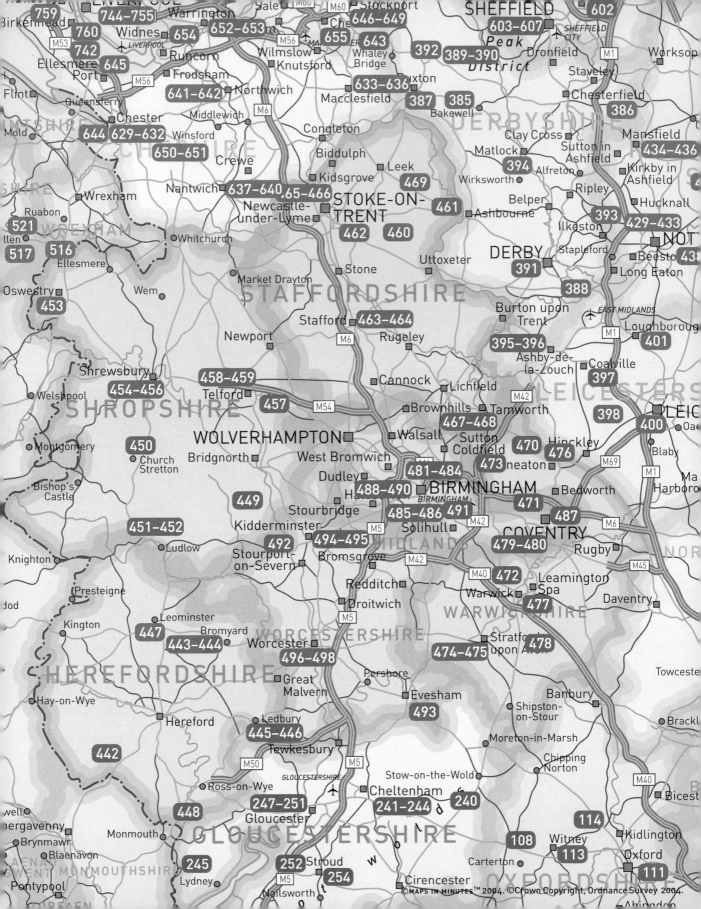

442 Abbeydore

Dore Abbey

1 hr   All year

Founded in 1147, Dore Abbey was once home to Cistercian or 'white' monks, so called because of their habits of undyed wool. They were famous for sheep farming and produced fine wools. The foundations of the settlement are still in evidence.

* Beautiful grounds, ideal for picnics

Location	Contact
In Abbeydore village on B4347	Abbeydore, Hereford HR2 0AD
Opening	w doreabbey.org.uk
Daily	
Admission	
Free	

443 Bromyard

Brockhampton Estate

1 hr   All year

This beautiful park and ancient woodland is a perfect habitat for wildlife including the dormouse, raven and buzzard. There are guided walks throughout the year and a C14 manor house with moat at the heart of the estate.

* Timber-framed gatehouse and ruined chapel
* Woodland is home to interesting range of wildlife

Location	Admission
2 miles E of Bromyard on A44	Adult £3.60, Child £1.80
Opening	**Contact**
House Mar Sat & Sun 12 noon–4pm	Greenfields, Bringsty WR6 5TB
Apr–Sep Wed–Sun 12 noon–5pm	t 01885 488099 / 482077
Oct Wed–Sun 12pm–4pm	w nationaltrust.org.uk
Estate all year dawn to dusk	e brockhampton@nationaltrust.org.uk

444 Bromyard

Shortwood Family Farm

4 hrs+   Easter–Oct

Shortwood is an organic farm with a walking trail and a pets corner. Guided tours are run between 2pm and 4pm every afternoon. Visitors can collect eggs, feed animals, milk a cow and watch a milking machine in action.

* Play area
* Trailer rides

Location	Admission
Signed from A417 between Burley Gate, Bodenham & from Pencombe village	Adult £4.50 Child £2.90
	Contact
Opening	Pencombe
Daily; from 10am	Bromyard HR7 4RP
	t 01885 400205
	w shortwoodfarm.co.uk

445 Ledbury

Eastnor Castle

2–3 hrs   Easter–Oct

This fairy-tale castle in the dramatic setting of the Malvern Hills is surrounded by a beautiful deer park, arboretum and lake. Many of the castle treasures are now displayed for the first time.

* Assault course & new night time maze
* Adventure playground & woodland & lakeside walks

Location	Admission
2 miles from Ledbury on A438 Ledbury–Tewkesbury road. 5 miles from M50 (junction 2) via Ledbury	*Castle & grounds:* Adult £7, Child £4, Concs £6
	Grounds: Adult £5, Child £3, Concs £4
Opening	**Contact**
Easter–3 Oct Sun & Bank Holiday Mon 11am–5pm; Jul & Aug daily except Sat	Eastnor, Ledbury HR8 1RL
	t 01531 633160
	w eastnorcastle.com

446 Ledbury

Glazydayz Ceramic Café

 2 hrs   All year

Paint pottery to your own design and personalize it. When you've created your masterpiece, staff glaze and fire the finished article and you collect three days later.

* Birthday parties & regular workshops
* Non-toxic & washable paint

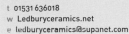

Location
In Ledbury within easy reach of Worcester, Gloucestershire & Herefordshire

Opening
Daily; Mon–Fri 11am–6pm, Sat & Sun 11am–5pm

Admission
Adult £5, Child £3

Contact
Homend Trading Estate, Ledbury HR8 1AR

t 01531 636018
w Ledburyceramics.net
e ledburyceramics@supanet.com

448 Symonds Yat West

Amazing Hedge Puzzle

 1 hr   Mar–Oct

Have fun finding your way to the centre of the maze but try to avoid the 13 dead-ends. By making your own labyrinths you too can follow in the footsteps of the heroes of Ancient Greece and India, Roman soldiers, native Americans, medieval monks and English kings.

* Hands-on displays allow you to build your own maze
* Set in the beautiful countryside of the Wye Valley

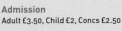

Location
Follow signs on B4164, off A40 between Ross-on-Wye & Monmouth

Opening
Good Friday–Sep daily 11am–5pm
Mar & Oct Sat–Sun 11am–4pm
Daily during half-terms

Admission
Adult £3.50, Child £2, Concs £2.50

Contact
Jubilee Park, Symonds Yat West, Ross-on-Wye HR9 6DA

t 01600 890360
w mazes.co.uk

447 Leominster

Berrington Hall

 2 hrs+   Mar–Oct

Berrington Hall is a C18 mansion with a Georgian dairy, a Victorian laundry, a walled garden and a children's play area. Orienteering courses are available.

* Ugly bug safaris
* Quizzes organised

Location
3 miles N of Leominster

Opening
6 Mar–4 Apr Sat–Sun 12 noon–4.30pm
5 Apr–31 Oct Sat–Wed 1pm–4.30pm

Admission
Adult £4.80, Child £2.40

Contact
Leominster HR6 0DW

t 01568 615721
w nationaltrust.org.uk
e berrington@nationaltrust.org.uk

449 Bridgnorth

Ray's Farm Country Matters

2–3 hrs   Feb–Nov

This attraction has unusual animals and birds, including red fallow, Sika and Axis deer, Bagot, pygmy, angora and other goats. Come and meet the owls, llamas, horses, ponies and donkeys, and visit the Sculpture Trail of Myth & Magic.

* Gold Award 2003
* At Christmas see Father Christmas & his reindeer

Location
Signposted off B4363 just S of Billingsley, halfway between Bridgnorth & Cleobury Mortime

Opening
Daily; 1 Mar–30 Nov 10am–5.30pm
Feb Sat & Sun & School Holidays 10am–5.30pm
Open Dec for Father Christmas

Admission
Adult £4.75, Child £3.25, Concs £4.25

Contact
Billingsley,
Bridgnorth WV16 6PF

t 01299 841255
w raysfarm.com

450 Church Stretton

Acton Scott

3 hrs   Apr–Oct

Learn about traditional skills and how horse-drawn machines operated. See hand-milking and butter-making, watch the work of the wheelwright, farrier and blacksmith, see the woodsman making rakes and gate hurdles, and visit animals in the farmyard and fields.

* Lambing, shearing, cider making in season
* Children's holiday activities

Location
Off A49, 17 miles S of Shrewsbury, 14 miles N of Ludlow

Opening
Mar 30–Oct 31 Tue–Sun & Bank Hols 10am–5pm

Admission
Adult £4.25, Child £2, Concs £3.75

Contact
nr Church Stretton SY6 6QN

t 01694 781306
w actonscottmuseum.co.uk
e acton.scott.museum@ shropshire-cc.gov.uk

451 Craven Arms

Secret Hills – Shropshire Hills Discovery Centre

2 hrs+   All year

Learn about ecology, geology, culture and more at this new hands-on discovery centre, set in a grass-roofed building in the Shropshire Hills. Visitors can also take a simulated balloon flight.

* Craft gallery and activities area
* Find out about earthquakes

Location
Off A49, 7 miles N of Ludlow

Opening
Daily; Apr–Oct 10am–4.30pm,
Nov– Mar 10am–3.30pm

Admission
Adult £4.25, Child £2.75

Contact
School Road, Craven Arms SY7 9RS

t 01588 676000 / 676040
w shropshire-cc.gov.uk/discover.nsf
e secrethills@shropshire-cc.gov.uk

452 Ludlow

Stokesay Castle

1 hr   All year

Stokesay Castle is the finest and best-preserved C13 fortified manor house in England. It includes a medieval Great Hall, a timber-framed Jacobean gatehouse, the parish church, and delightful cottage-style gardens.

* Magnificent Great Hall largely untouched
* Timber-framed Jacobean gatehouse

Location
Off A49, 7 miles NW of Ludlow

Opening
Daily; Apr–Sep 10am–6pm
Oct 10am–5pm
Nov–Mar Wed–Sun 10am–4pm

Admission
Adult £4.50, Child £2.30, Concs £3.40

Contact
Craven Arms SY7 9AH

t 01588 672544
w english-heritage.org.uk

453 Oswestry

Park Hall Countryside Experience

5 hrs+   All year

This is an all-weather farm visitor attraction. Popular with young and old alike, Park Hall puts on regular activities where you can meet and feed the animals. This unique experience combines education, fun and adventure. An impressive 80 per cent of the activities are indoors.

* Children's 4x4 off-road course with replica Land Rovers
* Indoor & outdoor adventure areas

WC 🏕 🍴 ♿

Location
In Oswestry, 30 minutes from Chester. Take A495 off the Oswestry bypass (A483)

Opening
Daily; Easter–30 Sep 10am–5pm;
1 Oct–31 Mar open Fri–Sun 10am–4pm;
Daily; school holidays & 1–24 Dec

Admission
Adult £4.95, Child £3.95, Concs £3.95

Contact
Park Hall,
Oswestry SY11 4AS

t 01691 671123
w parkhallfarm.co.uk
e rachel@parkhallfarm.co.uk

© English Heritage Photographic Library

454 Shrewsbury

Hawkstone Park

4 hrs   All year

Created in C18, Hawkstone became one of the greatest historic parklands in Europe. The park is centred around the Red Castle and the awe-inspiring Grotto Hill, and features intricate pathways, ravines, arches and bridges, the towering cliffs and follies.

* Woodland full of ancient oaks
* The attraction has won numerous awards

WC 🏕 🍴 ♿ 🐾

Location
Off A49, between Shrewsbury & Whitchurch

Opening
Times vary, phone for details

Admission
Adult £5.50, Child £3.50, Concs £4.50

Contact
Weston-under-Redcastle,
Shrewsbury SY4 5UY

t 01939 200611
w hawkstone.co.uk
e info@hawkstone.co.uk

©English Heritage Photographic Library/Jonathan Bailey

Mythstories, Museum of Myth & Fable

1 hr+   Apr–Oct

Enjoy colourful displays of traditional stories from Shropshire and around the world, with illustrations, photographs and artefacts. There are things to touch and play with, puzzles to do and live storytelling in the inglenook fireplace.

* Shropshire Family Attraction of the Year 2001
* Full programme of story walks

Location
On B5063 just off A49 near Whitchurch

Opening
Daily; Apr–Oct Sun–Thu 2pm–6pm; pre-booked group visits at other times

Admission
Adult £3.50, Child £2, Concs £2

Contact
The Morgan Library, Aston Street, Wem, Shrewsbury SY4 5AU

t   01939 235500
w   mythstories.com
e   info@mythstories.com

Wroxeter Roman City

1 hr   All year

The largest excavated Roman city in Britain to have escaped development, Wroxeter was once home to 6,000 people. The impressive remains include C2 municipal baths. The site museum offers insight into the lives of the people who lived here.

* Virtual reality Wroxeter visit
* Free children's activity sheet

Location
On B4380, 5 miles E of Shrewsbury

Opening
Daily; Apr–Sep 10am–6pm
Oct daily 10am–5pm
Nov–Mar 10am–1pm & 2pm–4pm

Admission
Adult £3.70, Child £1.70, Concs £2.80

Contact
Wroxeter,
Shrewsbury SY5 6PH

t   01743 761330
w   english-heritage.org.uk

The RAF Museum – Cosford

3 hrs+   All year

This museum houses one of the largest aviation collections in the UK. Over 70 historic aircraft are displayed in three wartime hangars on an active airfield. The collection spans nearly 80 years of aviation history and includes missiles, motor vehicles and aero engines.

* Visitor Attraction of the Year 2003
* State-of-the-art flight simulator

Location
On A41, less than 1 mile from M54 junction 3

Opening
Daily; 10am–6pm (last entry 4pm)

Admission
Free, charges for special events
Under 16s must be accompanied by an adult

Contact
Cosford, Shifnal TF11 8UP

t   01902 376 200
w   rafmuseum.org
e   cosford@rafmuseum.com

458 Telford

Enginuity

   2 hrs   All year

This new attraction within the World Heritage Site of the Ironbridge Gorge will appeal to children of all ages. There is plenty of hands-on, feet-on, full-on fun to be had as you explore the world of technology.

* World Heritage Site
* Be an apprentice engineer for the day

Location
Follow the brown tourist signs from M54 (junction 4)

Opening
Daily; 10am–5pm

Admission
Adult £5.30, Child £3.70, Concs £3.70
Please phone for latest prices

Contact
Ironbridge Gorge Museum Trust, Coach Road, Coalbrookdale Telford TF8 7DQ

t 01952 884391
w **ironbridge.org.uk**
e tic@ironbridge.org.uk

459 Telford

Ironbridge Gorge Museums

   1–6 hrs   All year

The Ironbridge Gorge was the scene of a remarkable breakthrough in technology that led to the Industrial Revolution. Nine museums catalogue these events and the men who made them happen.

* Various workshops, including ceramic and iron working
* Enginuity – hands-on design and tech experiences

Location
5 miles S of Telford, signed from M54 junction 4

Opening
Daily; 10am–5pm – some areas close in winter

Admission
Passport ticket to all ten attractions
Adult £12.95, Child £8.25, Concs £11.25

Contact
Ironbridge, Telford TF8 7DQ

t 01952 884 391
w ironbridge.org.uk
e visits@ironbridge.org.uk

460   Alton

Alton Towers

6 hrs+   Mar–Oct

This is a theme park with a blend of rides and attractions to suit every member of the family. It includes 200 acres of landscaped gardens, rides, live entertainment and the historic towers building. Come along and enjoy a fun-packed family day out.

* New family spinning roller-coaster
* Two on-site hotels incorporating an indoor water park

Location
Off B5030, near Uttoxeter (A50); take junction 15 or 16 from M6, or junction 23a or 28 from M1. Follow the brown tourist signs

Opening
Daily; Mar–end Oct 9.30am–5pm (later in summer). Please phone or check website before visiting

Admission
Please phone for details

Contact
Alton,
Stoke-on-Trent ST10 4DB

t 08705 204060
w altontowers.com

461   Ashbourne

Sudbury Hall & Museum of Childhood

3 hrs   Mar–Oct

This beautiful late C17 house is home to the Museum of Childhood with chimney climbs and coal tunnels, a Victorian schoolroom and nursery, and a great collection of toys, games and dolls. Discover how children worked and played in the past.

* Featured in the BBC's *Pride and Prejudice*
* 'Behind the Scenes' tours

Location
6miles E of Uttoxeter at junction of A50 Derby–Stoke and A515 Ashbourne

Opening
Hall 6 Mar–30 Oct Wed–Sun 1pm–5pm
Grounds 6 Mar–30 Oct Wed–Sun 11am–6pm; *Museum* 6 Mar–30 Oct, Wed–Sun, 1pm–5pm; 4–12 Dec Sat–Sun 11am–4pm

Admission
Hall Adult £5, Child £2
Museum Adult £5.50, Child £3.50
Hall & Museum Adult £ 9, Child £4.50

Contact
Sudbury, Ashbourne DE6 5HT

t 01283 585337
w nationaltrust.org.uk
e sudburyhall@nationaltrust.org.uk

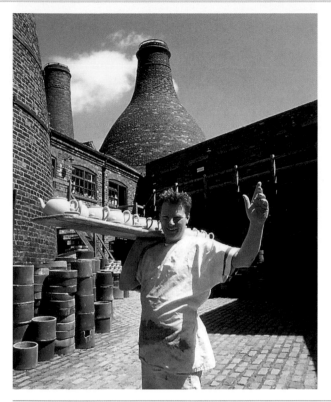

462 Longton

Gladstone Working Pottery Museum

2 hrs+   All year

A complete Victorian pottery factory where visitors can get to grips with the history and skills of the potteries. Throw your own pot or try your hand at a range of pottery crafts with the team of friendly expert presentation staff.

* Traditional skills and original workshops
* Cobbled yard and huge bottle kilns

Location
From M6, follow A500, take A50 to Longton

Opening
Daily; 10am–5pm

Admission
Adult £4.95, Child £3.50, Concs £3.95

Contact
Uttoxeter Road, Longton, Stoke-on-Trent ST3 1PQ

t 01782 319232
w stoke.gov.uk/gladstone
e gladstone@stoke.gov.uk

463 Stafford

British Wildlife Rescue Centre

2 hrs   All year

The whole family will enjoy a visit to this refuge set up for the treatment of sick and injured British wildlife. The farm facilities are available to visitors.

* Guided tours

Location
On A518 Stafford–Uttoxeter road, 1 mile from Weston

Opening
Daily; 10am–5pm; Apr–Sep 10am–6pm

Admission
Adult £1.50, Child 50p

Contact
Amerton Working Farm, Stowe-by-Chartley, Stafford ST18 0LA

t 01889 271308

464 Stafford

Stafford Castle

3 hrs+   All year

Built by William the Conqueror after 1066, the remains of this great castle provide fascinating insights into its 900-year history. The centre, built in the style of a Norman guard house, has archaeological artefacts and an audio-visual area.

* Try on armour & chainmail
* Host of archaeological finds

Location
Off A518, 1 mile SW of Stafford

Opening
Apr–Oct Tue–Sun & Bank Hols 10am–5pm
Nov–Mar Sat–Sun 10am–4pm

Admission
Free

Contact
Castle Bank, Newport Road, Stafford ST16 1DJ

t 01785 257698
w staffordbc.gov.uk
e castlebc@btconnect.com

465 Stoke-on-Trent

Etruria Industrial Museum

1 hr   All year

Etruria Industrial Museum is situated on the Calden, Trent and Mersey canals and includes the Etruscan Bone and Flint Mill.

* Family-friendly interactive exhibition & events programme
* Craft activities in holidays

Location
Signed from A500. The car park is off Etruria Vale Road

Opening
Jan–Mar Mon–Wed 12 noon–4.30pm;
Apr–Dec open Sat–Wed 12 noon–4.30pm

Admission
Adults £2.35, Child £1.20, Concs £1.20

Contact
Lower Bedford Street,
Stoke-on-Trent ST4 7AF
t 01782 233144
w stoke.gov.uk.museums
e etruria@swift.stoke.gov.uk

466 Stoke-on-Trent

Waterworld

3–4 hrs   All year

Children will enjoy this wacky and wild water park. It has 19 exciting rides and attractions including wave machines, flumes, rapids and slides. Some attractions include the Spacebowl, aqua assault course, the Python, the Black Hole & aquadisco parties are available.

* Best Practice Accolade 2002

Location
Off Junction 16 of M6. From M1 follow A50 to Stoke-on-Trent & then follow signs to Festival Park

Opening
Summer: Mon & Tue 10am–6pm, Wed & Thu 10am–7pm, Fri 10am–9pm, Sat & Sun 10am–6pm;
Winter: Wed & Thu 2pm–7pm, Fri 2pm–9pm, Sat & Sun 10am–6pm

Admission
Please phone for details

Contact
Etruria, Hanley,
Stoke-on-Trent ST1 5PU
t 01782 205747
w waterworld.co.uk

467 Tamworth

Ash End House Children's Farm

4 hrs   All year

This small family-owned farm has lots of friendly animals to feed and stroke. As well as outdoor activities and a play area, the farm offers lots of undercover attractions and some fascinating rare breeds. There are activities during weekends & holidays, including Make a Memento.

* Tours for groups
* Birthday parties on the farm

Location
In Middleton, near Tamworth in Staffordshire. Signed off A4091 & on the same road as Drayton Manor Park

Opening
Daily; in summer 10am–5pm;
in winter 10am–dusk;

Admission
Adult £2.90, Child £4.90 (includes feed for animals, pony ride, all activities)

Contact
Middleton Lane, Middleton
Nr Tamworth B78 2BL
t 0121 329 3240
w childrensfarm.co.uk
e contact@childrensfarm.co.uk

468 Tamworth

Drayton Manor Family Theme Park

6 hrs+   Mar–Nov

With over 100 rides and exciting attractions on offer, Drayton Park is a fantastic day out that's a firm favourite with all the family. Some attraction include aerial park, Pirate Cove, crazy golf, games booths & penny arcades.

* Museum, farm & zoo
* Live entertainment

Location
Near Tamworth on A4091. From M42 take junction 9 or 10

Opening
Daily; 22 Mar–2 Nov
Please phone or visit the website for details

Admission
Please phone or visit the website for details

Contact
Tamworth B78 3TW
t 01827 287979
w draytonmanor.co.uk
e info@draytonmanor.co.uk

Staffordshire

469 Winkhill

Blackbrook Zoological Park

2–4 hrs   All year

There is always something new to see at this fun and educational attraction, from rare birds, unusual animals and reptiles, to insects and aquatics.

* Pets area & aquarium & educational building
* Largest collection of birds from around the world

Location
From Leek, take A523 & 1st right, signed to the park, then 1st right again

Opening
Daily; 10.30am–5.30pm (earlier closing in winter)
Jan Café: open in summer only

Admission
Adult £6.25, Child £3.95, Concs £5.25

Contact
Winkhill ST13 7QR

t 01538 308293
w blackbrookzoologicalpark.co.uk

470 Atherstone

Twycross Zoo

3–4 hrs   All year

Twycross is the leading primate zoo in the country, but it also hosts hundreds of other animals from around the world including elephants, big cats, birds, reptiles and amphibians.

* Seal & penguin feeding times
* Pets' corner & rare breeds

Location
Just off M42 on A444 in Leicestershire, within easy reach of all the Midland counties

Opening
Daily; summer 10am–5.30pm; winter 10am–4pm

Admission
Please phone to confirm 2005 prices

Contact
Burton Road
Atherstone CV9 3PX

t 01827 880250
w twycrosszoo.com

471 Coventry

Brandon Marsh Nature Centre

1 hr+   All year

A haven for rare birds and wildlife. This 200-acre nature reserve is home to a series of pools and wetlands, nature trails and bird hides. Find out about the reserve's residents at the Eco-Zone centre, with touch-screen computers and interactive exhibits.

* Warwickshire Wildlife Trust Centre

Location
Off A45

Opening
Daily; Mon–Sat 9am–4.30pm
Sun 10am–4pm

Admission
Adult £2.50, Child £1, Concs £1.50

Contact
Brandon Lane, Coventry CV3 3GW

t 024 76308999
w wildlifetrust.org.uk
e admin@warkswt.cix.co.uk

472 Hatton

Hatton Country World

3 hrs+   All year

Hatton Country World offers acres of fun for everyone, with a fun-packed day of events and activities, such as Farmyard Favourites and Adventure Land. Finish off your day with a relaxing browse round the unique shopping village or a trip to see the animals.

* Daft Duck trials, children's show & Bird-obatics
* Soft play centre & Tristan the Runaway Tractor

Location
5 minutes from junction 15 off M40. Take A46 towards Coventry & turn onto A4177 & follow the brown tourist signs

Opening
Daily; summer 10am–5pm; winter open daily 10am–5pm

Admission
Please phone or look on website

Contact
Hatton House,
Hatton CV35 7LD

t 01926 843411
w hattonworld.com
e hatton@hattonworld.com

473 Kingsbury

Broomey Croft Children's Farm

2 hrs+   All year

Set in the North Warwickshire countryside, Broomey Croft Children's Farm provides an opportunity for a family day of fun and relaxation. Children can also meet and hand-feed the farm animals. Lambing & bottle-feeding lambs, baby goats, sheep shearing, baby chicks & a bee display.

* Free tractor & trailer rides
* Baby lambs

Location
10 minutes from junction 9 off M42. Follow A4091 towards Drayton Manor & follow the brown tourist signs

Opening
Daily; Easter–end Aug 10am–5pm; Oct–Mar open weekends & school holidays 10am–4pm

Admission
Adult £3.95, Child £3.45

Contact
Bodymoor Heath Lane,
Bodymore Heath,
Kingsbury B76 0EE

t 01827 873844
w childrens-farm.com
e info@childrens-farm.com

474 Stratford-upon-Avon

Shakespeare's Birthplace

1 hr   All year

Each of the five Shakespeare houses on show has its own unique character and family connection to William Shakespeare, and offers a different insight into the world of the famous playwright.

* Exhibitions tell the story of the house
* Exhibits of rare period items including *First Folio* 1623

Location
Signed from town centre

Opening
Daily; Nov–Mar Mon–Sat 10am–4pm
Sun 10.30–4pm
Apr–May & Sep–Oct Mon–Sat
10am–5pm Sun 10.30am–5p
Jun–Aug Mon–Sat 9am–5pm
Sun 10.30am–4pm

Admission
Adult £6.50, Child £2.50, Concs £5.50

Contact
Henley Street,
Stratford-upon-Avon CV37 6QW

t 01789 201823
w shakespeare.org.uk
e info@shakespeare.org.uk

475 Stratford-upon-Avon

Stratford Butterfly Farm

1 hr+ · All year

Wander through a tropical rainforest with a myriad of multi-coloured butterflies, birds and fish. See fascinating animals in Insect City and view deadly spiders in perfect safety in Arachnoland.

* Expert staff
* Wildlife video shows

Location
On the River Avon, opposite the Royal Shakespeare Theatre. Easily accessible from the town centre

Opening
Daily; summer 10am–6pm; winter 10am– dusk

Admission
Please phone for 2005 prices

Contact
Traway Walk, Swan's Nest Lane, Stratford-upon-Avon CV37 7LS

t 01789 299288
w butterflyfarm.co.uk
e sales@butterflyfarm.co.uk

476 Sutton Cheney

Bosworth Battlefield Visitor Centre & Country Park

2 hrs+ · Mar-Dec

Site of one of the most famous battles in English history, between Richard III and Henry Tudor. The result gave England a new king and marked the beginning of the Tudor dynasty.

* Extensive visitor centre
* Annual re-enactment of the battle

Location
2 miles S of Market Bosworth nr the village of Sutton Cheney

Opening
Visitor Centre Mar Sat-Sun 11am-5pm; Apr-Oct daily 11am-5pm; Nov-Dec Sun 11am-4pm
Country Park all year

Admission
Adult £3.25, Concs £2.25

Contact
Sutton Cheney, Nuneaton, Warwickshire CV13 0AD

t 01455 290429
w www.leics.gov.uk
e bosworth@leics.gov.uk

477 Warwick

Warwick Castle

2 hrs+   All year

Britain's greatest medieval experience – discover 1000 years of history at Warwick Castle. See the medieval preparation for battle in Kingmaker, join a Victorian Royal Weekend Party and enjoy special events throughout the year.

* Quality Assured Visitor Attraction

Location
2 miles from junction 15 off M40, Warwick Castle is easily accessible by road or rail

Opening
Daily; Apr–Sep 10am–6pm;
Oct–Mar 10am–5pm

Admission
Please phone for details

Contact
Warwick CV34 4QU

t 0870 442 2000
w warwick-castle.co.uk

478 Wellesbourne

Wellesbourne Watermill

2 hrs   Easter–Sep

Visitors to this historic watermill can see the mill's machinery being driven by one of the country's largest wooden waterwheels. There are regular demonstrations of how stoneground flour is milled. Coracles are used on the millpond, which is a tranquil haven for wildlife.

* Conservation award from SPAB
* Fishing lake

Location
On B4086, between Kineton & Stratford-upon-Avon

Opening
Easter–Sep Thu–Sun & Bank Hols 10am–5pm

Admission
Adult £3.50, Child £2.50, Concs £3

Contact
Kineton Road, Wellesbourne
CV35 9HG

t 01789 470237
w wellesbournemill.co.uk
e andrew@mill.spacomputers.com

479 Baginton

Lunt Roman Fort

2 hrs   Apr–Oct

Lunt Roman Fort features a timber reconstructed gateway, ramparts, a unique cavalry training ring, granary housing and archaeological objects.

* Events & re-enactments with the XIII Legion
* Museum of army life

Location
In Baginton Village, near Coventry. It can be approached from the A45 & the A46

Opening
Currently being refurbished; Re-opening Apr 2005; Please phone for details

Admission
2004; Adult £2, Child £1, Concs £1

Contact
Coventry Road, Baginton CV8 3AJ

t 02476 832565/303567

480 Baginton

Midland Air Museum

2 hrs   All year

A wide range of aircraft, both local and international. The collection includes Second World War aircraft and memorabilia and outside are a number of rare aircraft, including an anti-aircraft gun. A number of the aircraft have steps up to the cockpit area so you can look inside.

* Giant Armstrong Whitworth Argosy freighter of 1959
* Meteor, Vulcan, Hunter, Starfighter and Phantom

Location
Off A45, between roundabout & Baginton

Opening
Daily; Apr–Oct Mon–Sat 10am–5pm
Sun 10am–6pm
Nov–Mar 10am–5pm

Admission
Adult £4, Child £2.25, Concs £3.25

Contact
Coventry Airport, Baginton, Coventry CV8 3AZ

t 02476 301033
w midlandairmuseum.org.uk
e midlandairmuseum@aol.com

481 Birmingham

Lapworth Museum of Geology

1 hr   All year

For an educational few hours, take the children to visit one of the oldest specialist geological museums in the UK. Dating back to 1880, Lapworth has an extensive and fascinating collection of fossils, minerals and rocks.

* Over 250, 000 specimens
* 420 million-year-old fossils

Location
On A38 Bristol Road into Birmingham

Opening
Daily; Mon–Fri 9am–5pm; Sat & Sun 2pm–5pm;
Please phone for details
Other times by appointment

Admission
Free

Contact
University of Birmingham, Edgbaston Birmingham B15 2TT

t 0121 414 7294
e lapmus@bham.ac.uk

482 Birmingham

Think Tank

4 hrs   All year

A brand new science and discovery centre where kids are encouraged to get stuck in. Hands-on and interactive, there's a chance to hold polar bear blubber, drive a digger or detect a jewel thief. You'll also find an IMAX theatre with some stunning films.

* Unravel the mysteries of the body
* Medical tour covers techniques and instruments

Location
Follow blue banners, 15 mins walk from New Street

Opening
Daily; 10am–5pm

Admission
Adult £6.95, Child £4.95, Concs £5.50

Contact
Curzon Street, Birmingham B4 7XG

t 0121 2022222
w thinktank.ac
e findout@thinktank.ac

483 Birmingham

National Sea Life Centre

3 hrs   All year

This sea life centre has over 55 fascinating displays. Children can come face to face with literally hundreds of amazing sea creatures, from sharks to shrimps.

* Claws exhibition & transparent underwater tunnel
* New tropical ocean tank housing giant sea turtles

Location
Between National Indoor Arena & International Convention Centre

Opening
Daily; summer 10am–5pm; winter Mon–Fri 10am–4pm Sat & Sun 10am–5pm

Admission
Adult £8.95, Child £6.95, Concs £7.50

Contact
The Waters Edge, Brindleyplace, Birmingham B1 2HL

t 0121 643 6777 / 633 4700
w sealifeeurope.com
e slcbirmingham@ merlinentertainments.biz

484 Birmingham

Tolkien's Birmingham

2 hrs   Apr–Sep

Visit many of J.R.R Tolkien's childhood haunts and see the places that inspired him to write *The Hobbit* and *Lord of the Rings*. This is a fascinating guided tour, and a chance to experience the young imagination of a literary genius.

* In-depth knowledge from specialist tour guide for groups only
* Good footwear & waterproof clothing recommended

Location
Various areas of Birmingham

Opening
Apr–Sep by appointment
Phone for details of guided tours

Admission
£5 per person

Contact
50 Springfield Road, Kings Heath, Birmingham B14 7DU

t 0121 4444046
w birminghamheritage.org.uk
e balti1@compuserve.com

485 Bournville

Cadbury World

3 hrs   All year

Fun for all ages with the magical Cadabra journey and the Cadbury Fantasy Factory. Children can learn all about chocolate – where it came from and who first consumed this mysterious substance – and then visit the largest Cadbury shop in the world!

* Learn how chocolate is used to make famous brands
* Chocolate Coronation Street!

Location
Signed from M42

Opening
Times vary, phone for details

Admission
Adult £8.75, Child £6.60, Concs £7
Pre-booking recommended

Contact
Linden Road, Bournville, Brimingham B30 2LD

t 0121 4514159
w cadburyworld.co.uk
e cadbury.world@csplc.com

486 Bournville

Selly Manor

2 hrs   All year

Learn about medieval life, the Tudors, old houses and furniture in this amazing medieval timber-framed house which was moved piece by piece by George Cadbury to the village of Bournville. Portable notes, torches and magnifying glasses provided.

* In the village of Bournville, built by George Cadbury

Location
3 miles S of Birmingham city centre on Maple Road next to Bournville village green

Opening
Tues-Fri, 10am-5pm
Apr-Sep, Sat, Sun and Bank Holidays, 2pm-5pm

Admission
Adult £2.50, Child 50p, Concs £1.50

Contact
Bournville,
Birmingham B30 1UB

t 0121 472 0199
w www.bvt.org/sellymanor
e sellymanor@bvt.org.uk

487 Coventry

Ryton Organic Gardens

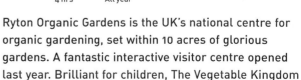

4 hrs   All year

Ryton Organic Gardens is the UK's national centre for organic gardening, set within 10 acres of glorious gardens. A fantastic interactive visitor centre opened last year. Brilliant for children, The Vegetable Kingdom is an exciting addition to this family day out.

* Children's garden
* Computer games

Location
Off A45 on the road to Wolston, 5 miles SE of Coventry

Opening
Daily; 9am-5pm

Admission
Adult £4.50, Child £2, Concs £4

Contact
Ryton-on-Dunsmore,
Coventry CV8 3LG

t 02476 303517
w hdra.org.uk
e enquiry@hdra.org.uk

The perfect vegetable?

The perfect vegetable plant would be totally edible.
It might look something like this!

488 Dudley

Black Country Living Museum

3 hrs+   All year

Discover a fascinating world where an old-fashioned village has been created beside the canal. Wander around original shops and houses, ride on a tramcar or fairground swingboat, go down the mine or just soak up the atmosphere.

* Tramcars and trolleybuses transport visitors
* Costumed demonstrators and working craftsmen

Location
On A4037, 3 miles from M5 junction 2

Opening
Daily; Mar–Oct 10am–5pm
Nov–Feb Wed–Sun 10am–4pm

Admission
Adult £9.60, Child £5.50, Concs £8.50

Contact
Tipton Road, Dudley DY1 4SQ

t 0121 5579643
w bclm.co.uk
e info@bclm.co.uk

489 Dudley

Critters Farm

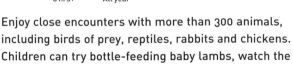

6 hrs+   All year

Enjoy close encounters with more than 300 animals, including birds of prey, reptiles, rabbits and chickens. Children can try bottle-feeding baby lambs, watch the duck racing and greet the goats.

* Disabled visitors please phone in advance

Location
Take the A463 or A459 or A457 into Sedgley. Signposted from Cotwall End Road or Catholic Lane

Opening
Daily; 1 Nov–28 Feb 9.30am–4pm; 1 Mar–31 Oct 9.30am–5pm

Admission
Adult £3, Child £2, Concs £2

Contact
Cotwall End, Catholic Lane, Sedgley, Dudley DY3 3YE

t 01902 674668
w crittersfarm.org.uk

490 Dudley

Dudley Zoological Gardens

3 hrs+   All year

Dudley Zoo is a modern zoo set in the 40-acre wooded grounds of Dudley Castle. Visitors can enjoy a varied day combining zoology, history and geology, as the zoo is built on an important limestone escarpment.

* Breathtaking views over the Black Country
* Audio-visual display & visitor centre

Location
Just 3 miles from junction 2 of M5

Opening
Daily; Mar–Oct 10am–4pm; Oct–Mar 10am–3pm

Admission
Adult £8.50, Child (4–15) £5.25

Contact
2 The Broadway, Dudley DY1 4QB

t 01384 215313
w dudleyzoo.org.uk

491 Edgbaston

Birmingham Botanical Gardens & Glasshouses

2 hrs+   All year

In a series of giant glasshouses each with different climatic conditions, you can visit a world of environments in just one day. There are four glasshouses, Tropical, Subtropical, Mediterranean and Arid, and a Study Centre running fun workshops aimed at children under 12.

* Designed by JC Loudon, a leading garden planner
* Sculpture trail, waterfowl and exotic birds

Location
Signed from Edgbaston

Opening
Daily; Mon–Sat 9am–5pm
Sun 10am–5pm

Admission
Adult £5.50, Child £3

Contact
Westbourne Road, Edgbaston, Birmingham B15 3TR

t 0121 4541860
w birminghambotanicalgardens. org.uk
e admin@birminghambotanical gardens. org.uk

492 Bewdley

West Midland Safari & Leisure Park

3 hrs+   Mar–Oct

This park is set in 200 acres comprising a drive-through animal safari with exotic species such as rhinos, lions, tigers, giraffes, wolves, emus, wallabies and many more. Come and see the Pets Corner, the reptile house, the sea lion show and Hippo Lakes.

* Safari Bus tours
* Discovery trail

Location
On A456 between Kidderminster & Bewdley

Opening
Mar–Oct
Please phone for details

Admission
Please phone for details

Contact
Spring Grove,
Bewdley DY12 1LF

t 01299 402114
w wmsp.co.uk
e info@wmsp.co.uk

493 Broadway

Broadway Magic Experience

1 hr   Feb–Dec

The Broadway Magic Experience has displays of new and old teddy bears, toys and magical animated scenes.

* Antiques & famous bears like Big Ted from *Playschool*
* Christmas-related items

Location
In Broadway just off the main A44 bypass road

Opening
1 Feb–31 Dec Tue–Sun 10am–4pm

Admission
Adult £2.50, Child £1.75, Concs £1.75

Contact
76 High Street,
Broadway WR12 7AJ

t 01386 858323
e janicelonghi@hotmail.com

494 Kidderminster

Mamble Craft Centre

3 hrs   All year

Mamble Craft Centre is housed in C17 barns on an ancient medieval site, with stunning views of the Clee Hills. It offers an insight into past and present crafts through its four craft workshops where you can see items being made.

* Award–winning tea rooms
* Enticing gift shop

Location
Off A456 in the village of Mamble, mid-way between Bewdley & Tenbury Wells

Opening
Tue–Sun & Bank Holidays
10.30am–5pm; Oct–Dec Mon
10.30am–5pm

Admission
Free

Contact
Mamble,
Kidderminster DY14 9JY

t 01299 832834
w mamblecraftcentre.co.uk

495 Kidderminster

Worcestershire County Museum

2 hrs   Feb–Nov

Housed in Hartlebury Castle, the museum tells the county's story from Roman occupation to the C20. Visitors can see the Castle State Rooms Tuesdays to Thursdays at no extra cost.

* Displays include a Victorian room & transport gallery
* Programme of temporary exhibitions & events

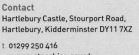

Location
Signed from A449,

Opening
Feb–Nov Mon–Thu 10am–5pm
Fri & Sun 2pm–5pm

Admission
Adult £2.50, Child & Concs £1.20

Contact
Hartlebury Castle, Stourport Road,
Hartlebury, Kidderminster DY11 7XZ

t 01299 250 416
w worcestershire.gov.uk
e museum@worcestershire.gov.uk

496 Worcester

Upton Heritage Centre

1 hr+   Apr–Sep

This restored bell tower is the oldest surviving building in the town and is a local landmark. It tells the story of the battle of Upton in 1651 during the Civil War. There are also exhibits on local history and the development of Upton-upon-Severn.

* Housed in the 'pepperpot'– an old church tower

Location
On B4211 from Great Malvern & A38 &
A4104 from Worcester

Opening
Daily; 1 Apr–30 Sep 1.30pm–4.30pm;
Open some mornings at other times
Please phone for details

Admission
Free

Contact
Church Street, Upton-upon-Severn,
Worcester WR8 0HT

t 01684 592679

497 Worcester

The Hop Pocket Craft Centre

4 hrs   All year

The Hop Pocket Craft Centre is situated in the beautiful Frome Valley. See over 300 different craftsmen's work on display, including pottery, glass engraving, jewellery, soft toys, paintings, and woodturning-gifts to suit every pocket.

* Demonstrations by appointment
* Situated in old hop kilns

Location
On the B4214 just off A4103
Worcester–Hereford road

Opening
Daily; Please phone for details

Admission
Free

Contact
New House Farm,
Bishops Frome,
Worcester WR6 5BT

t 01531 640323
w thehoppocket.com
e john@hoppocket.co.uk

498 Worcester

Worcester Cathedral

1 hr   All year

The present building was begun in 1084 and its many attractions include King John's tomb, Prince Arthur's chantry, St Wulstan's crypt, an early C12 chapter house, and a tower with amazing views over the city and county.

* Tower open 10am–4.30pm, Sat & summer holidays
* Magnificent Victorian stained glass windows

Location
City centre, off College Street

Opening
Daily; 7.30am–6pm
Services three times daily

Admission
Free, donations welcome

Contact
10A College Green, Worcester
WR1 2LH

t 01905 28854
w cofe-worcester.org.uk
e info@worcestercathedral.org.uk

Wales

Mid Wales North Wales South Wales

Carmel Head

Amlwch

Great Ormes Head

Kirkby

Bootle • Skelmersdale
• Crosby

Wallasey • LIVERPO

Birkenhead 759 744–755 • Widnes
760
M53 742 • LIVERPOO
645 • M56

Holyhead

Isle of Anglesey

Anglesey

Beaumaris

Llandudno • Colwyn Bay • Rhyl
Conwy 518 Abergele
Prestatyn
Holywell
St Asaph • Flint

Holy Island

Llangefni 511
512
Menai Bridge 519
510 Bangor
513–515 Caernarfon
Llanfairfechan

CONWY

Bethesda

522

Denbigh

Ruthin

FLINTSHIRE
Mold

Queensferry

644 629–632 • Chester

DENBIGHSHIRE

Ruabon • Wrexham

WREXHAM

Llangollen 521
517 516 Ellesmere • Wem

Lleyn Peninsula

Porthmadog
Criccieth 523
Pwllheli
Abersoch

Blaenau Ffestiniog
Ffestiniog 524
Bala

505

Oswestry
453

Shrewsbury
454–456

SHROPS

Bardsey Island

Barmouth
Dolgellau
Mallwyd

Welshpool

503
506–507 Machynlleth
Tywyn
Aberdyfi

Montgomery 450
Chur Stret

Newtown

Bishop's Castle

Cambrian Mountains

POWYS

451–4

499
Aberystwyth
500

Llanidloes

Llangurig

Knighton

Presteigne
451–4

Rhayader 509

Llandrindod Wells

Kington 447

WALES

Aberaeron
New Quay

Tregaron

Builth Wells

CEREDIGION

HEREFOR

Lampeter 508

Hay-on-Wye

Strumble Head

502
531 Cardigan

Newcastle Emlyn

Fishguard

St David's

PEMBROKESHIRE

CARMARTHENSHIRE

Llandovery

Brecon

Brecon Beacons

504

442

Carmarthen
534 Llandeilo
532 501

Crickhowell

Abergavenny

Narberth
537
St Clears

Haverfordwest

Milford Haven
Neyland
Pembroke Dock
Pembroke 541
Tenby

Kidwelly
Burry Port
Llanelli

Ammanford 533

NEATH TALBOT

Merthyr Tydfil
Rhymney

Ebbw Vale Brynmawr
Blaenavon

Monmouth

MONMOUTHSHI

535 Neath

Aberdare
Mountain Ash
Glyncorrwg

539 Bargoed 525
540

Pontypool

BLAENAU
GWENT

Cwmbran

Risca

Chepstow
536 M48
M4 Ca

Caldey Island

St Govan's Head

Port Eynon

Swansea
538

Port Talbot

Mumbles Head

Maesteg

Pontypridd

526 Caerphilly

NEWPORT Newport

M4

Avonmouth

M5

Porthcawl

Bridgend

Cowbridge

527–530

VALE OF GLAMORG

CARDIFF

CARDIFF

Clevedon

Barry

Weston-super-Mare

Congresbury

©MAPS IN MINUTES™ 2004. ©Crown Copyright, Ordnance Survey 2004.

499 Aberystwyth

Animalarium

3 hrs   All year

The Animalarium is a collection of small exotic and domestic animals, many of which have come from pet rescue centres. There are lots of activities for children, including pony rides in summer, the chance to touch snakes and watch crocodiles being fed.

Location
At Borth, between Aberystwyth & Machynlleth

Opening
Daily; summer 10am–6pm winter 11am–4pm

Admission
Adult £4.90, Child £2.80, Concs £4

Contact
Borth,
Ceredigion SY25 6RA

t 01970 871224

500 Aberystwyth

Vale of Rheidol Railway

1 hr+   Apr–Oct

Take a ride on a steam train for 11 miles from Aberystwyth to Devil's Bridge. During the hour-long journey you'll have spectacular views of the wooded Rheidol Valley. From Devil's Bridge, there are walks to Mynach Falls, Devil's Punchbowl and Jacob's Ladder.

* One of the Great Little Trains of Wales
* The last steam railway owned by British Rail

Location
Trains depart from Aberystwyth centre, beside the main railway station

Opening
Please phone for details

Admission
Return Adult £11.50, Child from £2.50, Concs £10.50

Contact
Park Avenue, Aberystwyth, Cardiganshire SY23 1PG

t 01970 625819
w www.rheidolrailway.co.uk
e vor@rheidolrailway.co.uk

501 Brecon

Brecon Beacons National Park Visitor Centre

1 hr+   All year

Situated among hills and mountains, the park covers an area of 520 square miles. Stretching from Hay on Wye in the east to Llandeilo in the west, it incorporates the Black Mountains, the Central Beacons and Fforest Fawr as well as moorland, forests, valleys, waterfalls, lakes, and gorges.

* Centre of internationally renowned festivals
* Selection of guided walks available

Location
The National Park Mountain Centre is 5½ miles SW of Brecon

Opening
Daily; Mar–Jun & Sep–Oct 9.30am–5pm
Jul–Aug 9.30am–6pm
Nov–Feb 9.30am–4.30pm

Admission
Free, car park charges vary

Contact
NPVC, Libanus, Brecon,
Powys LD3 8ER

t 01874 623366
w breconbeacons.org
e mountaincentre@breconbeacons.org

502 Cardigan

Felinwynt Rainforest & Butterfly Centre

1 hr+   Easter–Oct

This fascinating experience offers a glimpse into the rainforest with tropical butterflies and exotic plants, waterfalls and a stream. A personal guide can make the experience unique.

Location
Off the A487, 6 miles N of Cardigan.
Follow the brown tourist signs

Opening
Daily; Easter–Oct 10.30am–5pm
Limited opening in winter

Admission
Adult £3.75, Child £1.50, Concs £3.50

Contact
Felinwynt, Cardigan,
Ceredigion SA43 1RT

t 01239 810882/810250
w butterflycentre.co.uk

503 Corris

King Arthur's Labyrinth

2 hrs+   Mar–Nov

Take a boat ride underground and walk in spectacular caverns deep under the mountain, where Welsh tales of King Arthur unfold with magical sound and light effects. Back above ground join the bards' quest to search for legends lost in the maze of time.

* Large fully operational craft centre
* Shop sells items on the Arthurian theme

Location
On the A487 between Machynlleth and Dolgellau

Opening
Daily; 19 Mar–6 Nov 10am–5pm

Admission
Adult £5.15, Child £3.60, Concs £4.60

Contact
Corris, Machynlleth, Powys SY20 9RF

t 01654 761584
w kingarthurslabyrinth.com
e king.arthurs.labyrinth@corriswales.co.uk

504 Llangorse

Llangorse Rope & Riding Centre

2 hrs+   All year

The centre offers a range of indoor and outdoor activities, from climbing rock surfaces and rope bridges to trekking and hacking. A wide range, including junior bouldering, are designed specially for children over five. There are qualified instructors and on-site accommodation.

* Largest indoor climbing & riding centre in Wales
* WTB's Best New Business in Wales award

Location
On B4560, off A40
Brecon to Abergavenny road

Opening
Climb Daily; Mon–Sat 9am–10pm
Sun 9am–6pm
Ride Mon–Sun 9.30am–4.30pm;
closed 25,26 Dec and 1 Jan

Admission
Climb: £12, 2-hour trek £16

Contact
Gilfach Farm, Llangorse, Brecon Beacons, Powys, LD3 7UH

t 01874 658 272
w www.activityuk.com
e info@1001daysout.com

505 Llanwyddyn

Lake Vyrnwy Nature Reserve

2 hrs+   All year

This man–made lake was completed in 1888. In dry weather, if the water level drops far enough, the ruins of the old submerged village of Llanwyddyn reappear. With various hides, vantage points and nature trails, it is a spectacular place for birdwatching.

* Moorland, woodland & water habitats
* Good birdwatching all year round

Location
10 miles W of Llanfyllin

Opening
Daily; Apr–Dec 10.30am–5.30pm
Jan–Mar Sat & Sun; closed 25–31 Dec

Admission
Free

Contact
Brynawel, Llanwyddyn,
Powys SY10 0LZ

t 01691 870278
w rspb.org.uk
e vyrnwy@rspb.org.uk

506 Machynlleth

Celtica

1 hr+   All year

A unique and stimulating experience of Celtic heritage and culture. Your journey takes you through eight galleries – the foundry, the origins gallery, the village, the roundhouse, the forest, the otherworld, the vortex and Yma o Hyd. Special lightweight headset for children is provided.

* Award-winning attraction
* Member of Dyfi Valley Attractions

Location
In Machynlleth village

Opening
Daily 10am–6pm; closed Christmas

Admission
Adult £4.95, Child £3.95, Concs £4.30

Contact
Y Plas, Machynlleth,
Powys SY20 8ER

t 01654 702702
w www.celticawales.com
e celtica@celticawales.com

507 Machnylleth

Centre for Alternative Technology

3 hrs+   All year

Discover how we can work better with the earth's natural resources. Learn about solar, wind and wave power, have fun in the adventure playground and maze, and visit the smallholding and see many different animals. In summer travel on a unique water-balanced cliff railway.

* Largest public display centre of its kind in Europe
* Multi-award winner

Location
3 miles N of Machynlleth on the A487 to Dolgellau. Clearly signed

Opening
Daily; Sep–Oct 10am–5pm
Oct–Mar 10am–4pm
Mar–Jul 10am–5pm
Aug–Sep 9.30am–6pm

Admission
Adult £7.90, Child £4.50, Concs £5.50

Contact
Machynlleth,
Powys SY20 9AZ

t 01654 705950
w www.cat.org.uk
e information@cat.org.uk

508 Pumsaint

Dolaucothi Gold Mines

1 hr   Mar-Oct

Begun by the Romans, this mine was worked again in the C19 and C20. Visitors are taken on fascinating guided tours of the Roman and more recent underground workings (the latter are not open to children under five).

* Gold panning & way-marked walks
* Cycle hire, activity room & events

Location
On the A482 between Lampeter & Llanwrda

Opening
Daily; 31 Mar–31 Oct 10am–5pm

Admission
Adult £6.80, Child £3.40

Contact
Pumsaint,
Llanwrda SA19 8RR

t 01558 650177

509 Rhayader

Gigrin Farm

1 hr+   All year

This family-run sheep farm has 400 breeding ewes and other farm animals including donkeys, ponies, assorted ducks, chickens and pea fowl. It is also home to red kites which are fed daily. Watch live footage of badgers and learn about the animals from the touch-screen computers.

* Official Kite Country Red Kite Feeding station

Location
On the A470, ½ mile S of Rhayader

Opening
Daily 1pm–5pm

Admission
Adult £2.50, Child £1, Concs £2

Contact
South Street, Rhayader,
Powys LD6 5BL

t 01597 810243
w redkitecentre.co.uk
e kites@gigrin.co.uk

510 Anglesey

Anglesey Sea Zoo

2 hrs+   Mar–Nov

Underwater and undercover, this sea zoo offers many attractions, including a shipwreck, wave tanks, a lobster and sea horse nursery, tanks to walk over and under, conger eels, octopuses and British sharks.

* Major seahorse conservation project
* Lobster hatchery & gift shop

Location
Follow the lobster signs from the Britannia Bridge onto Anglesey

Opening
Daily; Mar–Nov 10am–6pm
(last admission 5pm)

Admission
Adult £5.95, Child £4.95, Concs £5.50

Contact
Brynsiencyn,
Anglesey LL61 6TQ

t 01248 430411
w info@seazoo.demon.co.uk
e www.angleseyseazoo.co.uk

511 Anglesey

Plas Newydd

3 hrs   Easter–Oct

This elegant C18 house is set in beautiful gardens, with access to a marine walk on the Menai Strait. Plenty of room to run around, relics from the Battle of Waterloo and the chance to take a boat ride if the weather's fine.

* Halloween family fun day
* Children's quiz trails

Location
Junction 7 & 8 off A55

Opening
19 Mar–2 Nov Sat–Wed
Gardens 11am–5pm
House 12pm–5pm

Admission
Adult £5, Child £2.50

Contact
Llanfairpwll,
Anglesey LL61 6DQ

t 01248 715272/714795
w nationaltrust.org.uk
e plasnewydd@nationaltrust.org.uk

512 Bordorgan

Henblas Country Park

4 hrs+   All year

There are 30 attractions on this site including falconry displays and sheep shearing, plus indoor and outdoor adventure playgrounds

* Tractor tours & pony rides
* Pets' corner & lamb feeding

Location
Just off the A55 & A5; take the B4422 from the A5, 10 miles from Britannia Bridge

Opening
Easter–Oct Sun–Fri 10.30am–5pm;
closed Sat (except Bank Holiday weekends)

Admission
Adult £4.25, Child £3.25

Contact
Bordorgan,
Anglesea LL62 5DL

t 01407 840440
w parc-henblas-park.co.uk

513 Caernarfon

Plas Menai National Watersports Centre

2–7 days   All year

An unrivalled choice of watersports and adventure training and courses for all abilities. Courses include dinghy and yacht sailing, kayaking, canoeing, wind-surfing and power sports. Live-in activity weeks during school holidays. Great for mountain activities too.

* Instructors are the most highly qualified in the UK
* National Watersports Centre for Wales

Location
2 miles N of Caernarfon on A487

Opening
Daily

Admission
Different prices for different courses, please phone or check website

Contact
Llanfairisgaer, Caernarfon, Gwynedd LL55 1UE

t 01248 670964
w plasmenai.co.uk
e plas.menai@scw.co.uk

514 Caernarfon

Welsh Highland Railway

3 hrs   All year

Take a 12-mile ride, from the coast to the slopes of Snowdon, on North Wales's newest railway. Enjoy spectacular scenery in comfort as you pass lakes, mountains and forest on the way to the heart of Snowdonia.

Location
Main station on St Helens Road in Caernarfon, signed from A487

Opening
Daily Mar–Nov, limited winter service, please phone for details

Admission
Adult £14, Child £7 (adult ticket includes 1 child)

Contact
Harbour Station, Porthmadog, Gwynedd LL49 9NF

t 01766 516073
w festrail.co.uk
e info@festrail.co.uk

515 Caernarfon

Inigo Jones Slateworks

1 hr   All year

See Welsh craftsmanship at first hand on a tour of the Inigo Jones Slateworks and learn about the development of the Welsh slate industry in the historical exhibition. The self-guided tour starts with a film on how slate is mined.

* Children's quiz with slate prize
* Engraving & calligraphy workshops

Location
On the A487, 6 miles from Caernarfon

Opening
Daily; summer 9am–5pm; winter 10am–5pm

Admission
Free entry to showroom; self-guided tour £3.80

Contact
Groeslon, Caernarfon LL54 7ST

t 01286 830242
w inigojones.co.uk
e slate@inigojones.co.uk

516   Chirk

Chirk Castle

2 hrs   Mar–Oct

Built in 1310, this National Trust property has a beautiful interior, medieval tower, dungeon and C18 servants' hall. Outside are a formal garden, a shrub garden, a rock garden and a thatched hawk house. Events for children include haunted tours and picture trails.

* Medieval tower and dungeon
* Hands-on activities

Location	Contact
1 mile off A5, 2 miles W of Chirk	Chirk,
	Wrexham LL14 5AF
Opening	
18 Mar–30 Oct Wed–Sun 12noon–5pm	t 01691 777701
	w nationaltrust.org.uk
Admission	e chirkcastle@ nationaltrust.org.uk
Adult £6.40, Child £3.20	

517   Chirk

Pony & Quad Treks

1 hr+   Easter–Oct

Enjoy the beautiful Ceiriod Valley on horseback. Choose from a variety of treks, from one hour to a full day, from ponies and horses to suit all ages. For the more adventurous over 12s, there's off-road quad biking. Safety equipment and protective clothing is available.

Location	Contact
8 miles from Chirk on B4500	Pont-y-Meibion, Pandy,
	Glyn Ceiriog, Chirk,
Opening	LlangollenLL20 7HS
Easter–Oct 10.30am–4pm	
	t 01691 718333/718413
Admission	w ponytreks.co.uk
Pony trekking day £45, 2 hrs £25,	e enquiry@ponytreks.co.uk
1 hr £15.	
Quad trekking 1 hr £25, 1/2 mins £15	

518   Colwyn Bay

The Welsh Mountain Zoo

4 hrs+   All year

A wildlife collection kept in a natural environment, with many attractions and activities for children, including Tarzan Trail adventure playground and virtual zoo tour.

* Children's farm
* Join the Zoo Club for regular animal updates

Location	Contact
3 mins from the A55 (Rhos-on-Sea	Old Highway, Colwyn Bay
exit); follow the signs	LL28 5UY
Opening	
Daily; summer 9.30am–6pm	t 01492 532938
winter 9.30am–5pm	w welshmountainzoo.org
Admission	
Adult £6.95, Child £4.95 Concs £5.95	

519 Gwynedd

Greenwood Forest Park

4 hrs+   Mar–Oct

From papermaking and wool spinning to archery and the Great Green sledge slide, there is a wide range of entertainment on offer at this award-winning adventure park.

* Jungle boats & toddlers' village

Location	Contact
Take the A4144 and then the B4366	Y Felinheli, Gwynedd LL56 4QN
Opening	t 01248 671493
Daily; 20 Mar–31 Oct 10am–5.30pm (5pm closing in Sep & Oct)	w greenwood-centre.co.uk
	e info@greenwood-centre.co.uk
Admission	
Please phone for details	

520 Llanberis

Snowdon Mountain Railway

2½ hrs   Mar–Nov

Travel on the only public rack and pinion railway in Britain to the summit of Snowdon – the tallest mountain in England and Wales. For those wishing to walk down, a single ticket to the summit station is available.

* 30-min stay at the top, single tickets available
* Breathtaking views from the train & the summit

Location	Admission
Llanberis Station on the A4086, 7½ miles from Caernarfon. 15 mins drive from A55/A5 junction at Bangor. Nearest train station is Bangor	Adult £20, Child £14, Concs £17
	Contact
	Llanberis, Gwynedd LL55 4TY
Opening	t 0870 4580033
Daily Mar–Nov	w snowdonrailway.co.uk
Please phone for details	e info@snowdonrailway.co.uk

521 Llangollan

Llangollan Wharf

1 hr+   Apr–Oct

You can embark on either a horse-drawn canal boat trip up to the spectacular Horseshoe Falls or a motorised cruise which takes you across Thomas Telford's famous aqueduct. There is also self-steer day hire available for groups of up to 10 people.

Location	Contact
Off the A5 Shrewsbury road & near the A483 to Chester	Welsh Canal Holiday Craft Ltd, The Wharf, Llangollen LL20 8TA
Opening	t 01978 860702
Daily; Easter–Oct 10am–5pm	
Admission	
Horse-drawn boats **Adult £4, Child £2.50** *Aqueduct cruise* **Adult £7.50, Child £6.50**	

522 Llanrwst

Amgueddfa Sir Henry Jones Museum

1 hr   May–Sep

This fascinating look at Victorian Welsh rural life is set in a C19 workman's cottage, the childhood home of Sir Henry Jones. Find out about his journey from shoemaker's apprentice to eminent professor in this true rags to riches story.

* Hear the shoemakers talk as they work
* See the tiny kitchen where 7 people took meals

Location
On the A548 Abergele to Llanrwst road in Llangernyw. Follow the signs from the car park

Opening
May–Sep Tue–Fri & Bank Hols
10.30am–1pm & 2pm–5pm
Sat & Sun 2pm–5pm

Admission
Adult £1.50, Child £1, Concs £1

Contact
Y Cwm, Llangernyw,
Abergele LL22 8PR

t 01745 860661
w sirhenryjones-museums.org
e info@sirhenryjones-museums.org

524 Porthmadog

The Ffestiniog Railway

4 hrs+   All year

Take a trip with the world's oldest independent railway company. The track runs through 13 miles of spectacular scenery from the sea up to the mountains. Special events are held throughout the year.

* Regular special events
* Refurbished café/bar at Harbour Station

Location
Next to harbour in Porthmadog on A487.

Opening
Daily Mar–Nov, limited winter service,
Please phone for details

Admission
Adult £14, Child £7
(Adult ticket includes 1 child)

Contact
Harbour Station, Porthmadog,
Gwynedd LL49 9NF

t 01766 516000
w festrail.co.uk
e info@festrail.co.uk

523 Minfford

Portmeirion

4 hrs+   All year

A private village created by Clough Williams Ellis on the coast of Snowdonia with woodland, gardens, shops, restaurants and hotels. Built in a fairy-tale style, it has grottos and cobbled squares. There is a sandy beach and playground for children.

* Used as location for cult TV series *The Prisoner*
* Cottages in the village let by Portmeirion Hotel

Location
Sign off the A487 at Minffordd between Penrhyndeudraeth and Porthmadog

Opening
Daily 9.30am–5.30pm

Admission
Adult £6, Child £3, Concs £5

Contact
Gwynedd, LL48 6ET

t 01766 770000
w portmeirion-village.com
e info@portmeirion-village.com

525 Blaenafon

Big Pit National Mining Museum

3 hrs+   Feb–Nov

This was a working coalmine until its closure in 1980. Now you can take an hour-long underground tour, led by ex-miners. Travel down in the pit cage and walk through underground roadways and engine houses. Above ground there's the colliery to explore.

* See simulated mining
* Winding engine–house, blacksmith's workshop

Location
Leave M4 at junction 25a/26, follow signs from the A465

Opening
Daily Feb–Nov 9.30am–5pm
Underground tours run frequently from 10am–3.30pm

Admission
Free

Contact
Blaenafon, Torfaen NP4 9XP
t 01495 790311
w nmgw.ac.uk
e bigpit@nmgw.ac.uk

526 Caerphilly

Caerphilly Castle

1 hr+   All year

One of the largest medieval fortresses in Britain, begun in 1268, the castle is famous for its leaning tower and its ringed stone and water defences. Enjoy the impressive great hall, two site exhibitions, an audio-visual display, and replica medieval siege weapons.

* 45-min audio tours
* Many summer demonstrations & events

Location
Exit the M4 at junction 32 and take the A470 or A469 for Caerphilly

Opening
Daily; 1 Apr–1 June 9.30am–5pm
2 Jun–28 Sep 9.30am–6pm
29 Sep–26 Oct 9.30am–5pm
27 Oct–31 Mar Mon–Sat 9.30am–4.30pm
Sun 11am–4pm

Admission
Adult £3, Child £2.50, Concs £2.50

Contact
Bridge Street, Caerphilly CF83 1JD
t 02920 883143
w cadw.wales.gov.uk
e caerphilly.castle@cadw.co.uk

527 Cardiff

Cardiff Castle

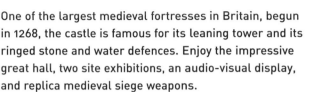

2 hrs+   All year

Discover 2000 years of history in the heart of the city. View the Roman wall, climb the Norman keep and take a guided tour of the fairy-tale apartments, created in the C19 for the 3rd Marquess of Bute.

* Guided tours of lavish & opulent interiors
* Set in beautiful grounds

Location
Cardiff city centre

Opening
Daily Mar–Oct 9.30am–6pm
Nov–Feb 9.30am–5pm

Admission
Adult £6, Child £3.70, Concs £3.70

Contact
Castle Street, Cardiff CF10 3RB
t 029 20 878100
w cardiffcastle.com
e cardiffcastle@cardiff.gov.uk

528 Cardiff

Millennium Stadium Tours

1 hr   All year

Explore the changing rooms, training areas and medical rooms; run down the players' tunnel; climb to the very top row of the highest tier in the stadium for breathtaking views; sit in the Royal Box, and have a trophy presented to you.

* World-class venue, home to 5 sporting bodies
* One of the proposed venues for the 2012 Olympics

Location
Cardiff city centre

Opening
Daily 10am–5pm

Admission
Adult £5, Child £2.50, Concs £3

Contact
Millennium Stadium Shop,
Gate 3, Westgate St
Cardiff CF10 1GE

t 02920 822040
w cardiff-stadium.co.uk

529 Cardiff

Museum of Welsh Life

3 hrs+   All year

Set in 100 acres of beautiful parkland, this is one of Europe's biggest and most exciting open-air museums. Over 40 buildings have been transported and rebuilt here to recreate 500 years of Welsh history. Events programme and craft demonstrations run throughout the year.

* Exhibitions of costume, daily life & farming tools
* Regular festivals of traditional music & dance

Location
4 miles W of Cardiff city centre
Exit junction 33 from the M4

Opening
Daily 10am–5pm

Admission
Free

Contact
St Fagan's, Cardiff CF5 6XB

t 02920 573500
w nmgw.ac.uk
e post@nmgw.ac.uk

530 Cardiff

Techniquest

2 hrs+   All year

Try some of the 160 hands-on exhibits in this amazing science discovery centre, or experiment in the laboratory and discovery room. Fire a rocket, launch a hot-air balloon or play a giant piano. Don't miss the science theatre and planetarium. Special toddler days.

* Explore the universe in the planetarium
* Enjoy a fascinating interactive Science Theatre Show

Location
Exit M4 at junction 33 & follow signs
on the A4232

Opening
Daily; Mon–Fri 9.30am–4.30pm
Sat, Sun & Bank Holidays
10.30am–5pm

Admission
Adult £6.90, Child £4.80, Concs £4.80

Contact
Stuart Street, Cardiff CF10 5BW

t 02920 475475
w techniquest.org
e info@techniquest.org

531 Cardigan

Cardigan Heritage Centre

1 hr   Mar–Oct

The heritage centre tells the story of Cardigan from Norman times to the present day. A child-friendly centre, it has arts activities for younger children and small quizzes for older children.

* Special summer interactive exhibitions
* Guided tours by appointment

Location
Take the A487 to Cardigan. The centre is on the bank of the River Teifi, next to Cardigan bridge

Opening
Daily; Mid Mar–Oct from 10am–5pm

Admission
Adult £2, Child £1, Concs £1.50

Contact
Teifi Wharf, Cardigan

t 01239 614404

532 Carmarthen

National Botanic Garden of Wales

2 hrs+   All year

Learn about the natural world in this 568-acre estate. Attractions include a discovery centre and a 'simply plants' interactive exhibition. Visit the mini-farm, maize maze, children's play area, and bee garden. Events include outdoor Shakespeare and helicopter rides.

* Outdoor art installations
* Regular calendar of special events

Location
On the A48 near Carmarthen, signed from the M4 and A40

Opening
Daily; Easter–Oct 10am–6pm
Nov–Mar 10am–4.30pm

Admission
Adult £6.95, Child £3.50, Concs £5

Contact
Garden of Wales,
Llanarthne SA32 8HG

t 01558 668768
w gardenofwales.org.uk
e reception@gardenofwales.org.uk

533 Dan-yr-Ogof

National Showcaves Centre for Wales

2 hrs+   Apr–Oct

Descend 500 metres below ground for a wonderland of stalactites, waterfalls and natural cave formations that extend over 10 kilometres. The showcaves are self-guided but commentaries play at selected points so you can explore at your own speed.

* Wales Top Day Out award winner 2003
* Heritage Education Trust winner 2003

Location
On A4067 between Swansea and Brecon. Signed from junction 45 of the M4

Opening
Daily Apr–Oct 10am–3pm

Admission
Adult £9, Child £6

Contact
Dan-yr-Ogof, nr Abercraf, Upper Swansea Valley, Powys SA9 1GJ

t 01639 730801
w www.showcaves.co.uk
e james@showcaves.co.uk

534 Llandeilo

Dinefwr

3 hrs   Mar–Oct

An eighteenth-century park which includes a medieval deer park. See the fallow deer and the herd of Dinefwr White Park Cattle, and take part in a badger watch. Special events include a Halloween evening and Christmas fair.

* Boardwalk through Bog Wood to Mill Pond Dam
* Children's quizzes & events

Location
On the outskirts of Llandeilo

Opening
Apr–Oct open Thu–Mon 11am–5pm

Admission
Adult £3.50, Child £1.70

Contact
Llandeilo SA19 6RT

t 01558 825912
w nationaltrust.org.uk

535 Neath

Aberdulais Falls

½ hr+   Mar–Dec

Aberdulais Falls features the largest electricity-generating water wheel in Europe. Get spectacular views of the falls, water wheel and fish pass or look around the ruins of a tin plate works dating from 1830. There are quiz trails for children.

Location
On A4109, 3 miles NE of Neath, 4 miles from junction 43 of M4

Opening
Mar Fri–Sun 11am–4pm
Apr–Nov Mon–Fri 10am–5pm
Sat & Sun 11am–6pm
7 Nov–21 Dec Fri–Sun 11am–4pm

Admission
Adults £3.20, Child £1.60

Contact
Aberdulais, nr Neath SA10 8EU

t 01639 636674
w nationaltrust.org.uk

536 Monmouth

Caldicot Castle & Country Park

2 hrs+   All year

A fine medieval castle set in 55 acres of beautiful parkland with plenty on offer for children. Audio tours are available for adults and children. At the activity station, children can find out about castles, play giant chess and draughts, and try on historical hats.

Location	Admission
From the M4 take junction 23 & the B4245. From the M48 take junction 2, the A48 & B4245. Signed from the B4245	Please phone for details
Opening	**Contact** Church Road, Caldicot NP26 4HU
Daily; Mar–Oct 11am–5pm	t 01291 420241
	w caldicotcastle.co.uk

537 Narberth

Oakwood Leisure Park

4 hrs +   Apr–Oct

One of the UK's top ten theme parks and one of Wales's largest tourist attractions. Oakwood has more than 400,000 visitors each year and boasts over 40 rides and attractions. You can be sure of a great day out, with much to please both older and younger children.

* Carousel, ferris wheel, pirate ship & more
* Megafobia roller-coaster & Hydro (water-coaster)

Location	Contact
Leave the M4 at junction 29, take the A48 to Carmarthen & follow the signs	Canaston Bridge Narberth SA67 8DE
Opening	t 08712 206211
3 Apr–3 Oct Please phone for details	w oakwood-leisure.com e park@oakwood-leisure.com
Admission	
Please phone for details	

538 Swansea

Craig-y-nos Country Park

2 hrs   All year

This beautiful historic garden is full of tall trees and rushing rivers. Now a country park, it is a great place to explore, have a picnic or simply enjoy the peace and quiet of the upper Swansea Valley – land of the Sleeping Giant.

Location	Contact
Mid-way between Brecon & Swansea on the A4067	t 01639 730395
Opening	w breconbeacons.org/cyncp
Please phone for details	e cyncp@breconbeacons.org
Admission	
Free. Car park charges apply	

539 Trelewis

Welsh International Climbing & Activity Centre

4 hrs+   All year

In addition to climbing, the centre offers a wealth of indoor and outdoor activities for all abilities, including abseiling, caving, potholing, gorge walking, kayaking, mountain walking and expeditions. It also has a fitness suite plus family and bunkhouse accommodation.

* One of the biggest indoor climbing walls in Europe
* High-ropes assault course

Location
From the B4255, follow signs to Bedlinog, then ½ mile from Trelewis

Opening
Daily; Mon–Fri 9am–10pm
Sat–Sun 9am–6pm

Admission
Prices vary according to activities

Contact
Taff Bargoed Centre, Trelewis,
Merthyr Tydfil CF46 6RD

t 01443 710749
w indoorclimbingwalls.co.uk
e enquiries@indoorclimbingwalls.co.uk

541 Tenby

Heatherton Country Sports Park

4hrs   All year

Heatherton is set in the beautiful West Wales countryside and hosts a range of activities for all the family including golf, karting, horse-riding and paintball. All equipment is provided.

Location
2 miles outside Tenby on the B4318
Tenby–Pembroke road

Opening
All year open daily; Jun–Sep 10am–10pm; Oct–May 10am–6pm; closed 25, 26 Dec & 1 Jan

Admission
Free admission
Pay-as-you-go activities

Contact
St Florence
Tenby SA69 9EE
t 01646 651025
w heatherton.co.uk

540 Treharris

Llancaiach Fawr Manor

1 hr+   All year

Llancaiach Fawr Manor offers a unique view of life in the middle of the English Civil War, through the eyes of the many servants. Hear tales of their everyday lives in 1645 and watch them at work. See an era brought to life.

* Listen to the gossip of the day – 300 years ago
* Children's workshops

Location
On the B4254 between Nelson and Gelligaer, about 2½ miles from the A470

Opening
Daily; Mon–Fri 10am–5pm
Sat–Sun 10am–6pm;
Nov–Feb closed Mon

Admission
Adult £4.95, Child £3.25, Concs £3.25

Contact
Nelson, Treharris CF46 6ER

t 01443 412248
w caerphilly.gov.uk/visiting

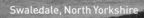

Yorkshire

**East Riding North Yorkshire
South Yorkshire West Yorkshire**

542 Bridlington

Bempton Cliffs Nature Reserve

1 hr+   All year

The best place in England to see seabirds – more than 200,000 nest on the cliffs. Rated one of Britain's most spectacular seabird colonies, it provides superb close-up views of breeding kittiwakes, fulmars, herring gulls, razorbills, guillemots, puffins, and gannets.

* Gannets first colonised cliffs in 1920s
*Puffins can be seen in spring and summer

WC

Location
On cliff road from Bempton, on B1229 from Flamborough to Filey

Opening
Visitor centre Daily; Mar-Nov 10am-5pm
Dec-Feb Sat/Sun only 9.30am-4pm

Admission
£3, car park fee for non-members

Contact
c/o 11 Cliff Lane, Bempton, Bridlington, YO15 1JD
t 01262 851179
w rspb.org.uk

543 Bridlington

Bondville Model Village

2 hrs   Easter–Sep

Town and countryside in miniature – Bondville is a masterpiece in landscape and gives lasting pleasure for young and old, complemented by hundreds of handmade model figures and buildings.

* One of the best model villages in the country
* 1 acre site

WC

Location
On A165

Opening
Daily; Easter–30 Sep 10am-5pm

Admission
Adult £2.50, Child £1.50, Concs £1.50

Contact
Sewerby Road,
Sewerby,
Bridlington YO15 1EL
t 01262 401736

544 Bridlington

Bridlington Leisure World

4 hrs+   All year

Attractions at this leisure centre include a wave pool with tropical rainstorm and a water slide. There are main and learner swimming pools, an expanded fitness suite, a refurbished sauna and solarium, a family entertainment centre, plus Kiddies Kingdom.

* 3 quality pools
* One of East Ridings premier attractions

Location
Off A165 (off M62). The nearest town is Scarborough

Opening
Varies, depending on activity
Please phone for details

Admission
Activities individualy priced

Contact
The Promenade,
Bridlington YO15 2QQ
t 01262 606715
w www.bridlington.net/leisureworld

545 Bridlington

Park Rose Owl &
Bird of Prey Centre

3 hrs   Mar–Oct

The owl sanctuary is set in natural woodland. There are 40 aviaries along a woodland walk displaying hundreds of owls and birds of prey. There are guided information tours and flying displays daily in summer season.

*Koi carp and aquatic centre opening March 2005

Location
On A165/A166, 2 miles S of Bridlington

Opening
Daily; Mar–Oct 10am-5pm

Admission
Adult £2.50, Child (3–16) £1.50

Contact
Carnaby Covert Lane,
Bridlington YO15 3QF
t 01262 606800

546 Bridlington

Sewerby Hall & Gardens

3 hrs   All year

Escape from your parents in the adventure playground, play a game of pitch and putt, hop on a train to the seaside, visit penguins, monkeys and wallabies in the zoo or take a woodland walk where you'll spot small animals, butterflies, birds and unusual plants.

* Display of Amy Johnson's awards and trophies
* Children's zoo includes monkeys and penguins

Location
From Bridlington follow signs for Flamborough and then Sewerby

Opening
Please phone for details

Admission
Adult £3.10, Child £1.20, Concs £2.40

Contact
Church lane, Sewerby, Bridlington YO15 1EA

t 01262 673769
w sewerby-hall.co.uk
e sewerbyhall@yahoo.com

547 Hull

Arctic Corsair

1 hr+   All year

The *Arctic Corsair* is the last remaining side-fishing trawler of the once proud Hull distant-water fishing fleet. The boat is fully restored to her original glory, and visitors can walk the decks and find out about life as a crewman on the frozen Arctic waters.

* Guided tours by former deep-sea trawlermen

Location
On River Hull between Drypool Bridge & Myton Bridge. Access is through the Wilberforce Museum at 25 High Street

Opening
Daily; Mon–Sat 10am–5pm & Sun 1.30pm–4.30pm

Admission
Free

Contact
Queen Victoria Square'
Hull HU1 3RA

t 01482 613902
w arctic-corsair.co.uk

548 Hull

The Deep

2 hrs+   All year

Discover the story of the world's oceans in this ship-shaped museum. See seven species of shark, huge marine dinosaurs, conger eels,rays and hundreds of other stunning sea creatures. Travel in the world's only underwater lift and see sharks swimming overhead.

* 10m deep tank containing 2.5 million litres of water
* Sharks galore

Location
Within walking distance of the town centre on the banks of the Humber

Opening
Daily; 10am-6pm

Admission
Adult £6.75, Child £4.75, Concs £5.25

Contact
Hull HU1 4DP

t 01482 381000
w thedeep.co.uk
e info@thedeep.co.uk

549 Hull

Ferens Art Gallery

1 hr   All year

This award-winning gallery combines an internationally renowned permanent collection with thriving programmes of exhibitions and live art.

* Dedicated children's gallery
* Live Art Space programme of events

Location
In the centre of Hull, off A63 & A1079

Opening
Daily; Mon–Sat
10am–5pm & Sun 1.30pm–4.30pm;

Admission
Free

Contact
Queen Victoria Square,
Hull HU1 3RA

t **01482 613902**
e **museums@hullcc.gov.uk**

550 Hull

Hull & East Riding Museum

1 hr+   All year

Discover the treasures of ancient Britain in a fascinating collection of archeological finds, including dinosaur bones and treasures from the Bronze and Middle ages. There is also an Iron Age village and a Roman bath-house to explore.

* Bronze Age warriors
* Treasures from Middle Ages

Location
City centre location, follow the signs for the Museum Quarter

Opening
Daily; Mon–Sat 10am– 5pm
& Sun 1:30–4:30pm

Admission
Free

Contact
36 High Street,
Hull HU1 1PSs

t **01482 613902**

551 Hull

Hands-On History

1 hr+   All year

The museum is a schools curriculum resource centre, created with children in mind. It features Egyptian treasures, Victorian inventions, The Story of the People of Hull exhibition, and more.

* Ancient Egyption mummy
* Victorian Britain exhibiton

Location
Take A63 to the town centre & A1079 from York

Opening
Daily; Mon–Sat 10am–5pm &
Sun 1.30pm–4.30pm

Admission
Free

Contact
South Church Side,
Hull HU1 1RR

t **01482 613902**
e **museums@hullcc.gov.uk**

552 Hull

Streetlife – Hull Museum of Transport

1 hr+   All year

Streetlife has some of the finest period displays in the country on railways, horse-drawn carriages, cycles, cars and trams. Come and meet the animated horses and experience a simulated carriage ride. Costumed figures and smells add to the visual display.

* New motor car gallery
* Hands-on interactive exhibition area

Location	Contact
Take A63 to the town centre, turn left into Old Town & High Street	6 High Street, Hull HU1 1PS
Opening	t 01482 613956
Daily; Mon–Sat 10am–5pm & Sun 1.30pm–4.30pm	w hullcc.gov.uk
	e museums@hull.gov.uk
Admission	
Free	

553 Pocklington

Burnby Hall Gardens

4 hrs+   All year

Home to more water lilies than anywhere else in Europe, Burnby Hall is also famous for its extensive range of ornamental trees, plants, shrubs, flowers and numerous birds and fish, including koi carp, which like to be fed by visitors. Fish food is on sale on site.

* The biggest collection of water lilies in Europe
* Two large lakes in 10 acres of beautiful gardens

Location	Contact
20 mins E of York off A1079	August Cottage, 48 Burnby Lane, Pocklington YO42 2QE
Opening	
Daily; Apr–Sep 10am–5pm	t 01759 302068
Oct–Mar Mon–Fri 10am–4pm	w burnbyhallgardens.co.uk
Admission	e burnbyhallgardens@hotmail.com
Adult £2.70, Child £1.20, Concs £2.20	

554 Selby

Barlow Common Local Nature Reserve

3 hrs   All year

Enjoy a family day out in a variety of wildlife habitats including woodland, meadow, ponds, a small lake and reedbed. Barlow Common is notable for its birdlife, wildflowers and butterflies.

* Coarse fishing facilities
* Nature trail

Location	Contact
Take A1041 Selby–Snaith road	c/o Selby District Council, Civic Centre, Portholme Road, Selby YO8 4SB
Opening	
Daily; all times	t 01757 617110
Admission	w selby.gov.uk
Free (except coarse fishing)	

555 Bedale

Big Sheep & Little Cow Farm

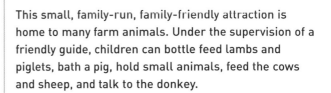

2 hrs   All year

This small, family-run, family-friendly attraction is home to many farm animals. Under the supervision of a friendly guide, children can bottle feed lambs and piglets, bath a pig, hold small animals, feed the cows and sheep, and talk to the donkey.

* Sand play area
* Quad bikes & play area

Location	Admission
11miles S of Scotch Corner & 1 mile from A1 on A684 towards Bedale. Follow brown 'Farm Visitor Centre' signs	Adult £4, Child £3, Concs £3.50
	Contact
	nr Bedale
Opening	t 01677 422125
Daily; Mar–Sep, 10.30am–5pm, Sep–Mar Sat–Wed 10.30am–5pm	w farmattraction.co.uk
	e enquiries@farmattraction.co.uk

556 Ebberston

The Quad Squad

1 hr+   All year

Enjoy the Quad Squad's trekking facility around the more scenic parts of Pheasant Hill Farm and parts of Dalby Forest. Children will be enthralled by this fun-packed and exhilarating adventure.

* Caters for everyone aged 6–65
* Situated on a working farm

Location	Contact
On A170 W of Scarborough & E of Pickering	Pheasant Hill Farm, Ebberston, Scarborough YO13 9BB
Opening	t 0771 575 7706
Daily; in summer 9.30am–5.30pm; in winter 9.30am–3pm	w quadbikes.fsnet.co.uk
	e johnharrison@quadbikes.fsnet.co.uk
Admission	
Adult £25, Child £20 per hour	

557 Harrogate

RHS Garden Harlow Carr

2 hrs+   All year

A spectacular 58-acre garden with renowned streamside, flower and vegetable trails, contemporary grass borders, scented herb and foliage gardens, woodland and an arboretum.

* Quality Assured Visitor Attraction
* Museum of Gardening

Location	Admission
Situated on Crag Lane, off Otley road (B6162) about 1½ miles from the centre of Harrogate	Adult £5, Child (6–16) £1, Senior £4.50
	Contact
	Crag Lane,
Opening	Harrogate HG3 1QB
Daily; 9.30am–6pm (or dusk if earlier)	t 01423 565418
	w rhs.org.uk

558 Harrogate

Ripley Castle

2 hrs+   All year

Ripley Castle has been the Ingilby family home since 1345. It's full of fine armour, furniture, chandeliers & panelling, as well as a priest's hiding hole. There are beautiful walled gardens, a deer park that is guaranteed to thrill children & an extensive tropical plant collection.

* Quality Assured Visitor Attraction
* Capability Brown deer park

Location
On the A61, 3½ miles N of Harrogate

Opening
Daily; Jun–Aug 10.30am–3pm;
Sep–May Tue, Thu, Sat & Sun
10.30am–3pm

Admission
Castle & Gardens: Adult £6, Child £3.80

Contact
Ripley,
Harrogate HG3 3AY

t 01423 770152
w ripleycastle.co.uk

559 Hawes

Dales Countryside Museum

1 hr+   All year

This wonderful museum tells the story of the Yorkshire Dales – its people and environment. There are exhibitions, events and demonstrations.

* Tourist Information & National Park Centre
* Guided tours for individuals

Location
Off A684 in the Old Station Yard

Opening
Daily; 10am–5pm

Admission
Adult £3, Child Free, Concs £2

Contact
Station Yard,
Hawes DL8 3NT

t 01969 667450
e hawes@ytbtic.co.uk

560 Hutton-le-Hole

Ryedale Folk Museum

1 hr+   Mar–Nov

Ryedale Folk Museum contains reconstructed local buildings including long-houses, an Elizabethan manor house and furnished cottages. See the oldest daylight photographic studio in the country and archaeological displays from prehistory to C10.

* Sanford award for Education 2003

Location
Take A170 from Helmsley into Hutton-le-Hole

Opening
Daily; 10 Mar–3 Nov 10am–5.30pm (last admission 4.30pm)

Admission
Please phone for details

Contact
Hutton-le-Hole YO62 6UA

t 01751 417367

561 Ingleton

White Scar Cave

2 hrs   All year

White Scar is the longest show cave in Britain. You can see underground waterfalls, thousands of stalactites, and the massive 330-ft Battlefield Cavern. Take the 80-minute guided tour which covers over a mile of underground adventure.

* Investigate a hidden world
* 200,000-year old cavern

Location
In the Yorkshire Dales National Park, 17 miles E of M6 (junction 35), 1½ miles from Ingleton on B6255 to Hawes

Opening
Daily; from 10am (weather permitting)

Admission
Adult £6.75, Child £3.75

Contact
Ingleton LA6 3AW

t 01524 241244
w whitescarcave.co.uk
e info@whitescarcave.co.uk

562 Knaresborough

Mother Shipton's Cave & Petrifying Well

3 hrs   Mar–Nov

First opened in 1630, Mother Shipton's Cave and Petrifying Well are the oldest tourist attractions in Britain. Children will particularly enjoy the cave, petrifying well, museum, playground and 12 acres of riverside grounds.

* Electronic information points
* Children's quiz with prize

Location
On A59 from Harrogate or York, the cave is in the centre of Knaresborough

Opening
Daily; 1 Mar–1 Nov 9.30am–5.30pm; Nov & Feb weekends only 10am–4.30pm

Admission
Adult £4.95, Child £3.75, Senior £4.25

Contact
Prophesy House, High Bridge, Knaresborough HG5 8DD

t 01423 864600
w mothershipton.co.uk

563 Kirby Misperton

Flamingo Land Theme Park & Zoo

6 hrs+   Apr–Dec

Flamingo Land offers something for all the family with a dozen white-knuckle thrillers, six great shows, kiddies' attractions and an extensive zoo, which is home to many rare and exotic species including rhinos, hippos, giraffes and tigers.

* Lost Kingdom display
* Children's farm

Location
In North Yorkshire, off A64 Scarborough–York road on the A169 Malton–Pickering road

Opening
Daily; Apr–Nov 10am–5pm or 6pm; *Theme park* closed Dec–Mar; *Zoo* open 6–7, 13–14 & 18–24 Dec 10am–5pm

Admission
Please phone for 2005 prices

Contact
Kirby Misperton, Malton YO17 6UX

t 01653 668287
w flamingoland.co.uk

564 Leyburn

Bolton Castle

1 hr+   All year

Bring the family along to this fascinating castle, which has dominated its beautiful Yorkshire Dales setting since its completion in 1399. One of the country's best preserved castles, Mary Queen of Scots was imprisoned here and it was besieged during the Civil War.

* *Heartbeat* filmed here

Location
6 miles W of Leyburn, just off A648. Signed from Wensley

Opening
Daily; Mar–Nov 10am–5pm; Dec–Feb 10am–4pm
Please phone for details

Admission
Please phone for details

Contact
Leyburn DL8 4ET

t 01969 623981
w boltoncastle.co.uk

565 Leyburn

Beech End Model Village

4 hrs+   Apr–Oct

At this fascinating model village, children can enjoy interactive fun controlling scale model boats and vehicles. They can push buttons for light and sound effects and peep inside the model houses.

* New scenery & interactive features

Location
Take A684 or A6108 to the centre of Leyburn, Wensleydale

Opening
Apr–Oct Mon, Wed & Fri 2pm–5pm, Sat & Sun 10.30am–5pm, & in school holidays open daily 10.30am–5pm

Admission
Adult £2, Child £1.60, Concs £1.80

Contact
Commercial Square, Leyburn DL8 5BP

t 01969 625400
w beech-end.co.uk
e ian@beech-end.co.uk

566 Middleham

Middleham Castle

1 hr All year

A spectacular C12 castle and fortress which became the childhood and favourite home of Richard III. There was once a Norman motte-and-bailey fortification on this site and its foundations can still be seen on high ground south-west of the castle.

* Childhood home of Richard III
* *James Herriot's Yorkshire* was filmed in the area

Location
2 miles S of Leyburn on A6108

Opening
Daily; Apr–Sep 10am–6pm
Oct 10am–5pm
Nov–Dec 10am–1pm & 2pm–4pm
Jan–Mar Wed–Sun 10am–1pm & 2pm–4pm

Admission
Adult £3, Child £1.50, Concs £2.30

Contact
Castle Hill, Middleham,
Leyburn DL8 4QR

t 01969 623899
w english-heritage.org.uk

567 Malton

Eden Camp

3 hrs+ All year

Eden Camp is the only history theme museum of its kind in the world. A visit here will transport you back to wartime Britain to experience the sights, the sounds and even the smells of those historic years.

* 1998 winner The England for Excellence Awards
* New military conflicts exhibit covering 1945–2003

Location
Just 100 yards from A64
(York–Scarborough) & A169
(Malton–Pickering) interchange

Opening
Daily; Second Mon in Jan–23 Dec
10am–5pm

Admission
Adult £4, Child £3, Senior £3

Contact
Malton YO17 6RT

t 01653 697777
w edencamp.co.uk
e admin@edencamp.co.uk

568 Ormesby

Ormesby Hall

2 hrs+   Apr–Nov

This Palladian mansion is full of fascination for visitors of all ages. You can wander around the gardens and enjoy the beautiful house and its famous stables.

* Large model railway on show
* Find out about 'wicked' Sir James Pennyman

Location
3 miles SE of Middlesbrough. Take A174, A172 & follow the signs

Opening
Apr–Nov Tue–Thu, Sun, Bank Holidays & Good Friday 1.30pm–4.30pm

Admission
Adult £3.90, Child £1.80

Contact
Ormesby Hall,
Ormesby TS7 9AS

t 01642 324188
e yorkor@smtp.ntrust.org.uk

569 Pickering

Pickering Castle

1 hr   Apr–Oct

Built shortly after the Norman Conquest, this splendid stone castle is well-preserved, with much of the original keep, towers and walls remaining. The exhibition in the chapel must be pre-booked.

* English Heritage Property

Location
In Pickering, 15 miles SW of Scarborough

Opening
Daily; Apr–Sep 10am–6pm; Oct, Thu–Mon 10am–4pm

Admission
Adult £3, Child £1.50, Concs £2.30

Contact
Pickering YO18 7AX

t 01751 474989
w english-heritage.org.uk

570 Pickering

North Yorkshire Moors Railway

3 hrs+   Mar–Nov

The North Yorkshire Moors Railway runs between the historic market town of Pickering and Grosmont near Whitby and is one of the world's oldest railway lines. Trains also call at the picturesque stations of Levisham and Goathland.

* Quality Assured Visitor Attraction

Location
Take A169 or A170 to Pickering

Opening
Daily; Mar–Nov some winter opening dates; times vary
Please phone for details

Admission
Please phone for details

Contact
Pickering Station, Park Street, Pickering YO18 7AJ

t 01751 472508
w northyorkshiremoorsrailway.com
e customerservices@nymr.fsnet.co.uk

571 Pickering

Pickering Trout Lake

4 hrs   Mar–Oct

Pickering lake is stocked with rainbow trout so that you can try fishing by float or fly methods. This is an ideal place for children to learn the art of angling – 99 per cent of visitors catch a fish!

* Guided tours for individuals
* Tackle available for hire or sale

Location
Signposted 'Fun Fishing' from Pickering, 400 yds past North Yorkshire Moors Railway Station

Opening
1 Mar–31 Oct open daily 10am–5pm (closing at dusk in summer)

Admission
Fun float fishing £5
Tackle hire £2.50

Contact
Newbridge Road,
Pickering YO18 8JD

t 01751 474219
e pickeringtroutlake@talk21.com

572 Richmond

Hazel Brow Visitor Centre

2 hrs+   Apr–Sep

Hazel Brow is an award-winning organic livestock farm in the heart of Swaledale. Farming is portrayed through displays, exhibitions and a farm video. Walk along the riverside nature trail or take the paths through the hay meadows, herb-rich pastures & wild heather moorland.

* Lambing time visits in April
* Sheepdog training

Location
From Richmond take A6108 signed Leyburn for approx 5 miles; branch off onto B6270 to Reeth; continue for 9 miles to Low Row Village

Opening
Apr–Sep Sat–Sun & Tue–Thu 11am–6pm

Admission
Adult £4, Child (2–16) £3.50

Contact
Low Row Village,
Richmond DL11 6NE

t 01748 886224
w yorkshirenet.co.uk/hazelbrow
e hazelbrowfarm@aol.com

573 Richmond

Richmond Castle

1 hr+   All year

One of the most imposing Norman remains in England, Richmond Castle towers over the town. The rectangular keep is 100ft high and is one of the finest in the country.

* Exhibition centre
* Set in beautiful countryside

Location
In Richmond town centre, on A6108

Opening
Daily; 1 Apr–30 Sep 10am–6pm; 14–22 Feb & 1–31 Oct 10am–4pm; 1 Nov–13 Feb & 23 Feb–31 Mar 10am–4pm;

Admission
Adult £3.50 , Child £1.80, Concs £2.60

Contact
Richmond DL10 4QW

t 01748 822493
w english-heritage.org.uk

574 Ripon

Fountains Abbey & Studley Royal Water Garden

3 hrs+   All year

The spectacular ruined C12 Cistercian abbey is the central feature of an eclectic mix of attractions. On some evenings the abbey is floodlit. The site also includes a watermill, Elizabethan mansion and a wonderful water garden.

* One of the National Trust's most visited sites
* World Heritage Site

Location
Four miles W of Ripon, off B6265 to Pateley Bridge

Opening
Daily; 1 Apr–30 Sep 10am–6pm;
1 Oct–31 Mar 10am–4pm

Admission
Adult £5, Child £3

Contact
Ripon HG4 3DY

t 01765 608888
w fountainsabbey.org.uk

575 Ripon

Newby Hall & Gardens

4 hrs   Apr–Sep

This beautiful late C17 house, built in the style of Sir Christopher Wren, has an Adam-designed interior. The extensive grounds include an adventure garden with swings, climbing frames, bridges, an aerial slide, pedalo boats, and a miniature railway.

* Featured in BBC television's *Heirs & Graces*
* A paddling pool & sandpit

Location
Off B6265 between Boroughbridge & Ripon

Opening
Apr–Sep Tue–Sun & Bank Hols 11am–5pm

Admission
Adult £7.20, Child £4.70, Concs £6.20

Contact
Ripon HG4 5AE

t 01423 322583
w newbyhall.com
e info@newbyhall.com

576 Scarborough

Atlantis

3 hrs+   May–Sep

Atlantis water theme park has two of the world's largest water slides, a river rapids run, a whirlpool bath and lots of water-based activities!

* Ice cream parlour
* Waveball

Location
Follow A64 into north Scarborough

Opening
Daily; May–Sep 10am–6pm
Please phone for details

Admission
Please phone for details

Contact
North Bay,
Scarborough YO12 7TU

t 01723 372744

577 Scarborough

Betton Farm Visitor Centre & Animal Farm

3 hrs   All year

Betton Farm offers an animal farm, a pets corner with a toy tractor area and a play area. There is also an indoor sandpit and a honey-bee exhibition.

* Birds of prey centre
* Meet farmyard friends

Location
Just off A170, W of Scarborough, towards Pickering & Hemsley

Opening
Daily 10am–5pm;

Admission
Please phone for details

Contact
Racecourse Road,
East Ayton,
Scarborough YO13 9HT

t 01723 863143
w bettonfarm.co.uk

578 Scarborough

Scarborough Castle

1 hr   All year

During the Iron Age a settlement was built on this great headland and in Roman times it was used as a look out. It was bombarded by German cruisers in 1914 and during the Second World War was used as a listening post. There are viewing platforms with great views of the Yorkshire coastline.

* Vast C13 fortress

Location
Castle Road, E of town centre

Opening
Daily; Apr–Sep, 10am–6pm; Oct–Mar, Thu–Mon, 10am–4pm

Admission
Adult £3.20, Child £1.60, Concs £2.40

Contact
Castle Rd, Scarborough,

t 01723 372 451
w english-heritage.org.uk

579 Scarborough

Sea Life & Marine Sanctuary

2 hrs+   All year

Meet creatures that live in the oceans around the British Isles, ranging from starfish, turtles and crabs to rays, seals and otters.

* Penguins, sharks & sea horses
* Feeding times

Location
Follow signs to North Bay Leisure Park, situated on Whitby Road, beyond Atlantis & Kinderland; look for white pyramids

Opening
Daily; 10am–6pm;

Admission
Adult £8.50, Child (3–14) £5, Concs £6.50

Contact
Scalby Mills,
Scarborough YO12 6RP

t 01723 376125
w sealife.co.uk

580 Scarborough

Staintondale Shire Horse Farm Visitor Centre

2 hrs+   May–Sep

Shire horse and Shetland pony lovers will love Staintondale. Live shows are a regular feature and include the Shire horses and Shetland ponies in full western roping rig. You can even learn how to spin a lariat, whatever the weather!

Location
Signposted from the A171

Opening
Spring Bank Holiday–mid Sep Tue, Wed, Fri & Sun 10.30am–4.30pm; Bank Holidays 10.30am–4.30pm

Admission
Adult £3.50, Child (2–15) £2.50, Concs £3

Contact
Scarborough YO13 0EY

t 01723 870458
w shirehorsefarm.yorks.net.co.uk

581 Scarborough

Wykeham Lakes

1 hr+   All year

Come to Wykeham Lakes to enjoy fishing, sailing, windsurfing, boat hire, scuba diving and canoeing. There are also nature trails and bird-watching facilities.

* Watersports lake
* Sailing & watersports tuition

Location
Situated 6 miles W of Scarborough off A170 between West Ayton & Wykeham

Opening
Boating & watersports lake Daily; dawn–dusk;
Fishing available all year;
Nature trails & bird-watching available all year

Admission
Prices vary according to activity/duration (please phone for details)

Contact
Charm Park, Wykeham
Scarborough

t 01723 863148

582 Skipton

Bolton Abbey Estate

2 hrs+   All year

You can enjoy nature trails, woodland walks, a tithe barn and picnic areas in this beautiful country estate alongside the River Wharfe.

* Quality Assured Visitor Attraction
* Strid Wood nature trails

Location	Contact
On B6160, off A59 Skipton–Harrogate road	Skipton BD23 6EX
Opening	t 01756 718009
Daily; dawn–dusk	w boltonabbey.com
Admission	
£4 per vehicle	
£2 for disabled badge holders	

583 Skipton

Skipton Castle

2 hrs   All year

For over 900 years Skipton Castle has stood at the gateway to the Yorkshire Dales through wars and sieges. One of the best preserved and most complete medieval castles in England, it can be explored in any season. Visit the dungeon, Watch Tower, chapel and Conduit Court.

* Quality Assured Visitor Attraction

Location	Admission
Take A59, A65, A629 to Skipton & follow the brown tourist signs	Adult £5, Child (5–17) £2.50, Concs £4.40
Opening	**Contact**
Daily; Mon–Sat from 10am & Sun from 12pm; last admission 6pm (4pm Oct–Feb)	Skipton BD23 1AQ
	t 01756 792442
	w skiptoncastle.co.uk

584 Thirsk

Monk Park Farm Visitor Centre

3 hrs+   Mar–Oct

This open farm in Hambleton Hills has indoor and outdoor viewing and feeding areas, a wildfowl lake and animal attractions. Meet breeds such as wallabies, rheas, llamas, lambs, piglets, goats, deer, ponies, ducks, geese, hens, swans and pheasants.

* Farm Walks
* Picnic Areas

Location	Contact
Bagby, just off A19 S of Thirsk	Monk Park Farm, Bagby, Thirsk YO7 2AG
Opening	t 01845 597730
Daily; Apr–Oct 11am–5.30pm Mar open weekends only	w monkpark.co.uk
Admission	
Adult £4, Child £3, Concs £3	

585 Whitby

Captain Cook Memorial Museum

1 hr+   Mar–Oct

This fascinating museum is in the harbourside house, with ship-timbered attic, where the young Cook lodged as an apprentice. Learn all about his ships, his companions and his amazing explorations.

* Quality Assured Visitor Attraction

Location	Admission
Take A171 to Whitby (or A169 from Pickering & York). Museum is in the town centre, 100 yards from the swing bridge	Adult £3, Child £2, Senior £2.50
Opening	**Contact**
Mar open weekends only 11am–3pm; Daily; Apr–Oct 9.45am–5pm	Grape Lane, Whitby YO22 4BA
	t 01947 601900
	w cookmuseumwhitby.co.uk
	e captcookmuseumwhitby@ukgate-way.net

586 York

Castle Howard

2 hrs   Feb–Oct

Built in 1699, Castle Howard is the private home of the Howard family. Inside are art treasure and sculptures; outside are temples, statues and monuments. There's a whole range of summer activities for children.

* Archaelogical dig, uncovering a medieval village
* Outdoor guided tours and historical characters

Location	Contact
15 miles NE of York	nr York YO60 7DA
Opening	t 01653 648333
Daily; Feb–Oct 11am–4pm	w castlehoward.co.uk
	e house@castlehoward.co.uk
Admission	
Adult £9.50, Child £6.50, Concs £8.50	

587 York

Jorvik Viking Centre

1 hr   All year

Discover what life was like in AD 975 and meet Vikings face to face. See over 800 items uncovered here, and journey through reconstructed Viking streets, complete with sounds and smells. Handle replica items, put your own skills to the test, and watch Viking craftsmen at work.

* Jorvik is the name given to York by the vikings in AD975
* Wheelchair users please ring 01904 543402

Location	Contact
A64 to York	Jorvik, Coppergate, York YO1 9WT
Opening	t 01904 543403 / 643211
Daily; Apr–Oct 10am–5pm	w jovik-viking-centre.co.uk
Nov–Mar 10am–4pm	e jorvik@yorkarchaeology.co.uk
Admission	
Adult £7.20, Child £5.10, Concs £6.10	

588 York

National Railway Museum

3 hrs+   All Year

A collection of over 103 trains from 1813 to the present day, including a palace on wheels. Learn all about railways from Rocket to the Eurostar. Take a ride on the miniature railway (weekends and school holidays) through the railway-themed children's play area.

* Home to 'Mallard', the world's fastest steam locomotive
* Literally millions of photographs and artefacts

Location
600 yards from railway station, signed from centre

Opening
Daily; 10am–6pm

Admission
Free except for special events

Contact
Leeman Road, YO26 4XJ

t 01904 621261
w nrm.or.uk
e nrm@nmsi.ac.uk

---

589 York

Rievaulx Abbey

4 hrs+   All year

Discover the spectacular and extensive remains of the first Cistercian monastery in northern England. Experience the unrivalled peace and serenity of this C12 site in the beautiful valley of the River Rye. Trace the past glories of the thriving community of monks who lived and worked here.

Location
In Rievaulx, 2¾ miles W of Helmsley on a minor road off B1257

Opening
Daily; 1 Apr–30 Sep 10am–6pm; 14–22 Feb & 1–31 Oct 10am–5pm; 1 Nov–13 Feb & 23 Feb–31 Mar 10am–4pm;

Admission
Adult £3.80, Child £1.90, Concs £2.90

Contact
Rievaulx,
York YO62 5LB

t 01439 798228
w wenglish-heritage.co.uk

---

590 York

York Dungeon

1 hr   All year

Take a spine-chilling tour through the plague-ravaged streets of C14 York. Brings more than 2000 years of gruesomely authentic history back to life.

* Confront the ghostly lost Roman Legion
* Follow Dick Turpin to the gallows

Location
York city centre

Opening
Daily; Oct–Mar 10.30am–4.30pm; Apr–Sep 10am–5.30pm

Admission
Adult £9.95, Child (5–9) £5.95 (10–14) £6.95, Concs £7.95

Contact
12 Clifford Street,
York YO1 9RD

t 01904 632599
w thedungeons.com
e yorkdungeon@merlinentertainments.biz

591 York

York Minster

1 hr+   All year

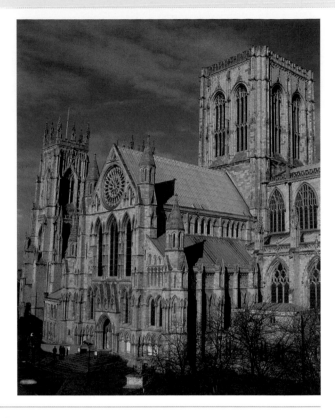

Built C12-C15, York Minster is the largest Gothic
cathedral in England. It is 524 feet long, 249 feet wide
and over 90 feet high. The present building was
constructed on the site of a Norman cathedral, which
was itself built on the foundations of a Roman fort.

* The largest Gothic cathedral in northern Europe
* Visited by 2 million people every year

Location
York city centre

Opening
Undercroft, treasury & crypt: **Summer**
Mon-Sat 9.30am-5pm, Sun 12noon-
5pm; Winter Mon-Sat 9.30am-5pm
Sun 12-5pm
Tower: Summer Mon-Sat 9am-5.30pm
Sun 12noon-5.30pm, Winter Mon-Sat,
9.30am

Admission
Adult £6.50, Child £1.50, Concs £4.50

Contact
Deangate, York YO1 2HG

t 01904 557216
w yorkminster.org
e info@yorkminster.org

---

592 York

Yorkshire Museum

1 hr+   All year

The European award-winning Yorkshire Museum is set
in 10 acres of botanical gardens located in the historic
centre of York. It displays some of the finest Roman,
Anglo-Saxon, Viking and medieval treasures ever
discovered in Britain.

Location
Town centre location, within walking
distance of rail station & bus stops.
A Park & Ride service is in operation
from the A64, A19, A1079 & A166

Opening
Daily 10am–5pm

Admission
Adult £4, Child £2.50, Concs £2.50

Contact
Museum Gardens, York YO1 7FR

t 01904 687687
w yorkshiremuseum.org.uk
e yorkshire.museum@york.gov.uk

---

593 York

Yorkshire Air Museum & Allied Air Forces Memorial

3 hrs   All year

This award-winning museum is housed on the largest
Second World War Bomber Command Station open to
the public. Experience fascinating displays, such as the
restored control tower, the Air Gunners Museum and
the Airborne Forces Display.

* Replicas of the pioneering Cayley Glider & Wright Flyer
* Also Halifax Bomber and modern jets, Harrier GR3

Location
Take A64 or A1079, then B1228

Opening
Daily; summer 10am–5pm;
winter 10am–3.30pm

Admission
Adult £5, Child (5–15) £3, Senior £4

Contact
Halifax Way,
Elvington,
York YO41 4AU

t 01904 608595
w yorkshireairmuseum.co.uk

594 Branton

Brockholes Farm Visitor Centre

3 hrs+   All year

This centre houses farm animals, including a pedigree herd of Limousin cattle, and exotic breeds, such as monkeys, zebras and wallabies. You can also see small animals, including rabbits, guinea pigs and hamsters, and there is a free pony ride for each child.

* Farm is 250 years old
* Woodland walks

Location
Take A638 from Doncaster towards Bawtry & turn onto B1396

Opening
Daily; 10.30am–5.30pm (last admission 4.30pm)

Admission
Adult £4, Child £3.50, Concs £3.50

Contact
Brockholes Lane,
Branton DN3 3NH

t 01302 535057
w brockholesfarm.co.uk

595 Barnsley

Barnsley Metrodome Leisure Complex

3 hrs+   All year

Barnsley Metrodome has a super pool complex offering a total water experience, including the Space Adventure, a fabulous new water theme park.

* Bowls & karate available
* Holiday activities

Location
Via A61/A628 interchange. Also signed from M1 at junction 37

Opening
Daily; 9am–10pm;
Pool opening times vary (please phone for details)

Admission
Please phone for details

Contact
Queens Ground, Queens Road,
Barnsley S71 1AN

t 01226 730060
w themetrodome.co.uk

596 Barnsley

Cannon Hall Farm

3 hrs   All year

This working farm is now open to visitors. Come and enjoy exhibits of cattle, pigs and sheep, as well as rabbits, ponies and horses. There are also exotic animals such as chinchillas, wallabies and llamas.

* White Rose Special Award for Tourism 2002
* Baby animals

Location
Take A635 from Barnsley just after Cawthorne village. Signed on right

Opening
Mon–Sat 10.30am–4.30pm, Sun & Bank Holidays 10.30am–5pm

Admission
Adult £2.95, Child £2.50, Senior £2.50

Contact
Barnsley S75 4AT

t 01226 790427
w cannonhallfarm.co.uk

597 Conisbrough

Conisbrough Castle

2 hrs+   All year

This spectacular medieval castle was built in the 1180s by the fifth Earl of Surrey, Hamelin Plantagenet, half brother of Henry II. It has been extensively restored with floodlighting and a visitor centre. Educational tours and children's parties are catered for.

* The finest circular Norman keep tower in the UK

Location
NE of Conisbrough town centre on A630

Opening
Daily; Apr–Sep 10am–5pm
Oct–Mar 10am–4pm

Admission
Adult £3.75, Child £2, Concs £2.50

Contact
Castle Hill,
Conisbrough DN12 3BU

t 01709 863329
w conisbroughcastle.org.uk
e info@conisbroughcastle.org.uk

598 Doncaster

The Earth Centre

3 hrs+   All year

The Earth Centre is a 400-acre visitor & education park with something for all the family. It includes showcased buildings, hands-on educational exhibitions, landscaping & gardens, including an ex-coalmine where a coal-spoil has been planted with over 1,000 trees.

* Activities include abseiling, climbing & archery
* Play areas

Location
Leave A1(M) at junction 36 & follow A630

Opening
Daily; in summer 10am–5pm; in winter 10am–3.30pm

Admission
Please phone for details

Contact
Denaby Main,
Doncaster DN12 4EA

t 01709 512000
w earthcentre.org.uk
e info@earthcentre.orq.uk

600 Doncaster

Thorne Memorial Park Railway

1 hr+   Varies

Thorne Memorial Park Railway Society operates, builds and maintains this miniature railway, which has recently opened a new second track. Juniors, pensioners and people with disabilities are welcome.

WC 🏕 ♿ 🐾

Location
Just 1 or 2 miles from M18, depending on whether you use junction 5 or 6. Next to Stainforth & Keadby Canal on A614 into the town centre

Opening
Please phone or visit website for details

Admission
Adult 30p, Child 30p, Under-3s Free

Contact
South Parade,
Thorne,
Doncaster

t 01302 842948
w thornerailway.org.uk

599 Doncaster

Doncaster Aeroventure

1 hr+   All year

A fascinating day out for any budding plane enthusiast. Come and see this collection of British jets and helicopters. Occupying the last part of the former Doncaster airfield, the site also features other buildings of the wartime period.

* DH Vampire T11, DH Chipmunk T10 & DH Dove
* Westland Scout, Whirlwind HAR 9 & Bell Sioux

WC 🏕 🍴 ♿ 🐾

Location
Leave M18 at junction 3 & turn onto A6182. Also reached via A638 Doncaster–Bawtry road

Opening
Thu–Sun including Bank Holidays 10am–5pm (4pm in winter)

Admission
Adult £3.50, Child £1, Concs £2

Contact
Sandy Lane,
Doncaster DN4 5EP

t 01302 761616
w aeroventure.org.uk

601 Doncaster South

Hatfield Water Park

2 hrs+   All year

This all-round watersports centre offers canoeing, kayaking, sailing, windsurfing and power-boating activities. The site also includes a three-star rated caravan and campsite and residential visitor centre.

* Adventure playground

WC 🏕 ♿ 🐾

Location
Off A18, just outside Hatfield Village on the road to Thorne

Opening
Daily; summer Mon–Fri 9am–4.30pm & Sat–Sun 9am–5.30pm; in winter open Mon–Fri 9am–4.30pm

Admission
Varies, depending on activity Please phone for details

Contact
Old Thorne Road,
Doncaster DN7 6EQ

t 01302 841572

602 Rotherham

Magna Science Adventure Centre

3 hrs+   All year

A high-tech, hands-on centre, organised according to the elements, where you can walk into a wind tunnel, blow a body noise, discover how fireworks work, squirt water on hot plates, find out how much water is in your body, make waves, or crawl through an underground tunnel.

* Multi-award winner
* Sci-Tek children's playground

Location
Just off M1, 1 mile along A6178 from Meadowhall shopping centre

Opening
Daily; 10am–5pm

Admission
Adult £9, Child £7, Concs £7

Contact
Sheffield Road, Templebrough, Rotherham S60 1DX

t 01709 720002
w visitmagna.co.uk
e info@magnatrust.co.uk

603 Sheffield

The Foundry Climbing Centre

2 hrs+   All year

The Foundry Climbing Centre provides indoor climbing experience for visitors of any age – from novices to experts. Instruction is available on request and children's climbing clubs are run regularly. Booking is essential.

* Special events held regularly

Location
Near Sheffield Ski Village, ½ mile from the city centre

Opening
Daily; summer Mon–Fri 10am–10pm & weekends 10am–6pm; winter Mon–Fri 10am–10pm & weekends 10am–8pm

Admission
£10 per person (includes entry, equipment & instruction)

Contact
45 Mowbray St,
Sheffield S3 8EN

t 0114 2796331
w greatadventures.co.uk
e fma@greatadventures.co.uk

604 Sheffield

Millennium Galleries, Sheffield

1 hr   All year

This new museum has four galleries: Special Exhibitions, Metalwork, Craft & Design and the Ruskin Gallery. Many of the exhibitions have hands-on elements that will appeal to children, and exhibitions in other galleries change regularly, keeping the galleries up to date.

* RIBA Architecture Award

Location
In the centre of Sheffield by Arundel Gate. Follow signs from the city centre

Opening
Daily; Mon–Sat 10am–5pm;
Sun 11am–5pm

Admission
Free, exhibitions may charge

Contact
Arundel Gate,
Sheffield S1 2PP

t 0114 2782600
w sheffieldgalleries.org.uk
e info@sheffieldgalleries.org.uk

605 Sheffield

Renishaw Hall Gardens

4 hrs+   Apr–Sep

Renishaw Hall gardens, museum and galleries are set in 300 acres of parkland with nature trails, reserves and a sculpture park. Children's events are organized regularly and there is a children's play area.

* Sculpture trail
* Regular children's events

Location
Just 2 miles from junction 30 of M1, between Ecrington & Renishaw on A6135

Opening
8 Apr–26 Sep Thu–Sun & Bank Holiday Mon 10.30am–4.30pm
Please phone for details of separate events

Admission
Adult £6, Child Free, Concs £4

Contact
Renishaw Hall, Sheffield

t 01246 432310
w sitwell.co.uk
e info@renishawhall.free-online.co.uk

606 Sheffield

Sheffield Cycle Speedway Club

2 hrs   All year

Sheffield Cycle Speedway Club is a British Cycling 'Go-Ride' club. It provides cycling experience for children of all ages and abilities.

* Free loan of equipment
* Experienced qualified coach in attendance

Location
Bochum Parkway, Sheffield

Opening
Mar–Oct Mon or Wed 7.30–9.30pm;
Nov–Feb Sun fortnightly 2pm–4pm.
Please phone before travelling

Admission
Joining fee £2, Admission Free

Contact
Bochum Parkway,
Sheffield S8 8JR

t 01246 824220
w sheffieldstars.net
e martin_gamble@hotmail.com

607 Sheffield

Sheffield Ski Village

3½ hrs   All year

If you are looking for a totally unique and exhilarating day out, the Ski Village at Sheffield is the perfect destination for all the family. Here at Europe's largest all-season ski resort, you can learn to ski and snowboard, or just chill out in the authentic Swiss atmosphere!

* Over 1 mile of piste
* Thunder Valley Toboggan Run

Location
5 minutes from Sheffield city centre, off A61 Penistone Road. Follow the brown tourist signs

Opening
Daily; summer Mon–Fri 4pm–10pm, Sat–Sun 10am–7pm, Bank Holidays 10am–10pm; winter Mon–Fri 11am–10pm, Sat, Sun, Bank Holidays & 26 Dec–2 Jan 9am–7pm;

Admission
Please phone for details

Contact
Vale Road, Sheffield S3 9SJ

t 0114 276959
w sheffieldskivillage.co.uk
e info@sheffieldskivillage.co.uk

608 Batley

Bagshaw Museum

1 hr+   All year

Bagshaw Museum surrounds you with the sights and sounds of past times and faraway places. On the way, journey through the vibrant colours of the Orient and tame the mythical beasts of four continents.

* Butterfly centre open in summer
* Enchanted Forest

WC 🪑 ♿

Location
The A652, A62 & M62 are all nearby & within easy access

Opening
Daily; Mon–Fri 11am–5pm;
Sat & Sun 12pm–5pm;

Admission
Free

Contact
Wilton Park,
Batley WF17 0AS

t 01924 326155
w kirkleesmc.gov.uk
e bagshaw.museum@kirkleesmc.gov.uk

609 Batley

Oakwell Hall Country Park

2 hrs   All year

History comes alive at Oakwell Hall. This beautiful Elizabethan manor house has delighted visitors for centuries. Stroll around the delightful period garden or check out the inhabitants of the wildlife access garden.

* Setting for Charlotte Brontë's *Shirley*
* 100 acres of estate to explore

Location
Take A652 Batley–Bradford road; the park is signed along this road. Take M62 exit at junction 26/27

Opening
Daily; Mon–Fri 11am–5pm, Sat & Sun 12noon–5pm

Admission
Adults £1.40, Child 50p

Contact
Nutter Lane, Birstall,
Batley WF17 9LG

t 01924 326240
w kirklees.gov.uk/museums
e oakwell.hall@kirklees.gov.uk

610 Bradford

Bradford Industrial Museum & Horses at Work

2 hrs   All year

The museum has an original C19 spinning mill complex, complete with mill owner's house, back-to-back cottages and job masters' stables with working Shire horses. There are spinning, weaving and horse demonstrations every day.

* Take a lesson in the Victorian school room
* Experience washday in Gaythorne Row

WC 🪑 ♿

Location
Take the A658 (Harrogate road),
A6177 (ring road)

Opening
Tue–Sat 10am– 5pm, Sun 12pm–5pm;
closed Mon (except Bank Holidays)

Admission
Free

Contact
Moorside Mills Moorside Road,
Bradford BD2 3HP

t 01274 435900
w bradford.gov.uk

611 Bradford

Colour Museum

3 hrs   All year

The Colour Museum is unique. Dedicated to the history, development and technology of colour, it is the only museum of its kind in Europe. A truly colourful experience for both kids and adults, it's fun, it's informative and it's well worth a visit.

* Workshop & educational programme (see website)

WC ♿

Location
Signed from B6144 (Westgate)

Opening
Tue–Sat 10am–4pm (last admission 3.30pm)

Admission
Adult £2, Child £1.25, Concs £1.50

Contact
Perkin House , PO Box 244,
Providence Street,
Bradford BD1 2PW

t 01274 390955
w sdc.org.uk/museum
e museum@sdc.org.uk

612 Bradford

National Museum of Photography, Film & TV

6 hrs+   All year

Take a voyage of discovery at the National Museum of Photography, Film & Television. Explore the five floors of interactive galleries where you can ride on a magic carpet, read the news or look back at your TV favourites from the past.

* Most visited national museum outside London
* IMAX Cinema

Location
City centre, follow the brown signs

Opening
Tue–Sun 10am–6pm; Mon during school & Bank holidays
Please phone to confirm

Admission
Free

Contact
Bradford BD1 1NQ

t 01274 202030
w nmpft.org.uk

613 Halifax

Eureka!
The Museum for Children

3 hrs   All year

Eureka! is Britain's first interactive museum designed for children. There are more than 400 exhibits and activities to encourage children to use their senses and imagination, including the new environmental gallery, Our Global Garden.

* Interactive music gallery

Location
Next to the railway station. From M62 (junction 24) follow signs to Halifax & then the brown tourist signs to Eureka!

Opening
Daily, 10am–5pm

Admission
Adult £5.95, Child £5.95, Under-3s Free

Contact
Discovery Road,
Halifax HX1 2NE

t 01422 330069
w eureka.org.uk

614 Halifax

Shibden Hall

1 hr+   All year

This magnificent C15 hall, home to the Lister family for over 300 years, is set in 90 acres of rolling parkland with a range of attractions including woodland walks, an orienteering course, children's rides, miniature railway, pitch and putt, and a boating lake.

* Regular events & special children's projects

Location
Signed from Hailifax & M62

Opening
Daily; Mar-Nov Mon-Sat 10am-5pm, Sun 12pm-5pm, Dec-Feb Mon-Sat 10am-4pm Sun 12 noon-4pm

Admission
Adult £3.50, Child £2.50, Concs £2.50

Contact
Lister's Road,
Halifax HX3 6XG

t 01422 352 246
w calderdale.gov.uk/tourism
e shibden.hall@calderdale.gov.uk

615 Harewood

Harewood House & Bird Garden

3 hrs+   Feb-Dec

This fine Yorkshire home is situated in stunning grounds with lakeside and woodland walks and a bird garden with 100 rare and endangered species.

* Yorkshire Visitor Attraction of the Year 2002
* Below Stairs exhibition

Location
On the junction of the A61/A659
Leeds–Harrogate road

Opening
House: Daily; 17 Mar–31 Oct 11am–5pm
Grounds & bird garden: Daily; 11 Feb–31 Oct 10am–6pm; garden open until mid-Dec 10am–dusk

Admission
Please phone for details

Contact
Harewood LS17 9LQ

t 0113 218 1010
e business@harewood.org

616 Hebden Bridge

Calder Valley Cruising

1 hr   Seasonal

Based in a converted barge, Calder Valley Cruising offers motorboat and hour-long horse-drawn cruises on the Rochdale Canal. Travel up and down locks and be legged through a tunnel by the crew.

* Special theme cruises
* Daily summer waterbus

Location
On A646 in the middle of Hebden Bridge, 7 miles from Halifax

Opening
Times vary (please phone for details)
Advance booking recommended

Admission
Adult £5.95, Child £2.95, Concs £5

Contact
Barge Branwell, The Marina,
New Road,
Hebden Bridge HX7 8AD

t 01422 845557
w caldervalleycruising.co.uk

617 Keighley

Cliff Castle Museum

1 hr+   All year

Originally a millionaire's mansion, the castle opened as a museum in 1959. It houses old dolls and toys, the fossil remains of a 300-million-year-old local giant newt, a working beehive of live honey bees, and a natural history gallery with an interactive birdsong unit.

* Collection of toys and dolls
* See fossil of local giant newt, 300 million years old!

Location
On A629 N of town centre

Opening
Tue-Sat & Bank Hols 10am-5pm Sun 12 noon-5pm

Admission
Free

Contact
Spring Gardens Lane,
Keighley BD20 6LH

t 01535 618231
w bradford.gov.uk/
tourism/museums

618 Keighley

Keighley & Worth Valley Railway

2 hrs+   All Year

The fully operational, preserved railway branch line is 5 miles long and runs from Keighley to Oxenhope. Along the line are six award-winning stations.

WC

Location
Take A650 or A629 to Keighley, or A6033 from Oxenhope

Opening
Sat & Sun from 9am; Easter & Christmas daily 11.30am–5pm; Jul–Sep daily from 9am
Please phone 01535 647777 for details

Admission
Adult £10, Child £5,

Contact
Haworth Station,
Keighley BD22 8NJ
t 01535 645214
w kwvr.co.uk

619 Leeds

Royal Armouries Leeds

4 hrs   All year

Learn about arms and armour from around the world in five themed galleries covering war, tournament, self-defence, hunting and the Orient. During the summer months you can watch displays of jousting, falconry and horsemanship. You can even shoot a crossbow.

* Britain's oldest national museum

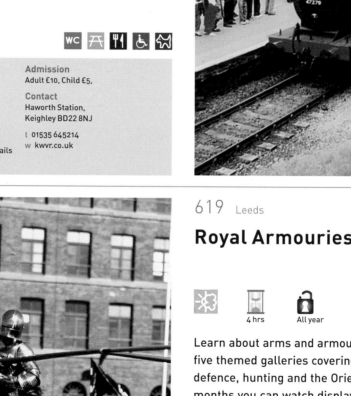

Location
S of Leeds city centre, near juction of M621

Opening
Daily; 10am–5pm

Admission
Free, on-site parking £3

Contact
Armouries Drive,
Leeds LS10 1 LT
t 08700 344344
w armouries.org.uk
e enquires@armouries.org.uk

620 Leeds

Temple Newsam House & Farm

2 hrs · All year

In the grounds of this beautiful country house is a farm with rare breeds of sheep, pigs, cattle and poultry. On special days visitors can join in with the laundry maids washing at the dolly tub, watch the blacksmith hammer out shoes and see logs cut at the saw-mill.

* The largest rare-breed centre in the world
* Grounds ideal for picnics

Location
Temple Newsam Road, off Selby Road, 4 miles from Leeds city centre, off A63

Opening
Nov-Mar Tue-Sat 10am-4pm; Sun 12-4pm; Apr-Oct Tue-Sat 10am-5pm; Sun 1pm-5pm

Admission
House Adult £3, Child £2
Farm Adult £3, Child £2

Contact
Temple Newsam Road, Leeds LS15 0AE

t 0113 2647321
w leeds.gov.uk/templenewsam
e tnewsamho.leeds@virgin.net

621 Leeds

Thackray Medical Museum

3 hrs · All year

This award-winning, interactive museum offers serious family fun. Explore the slums of Victorian Leeds as one of the city 'characters' and discover some of the weird treatments available.

* Quality Assured Visitor Attraction

Location
Next to St James's Hospital, 2 miles E of city centre; follow signs for St James's Hospital

Opening
Daily; 10am–5pm (last admission 3pm)

Admission
Adult £4.90, Child £3.50, Concs £3.90

Contact
Beckett Street, Leeds LS9 7LN

t 0113 247 0219 (info hotline)
w thackraymuseum.org
e info@thackraymuseum.org

622 Leeds

Tropical World

1 hr+ · All year

Walk into a tropical atmosphere among exotic trees, waterfalls and pools containing terrapins and carp. There are also meercats, lemurs, reptiles, insects and butterflies, as well as a recreated South American rainforest, a Desert House and a new tropical beach.

* Nocturnal zone
* Insect zone

Location
Off A58 at Oakwood, 3 miles N of Leeds city centre

Opening
Daily; 10am–6pm

Admission
Adult £3, Child (8–15) £2

Contact
Canal Gardens, Roundhay Park, Leeds, LS8 2ER

t 0113 266 1850

623 Shipley

Apollo Canal Cruises

1–3 hrs · All year

Both Water Prince, a traditional Leeds and Liverpool wide canal barge, and Apollo, a traditional canal narrow boat, will take you on a fantastic cruise through the beautiful Saltaire and Pennine hills.

Location
In central Shipley, off the junction of A657 & A6038

Opening
Daily; as per booking for restaurant boats; waterbus runs during school holidays & weekends

Admission
Please phone for details

Contact
Shipley Wharf, Wharf Street, Shipley BD17 7DW

t 01274 595914
w apollocanalcruises.co.uk

624 Shipley

St Leonard's Farm Park

2 hrs   Feb–Oct

Meet farmer James and his family on their award-winning farm. The farm has rare and modern breeds of animals (some of which you can feed), play areas, nature footpaths and listed barns and buildings.

* Junior ride-on electric tractors
* Tea room in C16 barn

Location
A6038 from Otley/Ilkley, A6038 from Shipley/Bradford

Opening
Daily; 10am–5pm throughout the school holidays

Admission
Adult £3, Child/Concs £2.50

Contact
Chapel Lane, Esholt, Shipley BD17 7RB

t 01274 598795
e farmerjames1@aol.com

625 Wakefield

Sandal Castle

1 hr+   All year

Sandal Castle is an excavated medieval castle overlooking the site of the Battle of Wakefield in 1460 and the scene of the Civil War siege. It has beautiful views of the Calder Valley.

* Site of 'The Grand Old Duke of York'
* Extensive fortifications

Location
On A61, 2 miles from the city centre in the direction of Barnsley

Opening
Daily dawn–dusk
Visitor centre: Easter–Oct half-term 11am–5pm otherwise weekends only Please phone for details

Admission
Free

Contact
Manygates Lane, Sandal, Wakefield WF2 7DG

t 01924 249779

626 Wakefield

Yorkshire Sculpture Park

3½ hrs   All year

A new award-winning centre with changing outdoor sculpture exhibitions sited in 500 acres of landscaped grounds, gardens and parkland. Families are invited to touch and explore the artworks which include monumental Henry Moore bronzes.

* Educational & community projects
* Workshops & courses

Location
Off A637 to Huddersfield, 1 mile from M1 (junction 38)

Opening
Grounds & centre: Daily; 10am–6pm (5pm in winter)
Facilities & indoor galleries: Daily; 11am–5pm (4pm in winter)

Admission
Free (Pay & Display parking)

Contact
Wakefield S73 4BX

t 01924 830302
w ysp.co.uk
e info@ysp.co.uk

North West

Cheshire Cumbria Greater Manchester
Lancashire Merseyside

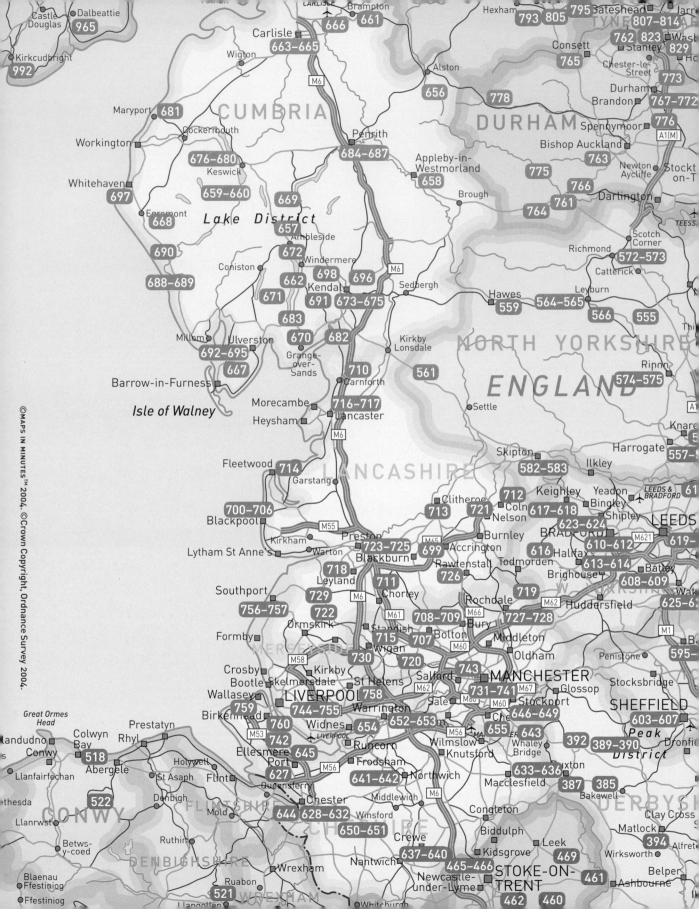

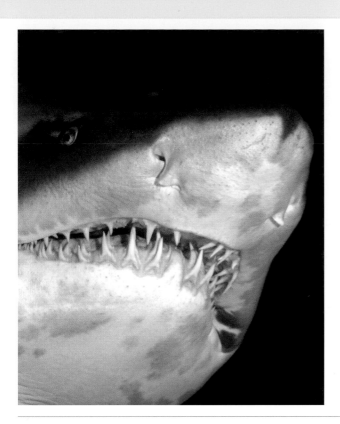

627 Cheshire Oaks

Blue Planet Aquarium

3 hrs   All year

One of Britain's largest aquariums, Blue Planet has two floors of interactive displays and exhibits. Take a voyage through the waters of the world, and see one of the largest collections of sharks in Europe.

* New exhibit for 2005, octopus adventure
* Good Guide to Britain 1999

Location
Take junction 10 off the M53 & follow the brown tourist signs.
8 miles from Chester train station

Opening
Daily from 10am, closing times vary, please phone for details

Admission
Adult £9.45, Child £7, Concs £7

Contact
Cheshire Oaks, Ellesmere Port
Cheshire CH65 9LF

t 0151 357 8804
w blueplanetaquarium.com
e info@blueplanetaquarium.co.uk

628 Chester

Cheshire Military Museum

1 hrs+   All year

Children will enjoy this museum, which houses an interactive Soldiers of Cheshire exhibition, telling the story of Cheshire's military history.

* Interactive computer displays
* Hands-on exhibits

Location
Close to the city centre

Opening
Daily; 10am–5pm (last admission 4.30pm)

Admission
Adult £2, Child £1, Concs £1

Contact
The Castle,
Chester CH1 2DN

t 01244 403933
w chester.ac.uk/militarymuseum

629 Chester

Chester Visitor Centre

½ hr+   All year

The ideal starting point for exploring Chester. The Interpretation Centre has a wide variety of features that aim to inform and entertain people of all ages. Activities include guided walks and brass rubbing.

* History of Chester displays
* Video show

WC ❚❙ ♿

Location
Accessible from the A483, A56, A51, A41, A55 & M53. Follow signs for the city centre

Opening
Daily; Mon–Fri 10am–5pm
Sat & Sun 10am–4pm

Admission
Free

Contact
Vicars Lane,
Chester CH1 1QX

t 01244 402111
w chestertourism.com
e tis@chestercc.gov.uk

630 Chester

Chester Zoo

5 hrs+   All year

The UK's largest zoological gardens, Chester Zoo has over 7000 animals housed in spacious enclosures. The zoo is set in 100 acres of beautiful landscaped gardens and has many attractions directed towards children.

* Zoo of the Year 2003
* Monkey islands

WC ⛱ ❚❙ ♿ 🐾

Location
Easily accessible from the M53 & M56; follow the brown tourist signs

Opening
Daily from 10am, closing times vary

Admission
Adult £13, Child £9.50, Concs £10.50

Contact

Upton-by-Chester,
Chester CH2 1LH

t 01244 380280
w chesterzoo.org
e reception@chesterzoo.co.uk

631 Chester

Dewa Roman Experience

1 hr   All year

Spend a few educational hours discovering what life was like in Roman Britain. Children can step aboard a Roman galley and stroll along reconstructions of Roman streets, experiencing the sights, sounds and smells of Roman Chester.

WC ♿

Location
Accessible from all major road routes; follow signs for Chester city centre

Opening
Daily; Feb–Nov 9am–5pm;
Dec & Jan 10am–4pm

Admission
Adult £4.25, Child £2.50, Concs £3.75

Contact
Pierpoint Lane, Bridge Street,
Chester CH1 1NL

t 01244 343407
w dewaromanexperiance.co.uk

632 Chester

Mouldsworth Motor Museum

2 hrs   Feb–Nov

Mouldsworth Motor Museum was built in 1937. The Art Deco building is set in its own grounds in the heart of the Cheshire countryside. With more than 60 veteran and classic cars and motorcycles, the museum is also home to a 1920s' replica garage, toys and pedal cars.

* Free quiz with prizes for children
* Motoring & motoring motif Art Deco collection

Location
On the B5393 into Ashton & Mouldsworth. 6 miles E of Chester; follow the brown tourist signs

Opening
3 Feb–Nov open Sun, Bank Hol Mons 12pm–5pm; Jul & Aug open Wed, Sat & Sun 12pm–5pm

Admission
Adult £3, Child £1.50

Contact
Smithy Lane, Mouldsworth
Chester, Cheshire CH3 8AR

t 01928 731781
w www.mouldsworthmotor
museum.com

---

634 Macclesfield

Jodrell Bank Science Centre & Arboretum

2 hrs   Mar–Oct

Travel aboard the spacecraft Elysium 7 en route to Mars for an amazing 3D flight over Martian volcanoes and canyons. Special events include meeting astronomers and guided walks of the arboretum for children. There are themed activity trails and hands-on exhibits.

* The 35-acre arboretum is a tree-lover's paradise
* Environmental discovery centre

Location
Between Holmes Chapel & Chelford, on A535, 8 miles W of Macclesfield

Opening
Mar–Oct 10.30am–5.30pm
The centre is under development, please check website for details

Admission
£1 per person, car park £3

Contact
Lower Withington,
Macclesfield SK11 9DL

t 01477 571339
w jb.man.ac.uk/scicen
e visitorcentre@jb.man.ac.uk

633 Macclesfield

Capesthorne Hall

2 hrs   Apr–Oct

Capesthorne Hall is where the Bromley-Davenports and their ancestors have lived since Domesday times. It contains a variety of treasures including fine paintings, furniture, marbles and Greek vases. It lies in gardens and parkland extending over 100 acres.

* Special events including craft fairs
* Car & Motorcycle events throughout the year

Location
Off A34 between Manchester & Stoke-on-Trent 3 miles S of Alderly Edge, Junction 6 of the M6

Opening
Apr–Oct Sun, Wed & Bank Hols 12noon–5pm

Admission
Adult £6, Child £3, Concs £5

Contact
Siddington,
Macclesfield SK11 9JY

t 01625 861221
w capesthorne.com
e info@capesthorne.com

635 Macclesfield

Macclesfield Riverside Park

1 hr+   All year

Take the whole family to enjoy this pretty country park with woodland, wetland, ponds and a wild flower meadow.

* Visitor centre

Location
Between Macclesfield & Prestbury.
Take the A538 out of Macclesfield

Opening
Park Daily
Visitor centre Daily 9am–4pm

Admission
Free

Contact
Beechwood Mews,
Macclesfield SK10 2SL

t 01625 511086
e bollin@cheshire.gov.uk

636 Macclesfield

Paradise Mill & New Macclesfield Silk Museum

2 hrs+   All year

Set in a restored mill, this venue gives an idea of working conditions in the 1930s. The silk museum is in the restored School of Art and includes six galleries and an audio visual presentation following the story of local silk manufacturing.

* Includes 26 Jacquard hand looms
* Craft club activities & exhibition room

Location
Take the A523 & follow signs for Macclesfield town centre. The museum is at the foot of the High Street

Opening
Daily; Mon–Sat 11am–5pm;
closed Good Fri, 25, 26 Dec & 1 Jan

Admission
Adult £3.75, Child £2.75, Concs £2.75

Contact
Park Lane, Macclesfield,
Cheshire SK11 6UT

t 01625 612045
w www.silk-macclesfield.org
e silkmuseum@tiscali.co.uk

637 Nantwich

Hack Green Secret Nuclear Bunker

2 hrs   Jan–Nov

A real government nuclear war headquarters, this place was a secret for over 50 years. It contains decontamination facilities, a Minister of State's office, life support systems and more. There are two cinemas and many hands-on activities for all age groups.

* Soviet Spy Mouse Trail for children
* World War II radar station

Location
From junction 16 on the M6 follow signs to Nantwich, then to Whitchurch on the A530

Opening
Daily; Mar–Oct 10.30am–5.30pm
Nov & Jan–Feb 11am–4.30pm

Admission
Adult £5.80, Child £4, Concs £5.50

Contact
PO Box 127, Nantwich CW5 8AQ

t 01270 629219
w hackgreen.co.uk
e coldwar@hackgreen.co.uk

638 Nantwich

Stapeley Water Gardens

3 hrs+   All year

A garden centre specializing in water gardening with display pools, pet centre and angling superstore. The Palms Tropical Oasis is a huge glass pavilion housing exotic plants, fish and animals, including sharks and toucans.

* Pet centre
* Santa in his grotto at Christmas

Location
1 mile S of Nantwich on the A51;
signed from the M6 (junction 16)

Opening
Stapely Water Gardens Daily;
closed Easter Sunday & 25 Dec
The Palms Tropical Oasis Daily

Admission
Adult £4.45, Child £2.60, Concs £3.95

Contact
London Road , Stapeley,
Nantwich CW5 7LH

t 01270 623868
e info@stapeleywg.com

639 Northwich

Marbury Country Park

1 hr+   All year

Set in 200 acres of woodland, this park has a large lake, self-guided trails and is great for orienteering. Ideal for walkers and picnickers.

* Children's play area
* Lakeside walks

Location	Contact
Leave the M56 at junction 10 & take the A523 & A559	Comberbach, Northwich CW9 6AT
Opening	t 01606 77741
Daily; May–Sep 8am–8pm Oct–Apr 8am–5pm	w northwichcommunitywoodlands.org.uk
Admission	e marbury@cheshire.gov.uk
Free, car park charge	

640 Nantwich

Stretton Watermill

1½ hrs   Apr–Sep

Visit this small working watermill set in beautiful Cheshire countryside and discover the traditional skills of flour milling.

* Displays on wildlife

Location	Admission
Near Farndon, 10 miles from Chester; signed from the A534	Adult £2, Child 75p
Opening	**Contact**
May–Aug Tue–Sun 1pm–5pm Apr & Sep Sat–Sun open 1pm–5pm, open Bank Hols	c/o Cheshire Museums, 162 London Road, Nantwich CW9 8AB
	t 01606 41331

641 Northwich

Stockley Farm

2 hrs+   Mar–Oct

Stockley Farm is a modern working organic dairy farm. It comprises 700 acres on the Arley Estate in the glorious Cheshire countryside. Visitors can watch a herd of 150 British Friesians being milked in one of the most modern computerised milking parlours in the country.

* Birds of prey display
* Bottle-feeding lambs & goats

Location	Admission
Leave the M56 at junction 7, 9 or 10; the M6 at junction 19/20 & follow the signs	Adult £4.75, Child £3.75, Concs £3.75
Opening	**Contact**
End Mar–early Oct Sat & Sun, Bank Hols & school hols 11am–5pm	Arley, Northwich CW9 6LZ
	t 01565 777323
	w stockleyfarm.co.uk
	e mark.walton@farming.co.uk

642 Northwich

Salt Museum

1 hr   All year

The museum tells the fascinating history of mid-Cheshire and the industry that has shaped the landscape and life of the area. With temporary exhibitions and special activities find out why salt is vital in so many ways.

* New galleries
* New disabled lift being installed for spring 2005

Location
Take the A533 N to Northwich & follow signs for the Salt Museum

Opening
Tue–Fri 10am–5pm,
Sat & Sun 2pm–5pm; Aug Mon
10am–5pm; Bank Hol Mons 10am–5pm

Admission
Adult £2.40, Child £1.20, Concs £2

Contact
162 London Road,
Northwich CW9 8AB

t 01606 41331
w saltmuseum.org.uk
e cheshiremuseums@cheshire.gov.uk

643 Poynton

Brookside Miniature Railway

1½ hrs   Apr–Sep

An extensive miniature railway layout that runs through the grounds of a large garden centre. There are lots of features of interest on the journey such as the river bridges, a pond filled with koi carp and a craft centre.

* Steam & diesel locomotives
* Santa Specials at Christmas

Location
On the A523 mid-way between Hazel Grove & Poynton. Follow the brown tourist signs

Opening
Apr–Sep weekends & Wed 11am–4pm;
daily mid Jul–mid Aug, Bank Hols &
school hols 11am–4pm

Admission
£1 (10 rides £8)

Contact
Macclesfield Road,
Poynton

t 01625 872919
e brooksidegc@absonline.net
w brookside-miniature-railway.co.uk

644 Saltney

KK5

1½ hrs   All year

KK5 is a fun-packed children's play centre that helps develop body and mind through play. Includes ball pools and café, with activities to keep your child amused all day.

* Unlimited play for toddlers until 3pm weekdays
* Discounts for childminders

Location
From the A483, travelling into Chester, take the A5104 into Saltney & turn right into Central Trading Estate

Opening
Daily 10am–7pm

Admission
Mon–Fri over-5 £3; under-5 £2
Weekends £3.50

Contact
Unit 11, Marley Way,
Central Trading Estate,
Saltney CH5 8SX

t 01244 677357

645 South Wirral

Rivacre Valley
Local Nature Reserve

1 hr+   All year

A natural area which has been landscaped with an orienteering trail, way-marked art and guided walks. A great place for kids to let off steam, and for adults to enjoy the surroundings.

* Guided tours
* Occasional events

Location
Leave the M53 at junction 7; follow signs for Overpool; take 1st right at Rivacre Road, then 2nd right

Opening
Daily 24 hrs

Admission
Free

Contact
Rivacre Road,
Ellesmere Port,
South Wirral CH64 2UQ

t 0151 3571991
w cheshire.gov.uk/countryside
e rivacre@cheshire.gov.uk

646 Stockport

Air Raid Shelters

1 hr+   All year

These air raid shelters were carved into the cliffs in the town centre. Now a visitor attraction, children can experience the sights and sounds of the Blitz and life in general in 1940s' Britain.

* Guided tours by arrangement
* Monthly explorer tour

Location
In Stockport town centre. Leave the M63 at junction 12 & take the A6 to Stockport

Opening
Daily 1pm–5pm

Admission
Adult £3.95, Child £2.50, Concs £2.95

Contact
61 Chestergate,
Stockport SK1 1NE

t 0161 4741940

647 Stockport

Alphabet Zoo

1½ hrs   All year

An indoor adventure playground with the emphasis on purposeful play in a safe environment. Children must be accompanied by an adult.

* Unlimited play for toddlers until 3pm weekdays
* Children's birthday parties

Location
Easily reached from the M60 (junction 1); on the corner of King Street West & Chestergate

Opening
Daily 10am–7pm

Admission
Mon–Fri over 4 £3, under 4 £2.50
Weekends £3.50

Contact
Mentor House,
King Street West,
Stockport SK3 0DY

t 01614 772225

648 Stockport

Lyme Park

½ day   All year

This Tudor house offers beautiful interiors plus extensive gardens and a medieval deer park of moorland, woodland and parkland. Visitors will recognise the place as the setting for Pemberley in the BBC adaptation of *Pride and Prejudice*.

* Children's guide to the house
* Children's quiz & trail

Location
The entrance is on the A6, 6½ miles SE of Stockport

Opening
Park Apr–Oct 8am–8.30pm
House Apr–Oct Fri–Tue 11am–5pm
Gardens Apr–Oct Fri–Tue 1pm–5pm

Admission
House Adult £5.80, Child £2.90
Gardens £2.70, £1.40

Contact
Disley,
Stockport SK12 2NX

t 01663 762023/76492
w nationaltrust.org.uk
e lymepark@nationaltrust.org.uk

649 Stockport

Reddish Vale Country Park

7 hrs   **All year**

A beautiful country park offering a variety of walks through woodlands, river valleys and meadows. It also features displays on the area's heritage, wildlife and future. Fishing is available on two large mill ponds.

* Cycle trail
* Butterfly park

Location	**Admission**
Take the B6167 Reddish road from Stockport	Free
	Contact
Opening	Mill Lane, Reddish,
Park Daily	Stockport SK5 7HE
Visitor centre Please phone for details	t 01614 775637

650 Tarporley

Cheshire Blue Lavender

2 hrs   **Jul–Aug**

A haven in the Cheshire countryside, visitors come to experience the unique qualities of this popular plant and enjoy a tranquil summer's day out.

* Jersey lavender ice cream
* Pick your own lavender

Location	**Admission**
7 miles E of Chester, 1 mile from Tarvin village & 3 miles from Tarporley	Free
	Contact
Opening	Burton Road, Duddon,
Jul & Aug; please phone for details	Tarporley CW6 0ET
	t 01829 741099
	w bluelavender.co.uk
	e sarah.evans@bluelavender.co.uk

651 Tarporley

Oulton Park Race Circuit

All day   **Apr–Oct**

Watch spectacular car and bike racing with British superbikes, Formula 3s and British touring cars. One-to-one instruction with the Racing & Rally Experiences and safe training with the Early Drive Experience are both on offer.

* Fairground rides
* Special events

Location	**Admission**
Take junction 18 off the M6 & follow the A54 to Chester for 12 miles. Turn left onto the A49 to Whitchurch & follow the signposts	Please phone for details
	Contact
	Brands Hatch Circuits Ltd,
Opening	Little Budworth, Tarporley,
Apr–Oct, Sat for minor meetings; Sun or Bank hols for major meetings	Cheshire CW6 9BW
	t 01829 760301
	w motorsportvision.co.uk

652 Warrington

Gulliver's World

7 hrs   Apr–Sep

A theme park for families set in beautiful woodlands around a lake. The park is aimed at children from 2 to 13 years old and has over 50 rides, attractions and shows. A fun day out for all.

* Lost World Dino area
* Special events

Location
Via the M6 (junction 21a) & the M62 (junction 8 or 9), then follow the signs

Opening
Please phone for details

Admission
Please phone for details

Contact
Warrington, Cheshire WA5 9YZ

t 01925 230088
w gulliversfun.co.uk

653 Warrington

Walton Hall & Gardens

2 hrs+   Apr–Oct

An ideal place for a family day out with attractions including ornamental gardens and woodland trails.

* Children's zoo
* Park ranger service & heritage centre

Location
Leave the M56 at junction 11 & follow the A56. 2 miles from Warrington town centre on A56

Opening
Daily; May–Sep 10.30am–5pm; Oct–Apr Sat, Sun, Bank Hol Mons & school holidays 10.30am–4.30pm;

Admission
Free

Contact
Walton Lea Road, Higher Walton, Warrington WA4 6SN

t 01925 601617
w warrington.gov.uk/waltongardens
e waltonhall@warrington.gov.uk

654 Widnes

Catalyst: Science Discovery Centre

3 hrs   All year

Science and technology come alive through a host of interactive exhibits and hands-on displays. Children and adults can tug, tease and test over 100 different exhibits in four action-packed galleries.

Location
Follow the road signs to Widnes (S), then the brown tourist signs

Opening
Sat & Sun 11am–5pm & Tue–Fri 10am–5pm; open Mon during school holidays, please phone for details

Admission
Adult £4.95, Child £3.50, Concs £3.95

Contact
Gossage Building, Mersey Road, Widnes, Cheshire WA8 0DF

t 01514 201121
w catalyst.org.uk
e info@catalyst.org.uk

655 Wilmslow

Quarry Bank Mill & Styal Estate

7 hrs   All year

A country park with a Georgian water-powered cotton mill, plus the Apprentice House, where visitors can see where pauper children stayed and the conditions in which they lived.

* Woodland & riverside walks
* New turbine in mill

Location
Leave the M56 at junction 5 & take the B5166

Opening
Daily, please phone for details

Admission
Adult £7.30, Child £4.50

Contact
Styal, Wilmslow, Cheshire SK9 4LA

t 01625 527468
e quarrybankmill@nationaltrust.org.uk

656 Alston

South Tynedale Railway

2 hrs   Apr–Oct

Visit England's highest narrow gauge railway and take a trip by diesel or steam from Alston to Kirkhaugh. The two-mile journey passes through the South Tyne valley and through an Area of Outstanding Beauty.

* Railway shop & picnic area
* Special events

Location
Alston is on the A686, A689, and B6277 16 miles NE of Penrith. Follow signs to railway from village centre

Opening
Apr–Oct, please phone for details

Admission
Please phone for details

Contact
Alston CA9 3JB

t 01434 382828 (timetable)
   01434 381696
w www.visitcumbria.com
e mail@strps.org.uk

657 Ambleside

Hawkshead Trout Farm

½ day+   All year

A well-stocked lake where you can fish by boat or from the shore. Suitable for inexperienced, intermediate and expert anglers. Tuition is available and children can feed and catch their own fish.

* Shop selling tackle, bait & local produce
* Purpose-built children's fishing area

Location
1½ miles S of Hawkshead, on the road to Newby Bridge

Opening
Daily 9am–6pm

Admission
Fishing Adult £20, Child £5.50, Concs £17

Contact
Ambleside LA22 0QF

t 01539 436541
w hawksheadtrout.com
e trout@hawkshead.demon.co.uk

658 Appleby-in-Westmorland

Appleby Castle

1 hr+   Apr–Oct

An eleventh-century castle and Norman keep with pleasant grounds. Climb the stairs to the top and see the magnificent views.

* Animals & rare breeds
* Brass rubbing

Location
Take the A66 & B260. Follow the M6 for 13 miles to junction 38 N or junction 40 S

Opening
Daily; Apr–Oct 10am–4.30pm

Admission
Adult £5, Child £3, Concs £4

Contact
Appleby-in-Westmorland CA16 6XH

t 01768 353823
w towersofeden.com

659 Borrowdale

Honister Slate Mine

1½ hrs   All year

An opportunity to see ancient craftsmanship and to learn the history of bygone years as you take an underground tour of this working mine.

* Quality Assured Visitor Attraction
* Guided tours compulsory

Location
From Keswick take the B5289 through Borrowdale & Rosthwaite for 9 miles; from Cockermouth follow the B5292 & B5289 for 14 miles

Opening
Daily; 9am–5pm
Sat & Sun 10am–5pm

Admission
Mine tour Adult £9.50, Child £4.50

Contact
Honister Pass, Borrowdale, Keswick CA12 5XN

t 017687 77230
w honister.com
e info@honister-slate-mine.co.uk

660 Borrowdale

Platty+

1 hr+   Mar–Oct

A family-based centre where visitors can enjoy canoeing, kayaking, dinghy sailing, dragonboating, rowing and a viking longship! Children and adults with special needs are welcomed.

* RYA training centre
* British Canoe Union approved

Location	Admission
From Keswick take the B5289 (Borrowdale road) for about 3 miles. Park in the Hilton Lodore Hotel car park & walk down to the boat landing	Activities priced individually
	Contact
Opening	Lodore Boat Landings, Derwentwater, Borrowdale, Keswick CA12 5UQ
Daily; Mar–Oct 10am–6pm Otherwise open by prior arrangment	t 01768777282 w plattyplus.co.uk e j.platt@plattyplus.co.uk

661 Brampton

Talkin Tarn Country Park

7 hrs   All year

Get active when you visit this 65-acre lake set amid 120 acres of farmland and woodland. A permanent orienteering course is laid out around the park, there are wooden rowing boats for hire, woods to explore or mountain bikes to ride.

* Sailing, boating, canoeing & windsurfing
* Coarse fishing available on a day-ticket basis

Location	Admission
On the B6413, 9 miles E of Carlisle & 2 miles S of Brampton	Free
Opening	Contact
Park Daily dawn–dusk. Please phone for details of other facilities	Brampton CA8 1HN t 01697 741050 w visitcumbria.com

662 Browness-on-Windermere

Blackwell, The Arts & Crafts House

1 hr+   Feb–Dec

Inspired by lakeland wild flowers, trees, berries and birds, Baillie Scott designed every last detail of this house. Outside from the garden terraces, there are wonderful views of Windermere. Children can have a go at the Blackwell quiz.

* Royal Institute of British Architects' award for excellence

Location	Admission
Follow the A5074 from Bowness (Lyth Valley road). Located 1 mile from Bowness	Please phone for details
	Contact
Opening	Bowness-on-Windermere LA23 3JR
Daily; Feb–Dec 10.30am–5pm; closes 4pm in Feb, Mar, Nov & Dec	t 01539 446139 w blackwell.org.uk e info@blackwell.org.uk

663 Carlisle

Border Regiment & King's Own Royal Border Regiment Museum

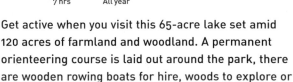
½ hr+   All year

This museum has a large collection of uniforms, weapons, medals, field and anti-tank guns, trophies, models, silver and pictures. Displays on two floors depict the 300-year history of Cumbria's County Infantry Regiment. The museum is located in Carlisle's medieval castle, the Regiment's home since 1873.

Location	Admission
On the N side of Carlisle city centre; accessible from the M6 (junction 43 or 44)	Adult £3.80, Child £1.90, Concs £2.90
	Contact
Opening	Queen Mary's Tower, The Castle, Carlisle CA3 8UR
Daily; Apr–Sep 9.30am–6pm Oct–Mar 10am–4pm;	t 01228 532774 e rhq@kingsownborder.demon.co.uk

664 Carlisle

Carlisle Castle

2 hrs   All year

A great medieval fortress with a thrilling past. Today visitors can explore fascinating and ancient chambers, stairways and dungeons.

* King's Own Regimental Museum here
* Lively exhibitions

Location
On the N side of the city, beyond the cathedral

Opening
Daily; Apr–Sep 9.30am–6pm
Oct 10am–5pm
Nov–Mar 10am–4pm

Admission
Adult £3.50, Child £1.80, Concs £2.70

Contact
Carlisle CA3 8UR

t 01228 591922

665 Carlisle

Laserquest

1 hr   All year

Unleash a volley of laser fire in the battle zone – the ultimate sci-fi action adventure for children over seven. Each game lasts for 20 minutes.

* Simple or complex games
* Play solo or in a team

Location
Carlisle city centre

Opening
Daily; Mon–Fri 11am–9pm
Sat 10am–9pm & Sun 10am–7pm

Admission
£3.50 for 1 game, £5.50 for 2, £7 for 3

Contact
Bush Brow,
Victoria Viaduct CA3 8AN

t 01228 511155
w lquk.com
e info@lquk.com

666 Crosby-on-Eden

The Edward Haughey Solway Aviation Museum

½ day   Apr–Oct

Young people interested in civil and military aviation history will be fascinated by this museum. Among the items on display are aircraft from the 1950s and 1960s and the Blue Streak Rocket Programme. Visitors can sit in the pilot's seat of the Vulcan B2.

* Mock-up control tower
* Vulcan B2, Canberra T4 & Sikorsky S-55a among aircraft

Location
3½ miles E of Carlisle on the A689

Opening
Apr–Oct open weekends & Bank Hols
10.30am–5pm; also Fri during school holidays

Admission
Adult £3.50, Child £1.75, Concs £2.25

Contact
Aviation House, Carlisle Airport,
Crosby-on-Eden CA6 4NW

t 01228 573823
w solway-aviation-museum.co.uk
e info@solway-aviation-museum.co.uk

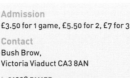

667 Dalton-in-Furness

South Lakes Wild Animal Park

4 hrs+   All year

One of Europe's leading conservation zoos, this rolling 17-acre park is home to some of the rarest animals on Earth. Many, such as lemurs, parrots, kangaroos and wallabies, have complete freedom to wander at will.

Location
Take junction 36 off the M6 & follow the signs on the A590.
At Dalton turn right at Tudor Square & continue for 1 mile

Opening
Daily 10am–5pm, 4.30pm in winter

Admission
Please phone for details

Contact
Dalton-in-Furness LA15 8JR
t 01229 466086
w wildanimalpark.co.uk

668 Egremont

Florence Mine Heritage Centre

3 hrs   All year

Based at the last deep iron ore mine in western Europe, this heritage centre offers a mining museum, a geology and mineral room and an authentic reconstruction of an underground mine.

* Guided underground tours

Location
Situated on the outskirts of Egremont, just off the A595 on the Haile/Wilton turn off

Opening
Mon–Fri 9.30am–4.30pm
also weekends 10am–4pm in summer
Please phone to book tours

Admission
Museum Adult £2, Child £1
Underground Adult £6.50, Child £4.50

Contact
Egremont CA22 2NR
t 01946 825830/820683
w florencemine.co.uk

669 Glenridding

Ullswater 'Steamers'

 2 hr+   All year

Cruises between Glenridding, Howtown and Pooley Bridge run daily from March to October, weather permitting. There is access to a variety of walks including Howtown to Glenridding and spectacular picnic spots in unspoilt scenery.

* New Sammy the Squirrel activity book and quiz sheet
* Best Large Visitor Attraction 2004

Location
Accessible from the M6 (junction 40) or over Kirkstone Pass from Windermere & Ambleside

Opening
Daily; sailing times vary, please phone or visit website for details

Admission
Please phone for details

Contact
Pier House, Glenridding LA11 0US

t 017684 82229
w ullswater-steamers.co.uk
e office@ullswater-steamers.co.uk

670 Grange-over-Sands

Lakeland Miniature Village

 1 hr   All year

Visit Lakeland in a day at Cumbria's only miniature village. It has more than 100 buildings made from local Coniston slate, including houses, farms, barns and tiny wishing wells. A new Japanese teahouse will be completed in 2005.

* See Beatrix Potter's house in miniature
* Play area for children

Location
From Grange-over-Sands take the B5277 to Flookburgh, follow the signs for Ravenstown & turn left after the post office

Opening
Daily 10.30am–dusk

Admission
Adult £3.50, Concs £3, Child £1.50

Contact
Winder Lane, Flookburgh, Grange-over-Sands LA11 7LE

t 015395 58500
w lakelandminiaturevillage.com

671 Grizedale Forest Park

Go Ape!

 2½ hrs   Feb–Nov

Discover the thrill of the high wire with an assault course of rope bridges, tarzan swings and zip slides. Scramble up rope nets and swing through the trees at this award-winning attraction.

* For children over ten only
* Pre-booking essential

Location
Off the Hawkshead–Satterthwaite road; follow the brown tourist signs to Grizedale Forest Park

Opening
Apr–Oct & Feb half-term daily
Mar & Nov open weekends
Please phone for details

Admission
Adult £18, Child £12

Contact
Grizedale Forest Centre

t 0870 4445562
w www.forestry.gov.uk

672 Hawkshead

Beatrix Potter Gallery

 ½ hr   Mar–Oct

Housed in what was once her husband's office, the gallery has an annually-changing exhibition of illustrations from Beatrix Potter's famous children's books, including *The Tale of Benjamin Bunny*, *The Tale of Jemima Puddle-Duck* and *The Tale of Squirrel Nutkin*.

* The interior remains substantially unaltered
* 2005 exhibition *The Tale of Mrs Tiggy-Winkle*

Location
Town centre

Opening
19 Mar–30 Oct Sat–Wed
10.30am–4.30pm

Admission
Adult £3.50, Child £1.70

Contact
Beatrix Potter Gallery,
Main Street, Hawkshead LA22 0NS

t 01539 436355
w nationaltrust.org.uk
e beatrixpottergallery@national-trust.org.uk

673 Kendal

Kendal Museum

1½ hrs   Feb–Dec

This museum houses displays of the archaeology and natural history of the Lake District, alongside a world wildlife exhibition. There are free quizzes, worksheets and activities for children and events throughout the year.

Location
On the A6 N of Kendal, opposite the railway station

Opening
Summer Mon–Sat 10.30am–5pm; winter Mon–Sat 10.30am–4pm closed Christmas to mid-Feb

Admission
Please phone for details

Contact
Station Road, Kendal LA9 6BT
t 01539 721374
w kendalmuseum.org.uk
e info@kendalmuseum.org.uk

674 Kendal

Low Sizergh Barn

2 hrs   All year

Walk on the farm trail and enjoy the beautiful countryside around this organic dairy farm. See the cows and hens, and watch out for wildlife and birds in the fields, pond and woods.

* Watch cows being milked at 3.45pm daily

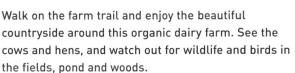

Location
On the A591, 4 miles S of Kendal. From the M6 (junction 36) take the A591 & follow signs

Opening
Daily 9am–5.30pm, 5pm closing Jan–Easter;

Admission
Free

Contact
Sizergh, Kendal LA8 8AE
t 01539 560426
w low-sizergh-barn.co.uk
e apark@low-sizergh-barn.co.uk

675 Kendal

Museum of Lakeland Life

1 hr+   Feb–Dec

The Museum of Lakeland Life shows how the Cumbrian people worked, lived and entertained themselves in the changing social climate of the past 200 years. Exhibits include a street scene, reconstructed workshops and a Victorian bedroom and parlour.

* Captain Flint children's room
* Arthur Ransome's study

Location
From the M6 (junction 36) follow signs for Kendal. From S Kendal follow the brown tourist signs for Abbot Hall

Opening
14 Feb–24 Dec Mon–Sat 10.30am–5pm
4pm closing Feb, Mar, Nov & Dec

Admission
Adult £2.75, Child £1.40

Contact
Abbot Hall, Kendal LA9 5AL
t 01539 722464
w lakelandmuseum.org.uk
e info@lakelandmuseum.org.uk

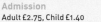

676 Keswick

Cumberland Pencil Museum

1 hr   All year

Cumberland Pencil Museum traces the history of pencil-making from the discovery of graphite to present-day methods of pencil manufacture. Children can see the world's largest pencil here.

* Brass rubbing
* Children's drawing area

Location
Follow the A66 to Keswick. Located 300 yards W of Keswick town centre

Opening
Daily 9.30am–4pm

Admission
Adult £2.50, Child £1.25, Concs £1.25

Contact
Southey Works,
Keswick CA12 5NG

t 01768 773626
w pencils.co.uk

677 Keswick

Derwent Water Marina

1 hr+   All year

This centre specializes in watersports with RYA sailing courses, windsurfing courses and canoe, kayak and dinghy hire available. Other activities include ghyll scrambling, abseiling, climbing and walking.

Location
From Keswick take the A66 & follow the signs for Portinscale

Opening
Daily 9am–5pm
closed 20 Dec–12 Jan

Admission
Activities priced individually

Contact
Portinscale,
Keswick CA12 5RF

t 017687 72912
w derwentwatermarina.co.uk
e info@derwentwatermarina.co.uk

678 Keswick

Keswick Holiday Arts Studio

1–3 hrs   All year

Make a special souvenir or gift at this creative arts and crafts studio for all ages to enjoy. The centre has a friendly, relaxed atmosphere and offers support for all activities, so no previous experience is needed.

WC ♿

Location
3 mins walk from Keswick town centre, on the Penrith road

Opening
Daily 10am–1pm & 2pm–5pm; Mon, Wed, Fri & Sun also open evenings 7pm–10pm

Admission
£5 per hr, £12 for 3 hrs

Contact
1 Wordsworth Street, Keswick CA12 4HU

t 01768 775990
w keswickstudio.co.uk
e info@keswickstudio.co.uk

679 Keswick

Trotters World of Animals

2–4 hrs   All year

At Trotters you will meet animals from all over the world, as well as many farmyard favourites. Handling of the animals is encouraged during audience participation sessions, plus there's a large soft play centre, picnic areas and special events.

* Pony & tractor trailer rides (weekends & holidays)
* Bird of prey centre

Location
Follow the brown tourist signs from the A591 & A66

Opening
Daily; Feb–Nov 10am–5.30pm (last admission 5pm)
Christmas holidays 11am–4.30pm (last admission 4pm)

Admission
Adult £5.25, Child £3.95

Contact
Coalbeck Farm, Bassenthwaite, Keswick CA12 4RD

t 01768 776239
w trottersworld.com
e info@trottersworld.com

680   Keswick

Whinlatter Forest Park

2 hrs+   All year

Nestling in England's only mountain forest, this park offers a wide variety of activities, from way-marked walks to orienteering courses, for all abilities and ages.

* Adventure playground
* Live TV pictures of nesting ospreys

Location	Admission
Signs on the A66 from Keswick	Free, car park charge
Opening	**Contact**
Daily; Oct–Easter 10am–4pm;	Braithwaite,
Easter–summer school holidays	Keswick CA12 5TW
10am–5pm;	t 01768 778469
school holidays 10am–5.30pm	w nwefd.co.uk
	e whinlatter@forestry.gsi.gov.uk

681   Maryport

The Lake District Coast Aquarium

1 hr+   All year

This independently owned aquarium has a comprehensive collection of native marine species. Exciting displays recreate natural habitats, including a 'walk-over' ray pool and 'hands-in' rock pool. There is also a new miniature golf attraction.

Location	Admission
Take junction 40 on the M6 & the A66	Adult £4.75, Child £3.10, Concs £4
to Maryport; or junction 44 & the A595	
S to connect with the A596 coastal	**Contact**
route	South Quay,
	Maryport, Cumbria CA15 8AB
Opening	
Daily 10am–5pm	t 01900 817760
	e info@ld-coastaquarium.co.uk

682   Milnthorpe

Lakeland Wildlife Oasis

1½ hrs+   All year

Enjoy a fascinating journey through the animal kingdom, from microbes to monkeys, in this unique, award-winning wildlife exhibition, with live animals and hands-on displays.

* Cumbria Winner, *Good Britain Guide*
* Animal handling sessions

Location	Admission
On the A6, 2½ miles S of Milnthorpe,	Please phone for details
near junction 35 on the M6	
	Contact
Opening	Milnthorpe LA7 7BW
Daily; summer 10am–5pm	t 015395 63027
winter 10am–4pm	w wildlifeoasis.co.uk

683   Newby Bridge

Aquarium of the Lakes

1 hr+   All year

This award-winning aquarium offers over 30 spectacular naturally themed habitats, bringing the natural history of the Lake District to life. Enjoy close encounters with many marine dwellers including eels, crabs, rays and many more.

* Quality Assured Visitor Attraction
* Interactive displays

Location	Admission
Situated just 1 mile from the A590 at	Adult £5.95, Child £3.75, Concs £4.95
Newby Bridge, on the S shore of	
Lake Windermere	**Contact**
	Newby Bridge LA12 8AS
Opening	
Daily 9am–6pm, 5pm in winter	t 01539 530153
(last admission 1 hr before closing)	w aquariumofthelakes.co.uk
	e aquariumofthelakes@reallive.co.uk

684 Penrith

Dalemain Historic House & Garden

  2 hrs — All year

Dalemain is a beautiful Tudor and Georgian house with fascinating interiors set among fine gardens, parkland with red squirrels and fallow deer and the Lakeland Fells. Children love the nursery, Mrs Mouse House on the back stairs and the hiding hole in the housekeeper's room.

* Children's garden
* Cruises available on nearby Ullswater

WC

Location
On the A592 Penrith–Ullswater road, 3 miles from the M6 (junction 40)

Opening
28 Mar–30 Aug Sun–Thu 10.30am–5pm
House 11am–4pm;
1 Sept–21 Oct Sun–Thu 10.30am–4pm
House 11am–3pm (last entry 2pm)

Admission
Adult £5.50, Child £3.50

Contact
Dalemain Estates,
Penrith CA11 0HB

t 01768 486450
w dalemain.com
e admin@dalemain.com

685 Penrith

Eden Ostrich World

2 hrs+ — All year

Come face to face with African black ostriches, rare breeds of cattle, donkeys, shire-horses, pigs, goats, red deer, ducks and geese.

* New indoor centre for 2005
* Tractor & trailer rides

WC

Location
In the Eden Valley, 5 miles from the M6 (junction 40), follow the A686 towards Alston

Opening
Daily Mar–Oct 10am–5pm
Nov–Feb open Wed–Mon 10am–5pm

Admission
Adult £4.50, Child £3.50, Concs £3.75

Contact
Langwathby Hall Farm, Langwathby, Penrith CA10 1LW

t 01768 881771
w ostrich-world.com

686 Penrith

Lakeland Bird of Prey Centre

2 hrs+   Apr–Oct

Situated in the walled garden of Lowther Castle and enclosed by parkland, this centre gives visitors the chance to see fascinating birds of prey at close quarters.

* Daily flying demonstrations at 1pm & 3pm

Location
From the N take the A6,
5 miles S of Penrith; from the S leave
the M6 at junction 39 onto the A6
through Shap, about
15 miles N of Kendal

Opening
Daily Apr–Oct 11am–5pm

Admission
Adult £6, Child £2, Concs £5

Contact
Old Walled Garden, Lowther,
Penrith CA10 2HH

t 01931 712746

687 Penrith

Rheged – The Village in the Hill

2 hrs+   All year

Award-winning Rheged is Europe's largest grass-covered building and home to a giant cinema screen showing epic movies daily. It also hosts the only international Everest exhibition, plus local craft and gift shops, a play area and activities for all the family.

* Cumbria Large Visitor Attraction of the Year 2002
* New bistro, toy shop and two exhibition halls

Location
Located only 2 mins from the M6
(junction 40) at Penrith, on the A66
towards Keswick

Opening
Daily 10am–6pm

Admission
Free parking & admission
(charge per activity or event)

Contact
Redhills, Penrith CA11 0DQ

t 01768 868000
w rheged.com
e enquiries@rheged.com

688 Ravenglass

Muncaster Castle

½ day   All year

Historic castle and headquarters of the World Owl Centre, Muncaster has 70 acres of gardens, a meadow vole maze and children's play area. It's also rumoured to be haunted...

* Small Visitor Attraction of the Year 2003
* Family Attraction of the Year 2001

Location
On the A595, 1 mile S of Ravenglass.
Take junction 40 off the M6
S & junction 36 off the M6 N

Opening
Gardens Daily 10.30am–6pm
Castle Sun–Fri 12pm–5pm
Please phone for winter times

Admission
Gardens Adults £6, Child £4
Castle Adult £3, Child £2

Contact
Ravenglass CA18 1RQ

t 01229 717614
w muncaster.co.uk
e info@muncaster.co.uk

689 Ravenglass

Ravenglass & Eskdale Railway

2 hrs+   All year

Take a gentle steam-train ride from the coast at Ravenglass to the foot of England's highest mountain at Eskdale, through the beautiful Lake District landscape. Depending on the weather, visitors can travel in open carriages or cosy covered ones.

* La'al Ratty, water vole stationmaster in summer hols

Location	**Admission**
On the A595 Whitehaven to Barrow road	*All-day return ticket*
	Adult £8.60, Child £4.30
Opening	**Contact**
Daily mid Mar–early Nov 9am–5pm, winter open weekends, Feb half-term & Christmas–New Year Please phone for details	Ravenglass CA18 1SW
	t 01229 717171
	e rer@netcomuk.co.uk

690 Seascale

Sellafield Visitor Centre

2 hrs+   All year

Ten zones outline what the nuclear industry is all about. There are hands–on interactive scientific experiments, shows and displays. For a closer look, take a tour of the Sellafield site on one of the sightseer coaches, where your host will explain the facts about the site operations in more detail and answer any questions.

Location	**Admission**
11 miles S of Whitehaven on the A595	Free
Opening	**Contact**
Daily; Apr–Oct 10am–6pm Nov–Mar 10am–4pm	Sellafield, Seascale CA20 1PG
	t 01946 727027
	w sparkingreaction.info

691 Sizergh

Sizergh Castle & Garden

2 hrs+   Easter–Oct

This small medieval castle includes a C14 tower and oak-panelled Elizabethan interiors. There are gardens, woodland, pasture and a rock garden with waterfalls and pools to explore.

* Identify butterflies in the ancient woods
* Try Trusty's Treasure Trail in the garden

Location	**Admission**
Signs from the A590, 3½ miles S of Kendal	*House* Adult £5.50, Child £3
	Garden Adult £3, Child £1.50
Opening	**Contact**
House Easter–Oct Sun–Thu 1.30pm–5.30pm	Sizergh, Nr Kendal LA8 8AE
Garden Easter–Oct Sun–Thu 12.15pm–5.30pm	t 01539 560070
	e ntrust@sizerghcastle.fsnet.co.uk

692 Ulverston

Bardsea Country Park

 2 hrs+   All year

A beautiful coastal country park with lovely sea views over Morecambe Bay. The large woodland area is ideal for walking. Seawood, a Site of Special Scientific Interest, is located next to the park and is owned by the Woodland Trust.

Location
Take the A5087 Ulverston–Barrow road

Opening
Daily

Admission
Free

Contact
Bardsea,
Ulverston LA12 9QL

693 Ulverston

National Trust Fell Foot Park

 4 hrs+   All year

This 18-acre restored Victorian park provides bathing, fishing and boating on Lake Windermere.

* Children's quiz & trail
* Hands-on family activities

Location
At the extreme S end of Lake Windermere, on the E shore, entrance from A592

Opening
Park Daily 9am–7pm or dusk if earlier
Shop & tea room Daily Easter–Oct 11am–5pm

Admission
Free, donations welcome

Contact
Newby Bridge,
Ulverston LA12 8NN

t 01539 531273
w nationaltrust.org.uk
e fellfootpark@ntrust.org.uk

694 Ulverston

Ulverston Heritage Centre

 1 hr   All year

An old spice warehouse that contains historical artefacts from Ulverston and reconstructions of old Ulverston shops and houses.

* Guided tours available

Location
The centre is clearly signed in Ulverston city centre

Opening
Mon–Sat 9.30am–4.30pm

Admission
Please phone for details

Contact
Hanover House, Victoria Road,
Ulverston LA12 0BY

t 01229 582491
e heritage@tower-house.demon.co.uk

695 Ulverston

Windermere Lake Cruises

 1 hr+   All year

Steamers and launches sail daily throughout the year from Ambleside, Bowness and Lakeside with connections for the Lake District Visitor Centre (Brockdale), the World of Beatrix Potter, the Aquarium of the Lakes and the Lakeside & Haverthwaite Railway.

* Cumbria Large Visitor Attraction of the Year 2003
* Rowing boats available

Location
Take junction 36 off the M6. Follow the brown tourist signs along the A590 to Lakeside or the A591 to Windermere for Bowness & Ambleside

Opening
Daily; summer open during daylight hours; winter 9.45am–4.30pm

Admission
Adult from £5, Child from £2.50

Contact
Lakeside, Newby Bridge,
Ulverston LA12 8AS

t 01539 531188
w windermere-lakecruises.co.uk
e mail@windermere-lakecruises.co.uk

696 Underskiddaw

Mirehouse, Keswick

2½ hrs | Feb–Oct

A comparatively small historic house, given to the Spedding family in 1802. Standing between mountains and lake, it is a living home with a tradition of giving a relaxed welcome. It has an interesting history and links with many famous writers.

* Best Property for Families in UK
* NPI Heritage Award 1999

WC | 🏕 | 🍴 | ♿

Location
On the A591, 3 miles N of Keswick

Opening
House Apr–Oct Sun & Wed.
Also open Fri in Aug
Grounds & tearoom Daily

Admission
Please phone for details

Contact
Underskiddaw,
Keswick CA12 4QE

t 01768 772287
w mirehouse.com
e info@mirehouse.com

697 Whitehaven

The Beacon

1½ hrs+ | All year

Discover the fascinating history of Whitehaven, West Cumbria's Georgian port. Situated on the harbourside, audio-visual, graphic and interactive presentations tell the story of the town's maritime, social and industrial heritage.

*Quality Assured Visitor Attraction

WC | 🏕 | 🍴 | ♿

Location
Follow the A595 to Whitehaven & then the town centre signs to S harbour

Opening
Tue–Sun 10am–5.30pm (4.30pm closing in winter)
please phone for details

Admission
Adult £4.40, Child £2.90, Concs £3.60

Contact
West Strand,
Whitehaven CA28 7LY

t 01946 592302
w copelandbc.gov.uk

698 Windermere

Lakeland Equestrian

1 hr+ | All year

This centre offers horse riding for all ages and abilities including short, hill, farm, pub and trail rides. All are undertaken with qualified staff and on suitable mounts, ranging from ex-competition horses to native breeds.

* Treks from 1 hour to 4 days
* Packed lunches available

 WC

Location
On the A592, 2½ miles from Windermere

Opening
Daily 10am–4pm, booking essential

Admission
From £13, please phone for details

Contact
Limefitt Park,
Trout Beck,
Windermere LA23 1PD

t 015394 31999
w lakelandequestrian.co.uk

699 Accrington

Oswaldtwistle Mills Shopping Village

2½ hrs   All year

A family attraction, set within a working mill and its grounds, Oswaldtwistle Mills offers an interesting range of facilities and shopping.

* Sweet factory
* Wendy House Village

Location
Accessible from the M65 (junction 7), the M62, A58 & the M6 junction 29

Opening
Daily; Mon–Sat 9.30am–5.30pm (8pm closing Thu) & Sun 11am–5pm; 11 Nov–19 Dec open Mon–Thu until 10pm

Admission
Free
Stockley Sweets Adult £1, Child 50p

Contact
Moscow Mill, Colliers Street, Oswaldtwistle, Accrington BB5 3DE

t 01254 871025
w o-mills.co.uk

700 Blackpool

Blackpool Illuminations

2hrs   Sep–Nov

Britain's biggest and brightest light show shines bright for 66 nights from September to November each year. It stretches for six miles and lights up the sky for miles around. Displays include alien space ships, pirates, jelly monsters and Tiffany lamps.

* View the giant clifftop tableaux
* 1879 electric arc lamps bathe promenade in light

Location
Central Promenade

Opening
2 Sep–6 Nov

Admission
Free

Contact
Blackpool Tourism, 1 Clifton Street, Blackpool FY1 1LY

t 01253 478222
w blackpooltourism.com
e tourism@blackpool.gov.uk

701 Blackpool

The Blackpool Piers

½ day+   Mar–Nov

Each pier has its own unique attractions and atmosphere. North Pier provides an atmosphere of romantic nostalgia with an original Venetian carousel ride, South Pier is home to heart-stopping daredevil rides, while Central Pier offers gentler fairground rides and games.

* Children's entertainer (all piers)
* Fairground rides (South & Central Pier)

Location
North Pier is located on the North Promenade; South Pier on the South Promenade & Central Pier on Central Promenade

Opening
Easter–Nov open daily from 10am

Admission
Free, except North Pier (30p toll)
Charge for individual rides

Contact
c/o Leisure Parks Ltd
97 Church Street, Blackpool FY1 1HU

t 01253 629600
w blackpoollive.com

702 Blackpool

Blackpool Pleasure Beach

4 hrs+   Mar–Nov

The entertainment adventure capital, with more rollercoasters than any other amusement park, including the Pepsi Max Big One and the new Spin Doctor. There's also the Beaver Creek Theme Park for younger children and award-winning shows.

* New ride in 2004 called Bling

Location
From the M6 (junction 32) follow the brown tourist signs to Blackpool S Shore, then to the Pleasure Beach

Opening
Mar–Nov, please phone for details

Admission
A range of tickets are available, please phone for details

Contact
Ocean Boulevard,
Blackpool FY4 1EZ

t 0870 444 5566
w blackpoolpleasurebeach.com

703 Blackpool

Blackpool Sea Life Centre

2 hrs   All year

The Sea Life Centre houses one of Europe's largest marine collections. It has more than 40 fascinating displays, allowing exciting close-up encounters with marine life, including sharks.

Location	Contact
On Blackpool promenade; leave the M55 at junction 4	The Promenade, Blackpool FY1 5AA
Opening	t 01253 622445
Daily 10am–8pm	w sealife.co.uk 1001daysout.com
Admission	e slcblackpool@leisureparks.com
Adult £7.95, Child £5, Concs £6	

704 Blackpool

Blackpool Tower & Circus

2–8 hrs   Apr–Nov

Visit Blackpool's answer to the Eiffel Tower to enjoy the aquarium, dinosaur ride, indoor adventure play area, plus family entertainment at the Hornpipe Gallery and the award-winning circus.

* Take the Walk of Faith 380 ft above the promenade

Location	Contact
Take the M55 to Blackpool	Promenade Blackpool FY1 4BJ
Opening	t 01253 622242
Daily; Easter–Nov, please phone or check website for details	w blackpooltower.co.uk
Admission	
Please phone for details	

705 Blackpool

Sandcastle Tropical Waterworld

½ day   All year

A water-based leisure complex with four pools, it offers a variety of thrills including water slides, a children's pool, a wave pool, white-knuckle water chutes and a new interactive water play area.

* Quality Assured Visitor Attraction
* Adventure playground

Location	Contact
On South Promenade	South Promenade, Blackpool FY4 1BB
Opening	t 01253 343602
Please phone for details	w sandcastle-waterworld.co.uk
Admission	
Please phone for details	

706   Blackpool

Wyreside Ecology Centre

2 hrs   All year

A visitor centre set in the heart of the Wyre Estuary Country Park, the Wyreside Ecology Centre provides an excellent base for nature trails and riverside walks.

* Riverside path suitable for blind visitors
* Cycles available for hire for disabled visitors

Location
Follow the M55, then the A585 & B5268

Opening
Daily; Nov–Apr 11am–3pm
Apr–Nov 10.30am–4.30pm

Admission
Free

Contact
Wyre Estuary Country Park, River Road, Thornton, Blackpool FY5 5LR

t 01253 857890
w wyrebc.gov.uk
e rreeves@wyrebc.gov.uk

707   Bolton

Bolton Museum, Art Gallery & Aquarium

2 hrs   All year

The museum contains permanent displays of Egyptology, natural and local history, geology, archaeology, art and sculpture and has an exciting programme of changing exhibitions. Children particularly enjoy the aquarium.

Location
Accessible from the A666; in the centre of Bolton, behind the Town Hall

Opening
Mon–Sat 10am–5pm;
closed Bank hols Mon & Christmas

Admission
Free

Contact
Le Mans Crescent, Bolton BL1 1SE

t 01204 332211
w boltonmuseums.org.uk
e museum@bolton.gov.uk

708   Bury

Burrs Activity Centre

1 hr+   All year

Children will have fun at this outdoor activity centre, where they can try canoeing, climbing, orienteering, hiking, kayaking and abseiling.

Location
Leave the M66 at junction 2, follow the A58 to Bolton & then take the B6214

Opening
Daily

Admission
Free, charges for activities

Contact
Woodhill Road, Bury BL8 1DA

t 0161 764 9649
w activity-centre.freeserve.co.uk/
e burrs@activity-centre.freeserve.co.uk

709   Bury

East Lancashire Railway

3 hrs+   All year

This mainly steam-hauled service runs between Bury, Ramsbottom, Rawenstall and Hayward every weekend. Visitors can break their journey at any station to visit the shops in quaint Ramsbottom and stalls at Bury Market.

Location
In the centre of Bury. Accessible from the A56, A58 & M66

Opening
Sat & Sun 9am–5pm;
also Apr–Sep Wed–Fri 10am–4.30pm

Admission
Adult £9.50, Child £6.50, Concs £6.50

Contact
Bolton Street Station, Bury BL9 0EY

t 0161 764 7790
w east-lancs-rly.co.uk
e admin@east-lancs-rly.co.uk

710 Carnforth

Docker Park Farm Visitor Centre

4 hrs+   All year

Get up close to the animals at this working livestock farm with horses, pigs, sheep, goats and poultry. Visitors can hold some of the animals, including rabbits and chickens, and enjoy pony trekking and lamb bottle-feeding.

* Collect eggs & feed poultry
* Tractor rides during holidays

Location
Exit the M6 at junction 35 onto the B6254

Opening
Daily; Mar–Oct 10.30am–5pm
Nov–Feb weekends only
10.30am–4pm

Admission
Adult £4.50, Child £3.50

Contact
Arkholme,
Carnforth LA6 1AR

t 01524 221331
w dockerparkfarm.co.uk

---

711 Chorley

Camelot Theme Park

4 hrs+   Apr–Oct

Fun for all the family, with breathtaking rides and nail-biting medieval jousting tournaments. The Whirlwind, a spinning roller-coaster, will keep even the most courageous thrill-seekers happy.

* Lancashire's Family Attraction of the Year 2002
* Water slides

Location
Leave the M6 at junction 27/28
& the M61 at junction 8

Opening
Daily; 3 Apr–31 Oct 10am–5pm
Please phone for details

Admission
Adult £14, Child £14, Concs £10

Contact
Park Hall Road, Charnock Richard,
Chorley PR7 5LP

t 01257 452100
w camelotthemepark.co.uk
e kingarthur@camelotthemepark.co.uk

---

712 Colne

British in India Museum

2 hrs   All year

An interesting museum full of artefacts relating to the British in India. On display are Indian regimental ties, paintings, photographs of military and civilian subjects, model soldiers, medals, coins, toys and examples of Indian dress.

Location
Take the A56/A6068 from
Burnley–Keighley

Opening
Wed & Sat 2pm–5pm;
closed 20 Dec–7 Jan

Admission
Adult £3, Child 50p

Contact
Newtown Street,
Colne BB8 0JJ

t 01282 613129

713 Clitheroe

Clitheroe Castle Museum

1 hr   All year

Clitheroe Castle Museum brings to life the history and geology of the Ribble Valley. It has an Edwardian kitchen, cloggers shop and C18 mine.

* Special events
* Set in 16 acres of grounds

Location
Off the A59 Preston–Skipton bypass. Follow the brown tourist signs. The museum is situated alongside the castle keep

Opening
Daily 11am–5pm (4.30pm closing in winter); please phone for details

Admission
Adult £1.65, Child 25p, Senior 80p

Contact
Castle Hill, Castle Gate, Clitheroe BB7 1BA

t 01200 424635
w ribblevalley.gov.uk
e museum@ribblevalley.gov.uk

714 Fleetwood

Farmer Parr's Animal World

3½ hrs   All year

More than 20 acres of farmland with a collection of over 200 farm animals and rare breeds, including poultry and pets. There are outdoor and indoor areas.

* Autism Initiatives pottery shop
* Pony & tractor rides

Location
Follow the M55 to Fleetwood & then take the A585 (Fleetwood Road & Amounderness Way). Opposite Cala Gran Caravan Park

Opening
Daily 10am–5pm

Admission
Adult £3.50, Child £2.50

Contact
Wyrefield Farm, Rossall Lane, Fleetwood FY7 8JP

t 01253 874389/770484
w farmerparrs.com

715 Haigh

Haigh Country Park

2 hrs+   All year

Explore and enjoy this country park which offers woodland trails and a wide variety of events and activities including archery, rock climbing and abseiling.

* Free Sunday afternoon entertainment
* Children's craft workshops

Location
From the M6 take the A49 to Standish, then the B5239 to Haigh

Opening
Daily

Admission
Charge per activity, car park £1 per day

Contact
Haigh Country Park, Haigh, Wigan WN2 1PE

t 01942 832895
w haighhall.net
e hhgen@wiganmbc.co.uk

716 Lancaster

Leighton Hall

2 hrs   May–Sep

This interesting historical building has large grounds with a maze, woodland walk and a collection of birds of prey.

*Guided tours compulsory

Location
Leave the M6 at junction 35 & follow the signs on the A6

Opening
May–Sep Sun, Tue–Fri & Bank Hol Mons from 2pm

Admission
Adult £5, Child £3.50

Contact
Lancaster LA5 9ST

t 01524 734474
e info@leightonhall.co.uk

717 Lancaster

Williamson Park & Butterfly House

1½ hrs   All year

Take the family to visit the Ashton Memorial, a Victorian folly, a conservation garden and a tropical butterfly house.

* Mini beast centre
* Small mammal enclosure

Location
Follow the Lancaster signs from the A6/M6 (junction 33 or 34). Follow the brown tourist signs from the city

Opening
Daily; Apr–Sep 10am–5pm
Oct–Mar 10am–4pm

Admission
Adult £3.50, Child £2, Concs £3

Contact
Williamson Park, Quernmore Road, Lancaster LA1 1UX

t 01524 33318
w williamsonpark.com

718 Leyland

Worden Arts & Crafts Centre

2 hrs+   Summer

Set in 157 acres of parkland, this arts and crafts centre has a fully-equipped theatre, six craft workshops and an exhibition display room.

* Maze
* Garden for the blind

Location
Leave the M6 at junction 28 & follow the signs for Worden Arts Centre

Opening
Daily; summer 8.30am–8.30pm

Admission
Free

Contact
Worden Park,
Worden Lane,
Leyland PR25 1DJ

t 01772 455908
w worden-arts.co.uk

719 Littleborough

Hollingworth Lake Country Park

4 hrs+   All year

A country park consisting of lake and surrounding countryside, with boating, nature reserve, trails, events, guided walks, visitor centre, play areas and picnic sites.

Location
Leave the M62 at junction 21 & take the B6225; follow the brown tourist signs

Opening
Daily Oct–Apr 11am–4pm,
Apr–Sep 10.30am–6am

Admission
Free

Contact
Rakewood Road,
Littleborough OL15 0AQ

t 01706 373421
w rochdale.gov.uk

720 Leigh

Pennington Flash Country Park

4 hrs+   All year

Nearly 500 acres of Country Park, centred on a 172 acres lake. World-renowned as a bird-watcher's paradise, this is a popular beauty spot, lake and nature reserve. Over 230 bird species recorded on site.

* Fishing & sailing
* 7 viewing hides

Location
Take the A572 from Leigh town centre & the A580 from Manchester & Liverpool

Opening
Daily; ranger on site dawn–dusk

Admission
Free, car park charge

Contact
Helens Road,
Leigh WN7 3PA

t 01942 605253

721 Nelson

Pendle Heritage Centre

2 hrs+   All year

Situated in the beautiful Pendle landscape, the Heritage Centre is the perfect starting point for a variety of local walks. Stroll through the 18th Century Walled Garden or take the Woodland Walk, stopping at the Medieval Cruck Barn to visit the farmyard animals.

* Cruck-frame barn
* Farm animals

Location
Leave the M65 at junction 13 & take the A682 onto the B6247

Opening
Daily 10am–5pm;

Admission
Please phone for details

Contact
Park Hill, Barrowford,
Nelson BB9 6JQ

t 01282 661701
e tic@htnw.co.uk

722 Ormskirk

Cedar Farm Galleries

½ day   All year

There are contemporary crafts, farm animals and a funky playground at these galleries, which include nine working craft retail studios, where makers can be seen at work and commissions are taken.

* New art and Yoga workshops
* 'Pots of fun' pottery painting studio

Location
From the M6 (junction 27), follow the brown tourist signs. At the crossroads in Mawdesley Village turn into Gorsey Lane & then into Back Lane

Opening
Tue–Sun & Bank Hol Mons 10am–5pm

Admission
Free

Contact
Back Lane,
Mawdesley,
Ormskirk L40 3SY

t 01704 822616
w cedarfarm.net

723 Preston

Beacon Fell Country Park

2 hrs+   All year

Spend a relaxing few hours walking in this country park with 271 acres of extensive conifer woods and moorland. It is situated in the Forest of Bowland, an area of outstanding natural beauty.

* Events held throughout the year

Location
Signed from the A6 at Broughton

Opening
Daily Easter–Sep;
Oct–Easter weekends & Wed
Please phone for details of times

Admission
Free

Contact
Goosnargh,
Preston PR3 2NL

t 01995 640557
w lancsenvironment.com
e judy.campbell-ricketts@env.lancscc.gov.uk

Leisure Lakes

4 hrs+   All year

The 30-acre lakes with sandy beaches provide the perfect base for a range of water pursuits, from windsurfing and canoeing to sailing and jetskiing. A 20 bay driving range offers professional tuition for adults and children.

* Jet-ski centre
* Mountain bike centre

Location
Off the A565, 6 miles from Southport & 10 miles from Preston

Opening
Daily 9am–7pm

Admission
£5 per car or Adult £2.50, Child £2
Additional charges for some activities

Contact
Mere Brow, Tarleton, Preston PR4 6JX

t 01772 813446
e gab@leisurelakes.co.uk

West Lancashire Light Railway

1 hr+   All year

Ride on a narrow-gauge steam railway and visit a historic collection of locomotives and rolling stock at this light-railway centre.

Location
Leave M6 at junction 31 & head for Preston; take the A59 to Tarleton, then the unclassified road to Hesketh Bank

Opening
Daily; Apr–Oct & Bank Hols Mon 12pm–5.30pm;
Nov–Mar Sun 12.30pm–5pm;
Steam trains operate Apr–Oct only

Admission
Adult £2, Child £1.25

Contact
Station Road, Hesketh Bank Preston PR4 6SP

t 01772 815881
w westlancs.org
e publicity@westlancs.org

Ski Rossendale

1 hr+   All year

Ski Rossendale is the North's premier ski centre. Open all year round, the centre is ideal for beginners and expert skiers alike. Set amid trees and parkland, Ski Rossendale commands a superb view over the Rossendale Valley.

* Intermediate slope is 80 yards
* Novices please ring before visiting

Location
Follow the M66 to Rawtenstall. The centre is located on the town's outskirts

Opening
Daily; Mon–Fri 10am–9.30pm, weekends 9am–4.30pm

Admission
Adult £10.75, Child £6.50

Contact
Haslingden Old Road, Rawtenstall BB4 8RR

t 01706 226457
w ski-rossendale.co.uk
e info@ski-rossendale.co.uk

727 Rochdale

Ellenroad Engine House

2 hrs   Feb–Dec

A fascinating engine house which contains the world's largest working steam cotton-mill engine, together with its original steam-raising plant.

* Guided tours

Location
Leave the M62 at junction 21

Opening
Feb–Dec open 1st Sun of each month 12pm–4pm

Admission
Adult £2.50, Child £1.50, Concs £1.50

Contact
Elizabethan Way, Milnrow
Rochdale OL16 4LG
t 01706 881952
w ellenroad.org.uk
e ellenroad@aol.com

728 Rochdale

Whitworth Water Ski & Recreation Centre

4 hrs+   Apr–Oct

The aim of the centre, run in conjunction with an able-bodied ski club, is to teach people of all disabilities how to water-ski and to help them integrate with able-bodied members. Full instruction and equipment are provided.

* Banana & Ringo rides
* Bikes for disabled visitors

Location
Take the A671 from Rochdale

Opening
Daily; Apr–Oct 9.30am–dusk

Admission
Adults £13 Child £8.50, Concs £8.50
all other activities priced individually

Contact
Cowm Reservoir, Tong Lane
Whitworth,
Rochdale OL12 8BE
t 01706 852534
w whitworth-waterski.co.uk
e andynflo@whitworthwaterski.co.uk

729 Rufford

Rufford Old Hall

2 hrs+   Apr–Oct

Rufford is one of Lancashire's finest C16 buildings, famed for its spectacular Great Hall, where it is believed Shakespeare once performed. There's lots to entertain children here, with quizzes and trails through the house and garden.

Location
7 miles north of Ormskirk, in the village of Rufford, on the E side of the A59

Opening
House Apr–Oct Sat–Wed 1pm–5pm
Garden Apr–Oct Sat–Wed 11am–5.30pm

Admission
Adult £4.30, Child £2

Contact
Rufford,
Nr Ormskirk L40 1SG
t 01704 821254
w nationaltrust.org.uk
e ruffordoldhall@nationaltrust.org.uk

730 Wigan

Rumble Tumble

1½ hrs   All year

Children can have fun and be challenged in this giant indoor adventure zone, which includes a supervised free-fall slide (for children over five only).

Location
Off the A49, in Wallgate

Opening
Daily 10am–7pm;

Admission
Before 3pm: under-4s £1.85. After 3pm Child £3. Weekends & holidays Child £3.50 for 1½ hrs

Contact
10 Tower Enterprise Park,
Great George Street,
Wigan WN3 4DP
t 01942 494922

731 Manchester

Adventures of Dreamieland

¼ hr+ All year

Children will enjoy this spooky interactive ride based on dreams. Travel through nine dream scenes on a dreamie car and zap the Dream Guzzlers!

* Children's activity centre
* Arts & crafts sessions

Location
At junctions 9 & 10 off the M60

Opening
Daily; Mon–Fri 10am–9pm, Sat 10am–8pm & Sun 12pm–6pm (Dec 11am–6pm)

Admission
Member £2, Non-member £3

Contact
203 The Dome,
The Trafford Centre,
Manchester M17 8DF
t 01260 223137
w www.dreamieland.com
e info@dreamieland.com

732 Manchester

Airport Tour Centre

2 hrs+ All year

Children interested in aeroplanes will love this trip to the airport. Trained guides explain in detail the inner workings of the airport's various departments. Pre-booking is essential.

Location
Leave the M56 at junction 5

Opening
Daily 9am–9pm

Admission
Adult £5, Child £4, Concs £5

Contact
Terminal 1,
Manchester Airport,
Manchester M90 1QX
t 0161 489 2442
w www.webmaster.tasmanchester.com
e tourcentre@tasmanchester.com

733 Manchester

Castlefield Urban Heritage Park & Visitor Centre

1 hr+ All year

For a great family day out, Castlefield has it all – numerous museums, the remains of the Roman fort of Mamucium, a canal, pleasant walks, boat trips and frequent events in the outdoor arena. Perfect for picnics on a fine day.

* Britain's first urban heritage park

Location
Manchester city centre, follow signs for the Museum of Science & Industry

Opening
Park Daily
Centre Daily; Mon–Fri 10am–4pm; Sat, Sun & Bank Hols 12noon–4pm

Admission
Free

Contact
Castlefield, Manchester
w manchester.gov.uk

734 Manchester

Manchester Art Gallery

½ day Mar–Sep

Discover art and design in Manchester. The gallery includes a lively new space with hands-on activities for families with children aged 5–12 years.

* See paintings 'come alive'
* Morph your face into a mythical creature

Location
City centre. The nearest Metrolink stations are St Peter's Square & Mosley Street

Opening
Tue–Sun 10am–5pm; open Bank Hols Mon; closed Good Fri & Christmas

Admission
Free

Contact
Mosley Street,
Manchester M2 3JL
t 0161 235 8888

Manchester Museum

1 hr   All year

The museum's collections include fossils, minerals, natural history specimens, archaeology, a unique collection from Ancient Egypt, living reptiles and amphibians in the award-winning vivarium, and an interactive exhibition on the human body.

* Ethnology collections from South America
* Collections of fossils & minerals

Location
In Oxford Road to the S of the city centre

Opening
Daily; Mon–Sat 10am–5pm
Sun & Bank Hols 11am–4pm

Admission
Free, exhibitions may charge

Contact
The University of Manchester,
Oxford Road,
Manchester M13 9PL

t 0161 275 2634
w museum.man.ac.uk
e michael.rooney@man.ac.uk

Museum of Science & Industry

3 hrs+   All year

The museum comprises 5 buildings over a 7½ acre site and tells the story of the history, science and industry of Manchester, the world's first industrial city.

* Steam engines & locomotives
* Morphis simulator rides

Location
Near the city centre

Opening
Daily 10am–5pm;

Admission
Free (permanent galleries)
Under-16s must be accompanied

Contact

Liverpool Road
Castlefield
Manchester M3 4FP

t 0161 832 2244
e marketing@msim.org.uk

Museum of Transport

2 hrs   All year

Housed in a former bus depot, this wonderfully quirky museum is packed with vintage vehicles, including buses, fire engines and lorries, some 100 years old. There are horse-drawn vehicles right through to the earliest models of the Metrolink trams.

* The biggest collection of vintage buses in the UK

Location
1 mile N of city centre at the N end of Boyle Street, next to Queen's Road bus garage

Opening
Wed, Sat, Sun & Bank Hols (except Christmas & New Year)
Mar–Oct 10am–5pm;
Nov–Feb 10am–4pm

Admission
Adult £3, Child £1.75, Concs £1.75

Contact
Boyle Street, Cheetham,
Manchester M8 8UW

t 0161 205 2122
w www.gmts.co.uk
e email@gmts.co.uk

738 Manchester

Old Trafford Museum & Tour

2 hrs   All year

See the Manchester United trophy room, kits through the ages, and memorabilia of the 'greats', from Charlton to Cantona, Best to Beckham. A stadium tour takes you to the players' tunnel, the dressing room, the dugout and more.

Location
From Chester Road (A56), turn into Sir Matt Busby Way; or use Old Trafford Metrolink station

Opening
Daily 9.30am–5pm (museum closes 30 mins before kick-off). Please phone for details of times and to book tours

Admission
Museum Adult £5.50, Child £3.75, Concs £3.75

Contact
Sir Matt Busby Way, Old Trafford, Manchester M16 0RA

t 0870 442 1994
w www.manutd.com

739 Manchester

People's History Museum

2 hrs   All year

Discover the extraordinary story of ordinary people, with interactive exhibits looking at their lives at work, home and leisure over the last 200 years.

* From mill workers to the first professional footballers
* Housed in an Edwardian pumping station

Location
Via the A6, M602, M62, A56, follow the signs to Castlefield

Opening
Tue–Sun & Bank holidays 11am–4.30pm; closed Good Fri

Admission
Adult £1, Child free, Concs free (free to all on Fridays)

Contact
The Pump House, Bridge Street, Manchester M3 3ER

t 0161 839 6061
w www.peopleshistorymuseum.org.uk
e info@peopleshistorymuseum.org.uk

740 Manchester

Trafford Ecology Park

Trafford Ecology Park is a peaceful oasis in the middle of Trafford Park Industrial Estate. Visitors can come to the centre to see the displays, take part in the special events, or simply discover the wealth of wildlife that lives there.

Location
Take the A56 towards Old Trafford Stadium, then Trafford Park Road onto Lake Road

Opening
Mon–Fri 9am–5pm

Admission
Free

Contact
Lake Road,
Trafford Park,
Manchester M17 1TU

t 0161 873 7182
w www.groundwork.org.uk
e st@groundwork.org.uk

741 Northenden

Wythenshawe Park

 4 hrs+ · All year

This C16 hall is set in 275 acres of parkland, offering a range of leisure facilities. Beautifully maintained, it has numerous facilities and sporting attractions including several football pitches, tennis courts, bowling greens and children's play areas

* Museum, gallery & glasshouses
* Farm centre

Location
Just off the M56, 4 miles from Manchester Airport

Opening
Park Daily dawn–dusk
Please phone for opening times of other facilities

Admission
Please phone for details

Contact
Wythenshawe Road, Northenden, Manchester M23 0AB
t 0161 998 2117
e s.downey@notes.manchester.gov.uk

742 Ellesmere Port

The Boat Museum

 3 hrs · All year

This unique award winning canal museum has over 5,000 artefacts ranging from large boats to canal company buttons. It covers over 7 acres of the historic canal port. New interactive exhibition.

* Programme of events throughout the year
* World's largest collection of traditional canal craft

Location
Off M53 at Junction 9 & follow the signs

Opening
Daily; Apr–Oct 10am–5pm
Nov–Mar Sat–Weds 11am–4pm

Admission
Adult £5.50, Child £3.70, Concs £4.30

Contact
South Pier Road,
Ellesmere Port CH65 4FW
t 0151 355 5017
w boatmuseum.org.uk
e bookings@thewaterwaystrust.org

743 Salford

Ordsall Hall Museum

 2 hrs · All year

Ordsall Hall is a haunted Tudor manor house in the surroundings of inner city Salford. Visitors can enjoy the impressive Great Hall, Star Chamber and Tudor Kitchen.

* Family events
* Exhibitions programme

Location
Signed from the A57 & A5063

Opening
Mon–Fri 10am–4pm & Sun 1pm–4pm; closed Good Friday, Easter Sun, & Christmas

Admission
Free

Contact
Ordsall Lane,
Salford,
Manchester M5 3AN
t 0161 872 0251
w ordsallhall.org
e ordsall@btopenworld.com

744 Liverpool

Croxteth Hall & Country Park

 2 hrs+ · Apr–Sep

An Edwardian stately home set in 500 acres of countryside, featuring a Victorian walled garden and a visitor farm.

* Rare breeds of livestock
* Miniature railway

Location
Leave the M57 at junction 4 & take the A580 towards Liverpool

Opening
Daily; Easter–Sep 10.30am–5pm

Admission
Adult £4.20, Child £2.10, Concs £2.10

Contact
Croxteth Hall Lane,
Liverpool L12 0HB
t 0151 228 5311
w croxteth.co.uk
e croxtethcountrypark@liverpool.gov.uk

745 Liverpool

The Beatles Story

1½ hrs   All year

The award-winning Beatles Story is the ultimate tribute to Liverpool's most famous sons – John, Paul, George and Ringo. The magical history tour takes the visitor on a trip from the Cavern Club, through the years of Beatlemania and flower power to the eventual break-up of the group.

* Visitor Attraction of the Year 2002
* New exhibition on McCartney's solo years

Location
Follow the brown tourist signs from the M62 or the city centre to the Albert Docks

Opening
Daily 10am–6pm (last admission 5pm)

Admission
Adult £8.45, Child £4.95, Concs £5.45

Contact
Britannia Vaults, Albert Dock, Liverpool L3 4AA

t 0151 709 1963
w beatlesstory.com
e info@beatlesstory.com

746 Liverpool

Everton Football Club

2 hrs   All year

Discover at first hand what goes on behind the scenes at Goodison Park. Walk down the tunnel to the roar of 40,000 fans, visit the dressing room where the players get changed and see where they relax after the game.

WC

Location
3 miles N of Liverpool city centre

Opening
Daily, except on match days

Admission
Adult £8.50, Child £5, Concs £5
Pre-booking essential

Contact
Goodison Park,
Liverpool L4 4EL

t 0151 330 2277
w evertonfc.com
e boxoffice@evertonfc.com

747 Liverpool

Knowsley Safari Park

3 hrs+   All year

Enjoy a drive through Knowsley Safari Park: 500 acres of rolling countryside, where some of the world's wildest animals roam free.

Location
Leave the M62 at junction 6, the M57 at junction 2 & follow the signs

Opening
Daily; Mar–Oct 10am–4pm; Nov–Feb 10.30am–3pm

Admission
Adult £9, Child £6, Concs £6

Contact
Prescot L34 4AN

t 0151 430 9009
w knowsley.com
e safari.park@knowsley.com

748 Liverpool

Liverpool Football Club Museum & Tour Centre

4 hrs+   All year

A must for any Liverpool fan, young or old. The museum includes a display of the club's trophies and films on the history of the club. Visit the dressing room, walk down the tunnel to the sound of 45,000 cheering fans, touch the famous This is Anfield sign, and sit in the team dugout.

Location
Easily reached from the city centre, the M62, M57 & M58; well signed

Opening
Daily 10am–5pm (last admission 4pm); last admission 1 hr before kick-off on match days; no stadium tours on match days; please book tours in advance

Admission
Adult £5, Child £5, Concs £3

Contact
Anfield Road L4 0TH

t 0151 260 6677
w liverpoolfc.tv

749 Liverpool

Liverpool Planetarium

1 hr   All year

Enjoy an exciting visual experience of space in a domed auditorium at this planetarium. The support programme *Nightwatch* takes a look at the night sky.

* 40-minute performance

Location
In Liverpool city centre. Follow the signs from the M62

Opening
Tue–Fri with shows at 3.15pm, Sat & Sun at 1.15pm, 2.15pm, 3.15pm & 4.05pm

Admission
Free

Contact
William Brown Street, Liverpool L3 8EN

t 0151 478 4283
w liverpoolmuseums.org.uk

750 Liverpool

Museum of Liverpool Life

1 hr+   All year

The museum celebrates the unique character of the vibrant city of Liverpool, with galleries depicting various aspects of city life, including Mersey Culture, Making a Living, the River Mersey and City Soldiers, which tells the story of the King's Regiment.

Location
Situated at the pier head.
Follow the A565

Opening
Daily 10am–5pm (last admission 4.30pm)

Admission
Free

Contact
Albert Dock
Liverpool L3 1PZ

t 0151 478 4499
w museumofliverpoollife.org.uk
e liverlife@nmgm.org

751 Liverpool

National Wildflower Centre

2 hrs+   Apr–Sep

A family-friendly visitor attraction that promotes the creation of new places for wildflowers and their importance to the environment. There are demonstration gardens, a plant nursery and a rooftop walkway.

* Children's play area
* Wall with climbing handles

Location
Junction 5 off the M62.
Follow the brown tourist signs

Opening
Daily; Apr–Sep 10am–5pm
(last admission 4pm)

Admission
Adult £3, Concs £1.50

Contact
Court Hey Park, Roby Road,
Liverpool L16 3NA

t 0151 737 1819
w nwc.org.uk
e info@nwc.org.uk

752 Liverpool

Speke Hall, Gardens & Woodland

 3 hrs+   Apr–Nov

One of the most famous half-timbered houses in the country, dating from 1530. A fully equipped Victorian kitchen and servants' hall enable visitors to see behind the scenes. The nearby Home Farm is a restored model Victorian farm building with orchard.

WC

Location
On the N bank of the Mersey, 1 mile off the A561 on the W side of Liverpool Airport. Follow airport signs from M62 (junction 6) & M56 (junction 12); follow brown tourist signs from A5300

Opening
House Easter–Oct Wed–Sun 1pm–5.30pm; Nov Sat & Sun 11am–4.30pm.

Garden **Daily; Easter–Nov** 11am–5.30pm (4.30pm closing in Nov)

Admission
Adult £5.50, Child £3.50

Contact
The Walk, Liverpool L24 1XD
t 0151 427 7231
w spekehall.org.uk
e spekehall@nationaltrust.org.uk

753 Liverpool

Tate Liverpool

 1 hr+   All year

Take the children for a cultural day out at Tate Liverpool, the home of the National Collection of modern art in the North of England. Part of the historic Albert Dock, it has four floors of art, free daily talks, a shop and café.

WC

Location
In Liverpool city centre

Opening
Daily; Tue–Sun & Bank Hol Mons 10am–5.15pm; closed Good Fri & Christmas

Admission
Admission to Tate collection **Free**

Charges for special exhibitions
Adult £4, Child free, Concs £3

Contact
Albert Dock Liverpool,
Merseyside L3 4BB
t 0151 7027400
w www.tate.org.uk/liverpool/
e liverpoolinfo@tate.org.uk

754 Liverpool

Williamson Tunnels

45 mins   All year

When you enter Williamson Tunnels, you enter a strange underground kingdom which has lain beneath the city of Liverpool since the early 1800s. Visitors can see and touch the brick and sandstone workings of this key section of the tunnels, while enjoying entertaining commentary from an expert guide.

Location
From M62 into Liverpool look for the brown tourist signs.

Opening
Summer 10am–5pm Tue–Sun, winter open Thu–Sun 10am–4pm, Tue & Wed open by arrangement; Oct & Feb half-terms open daily

Admission
Adult £3.50, Child £2, Concs £3

Contact
The Old Stableyard, Smithdown Lane Liverpool L7 3EE

t 0151 709 6868
w willliamsontunnels.co.uk
e enquiries@willliamsontunnels.co.uk

755 Liverpool

Yellow Duckmarine

1 hr   All year

This unique amphibious city tour takes you through the historic city, docks and waterfront. On dry land, visit the Pier Head, St George's Hall, both cathedrals, Chinatown and the Philharmonic Hall, before you 'splash down' into the Salthouse Dock.

Location
Follow the brown tourist signs from the M62 or the city centre to the Albert Docks

Opening
Daily Mid Feb–Christmas from 11am–4pm

Admission
Adult £9.95, Child £7.95, Concs £8.95

Contact
32 Anchor Courtyard, Britannia Pavilion, Albert Dock, Liverpool L3 4AS

t 0151 708 7799
w theyellowduckmarine.co.uk

756 Southport

Formby

2hrs   All year

This nature reserve is home to one of Britain's last thriving colonies of red squirrels. These squirrels can be seen in the pine trees and the shoreline attracts waders such as oystercatchers and sanderlings. As well as the beautiful beach there are miles of walks across the sand dunes.

Location
15 miles N of Liverpool, 2 miles W of Formby, 2 miles off A565 & 6 miles S of Southport

Opening
Daily dawn to dusk

Admission
Free, car park £3.10

Contact
Blundell Avenue, Formby L37 1PH

t 01704 878 591
w nationaltrust.org.uk
e formby@nationaltrust.org.uk

757 Southport

Model Railway Village

2 hrs   Apr–Sep

Set within sheltered gardens, this beautiful miniature village has more than 200 1:18 scale models including watermills, churches, shops and houses. There is also a garden gauge railway.

Location
From M6 (junction 26 N or junction 31 S). Situated opposite the Royal Clifton Hotel, next to the marine lake footbridge

Opening
Daily; Easter–end Sep 11am–5pm 6pm closing in Jul & Aug (last admission 1 hr before closing)

Admission
Adult £3.50, Child £2.50, Concs £2

Contact
Lower Promenade, Kings Gardens, Southport PR8 1RB

t 01704 214266
w southportmodelrailwayvillage.co.uk

758 St Helens

World of Glass

2 hrs   All year

Take a journey of discovery into one of the most common substances on earth. See live demonstrations of glass-blowing by resident artists and wander through a maze of tunnels which are the remains of the oldest glass-making tank furnace in the world.

* Underground maze of tunnels to explore
* Fun zone with distorting mirrors & kaleidoscopes

Location
Leave the M62 at junction 7 & the M6 at junction 24, then head into the town centre

Opening
Tue–Sun & Bank Hols 10am–5pm

Admission
Adult £5.30, Child £3.80, Concs £3.80

Contact
Chalon Way, St Helens WA10 1BX

t 08700 114466
w worldofglass.com
e info@worldofglass.com

759 Wallasey

Mersey Ferries River Explorer Cruise

1 hr+   All year

This cruise along the Mersey takes 50 minutes and has a recorded commentary. A stop-off at the Wirral Terminal allows for a visit to an aquarium, children's play area, shop and café.

* Pirate-themed children's play area at Seacombe
* Aquarium at Seacombe

Location
Pier Head Liverpool is signed from Albert Dock. Follow the signs on the M53 for Seacombe & Woodside-on-Wirral

Opening
Daily: Mon–Fri 10am–3pm,
Sat, Sun & Bank Hols 10am–6pm

Admission
Adult £4.65, Child £2.60, Concs £3.40

Contact
Victoria Place, Seacombe,
Wallasey CH44 6QY

t 0151 330 1444
w merseyferries.co.uk
e info@merseyferries.co.uk

760 Wirral

Historic Warships at Birkenhead

2 hrs+   All year

Visitors to HMS *Plymouth* will experience what life is like on the high seas. On *Onyx* visitors can imagine shadowing a target vessel while looking through the periscope. Guided tours available.

Location
Follow the signs from the M53

Opening
Daily; Apr–Aug 10am–5pm
Sep–Mar 10am–4pm
5 Jan–17 Feb open Mon–Fri only

Admission
Adult £5.50, Child £3.50, Concs £4.50

Contact
Dock Road, Birkenhead,
Wirral CH41 1DJ

t 0151 650 1573
w warships.freeserve.co.uk
e manager@warships.freeserve.co.uk

North East

Durham Northumberland Tyne & Wear

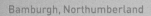

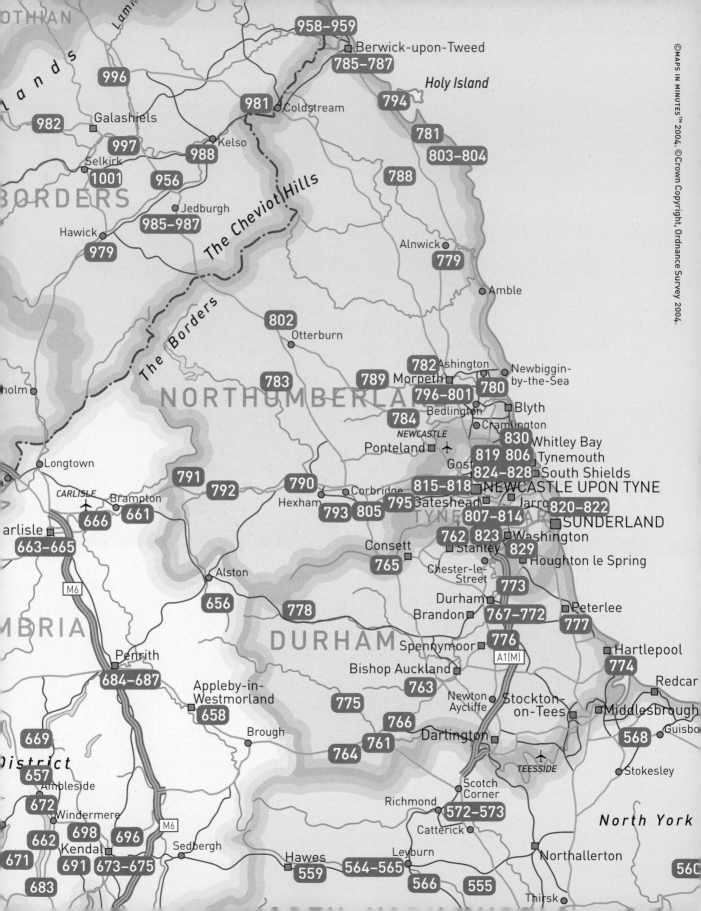

OTHIAN

Lammer...

958–959
785–787 Berwick-upon-Tweed

Holy Island

996

794

982 Galashiels

981 Coldstream

997

781

988 Kelso

803–804

1001

956

Selkirk

788

The Cheviot Hills

Jedburgh

985–987

Hawick

Alnwick

979

779

Amble

The Borders

802

Otterburn

NORTHUMBERLAND

783

782 Ashington

Newbiggin-
by-the-Sea

789 Morpeth

780

holm

796–801

Blyth

784

Bedlington

Cramlington

NEWCASTLE

830 Whitley Bay

Ponteland

819 **806** Tynemouth

Gos...

824–828 South Shields

Longtown

815–818 NEWCASTLE UPON TYNE

CARLISLE

791

792

790

Corbridge

795 Gateshead

820–822 Jarro...

Brampton

Hexham

793 **805**

807–814 SUNDERLAND

661

666

762 **823** Washington

arlisle

763–665

829

Consett

765

Stanley

Houghton le Spring

Chester-le-
Street

M6

773

Alston

Durham

767–772 Peterlee

656

778

Brandon

777

MBRIA

DURHAM

Spennymoor

776 Hartlepool

A1(M)

Penrith

Bishop Auckland

774

684–687

763

Redcar

Appleby-in-
Westmorland

775

Newton
Aycliffe

Stockton-
on-Tees

Middlesbrough

658

766

Dartington

Guisbo...

Brough

761

568

669

764

TEESSIDE

Stokesley

657

Ambleside

Scotch
Corner

672

Richmond

Windermere

572–573

North York

M6

Catterick

662

698

696

Northallerton

671

Kendal

Sedbergh

Leyburn

691 **673–675**

Hawes

564–565

683

559

566

555

Thirsk

560

761 Barnard Castle

Barnard Castle

1 hr+   All year

Towering high above the River Tees, this C12 stone castle was once one of the largest castles in northern England, the principal residence of the Baliol family, and a major power base in the many conflicts between England and Scotland.

Location
In Barnard Castle town, off Galgate on A688

Opening
Daily; Apr-Sep 10am-6pm;
Oct 10am-4pm; Nov-Mar
Wed-Sun, 10am-4pm
Closed 24-26 Dec & 1 Jan

Admission
Adult £3.00, Child £1.50, Concs £2.30

Contact
Barnard Castle

t 01833 638212
w english-heritage.org.uk

762 Beamish

Beamish, The North of England Open Air Museum

2-5 hrs   All year

Beamish is an extraordinary day out for the whole family. Touch, taste and experience the past at this living open-air museum which vividly illustrates life in the Great North in the early 1800s and early 1900s.

* Living Museum of the Year 2002
* Northumbria Family Attraction of the Year 2002

Location
Between Durham City & Newcastle upon Tyne. From A1(M) (junction 63) follow A693 towards Stanley

Opening
Daily: in summer 10am-5pm
(last admission 3pm); in winter
10am-4pm (last admission 3pm);
Closed Mon & Fri

Admission
Summer Adult £14, Child (5-16 yrs) £7,
Senior £11; *Winter* £5 per person.
Please phone to confirm 2005 prices

Contact
DH9 0RG

t 0191 370 4000
w beamish.org.uk
e museum@beamish.org.uk

763 Bishop Auckland

Hamsterley Forest

2–4 hrs   All year

Hamsterley has exhibits on forestry and wildlife in its visitor centre. There are also fascinating walks and a forest drive.

* Play park now open
* Tearoom & shop

Location
From A68 at Witton-le-Wear follow the brown tourist signs

Opening
Forest Daily: 7.30am–sunset
Visitor Centre Daily; Apr–Oct Mon–Fri 10am–4pm, Sat & Sun 11am–5pm
Please phone for details in Nov & Dec

Admission
Free. Toll for forest drive & car park charge (£2 per car)

Contact
Redford,
Bishop Auckland DL13 3NL

t 01388 488312
w forestry.gov.uk

764 Bowes

The Bowes Museum

2–3 hrs   All year

A French-style chateau housing one of Britain's finest museums. Collections in the museum include paintings, textiles, furniture and ceramics. There are beautiful gardens for children to wander through and fascinating exhibitions throughout the year.

* Investing in Children Award 2003
* Exhibits excavated from Roman forts

Location
In the historic town of Barnard Castle, just off A66

Opening
Daily; 11am–5pm;
Closed 25, 26 Dec & 1 Jan

Admission
Adult £6, Under-16s Free, Concs £5

Contact
Newgate,
Barnard Castle DL12 8NP

t 01833 690606
w bowesmuseum.org.uk
e info@bowesmuseum.org.uk

765 Consett

Mister Twisters, Consett

1 hr+   All year

This exciting indoor play and party centre includes a multi-level soft play climbing frame, inflatable temple and spooky tomb. There is a separate under-5s play village with a baby crawling pit and activity room. (Also centres in Gateshead and Hartlepool.)

* Large Visitor Attraction of the Year Finalist 2003

Location
From A1(M) take A691 to Consett; from Gateshead take A692 to Consett

Opening
Daily; Sun–Thu 9am–8pm,
Fri & Sat 9am–9pm

Admission
Under 3 £1.95, 3–4 £2.95, 5+ £3.95

Weekends and Bank Hols £2.95, £3.45, £3.95, Additional adults 50p

Contact
Unit 40, No1 Industrial Estate,
Medomsley Road,
Consett DH8 6TW

t 01207 500007
w mistertwisters.co.uk

766 Darlington

Raby Castle

3 hrs+   May–Sep

Raby Castle is a magnificent example of a medieval castle in Teesdale. A wonderful day out for the family, with stunning rooms to wonder at.

* Quality Assured Visitor Attraction
* Extensive gardens

Location
On A688, 8 miles NE of Barnard Castle

Opening
Jun–Aug Sun-Fri; May & Sep Wed & Sun only; Bank Holidays Sat–Wed
Castle 1pm–5pm
Grounds 11am–5.30pm

Admission
Adult £7, Child £3, Senior £6

Contact
Staindrop,
Darlington, DL2 3AH

t 01833 660202
w rabycastle.com

767 Durham

Diggerland

3 hrs+   Feb–Nov

Based on the world of construction machinery, this is a unique adventure park where children and adults can experience the thrill of riding and driving real JCBs and dumpers in safety.

* Educational day out with a difference
* Learn about road safety

Location
Exit M5 (junction 27), head E on A38, turn right at the roundabout onto B3181 & the park is 3 miles on the left

Opening
Feb–Nov weekends, Bank Holidays & school holidays 10am–5pm

Admission
Adult/Child £2.50, Under-2s Free, Senior £1.25

Contact
Langley Park, DA7 9TT

t 08700 344437
w diggerland.com

768 Durham

Crook Hall Gardens

1 hr   Easter–Sep

Crook Hall is a Grade 1-listed, medieval manor house. If you are scared of spooks avoid the haunted Jacobean room, home to the ghost of the White Lady. Outside you can visit the moat pool, wildflower meadow and orchard or find your way out of the maze.

* Fruit trees wreathed in rambling roses
* 'A tapestry of colourful blooms', Alan Titchmarsh

Location
Short walk from Millburngate shopping centre, opposite the Gala theatre

Opening
Easter, Bank Hols & Sun in May & Sep, Jun–Aug Sun–Fri 1pm–5pm

Admission
Adult £4, Concs £3.50

Contact
Frankland lane,
Sidegate, Durham DH1 5SZ

t 01913 848028
w crookhallgardens.co.uk
e info@crookhallgardens.co.uk

769 Durham

The DLI Museum

2 hrs+   All year

Enter the world of County Durham Light Infantry soldiers and their families. Dramatic and interactive displays and a set walk let you see for yourself what their lives were like.

* Dress up as a soldier
* Hands-on experience of exhibits

Location
1/2 mile NW of Durham city centre, off A691, near the railway station

Opening
Daily; Apr–Oct 10am–5pm; Nov–Mar 10am–4pm
Closed 25, 26 Dec

Admission
Adult £3, Concs £2 Child £1.25

Contact
Aykley Heads, Durham DH1 5TU

t 0191 384 2214
w durham.gov.uk
e dli@durham.gov.uk

770 Durham

Durham Castle

1 hr   Easter–Sep

Built by William the Conqueror in 1072 as a mighty fortress, the castle has been in constant use for over 900 years and is one of the largest Norman castles in England. It was also once a bishop's palace and today provides accommodation for the university. Entrance by guided tour only.

* World Heritage Site

Location
Durham city centre. Uphill walk or bus service 40 to Palace Green

Opening
Mid-Mar–mid Apr, Jul, Aug & Sep, daily 10am–12.30pm & 2pm–4.30pm. Other times usually Mon, Wed, Sat & Sun afternoons but phone to confirm

Admission
Adult £5, Child/ Concs £2.50

Contact
Durham DH1 3RW

t 0191 334 3800
w durhamcastle.com
e university-college.www@durham.ac.uk

771 Durham

Kascada Leisure Complex

2 hrs   All year

Situated in the heart of historic Durham, the Kascada Leisure Complex has excellent leisure facilities, with 20 bowling lanes using the latest computerized technology.

*Arcadia – fully interactive video arcade
* Diner Express fast food bar

Location
From A1(M) take A690 towards Durham, take last right at Gilesgate roundabout, into Claypath, right at traffic lights then left into The Sands (follow signs for coach park)

Opening
Daily; Mon–Fri 11am–11pm, Sat & Sun 10am–11pm

Admission
Adults £3.95, Child/Concs £2.95 (90p shoe hire)

Contact
Walkergate DH1 1SQ

t 0191 383 0300
w kascadabowl.com

772 Durham

Prince Bishop River Cruiser

1 hr   All year

The *Prince Bishop* river cruiser sails on the River Wear. It offers the best views of Durham Cathedral, Durham Castle and the bridges. The trip includes a commentary that will suit children of all ages.

* Sun deck & on-board BBQ
* 1-hour Santa Cruises in Dec

Location	**Admission**
The cruiser is found below the Prince Bishop shopping centre in Durham	Adult £4.50, Child £2 Senior £4
Opening	**Contact**
Sailing times 12.30pm, 2pm, 3pm	Durham River Trips Ltd, The Boathouse, Elvet Bridge DH1 3AH
	t 0191 386 9525

773 Gilesgate Moor

Top Gear Indoor Karting

2 hrs+   All year

Top Gear is a leisure karting centre. It provides indoor karting fun for everyone aged 8–88 (minimum height requirement 1.4m) and is a great place for family birthdays.

* New karts recently arrived
* Regular race meetings

Location	**Admission**
From A1(M) take A690 towards Durham and follow the brown tourist signs	£20 per person for 30 laps £25 per person for 40 laps
Opening	**Contact**
Daily; Mon–Fri 12 noon–9pm Sat & Sun 9am–7pm Closed 25, 26 Dec & 1 Jan	13 Renny's Lane, Gilesgate Moor DH1 2RS
	t 0191 386 0999
	w durhamkarting.co.uk
	e durhamkarting@lineone.net

774 Hartlepool

HMS Trincomalee

1 hr   All year

Built in Bombay in 1816-17 for the princely sum of £23,000, HMS *Trincomalee* is the oldest ship afloat in the UK. Today you can experience what life was like on board. Visit the captain's cabin, the bread room, the sleeping quarters, the quarter deck, even the toilets.

* World Ship Trust's Maritime Heritage award winner
* NTB's Visitor Attraction of the Year

Location	**Contact**
Follow signs for Hartlepool historic quay	HMS Trincomalee Trust, Jackson Dock, Hartlepool TS24 0SQ
Opening	t 0149 223193
Daily; Apr-Oct 10.30am-5pm Nov-Mar 10.30am-4pm	w hms-trincomalee.co.uk e office@trincomalee.co.uk
Admission	
Adult £4.25, Child £3.25, Concs £3.25	

775 Middleton-in-Teesdale

Bowlees Picnic Area

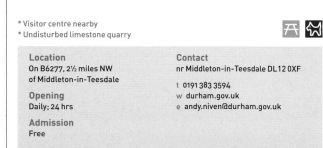
½ day   All year

This picnic area is in a sheltered side valley of Teesdale. There are four beautiful waterfalls in the site and more falls alongside a footpath that leads to Gibson's Cave.

* Visitor centre nearby
* Undisturbed limestone quarry

Location	**Contact**
On B6277, 2½ miles NW of Middleton-in-Teesdale	nr Middleton-in-Teesdale DL12 0XF
Opening	t 0191 383 3594
Daily; 24 hrs	w durham.gov.uk
Admission	e andy.niven@durham.gov.uk
Free	

776   Spennymoor

Whitworth Hall Country Park

 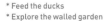

3 hrs   All year

Hand-feed the red and fallow deer in this 73-acre historic parkland. There is also an ornamental lake, a Victorian walled garden, a woodland garden and indoor and outdoor play facilities for children.

* Feed the ducks
* Explore the walled garden

Location
7 miles W of Durham & A1.
At A1 (junction 61) join A688
'Spennymoor'. Continue following
signs for Whitworth Hall Hotel

Opening
Daily; noon–dusk

Admission
Free

Contact
nr Spennymoor DL16 7QX

t 01388 811772
w whitworthhall.co.uk

777   Stanhope Chase

Castle Eden Dene National Nature Reserve

4 hrs+   All year

At Castle Eden Dene Nature Reserve you can enjoy 12 miles of walks through a wooded valley. There is a fantastic diversity of flora and fauna, and parts of the reserve remain almost unaltered since the Ice Age.

* Enjoy the woodland birds
* Spot a red squirrel

Location
Situated on the southern side of
Peterlee, signed from A19

Opening
Daily; at any reasonable time

Admission
Free

Contact
Oakerside Dene Lodge,
Stanhope Chase,
Peterlee SR8 1NJ

t 0191 586 0004

778   Upper Weardale

Killhope Lead Mining Museum

3 hrs+   Apr–Oct

With hard hat, lamp and wellies, you are guided down the original tunnel of a lead mine to find out about the lives of the miners.

* New exhibition on C19 emigration
* Woodland walks

Location
Between Stanhope & Alston on A689

Opening
Daily; Apr–Sep 10.30am–5pm (5.30pm
on Bank Holidays & summer holidays)
Oct Sat, Sun & half term 10.30am–5pm
Also open 4, 5, 11 & 12 Dec

Admission
Please phone for 2005 prices

Contact
nr Cowshill,
Upper Weardale DL13 1AR

t 01388 537505
w durham.gov.uk/killhope

779   Alnwick

Alnwick Castle

1 hr+   Apr–Oct

This medieval castle has wonderful Renaissance furnishings inside its walls. The Regiment Museum of Royal Northumberland Fusiliers is housed in the Abbott's Tower along with the museum of local archaeology and the Percy Tenantry volunteers.

* Venue for Harry Potter films
* Award-winning gardens

Location
Off A1 or A697 on the outskirts of Alnwick town

Opening
Daily; Apr–Oct 11am–5pm
(last admission 4.15pm)

Admission
Adult £7.50, Child £1.50, Concs £7

Contact
Alnwick NE66 1NQ

t 01665 510777
e enquiries@alnwickcastle.com

---

780   Ashington

Wansbeck Riverside Park

2–5 hrs   All year

An award-winning country park with a delightful camping and caravan site, plus a wide range of activities on hand, many of which are on the water. There is a play area, a paddle pool, and an island nature reserve.

* Wonderful wildlife walks
* Sailing and fishing available

Location
On A1068. The park is located between Ashington & Bedlington

Opening
Daily; 8am–dusk

Admission
Free

Contact
Green Lane,
Ashington NE63 8TX

t 01670 843444

---

781   Bamburgh

Bamburgh Castle

2 hrs   Mar–Oct

This magnificent coastal castle contains collections of furniture, paintings, arms and armour. The rocky outcrop became a royal centre by AD 547. The present fortress has a museum room, grand kings' hall, cross hall, armoury and the Victorian scullery for children to explore.

* Quality Assured Visitor Attraction
* Guided tours for individuals

Location
On B1340. From A1 Belford bypass take either B1341 or B1342 to Bamburgh

Opening
Daily; 13 Mar–31 Oct 11am–5pm
(last admission 4.30pm)

Admission
Adult £5, Child (6–15) £2, Concs £4

Contact
Bamburgh NE69 7DF

t 01668 214515
w bamburghcastle.com
e bamburghcastle@aol.com

782 Bedlington

Plessey Woods Country Park

2–4 hrs   All year

This country park is set in 100 acres of woodland, meadow and riverside, with a good network of paths and bridleways linking the surrounding area.

* Children's play area
* Visitor centre with displays

Location
On A192; just off A1068 & close to A1

Opening
Parkland Daily; at all reasonable times
Car park Daily; dawn–dusk

Admission
Car park £1

Contact
nr Bedlington NE22 6AN

t 01670 824793
w northumberland.gov.uk
e plesseywoods@
northumberland.gov.uk

783 Bellingham

Heritage Centre, Bellingham

2 hrs   Apr–Oct

This small folk museum situated in the old railway station yard houses photographs, artefacts and memorabilia recording the life and times of the people in the North Tyne Valley and Redewater Valley.

* The Border Counties Railway
* Special attractions for children

Location
Follow B6320 from Hexham–Bellingham (17 miles). The Heritage Centre is in Woodburn Road, in Station Yard opposite the Hillside Estate

Opening
Easter–Oct Thu–Mon
10.30am–4.30pm
Please phone for details

Admission
Adult £1, Child (5–16) 50p, Concs 50p

Contact
Station Yard, Woodburn Road, Bellingham, Hexham NE48 2DF

t 01434 220050

784 Belsay

Bolam Lake Country Park

2–4 hrs   All year

Bolam Lake Country Park has everything for a family day out. There is a lake surrounded by beautiful woodland and meadows with paths and picnic areas. It is ideal for bird-watching.

* Lakeside walk by local architect – John Dobson

Location
Signed from A696 at Belsay & B6524 at Whalton

Opening
Park Daily; at all reasonable times
Car park Daily; dawn–dusk
Café Weekends, Bank Holidays & school holidays
Please phone for details

Admission
Free, *Car park* 2hrs 50p, 8hrs £1

Contact
nr Belsay NE20 0HE

t 01661 881234

©National Trust Photographic Library

Bewick Barracks Museum & Art Gallery

All year

The barracks are home to a number of attractions, including 'By Beat of Drum' – showing what life was like for British infantry soldiers until Queen Victoria's reign – the regimental museum of the King's Own Scottish Borderers and a contemporary art gallery.

* One of the first purpose-built barracks
* Walk on ramparts affords great views of River Tweed

Location
Off Church Street in centre of town

Opening
Daily; Easter–Sep 10am–6pm
(till 5pm in Oct);
Nov–Mar Wed–Sun 10am–4pm

Admission
Adult £3, Child £1.50, Concs £2.30

Contact
The Parade,
Berwick-upon-Tweed PD15 1DF

t   01289 304493
w   english-heratage.org.uk

Lindisfarne Castle

2 hrs+   Mar–Nov

Perched atop a rocky crag, only accessible over a causeway at low tide, a visit to this Tudor fort is a real adventure.

* Walled garden
* Family guide

Location
On Holy Island, 6 miles E of A1

Opening
Mar–Nov Sat–Thu; open Good Fri
It is impossible to cross to the island between the 2 hrs before and 3 hrs after high tide. Tide tables are printed in local newspapers and are displayed on the causeway

Admission
Adult £4.20, Child £2.10

Contact
Holy Island,
Berwick-upon-Tweed TD15 2SH

t   01289 389244
w   nationaltrust.org.uk

Pot-a-Doodle-Do

2 hrs   Feb–Dec

An oasis of creativity for all – there is a wide range of art and craft activities to try, as well as a large children's play area, Quad bike trekking, fishing and country walks. Friendly staff are on hand to help make sure your day is the best it can be.

* Potting – from raw clay to glazed item
* Mosaicking – part of national curriculum in History

Location
On A1, S of Berwick

Opening
Daily; Easter–Oct 10am–5pm;
31 Oct–Easter Wed–Sun 10am–4pm
Closed Jan

Admission
Free (pay-as-you-go activities)

Contact
Borewell Farm, Scremerston,
Berwick-upon-Tweed TD15 2RJ

t   01289 307107
w   potadoodledo.com
e   info@potadoodledo.com

788 Chillingham

Chillingham Castle

1 hr   Easter–Sep

This medieval fortress has Tudor additions, a torture chamber and dungeon, and a woodland walk. It has beautifully furnished rooms and an Italian topiary garden with herbaceous borders.

* See a real 'Iron Maiden'
* Most haunted castle in England

Location
From Newcastle upon Tyne take A1 & A697, then follow signs from Wooler; from the north take A1 south & follow the brown tourist signs

Opening
Daily; Easter–30 Sep except Sat;
Castle 1pm–5pm
Grounds & tearoom 12 noon–5pm

Admission
Adult £5, Under-16s £2, Concs £4.50

Contact
Chillingham NE66 5NJ

t 01668 215359
w chillingham-castle.com

789 Cambo

Wallington Estate

2-4 hrs   All year

The impressive grounds surrounding the historic house of Wallington have plenty of walks, covering formal gardens, woodland and high moorland, plus an adventure playground.

* Redecorated and refurbished in 2004
* Fine collection of doll's houses

Location
12 miles W of Morpeth &
6 miles NW of Belsay

Opening
House 1 Apr–5 Sep Mon & Wed-Sun 1pm-5.30pm (4.30 in Oct)
Grounds Daily; Apr–Oct 10am–7pm (6pm in Oct); Nov–Mar 10am–4pm

Admission
House & grounds Adult £7, Child £3.50
Grounds only Adult £5, Child £2.50

Contact
Cambo, Morpeth NE61 4AR

t 01670 773600
w wallington@nationaltrust.org.uk

790 Falstone

Kielder Water Leaplish Waterside Park

6 hrs+   All year

Situated in the North Tyne Valley, this waterside park is set in breathtaking scenery and has a 27-mile shoreline. There are facilities and activities to suit all ages.

* *Daily Telegraph* Awards 2000
* Adventure playground

Location
8 miles from the Scottish border, 20 miles N of Bellingham at the top of the Kielder Reservoir; 1 hour N of Hexham

Opening
Daily; some facilities are seasonal
Please phone for details

Admission
Activities priced individually

Contact
Leaplish Waterside Park,
Falstone, Hexham

t 01434 250294
w kielder.org

791 Greenhead

Roman Army Museum

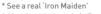

2 hrs   Feb-Nov

Ever wanted to be a Roman soldier? Here you can watch the recruiting film, fill in the join-up sheet and join the Roman army for a day. Learn about weapons, uniforms, pay, training and what soldiers did in their free time.

* Situated on Hadrian's Wall
* Life-size figures, models and displays

Location
Off B6318, nr Greenhead, 3 miles from Haltwhistle. Follow heritage signs for Hadrian's Wall & Roman Museum

Opening
Daily; Feb-Mar 10am-5pm; Apr-Sep 10am-6pm; Oct-Nov 10am-5pm

Admission
Adult £3.50, Child £2.20, Concs £3

Contact
Greenhead CA6 7JB

t 01697 747485
w vindolanda.com
e info@vindolanda.com

792 Haltwhistle

South Tyne Trail

3 hrs+   All year

This former railway line is open to walkers of all ages, and for much of its length to cyclists and horse-riders. The trail has excellent views of the South Tyne Valley and it includes the spectacular Lambley Viaduct.

* Interpretation displays near Coanwood
* Self-guided trail

Location	Admission
Runs for 13 miles between Haltwhistle & Alston parallel to A689. Best access from Haltwhistle, Alston & car parks at Featherstone Park & Coanwood (for Lambley Viaduct)	Free
	Contact
	South Tyne Trail, Haltwhistle
Opening	
Daily; at any reasonable time	

793 Hexham

Housesteads Roman Fort, Hadrian's Wall

1 hr+   All year

Children will be fascinated to encounter life as it was on Rome's northernmost frontier at Housesteads – a jewel in the crown of Hadrian's Wall and the most complete Roman fort still standing in Britain. There is also an indoor museum to explore.

* The best preserved of 16 forts along the Wall
* Dramatic countryside

Location	Admission
Take B6318, 2¾ miles NE of Bardon Mill	Adult £3, Child (5–16) £1.50, Concs £2.30
Opening	**Contact**
Daily; Apr–Sep 10am–6pm Oct 10am–5pm; Nov–Mar 10am–4pm Closed 24–26 Dec & 1 Jan	Hexham NE47 6NN
	t 01434 344363
	w nationaltrust.org.uk

794 Holy Island

Lindisfarne Priory

1 hr+   All year

Lindisfarne was founded in C7 by St Aidan, destroyed by the Vikings in 793, rebuilt in C12 and destroyed again by Henry VIII in C16 who used the stones to build Lindisfarne Castle. The priory is reached by a causeway only accessible at low tide so check tide times before visiting.

* One of the most important early centres of Christianity in Anglo-Saxon England

Location	Admission
Holy Island, 6 miles E of A1, across causeway	Adult £3, Child £1.50, Concs £2.30
Opening	**Contact**
Daily; Apr–Sep 10am–6pm, Oct 10am–5pm, Nov–Mar 10am–4pm – subject to tides	Holy Island, Berwick-Upon-Tweed
	t 01289 389200
	w english-heritage.org.uk

795 Low Prudhoe

Tyne Riverside Country Park

2-4 hrs   All year

This delightful country park includes a riverside walk that links through to Newcastle upon Tyne.
It can also offer canoeing access to the river.

* Off-road cycle route
* Children's play area

Location
On A695, just off A69

Opening
Daily; at all reasonable times (car park dawn–dusk)

Admission
Free

Contact
Station Road,
Low Prudhoe NE42 5PR

t 01661 834135

796 Morpeth

Belsay Hall Castle & Gardens

3 hrs   All year

This wonderful estate has a C14 castle, C17 manor house and C19 neoclassical hall set in 30 acres of landscaped gardens and grounds, including quarry gardens with a micro-climate where rhododendrons are found in bloom even in the middle of winter.

* Two acres of rhododendrons at best May & June
* Formal terraces and winter garden, original planting

Location
In Belsay, 14 miles NW of Newcastle on A696

Opening
Daily; Apr-Sep 10am-6pm, Oct 10am-5pm, Nov-Mar 10am-4pm

Admission
Adult £4.50, Child £2.30, Concs £3.40

Contact
Belsay NE20 0DX

t 01661 881636
w english-heritage.org.uk

©National Trust Photographic Library

797 Morpeth

Carlisle Park

1–3 hrs · All year

Situated on the riverside in Morpeth, Carlisle Park's attractions include woodland and riverside walks, a castle, the William Turner Herb Garden, an aviary, tennis courts, bowling greens and a play area.

* Quality Assured Visitor Attraction
* Paddling pool & boating on the river

Location
From A1 follow the signs to Morpeth town centre

Opening
Park Daily; at all reasonable times
Turner Garden Daily; dawn–dusk

Admission
Free

Contact
Castle Morpeth Borough Council,
Kylins Centre,
Morpeth NE61 2EQ

t 01670 500789
w castlemorpeth.gov.uk
e sam.talbot@castlemorpeth.gov.uk

798 Morpeth

Cragside House, Gardens & Estate

2 hrs+ · Apr–Dec

Described as the Palace of a Modern Magician, Cragside was at the cutting edge of technology when built in the 1880s. It had hot and cold running water, central heating, telephones, a passenger lift, a Turkish bath suite and was lit by hydroelectricity.

* See the first flushing loos
* Rhododendron maze

Location
13 miles SW of Alnwick (B6341) and 15 miles NW of Morpeth on the Wooler road (A697); turn left onto B6341 at Moorhouse crossroads

Opening
House: Apr–Oct Tue–Sun 1pm–5.30pm (4.30pm closing in Oct)
Estate: Apr–Oct Tue–Sun

10.30am–7pm; Nov–Dec Wed–Sun 11am–4pm

Admission
Adult £7.20, Child £3.60

Contact
Rothbury, Morpeth NE65 7PX
t 01669 620333
w nationaltrust.org.uk
e cragside@nationaltrust.org.uk

799 Morpeth

Cresswell Dunes

1 hr+ · All year

This site is in the southern section of Druridge Bay, a 5-mile sandy beach with nationally important wildlife and beautiful dunes. Close by are the amenities of Cresswell village and the birdwatching hide at Cresswell Pond.

* Go rockpooling
* Expert guides available

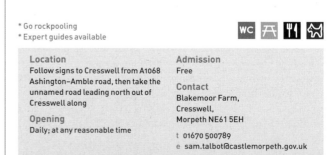

Location
Follow signs to Cresswell from A1068 Ashington–Amble road, then take the unnamed road leading north out of Cresswell along

Opening
Daily; at any reasonable time

Admission
Free

Contact
Blakemoor Farm,
Cresswell,
Morpeth NE61 5EH

t 01670 500789
e sam.talbot@castlemorpeth.gov.uk

800 Morpeth

Druridge Bay Country Park

2-4 hrs   All year

At Druridge Bay you can enjoy lakeside walks and 5 miles of beautiful beach. Visitors can also windsurf and use non-motorised boats (by permit, available from the information centre or ticket machine).

* Ladyburn Lake watersports centre
* Annual kite festival

Location
Off A1068

Opening
Park: Daily; at any reasonable time (car park open dawn–dusk)
Café: Weekends, Bank Holidays & local school holidays
Please ring for details

Admission
Free
Car park 2 hrs 50p, 8 hrs £1

Contact
Hadston,
Morpeth NE61 5BQ

t 01670 760968

801 Morpeth

Scotch Gill Woods Local Nature Reserve

1-3 hrs   All year

Otters and dippers can be seen in the River Wansbeck which runs along Scotch Gill Woods. Red squirrels are present here, as well as at the adjacent nature reserves of Bracken Bank and Davies Wood (accessible from the same car park).

* Always wear appropriate clothing and footwear

Location
Follow B6343 from Morpeth for ½ mile, turn right into the car park at the 1st bridge over the river

Opening
Daily; at any reasonable time

Admission
Free

Contact
Mitford Road,
Morpeth NE61 1RG

t 01670 500789
w castlemorpeth.gov.uk
e sam.talbot@castlemorpeth.gov.uk

802 Rochester

Brigantium

1 hr   All year

This archaeological reconstruction centre has plenty to stimulate the young explorer. Wander round the Roman British farm, roundhouse, mesolithic hunting camp, Roman defences and road, and marvel at the Bronze Age burial and stone circle.

* Display & video room
* Dowsing course

Location
On A68 from Jedburgh or Corbridge or A696 from Newcastle

Opening
Daily; 9.30am–4.30pm
Closed Christmas & New Year
Special visits & guided tours can be booked in advance

Admission
Adult £2.50, Child/Concs £1.50

Contact
Rochester Café,
Rochester NE19 1RH

t 01830 520801

803 Seahouses

Farne islands

2-3 hrs   Varies

Take the whole family on a boat trip to the Farne Islands. They house a bird reserve holding around 70,000 pairs of breeding birds, from 21 species. Puffins can be seen in season, and the islands are also home to a large colony of grey seals throughout the year.

* Most famous seabird sanctuary on the British Isles

Location
The islands are 2-3 miles off the north Northumberland coast. Take B1340 & then a boat from Seahouses harbour

Opening
Please phone for details

Admission
Please phone for details

Contact
Seahouses

t 01665 721099
w nationaltrust.org.uk

804 Seahouses

Marine Life Centre & Haunted Kingdom

2-3 hrs   Feb–Oct

The museum and aquarium includes a touch pool for crabs and other sea life and an exhibition with audio-visual conversations between fishing families. The centre also houses Northumbria's Haunted Kingdom, an adventure for children and adults.

* 50,000 litre trout pond
* Reconstructed fisherman's house

Location
Off B1340 on the coast

Opening
Daily; 28 Feb–31 Oct 10.30am–5pm

Admission
Adults £2.50, Concs/Child £2

Contact
8–10 Main Street,
Seahouses NE68 5RG

t 01665 721257
w marinelifecentre.co.uk

806 Tynemouth

Tynemouth Priory & Castle

1 hr   All year

A burial place of saints and kings, this commanding castle has provided defence against the Vikings, medieval Scotland, Napoleon and C20 Germany. The Benedictine priory was founded in 1090 on the site of an ancient Anglian monastery.

* Restored magazines of a coastal defence gun battery on view at weekends

Location
In Tynemouth, nr North Pier

Opening
Daily; Apr-Sep 10am-6pm;
Oct 10am-4pm;
Nov-Mar Thu-Mon, 10am-4pm
 Closed 24-26 Dec and 1 Jan

Admission
Adult £3, Child £1.50, Concs £2.30

Contact
Tynemouth,

t 0191 257 1090
w english-heritage.org.uk

805 Stocksfield

Cherryburn

2 hrs   End Mar–Oct

This delightful cottage, with farmyard, garden and play lawn, was once home to the artist, engraver and naturalist Thomas Bewick. Visitors can enjoy an exhibition of his work and see demonstrations of wood engraving and hand printing from wood blocks.

* Friendly farm animals in the cobbled courtyard
* Beautiful walks along the bank of the Tyne

Location
11 miles W of Newcastle; ¼ mile N of Mickley Square; leave A695 at Mickley Square onto Riding Terrace, leading to Station Bank; Cherryburn is close to the south bank of the River Tyne

Opening
End Mar–end Oct Thu–Mon
1pm–5.30pm

Admission
Adult £3, Child £1.50

Contact
Station Bank, Mickley,
nr Stocksfield NE43 7DD

t 01661 843276
w nationaltrust.org.uk

©National Trust Photographic Library

807 Burnopfield

Gibside

½ day   All year

Gibside is one of the North's finest landscapes, embracing many miles of riverside and forest walks. The park is very child-friendly with woods to explore, streams to paddle in and wildlife to look out for, including deer, kingfishers, herons and even badgers.

* Information centre
* Children's days & special events

Location
20 miles W of Durham and 6 miles SW of Gateshead; entrance is on B6341 between Burnopfield & Rowlands Gill. From A1 take the exit N of the Metro Centre and follow brown tourist signs

Opening
Tue–Sun 10am–6pm (4pm closing in winter); Bank Holiday Mons

Admission
Adult £3.50, Child £2

Contact
Nr Rowlands Gill, Burnopfield, Newcastle upon Tyne NE16 6BG
t 01207 542255
w nationaltrust.org.uk
e gibside@nationaltrust.org.uk

808 Dunston

Whickham Thorns Outdoor Activity Centre

1 hr+   All year

This activity centre offers plenty of excitement, including an assault course, a climbing wall, cycle hire, a ski slope, archery and orienteering. There is also a snowboarding club.

* Pre-booking essential for activities
* First Boulder Park in the North East

Location
Off A1 on the opposite side of the motorway to the MetroCentre

Opening
Daily; Mon–Fri 11am–10pm, Sat 11am–6.30pm, Sun 12 noon–3pm; Closed during certain holidays Please phone for details

Admission
Free; please phone for activity prices

Contact
Market Lane,
Dunston,
Gateshead NE11 9NX

t 0191 433 5767
w gateshead.gov.uk

809 Gateshead

BALTIC

1 hr+   All year

Housed in a 1950s' grain warehouse, this contemporary art centre has five galleries, artists' studios, cinema/lecture space, a media lab, a library, an archive for the study of contemporary art and a retail outlet. Exhibitions are free and change regularly.

* Constantly changing programme of exhibitions
* Displays of artists in residence

Location
Gateshead Quayside, 10 mins walk from town centre

Opening
Daily; Mon, Tue, Wed, Fri & Sat 10am–7pm; Thu 10am–10pm, Sun 10am–5pm

Admission
Free

Contact
South Shore Road,
Gateshead NE8 3BA

t 0191 4781810
w balticmill.com
e info@balticmill.com

810 Gateshead

Bill Quay Farm

2 hrs   All year

Bring your children to this lovely urban farm to enjoy spectacular views of the Tyne and to meet farmyard breeds, both traditional and unusual. The farm includes a green retreat for wildlife.

* Outstanding panoramic views of the Tyne
* Family picnic area

Location
Take A185 from Heworth interchange, turn left down Station Road (¼ mile from Heworth) & take 1st left at crossroads

Opening
Daily; 12 noon–5pm
Some buildings have restricted access (please phone for details)

Admission
Free

Contact
Hainingwood Terrace,
Bill Quay,
Gateshead NE10 0TE

t 0191 433 5780

811 Gateshead

The New Metroland

 3 hrs+ — All year

Among the many children's attractions are a roller-coaster, a pirate ship, swinging chairs, dodgem cars, a children's railway, a Ferris wheel, aeroplanes, helicopters, slides and climbing nets.

* Europe's largest indoor funfair
* Mr B's Amusement Arcade

Location
Take A1(M) to Gateshead MetroCentre

Opening
During term time Mon–Fri from
12 noon; in school holidays Mon–Sat
10am–8pm & Sun 11am–6pm
Closed 25 Dec

Admission
Please phone for details

Contact
39 Garden Walk,
MetroCentre,
Gateshead NE11 9XY

t 0191 493 2048
w metroland.uk.com

812 Gateshead

Saltwell Park

 1–3 hrs — All year

At Saltwell Park you can enjoy bedding displays, a rose garden, a wooded den, a children's play area and a boating lake. There are brass bands at the bandstand and bowls during the summer.

* An original and genuine Victorian public garden
* Undergoing extensive renovation

Location
Off A184 or A692 S of Newcastle upon
Tyne

Opening
Daily; 7.30am–dusk

Admission
Free

Contact
Park Road,
Gateshead NE8 4SF

t 0191 433 5900
w gateshead.gov.uk

813 Gateshead

Shipley Art Gallery

 2 hrs — All year

Shipley Art Gallery is home to a collection of over 700 pieces by the country's leading craftmakers. It includes studio ceramics, glass, metal work, jewellery, textiles and furniture. The exhibition 'Made in Gateshead' tells the fascinating history of the town.

* Activity room
* Art Kart

Location
Off A167. The nearest Metro station is
Gateshead. There is limited free
street parking outside the gallery

Opening
Daily; Mon–Sat 10am–5pm & Sun
2pm–5pm
Closed Good Fri, 25, 26 Dec & 1 Jan

Admission
Free

Contact
Prince Consort Road,
Gateshead NE8 4JB

t 0191 477 1495
w twmuseums.org.uk

814 Jarrow

Bede's World & St Pauls' Church

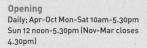

3hrs   All year

Discover what life was like for Bede who established a monastery and church here in C7. During the summer enjoy a range of children's activities, including tours of an Anglo-Saxon demonstration farm, story telling, tile-making, archery and bread-making.

* Herb garden based on Anglo-Saxon & medieval plants
* Anglo-Saxon Domo farm, complete with animals

Location
Near S end of Tyne tunnel, off A185

Opening
Daily; Apr-Oct Mon-Sat 10am-5.30pm
Sun 12 noon-5.30pm (Nov-Mar closes 4.30pm)

Admission
Adult £4.50, Child £2.50, Concs £3

Contact
Church Bank NE32 3DY

t 0191 4892106
w bedesworld.co.uk
e visitorinfo@bedesworld.co.uk

815 Newcastle upon Tyne

Centre For Life

3 hrs+   All year

There's always something new at the Centre for Life. Meet your 4-billion-year-old family, explore what makes us all different, test your brain power and enjoy the thrill of the crazy motion ride.

* Escape from Dino Island 3D ride
* Open-air ice rink in Times Square during Christmas period

Location
From S take A19, A184, A69 or A1 into Newcastle upon Tyne; from N take A69 into Newcastle upon Tyne

Opening
Daily; Mon-Sat 10am-6pm, Sun 11am-6pm (last admission 4.30pm); Closed 25 Dec & 1 Jan

Admission
Adult £6.95, Child (5–16) £4.50

Contact
Times Square,
Newcastle upon Tyne NE1 4EP

t 0191 243 8210
w centre-for-life.co.uk
e general@centre-for-life.co.uk

816 Newcastle upon Tyne

Discovery Museum

2-3 hrs   All year

Explore Newcastle's past, from Roman times to the present day. See Tyneside inventions that changed the world and take a walk through changing fashions. The Discovery Museum offers a fun approach to science and a great day out for all the family.

* Region's biggest free museum
* New 'Story of the Tyne' exhibition

Location
A short walk from Newcastle Central Station (Metro and mainline); Pay & Display parking available outside museum

Opening
Daily; Mon-Sat 10am-5pm & Sun 2pm-5pm
Closed Good Fri, 25, 26 Dec & 1 Jan

Admission
Free

Contact
Blandford Square,
Newcastle upon Tyne NE1 4JA

t 0191 232 6789
w twmuseums.org.uk

817 Newcastle upon Tyne

Hancock Museum

2–3 hrs   All year

The museum combines traditional natural history displays with live animals and interactive displays to show how our world has evolved. An activity area for young children brings the natural world to life through specimens, live animals, toys and games.

* Land of the Pharaohs exhibition
* World premier exhibitions

Location
In the city centre between Barras Bridge & Claremont Road. Nearest Metro station is Haymarket. For drivers, take A167 and follow the yellow AA signs to the museum

Opening
Daily; Mon–Sat 10am–5pm & Sun 2pm–5pm. Closed 25 Dec & 1 Jan

Admission
Please phone for details

Contact
Barras Bridge
Newcastle upon Tyne NE2 4PT

t 0191 222 7418
w twmuseums.org.uk

818 Newcastle-upon-Tyne

The People's Museum of Memorabilia

1 hr   All year

This small but fascinating museum and shopping arcade recreates Newcastle's past in miniature with C18 and C19 cottages, shops and alleyways. The museum houses artefacts and memorabilia from the past 200 years of the region's history.

* Shop sells period toys and gifts

Location
Grainger St, Newcastle town centre

Opening
Mon–Sat, 10am–5pm

Admission
Free

Contact
Newcastle-upon-Tyne NE1 5JG

t 0191 221 1688

819 North Shields

Stephenson Railway Museum

1 hr+   May–Sep

Relive the glorious days of the steam railway at the Stephenson Railway Museum. Take a ride on a steam train and discover the impact of coal and electricity on the lives of ordinary people. There are activities and events to suit all ages.

* Home to 'Billy' and 'Jackie Milburn' engines
* The Electric Century exhibition

Location
Well signed from A19/A1058 junction, opposite the Atmel factory & adjacent to the Blyth & Tyne cycle route. Nearest Metro station is Percy Main

Opening
5 May–28 Sep Tue–Thu 11am–3pm & Sat–Sun & Bank Holidays 11am–4pm

Admission
Free

Contact
Middle Engine Lane,
North Shields NE29 8DX

t 0191 200 7146
w twmuseums.org.uk

820 Sunderland

Monkwearmouth Station Museum

1 hr+   All year

This splendid Victorian railway station recreates rail travel of the past. Explore the ticket office, guard's van and goods wagon. There is also a children's gallery with a range of toys, books and dressing-up clothes.

* Children's gallery for under 5s
* Model railways

Location	Admission
On A1018. 1 minute walk from St Peter's Metro station	Free
Opening	**Contact**
Daily; Mon–Sat 10am–5pm & Sun 2pm–5pm Closed Good Fri, 25, 26 Dec & 1 Jan	North Bridge Street, Sunderland SR5 1AP t 0191 232 7734 w twmuseum.org.uk

821 Sunderland

National Glass Centre

1 hr+   All year

Discover how glass has been used since it was invented in 5000 BC. See it magnify a bee's knee and a fly's tongue 100 times, listen to a glass orchestra, have fun with crazy mirrors, and hear how glass is used to protect astronauts when they re-enter the earth's atmosphere.

* Home of International Institute for research in glass

Location	Contact
Signed from all major roads	Liberty Way, Sunderland SR6 0GL
Opening	t 0191 515 5555
Daily; 10am–5pm	w nationalglasscentre.co.uk
Admission	e info@nationalglasscentre.co.uk
Adult £5, Child/Concs £3	

822 Sunderland

Sunderland Museum & Winter Gardens

2–3 hrs   All year

This museum tells the story of Sunderland. It includes paintings by L. S. Lowry and exciting hands-on exhibits and interactive displays. The stunning winter gardens will stimulate the senses with over 1,500 flowers and plants – a showcase of the world's natural beauty.

* Computer and video presentations
* Treetop walkway in winter gardens

Location	Admission
In Sunderland city centre, a short walk from Sunderland & Park Lane Metro stations	Free
Opening	**Contact**
Daily; Mon–Sat 10am–5pm & Sun 2pm–5pm Closed Good Fri, 25, 26 Dec & 1 Jan	Mowbray Park, Burdon Road, Sunderland SR1 1PP t 0191 553 2323 w twmuseum.org.uk

823 Sunniside

Tanfield Railway

2 hrs+   All year

Tanfield is a 3-mile steam railway & the oldest existing railway in the world. Travel into the scenic Causey Woods where the 1727 Causey Arch bridge is the centrepiece in a deep valley with walks & display boards giving the C18 railway history of the area.

* Large collection of locally built locomotives
* The oldest working engine shed in Britain

Location
On A6072 Stanley–Gatehead road

Opening
Daily (viewing only)
Please phone or visit website for details

Admission
Train ride Adult £5, Child (5–14) £2.50,
Senior £3.50

Contact
Old Marley Hill,
Sunniside,
Gateshead NE16 5ET

t 0191 388 7545
w tanfield-railway.co.uk
e tanfield@ingsoc.demon.co.uk

©National Trust Photographic Library

824 South Shields

Arbeia Roman Fort

2 hrs   All year

Arbeia was an essential part of a mighty frontier system. Built in approximately AD 160, it guarded the entrance to the River Tyne. Excavated remains, plus stunning reconstructions of original buildings and displays of finds discovered at the site.

* Three reconstructed buildings on their original sites
* 'Time Quest' archaeological dig

Location
Just a 10 minute walk from South
Shields Metro & bus station;
signed from Ocean Road

Opening
Daily; Easter–Sep Mon–Sat
10am–5.30pm & Sun 1pm–5pm;
Oct–Easter Mon–Sat 10am–4pm &
closed Sun

Admission
Free

Contact
Baring Street,
South Shields NE33 2BB

t 0191 456 1369
w twmuseums.org.uk

825 South Shields

Pier Amusements Centre

2 hrs   All year

At the Pier Amusements Centre you can play Quasar, a futuristic game where each player is armed with a laser gun and shoots the opposition to win points.

Location
On the pier front at South Shields.
Reached via A183, A1018 or A185

Opening
Daily; 10am–10pm

Admission
Please phone for details

Contact
Pier Parade, South Shields NE33 2JS

t 0191 455 3885

826 South Shields

Souter Lighthouse

1 hr+   Feb–Oct

Built in 1871, Souter boasted the most advanced lighthouse technology of its day. The lighthouse is full of interest for children. They can see the engine and rooms, the Victorian keeper's cottage and the light tower.

* Pirates & smugglers activity
* Lighthouses & Lighthouse Life exhibition

Location
Take A183 coast road from Sunderland to South Shields

Opening
Daily (except Fri); 14 Feb–29 Feb & 27 Mar–31 Oct 11am–5pm (last admission 4.30pm)

Admission
Adult £3.50, Child (5–16) £2

Contact
Coast Road, Whitburn,
South Shields SR6 7NH

t 0191 529 3161
w nationaltrust.org.uk

827 Tynemouth

Blue Reef Aquarium

1 hr+   All year

The ultimate undersea safari, Blue Reef brings the magic of the undersea world alive. Explore the drama of the North Sea and the dazzling beauty of a spectacular coral reef. This giant tropical ocean tank, with its own underwater tunnel and more than 30 living displays.

Location
From A19, take A1058 to the town centre & follow the brown tourist signs

Opening
Daily; Mar–Oct 10am–5pm; Nov–Feb 10am–4pm

Admission
Adult £5.50, Child £3.75, Concs£4.95

Contact
Grand Parade,
Tynemouth NE30 4JF

t 0191 258 1031
w bluereefaquarium.co.uk
e tynemouth@bluereefaquarium.co.uk

828 Wallsend

Segedunum Roman Fort, Baths & Museum

2 hrs+   All year

The last outpost of Hadrian's Wall, Segedunum has stood on the banks of the Tyne since AD 122. It was built to protect the coast from barbarians in the north, and was once home to 600 Roman soldiers.

* Spectacular views from 100-ft-high tower
* Full-sized reconstruction of Roman baths

Location
Just one minute's walk from Wallsend Metro & bus station

Opening
Daily; 10am–5pm (3.30 pm 1 Nov–31 Mar)
Closed Good Fri, 25, 26 Dec & 1 Jan

Admission
Adult £3.50, Child/Concs £1.95

Contact
Buddle Street,
Wallsend NE28 6HR

t 0191 236 9347
w twmuseums.org.uk

830 Whitley Bay

Whitley Bay Ice Rink

½ day   All year

Whitley Bay Ice Rink offers something for everyone. Come and enjoy a morning of tenpin bowling and then have a brisk swim or a leisurely paddle in the swimming pool. The ice rink is also a concert venue.

* Fantastic fun on the ice
* Snacks and drinks available

Location
From S take A1 through the Tyne Tunnel, then A1058; from Newcastle upon Tyne take A1058

Opening
Daily; closed 25 Dec
Please phone for details

Admission
Adult £3.80, Child £3.30 (£1.50 boot hire)

Contact
Hillheads Road,
Whitley Bay NE25 8HP

t 0191 291 1000
e icerink@ukonline.co.uk

829 Washington

Wildfowl & Wetlands Trust Washington

3 hrs+   All year

The trust is home to more than 500 ducks, geese, swans and flamingos. Many birds will take food from your hand. The annual highlight is the downy duckling days (May to July) when visitors can see young birds take their first wobbly steps in the nursery.

* Quality Assured Visitor Attraction
* 100 acres of wetland & woodland

Location
Signed from A195 & A1231. The Trust is 4 miles from A1(M) & 1 mile from A19

Opening
Daily 9.30am–5pm (4pm in winter)
Closed 25 Dec

Admission
Adult £5.50, Child £3.50, Concs £4.50

Contact
District 15,
Washington NE38 8LE

t 0191 416 5454
w wwt.org.uk
e wetlands@euphony.net

Silver Sands Beach, Morar

Scotland

Central Scotland Grampian
Highlands and Islands Southern Scotland

831 Aberfoyle

Forest Hills Watersports

4–6 hrs   Mar–Dec

The centre offers a range of 'wet' and 'dry' activities which can be combined or enjoyed individually. Watersports of all descriptions are available in addition to quad biking, mountain biking and 4x4 drives.

* Cliff jumps
* Kayaking

Location
Off junction 10 of M9 & junction 16 of M8. Follow the signs for Aberfoyle, then to Forest Hills Watersports, 4 miles along B829

Opening
Daily; Mar–Dec, in summer 9.30am–7pm; in winter 10.30am–5pm

Admission
Activities priced individually

Contact
Kinlochard, Aberfoyle, Stirlingshire FK8 3TL

t 01877 387775
w goforth.co.uk
e info@goforth.co.uk

833 Brechin

Brechin Castle Centre

2 hrs+   All year

Brechin Castle is a country park with a working model farm and a children's activity area.

* 4-Star Visitor Attraction, Scottish Tourist Board
* Santa at Christmas

Location
Between Aberdeen & Dundee, off A90; on A935 to Brechin turn off; it is well signed from there

Opening
Daily; Mon–Sat 9am–6pm, Sun 10am–6pm

Admission
Adult £2 , Child £1

Contact
Haughmui, by Brechin, Angus DD9 6RL

t 01356 626813
w brechincastlecentre.co.uk
e enquiries@brechincastlecentre.co.uk

832 Angus

J.M. Barrie's Birthplace

2 hrs   Apr–Sep

J.M. Barrie, the creator of Peter Pan, was born here in 1860, one of a handloom weaver's ten children. See the imaginative exhibition and discover how the outside wash-house served as Barrie's first theatre.

Location
Off the A90 & A926, 6 miles NW of Forfar

Opening
1 Apr–30 Jun & 1–30 Sep open Fri–Tue 12 noon–5pm; 1 Jul–31 Aug daily 12 noon–5pm

Admission
Please phone for details

Contact
9 Brechin Road, Kirriemuir, Angus

t 01575 572646

834 Callander

Rob Roy & Trossachs Visitor Centre

3 hrs+   All year

Visit this reconstructed farmhouse, just as Rob Roy would have experienced it. Children can meet the Children of the Mist dressed in authentic period clothing as well as enjoying the indoor play area.

* 4–Star Visitor Attraction

Location
Off A84

Opening
Daily; 1 Apr-31 May 10am-5pm,
1 Jun-30 Sep 10am-6pm,
1 Nov-28 Feb 11pm-4pm
Oct & Mar 10am-5pm,

Admission
Adult £3.25, Child £2.25, Concs £2.25

Contact
Ancaster Square, Callander FK17 8ED

t 01877 330342
e info@callender.visitscotland.com

835 Comrie

Auchingarrigh Wildlife Centre

4 hrs+   All year

Set in 100 acres of Perthshire countryside, the centre has animals and birds from all over the world. Attractions include falconry displays, indoor and outdoor play areas, animal and chick handling, a unique bird hatchery and trout fishing ponds.

* Coffee shop & Gift Shop

Location
2 miles S of Comrie on B827, 25 miles
W of Perth & 20 miles N of Stirling.
Follow the signs for Crieff

Opening
Daily; 10am–dusk

Admission
Please Phone for details

Contact
Comrie
Perthshire PH6 2JS

t 01764 679469/670486

836 Crieff

Famous Grouse Experience at Glenturret Distillery

2 hrs+   All year

Take an airborne journey with The Famous Grouse. Setting off over the Highlands, visitors swoop over numerous famous Scottish landmarks – from Loch Ness to Edinburgh Castle. Afterwards stroll along a nature trail or enjoy a picnic in the grounds.

* BAFTA award-winning attraction
* State-of-the-art audio-visual presentation

Location
Off A85, 1 mile from Crieff

Opening
Daily; 9am-6pm
Tours from 9.30am-4.30pm

Admission
Adult £5.95 Child £3, Concs £4.95

Contact
Glenturret Distillery, The Hosh, Crieff,
Perthshire PH7 4HA

t 01764 656565
w famousgrouse.com
e enquiries@famousgrouse.com

837 Crieff

Stuart Crystal Factory Shop

 ½ hr · All year

Come and see the wonderful craft of crystal at the Stuart Crystal Factory Shop. There is a crystal engraving service for that personalised special gift or memento. A large display of Stuart Crystal, Waterford Crystal and Wedgwood China, with factory seconds.

* Souvenir gift shop
* Chip repair service

Location	Admission
Signed from town centre	Free
Opening	**Contact**
Daily; Jun–Sep 10am–6pm	Muthill Road, Crieff
Oct–May Mon–Sat 10am–5pm	Perthshire PH7 4HQ
Sun 11am–5pm	t 01764 654 004

838 Dundee

Discovery Point

 1 hr+ · All year

Discovery Point is home to Captain Scott's ship, *Discovery*, which was built in Dundee for his expedition to the Antarctic, and the Verdant Works, winner of the European Industrial Museum of the Year award. It has original working machinery, computer and hands-on displays.

* State-of-the-art multimedia exhibitions
* Voted Scotland's Family Attraction of the Year 2004

Location	Admission
City centre, opposite train station	Adult £6.25, Child £3.85, Concs £4.70
Opening	**Contact**
Daily; Apr–Oct Mon–Sat 10am–6pm	Discovery Quay, Dundee DD1 4XA
Sun 11am–6pm	t 01382 201245
Nov–Mar Mon–Sat 10am–5pm	w rrsdiscovery.com
Sun 11am–5pm	e info@dundeeheritage.co.uk

839 Dundee

Sensation: Dundee

 1 hr+ · All year

If you thought science was boring, this centre may help you rethink. The hands-on experiments, live workshops and investigations bring science to life.

* Scottish Family Attraction of the Year 2003
* Gyroscope

Location	Contact
In Dundee city centre, 5 min walk from Dundee Station. Follow the brown tourist signs	Greenmarket, Dundee DD1 4QB
	t 01382 228800
Opening	w sensation.org.uk
Daily; 10am–6pm (5pm in winter)	e staff@sensation.org.uk
Admission	
Adult £6.50 , Child £4.50, Concs £4.50	

840 Dunfermline

Knockhill Racing Circuit

 3 hrs · All year

Get behind the wheel of a Formula First single-seater racing car or rally car, go off-road in a 4x4 or be driven round the racing circuit by a professional. Alternatively, sit back and enjoy the races. Choose from British touring cars, superbikes, stock cars and Formula Woman.

* Scotland's national race centre

Location	Contact
Signed from M90 junction 4	Dunfermline, Fife KY12 9TF
Opening	t 01383 723337
Daily; 9am–6.30pm	w knockhill.co.uk
Admission	e enquiries@knockhill.co.uk
Prices vary depending on the event, telephone for details	

841 East Lothian

Museum of Flight

1 hr+   **All year**

A superb aviation collection with aircraft, engines, rockets, photographs, a reference library, archives, models, flying clothing, instruments and propellers.

* Post-war military aircraft
* Exhibitions on 1914–18 & 1939–45

Location
Close to A1 near Haddington;
well signed from A1 in both directions

Opening
Daily; Apr–Oct 10am–5pm;
Nov–Mar weekends only 11am–4pm

Admission
Adult £3, Child Free, Concs £1.50

Contact
East Fortune Airfield,
East Lothian EH39 5LF

t 01620 880308
w nms.ac.uk/flight
e info@nms.ac.uk

842 Edinburgh

Almond Valley Heritage Centre

3 hrs   **All year**

An innovative museum exploring the history and environment of West Lothian with award-winning children's activities and interactive displays.

* Demonstrations & seasonal activities
* Narrow-gauge railway

Location
Signed from M8 (junction 3)
2 miles from the motorway

Opening
Daily; 10am–5pm

Admission
Adult £3, Child £2

Contact
Millfield, Livingston
West Lothian EH54 7AR

t 01506 414957
w almondvalley.co.uk
e info@almondvalley.co.uk

843 Edinburgh

Bedlam Paintball, Edinburgh

3 hrs+   **All year**

Find the ultimate adrenaline rush at Bedlam Paintball. Be prepared to utilize tactics, teamwork and quick thinking as you experience all five of the game scenarios available here.

* Other venues at Glasgow & Edzell
* For children aged 12 yrs+

Location
If travelling from Edinburgh, Fife, Falkirk, Stirling, Livingston & the surrounding areas, Bedlam is off the A8000

Opening
Daily; 9am–12 noon & 1pm–4pm
May–Mid Sept 5pm-8pm

Admission
From £20 per person, please phone for details

Contact
Milton Wood, Dundas Estate
South Queensferry, Edinburgh
t 07000 233526
e bedlam.co.uk
w info@bedlam.co.uk

844 Edinburgh

The Cadies & Witchery Tours

1-2 hrs   All year

Witchery Tours take a light-hearted look at tales of witchcraft, plague and torture. Explore the eerie alleyways and creepy courtyards of the Old Town with your ghostly guide, who will blend history with humour and fact with fable.

* 'Jump-ooters' make ghastly appearances
* Re-enactments & live performances

Location
Off the Royal Mile

Opening
Daily; tours operate 7pm-10pm;
Please phone to check times and avail-
ability

Admission
Under-5s Free
Please phone for details

Contact
84 West Bow (Victoria Street),
Edinburgh EH1 2HH

t 0131 225 6745
w witcherytours.com
e lyal@witcherytours.demon.co.uk

845 Edinburgh

Edinburgh Butterfly & Insect World

3 hrs+   All year

Walk through an indoor tropical rain forest inhabited by thousands of the world's most beautiful butterflies.

*Bugs & Beasties section
* Meet the Beasties handling sessions

Location
3 miles S of Edinburgh city centre on A702. Just off the Edinburgh city bypass, A720 at the Gilmerton exit

Opening
Daily; in summer 9.30am-5.30pm;
in winter 10am-5pm

Admission
Adults£4.70, Child £3.60, Concs £3.60

Contact
Dobbies Garden World
Lasswade, Edinburgh EH18 1AZ

t 0131 663 4932
e info@edinburgh-butterfly-
world.co.uk

846 Edinburgh

Edinburgh Crystal Visitor Centre

2 hrs   All year

Watch the craftsmen at work and experience for yourself the thrill of blowing and cutting crystal, it will take your breath away.

* VIP 'Hands On' Tour

Location
30 mins S of Edinburgh city centre.
From the city bypass, take A701 S for 4 miles, following the signs for Penicuik

Opening
Mon-Sat 10am-5pm

Admission
Free

Contact
Penicuik, Midlothian EH26 8HB

t 01968 675128
e edinburgh-crystal.com
w visitorcentre@edinburgh-
crystal.co.uk

847 Edinburgh

Edinburgh Castle

1 hr+ All year

A majestic landmark that dominates the city's skyline, Edinburgh Castle is the most visited of Scotland's historic buildings. Perched on an extinct volcano and offering stunning views, this fortress is a powerful national symbol, and part of Edinburgh's World Heritage Site.

* Guided & audio tours
* The Scottish Crown Jewels and the Stone of Destiny

Location
Castle Hill, at the top of the Royal Mile

Opening
Daily; Apr–Oct 9.30am–6pm
Nov–Mar 9.30am–5pm

Admission
Adult £9.50, Child £2, Concs £7

Contact
Castle Hill, Edinburgh EH1 2NG

t 0131 2259846
w historic-scotland.gov.uk

---

848 Edinburgh

Edinburgh Dungeon

1 hr All year

Buried beneath the paving stones of Edinburgh, lies this chilling horror attraction where scenes from the more terrible chapters of Scottish history unfold. Witch-hunters, grave-robbers, murderers, cannibals, and executioners – they're all here.

* Actors bring history to life
* Horror rides

Location
Edinburgh city centre

Opening
Please phone for details

Admission
Adult £8.95, Child (10–14) £6.95, (4–9) £4.95, Under-4s Free

Contact
31 Market Street,
Edinburgh EH1 1QB

t 0131 240 1000
e edinburghdungeon@merlinentertainments.biz

---

849 Edinburgh

Edinburgh Zoo

4 hrs All year

This is Scotland's most popular wildlife attraction, with over 1000 animals, including meerkats, pygmy hippos, tigers, lions and blue poison arrow frogs. Set in beautiful parkland, the zoo has the world's biggest penguin pool.

* African Plains Experience, the Maze, the Magic Forest
* Hilltop Safari Tour

Location
10 mins from the centre of Edinburgh

Opening
Daily; Apr–Sep 9am–6pm
Oct & Mar 9am–5pm
Nov–Feb 9am–4.30pm

Admission
Adult £8.50, Child £5.50, Concs £6

Contact
134 Corstorphine Road,
Edinburgh EH12 6TS

t 0131 3349171
w edinburghzoo.org.uk
e marketing@edinburghzoo.org.uk

850 Edinburgh

Museum of Scotland

2 hrs+ · All year

This magnificent museum tells the story of Scotland–its land, people and culture–through the rich national collections. The stunning themed galleries cover landscape and wildlife, early people, kingdom of the Scots, industry and empire, Scotland transformed and C20.

* Free events for all the family every Sunday
* Family funshops during the summer holidays

Location
Off A7 South Bridge, in city centre

Opening
Daily; Mon–Sat 10am–5pm Tue 10am–8pm Sun 12 noon–5pm

Admission
Free

Contact
Chambers Street, Edinburgh EH1 1JF
t 0131 247 4422
w nms.ac.uk
e info@nms.ac.uk

851 Edinburgh

National Portrait Gallery

2 hrs · All year

The gallery provides a visual history of Scotland, told through portraits of those who shaped it: royals and rebels, poets and philosophers, heroes and villains. Mary, Queen of Scots, Robert Burns, Sir Walter Scott and Sean Connery are all here.

* Works by Gainsborough, Copley and Rodin
* Unparalleled collection of Scottish portraits

Location
E end of Queen Street, Edinburgh city centre

Opening
Daily; 10am–5pm, Thu 10am–7pm; 1 Jan, 12 noon–5pm

Admission
Free

Contact
1 Queen Street, Edinburgh EH2 1JD
t 0131 624 6200
w nationalgalleries.org
e enquiries@nationalgalleries.org

852 Edinburgh

Our Dynamic Earth

1 hr+ · All year

Take a fantastic journey of discovery. Travel back in time to witness the Big Bang from the deck of a space ship, then forward through the history of our planet. You'll be shaken by earthquakes, dive deep beneath the ocean, feel the chill of polar ice and even get caught in a tropical rainstorm.

* Find out if there's a monster in Loch Ness
* Live 4500 million years in a day

Location
At the foot of Arthur's Seat, adjacent to the new Scottish Parliament

Opening
Daily; Mar–Aug 10am–6pm Sep–31 Oct 10am–5pm; Nov–Mar Wed–Sun 10am–5pm

Admission
Adult £8.95, Child & Concs £5.45

Contact
112 Holyrood Road, Edinburgh EH8 8AS
t 0131 550 7800
w dynamicearth.co.uk
e enquiries@dynamicearth.co.uk

853 Edinburgh

Polkemmet Country Park

2 hrs+ · All year

Polkemmet Country Park is a very attractive area of mixed mature woodlands and grassy open spaces along the upper reaches of the River Almond.

* Fantasy Forest
* 9-hole golf course

Location
Between junctions 4 & 5 of the M8, mid-way between Edinburgh & Glasgow. Entry is from the B7066, on the outskirts of Whitburn

Opening
Daily; 7am–9pm

Admission
Free

Contact
Whitburn
West Lothian EH47 0AD
t 01501 743905
e mail@beecraigs.com

854 Edinburgh

The Royal Yacht *Britannia*

4 hrs   All year

The *Britannia* Experience starts in the visitor centre where you can discover her fascinating story. Then step aboard her for a self-led audio tour, giving a unique insight into what life was like on board.

* Children's audio handset available
* Best UK Attraction Runner-up 2003

Location	**Admission**
Leith, north Edinburgh. Follow signs to Leith & Ocean Terminal	Adult £9, Child £5, Concs £7
Opening	**Contact**
Daily; Mar–Oct 9.30am–4.30pm Nov–Feb 10am–3.30pm	Ocean Terminal, Leith, Edinburgh EH6 6JJ
	t 01315 555566
	w royalyachtbritannia.co.uk
	e enquiries@tryb.co.uk

855 Edinburgh

Royal Botanic Garden Edinburgh

2 hrs   All year

Founded in the 17th century as a 'physic garden', growing medicinal plants, the garden is now acknowledged to be one of the finest in the world where unusual and beautiful plants can be found. It's a place to rest and relax away from the city's hustle and bustle.

* Guided and themed tours
* Rock/ peat/woodland gardens, chinese plants

Location	**Contact**
Off A902, 1 mile N of the City Centre	20A Inverleith Row, Edinburgh EH3 5LR
Opening	t 0131 552 7171
Daily; Apr–Sep 10am–7pm Mar & Oct 10am–6pm Nov–Feb 10am–4pm	w rbge.org.uk e info@rbge.org.uk
Admission	
Free (Donations welcome)	

856 Edinburgh

Royal Museum of Scotland

2 hrs   All year

Explore 36 galleries of exhibits covering decorative art, the natural world, science and industry. See steamships and sculptures, black holes and brown bears. Check out the communicate gallery to test how fast you can text and see what your name looks like in morse code.

Location	**Admission**
Edinburgh city centre, close to Prince's Street & the Royal Mile	Free
Opening	**Contact**
Daily; Mon–Sat, 10am–5pm; Tue 10am–8pm; Sun 12 noon–5pm	Chambers Street, Edinburgh EH1 1JF
	t 0131 247 4422
	w nms.ac.uk/royal
	e web@nms.ac.uk

857 Edinburgh

Scottish Railway Exhibition

1 hr   Apr–Oct

The Scottish Railway Exhibition tells the story of the railways in Scotland. Carriages, locomotives and wagons are on display, including Glen Douglas and a Royal saloon coach. The Bo'ness and Kinneil railway offers a 7-mile round trip by steam train.

* Demonstrations workshop
* 100 years of railways

Location
Access by footbridge from Bo'ness Station, West Lothian, 8 miles W of the Forth bridges. Access via junction 3 or 5 of M9

Opening
Apr–Oct weekends 11am–4.30pm; Jul & Aug Tue–Sun 11am–4.30pm

Admission
Adult £4.50, Child £2, Concs £3.50

Contact
Bo'ness Station, Union Street, Bo'ness, West Lothian EH51 9A
t 01506 822298
w srps.org.uk

858 Edinburgh

Scottish Seabird Centre

1 hr+   All year

Set on a dramatic promontory at North Berwick, the centre allows visitors to explore the fascinating world of seabirds, including puffins, via remote cameras on the nearby islands of Fidra, May and Bass Rock.

* 5-Star Visitor Attraction
* Queen's award for sustainability

Location
North Berwick Harbour, 25 miles from Edinburgh (regular train & bus services from the city)

Opening
Please phone for details

Admission
Adult £5.95, Child £3.95, Concs £3.95

Contact
Scottish Seabird Centre, The Harbour, North Berwick, East Lothian EH39 4SS
t 01620 890202
w seabird.org

859 Falkirk

Callendar House Museum

3 hrs   All year

Callendar House is an imposing mansion with a 600-year history, where you can go back in time to experience life in the 1820s.

* Costumed interpreters
* Boating

Location
From Callendar Road (A803) enter Estate Avenue. Located ½ mile E of the town centre

Opening
Mon–Sat 10am–5pm; Apr–Sep also Sun 2pm–5pm

Admission
Adult £3, Child £1, Concs £1.50

Contact
Callendar Park, Falkirk FK1 1YR
t 01324 503770
w falkirkmuseum.gov.uk

860 Falkirk

Megazone

1 hr+   All year

Megazone laser adventure is a futuristic wasteland filled with smoke, sounds, flashing lights – and enemies. Stalk your opponents with the latest technology. Use stealth and cunning, strategy and skill to score points.

* Regular family nights
* Expert retail store

Location
5 minutes' walk from Grahamston Railway Station & Central Retail Park

Opening
Daily; Mon 4pm–10pm, Tue–Fri 12 noon–10pm & Sat–Sun 10am–10pm

Admission
1st game £3.50 per person, further games £2.50 per person

Contact
104 Grahams Road Falkirk FK2 7BZ
t 01324 634828

861 Falkirk

The Falkirk Wheel

1 hr   Feb-Dec

For a truely uplifting experience visit the world's first and only rotating boat lift, linking two canals. There is a fascinating visitor centre with interactive exhibits and a viewing gallery.

* Boat trips available (please phone for admission details)
* Fun factory for kids

Location
Signed from M9

Opening
Daily; Apr–Nov 9am–6pm; Nov–Mar
10am–5pm

Admission
Visitor centre: **Free**

Contact
Lime Road, Tamfourhill,
Falkirk FK1 4RS

t 01324 676902
w thefalkirkwheel.co.uk
e info@thefalkirkwheel.co.uk

862 Fife

Deep Sea World

2 hrs+   All year

Explore the undersea world at the triple award-winning National Aquarium of Scotland. Situated on the banks of the Firth of Forth, below the Forth Railway Bridge this spectacular attraction is perfect for a family day out.

* Also known as Scotland's Shark Capital

Location
Signed 1mile from M90 on the N side
of the Forth Road Bridge

Opening
Daily; Apr–Oct 10am–6pm
Nov–Mar Mon–Fri 1am–5pm
Sat & Sun 10am–6pm

Admission
Adult £8.25, Child £6, Concs £6

Contact
North Queensferry, Fife KY11 1JR

t 01383 411411
w deepseaworld.com
e info@deepseaworld.com

Inverkeithing Museum

1 hr +   All year

Housed in the hospitium of the old Friary, this local history museum tells the story of Inverkeithing and nearby Rosyth. It contains artefacts belonging to Admiral Sir Samuel Greig, a son of Inverkeithing and the father of the modern Russian Navy.

* Please note: very steep external staircase   WC

Location	Contact
Located in Inverkeithing. Take the 1st exit over the Forth Road Bridge from Edinburgh, junction 1 on M90	The Friary, Queen Street, Inverkeithing KY11 1LS
Opening	t 01383 313838
Thu–Sun 11am–12.30pm & 1pm–4pm; open public holidays	e Lesley.Botten@fife.gov.uk
Admission	
Free	

864 Fife

Scottish Deer Centre

2 hrs +   All year

Enjoy a visit to this beautiful countryside centre, where a large herd of deer roam free. Under the guidance of expert rangers you are able to meet these majestic animals or even enjoy a nose-to-nose encounter with a stag.

* Adventure play parks
* Falconry displays

Location	Contact
On the outskirts of Cupar, 12 miles from St Andrews on A91	Rankeilour Park, Bow-of-Fife, Cupar, Fife KY15 4NQ
Opening	t 01337 810391
Please phone for details	e simplythebest@ewm.co.uk
Admission	
Adult £4.95, Child £3.45, Concs £3.95	

865 Fife

Scottish Fisheries Museum

1 hr+   All year

The Scottish Fisheries Museum tells the story of Scottish fishing and its people from the earliest times to the present. There are many fine paintings and photographs on display as well as a variety of real and model boats, fishing gear and other accoutrements.

* Overlooks a beautiful harbour
* Regular calendar of events and exhibitions

Location
Leave M90 at junction 3, follow A92 to Anstruther

Opening
Daily; Apr–Sep Mon–Sat 10am–5.30pm Sun 11am–5pm, Oct–Mar Mon–Sat 10am–4.30pm Sun 12 noon–4.30pm

Admission
Adult £4.50, Child Free, Concs £3.50

Contact
St Ayles, Harbourhead, Anstruther, Fife KY10 3AB

t 01333 310628
w scottish-fisheries-museum.org
e info@scottish-fisheries-museum.org

866 Fife

Scottish Vintage Bus Museum

2 hrs   Apr–Oct

Possibly Britain's largest collection of historic buses dating from the 1920s to 1980s. There are beautifully restored buses to see in the main exhibition hall, as well as buses under restoration in the large workshops.

* Regular bus rallies
* Fire engines

Location
On B915, near Dunfermline; follow signs to 'Commerce Park' from M90 (junction 4)

Opening
Easter–early Oct Sun only 12.30pm–5pm

Admission
Adult £3, Concs £1.50

Contact
Commerce Park, Lathalmond, Nr Dunfermline, Fife KY12 0SJ

t 01383 623380
w busweb.co.uk/svbm

867 Fife

St Andrews Aquarium

1 hr+   Apr–Oct

Enjoy a sense of discovery and enjoyment at St Andrews Aquarium, which welcomes you to the wonderful world of the sea and its inhabitants – from shrimps to sharks, octopuses to eels, rays to seals.

* Over 30 exhibition tanks
* Touch some of the rays and fish

Location
At the Bruce Embankment near the Royal & Ancient Golf Club

Opening
Daily; Easter–end Oct 10am–6pm

Admission
Adult £5.85, Child £3.85, Concs £4.85

Contact
The Scores, St Andrews, Fife KY16 9AS

t 01334 474786
w standrewsaquarium.co.uk
e info@standrewsaquarium.co.uk

868 Glamis by Forfar

Glamis Castle

 2 hrs+   Mar–Oct

This is a place of legends and fairytales. It has been a royal residence since 1372 and was the childhood home of HM Queen Elizabeth The Queen Mother, birthplace of HRH The Princess Margaret and the legendary setting for Shakespeare's famous play *Macbeth*.

* Free guide books for all children visiting the castle
* Beautiful gardens & nature trail

Location
On A94, between Aberdeen & Perth

Opening
Daily; Mar–Oct 10am–6pm
Nov–24 Dec 11am–3pm

Admission
Adult £7, Child £3.80, Concs £5.70

Contact
The Castle Administrator,
Estates Office, Glamis by Forfar,
Angus DD8 1RJ

t 01307 840393
w glamis-castle.co.uk
e enquiries@glamis-castle.co.uk

869 Glasgow

Calderglen Country Park

 2 hrs   All year

This is a large country park with a visitor centre, children's zoo, conservatory, adventure playground and miles of fascinating trails to follow.

* 4-Star award by the Scottisch Tourist Board

Location
In Calderglen Country Park in East Kilbride on the Strathaven road, just out of town

Opening
Park: Daily; at any reasonable time
Visitor centre: Daily; in summer
10.30am–5pm; in winter 11.30am–4pm

Admission
Free

Contact
East Kilbride G75 0QZ

t 01355 236644

870 Glasgow

Clydebuilt Scottish Maritime Museum

 2 hrs   All year

Clydebuilt charts the development of Glasgow and the Clyde from 1700 to the present day. It tells the story of Glasgow's rivers, its ships and its people, through award-winning audio-visuals, computer interpretation, hands-on displays and video.

* 5-Star Museum Attraction
* Take control of a real steam engine

Location
At junctions 25 & 26 on Glasgow's M8

Opening
All year open Mon–Thu & Sat
10am–5.30pm & Sun 11am–5.30pm
Closed Fri

Admission
Adult £3.50, Child £1.75, Concs £1.75

Contact
Braehead Shopping Centre,
Kings Inch Road,
Glasgow G51 4BN

t 0141 8861013
w scottishmaritimemuseum.org
e clydebuilt@tinyworld.co.uk

871 Glasgow

Falls of Clyde Visitor Centre and Wildlife Reserve

 2 hrs+   All year

The Falls of Clyde Wildlife Reserve includes ancient gorge woodland along both sides of the River Clyde, with its famous and spectacular waterfalls. The Visitor Centre includes an exhibition and offers a programme of educational events and guided walks on the reserve.

* Network of paths
* Badger watching

Location
The Visitor Centre is in New Lanark, which is signed from all major routes and lies 1 mile S of Lanark

Opening
Reserve: Daily; in summer 8am–8pm; in winter during daylight hours

Admission
Free

Contact
Falls of Clyde Reserve,
New Lanark,
Lanarkshire ML11 9DB

t 01555 665262
w swt.org.uk
e fallsofclyde@swt.org.uk

873 Glasgow

Glasgow Science Centre

2 hrs+   All year

The Glasgow Science Centre has hundreds of hands-on exhibits over three floors, where visitors can interact with real experiments and phenomena.

* IMAX theatre
* Space theatre with planetarium projector

Location
Opposite the Scottish Exhibition Centre & the Moat House Hotel on the Clyde

Opening
Daily; 10am–6pm

Admission
Adult £6.95, Child £4.95, Concs £4.95

Contact
50 Pacific Quay,
Glasgow G51 1EA

t 0141 420 5000
w glasgowsciencecentre.org
e admin@gsc.org.uk

872 Glasgow

Glasgow Police Museum

1 hr+   All year

Visit the museum of Britain's first police force to gain historical insight into the people and the events that contributed to the founding, development and progress of the force.

* International police exhibition

Location
From London Road, via James Morrison Street, or Saltmarket via St Andrew's Street, or Greendyke Street via Turnball Street

Opening
Daily; Apr–Oct 10am–4.30pm (12 noon opening on Sun); Nov–end Mar Tue 10am–4.30pm & Sun 12 noon–4.30pm

Admission
Free

Contact
68 St. Andrew's Square, Glasgow,

t 07788532691
w policemuseum.org.uk

874 Glasgow

Glasgow Ski & Snowboarding Centre

1 hr+   All year

An artificial ski and snowboarding centre with three slopes that caters for children of all levels and offers lessons in group or private sessions.

* Race training & freeride clubs
* Kids' toboggan parties (5 yrs+)

Location
In Bellahouston Park

Opening
Daily; In summer Mon–Fri 9.30am–9pm & Sat–Sun 9.30am–6pm; in winter Mon–Thurs 9.30am–11pm & Fri–Sun 9.30am–9pm

Admission
Adult £13, Child £10

Contact
16 Dumbreck Road,
Glasgow G41 5BW

t 0141 4274991
w ski-glasgow.co.uk
e info@ski-glasgow.co.uk

875 Glasgow

Lamont City Farm

2 hrs   All year

Come and meet all sorts of animals, including sheep, goats, horses, ponies, pigs, rabbits, chinchillas, chipmunks, guinea pigs, hens, ducks and geese.

* Donkey rides
* Snack bar

Location
On M8 travel to St James roundabout & take the Erskine cut-off. At the 3rd roundabout, turn left then 1st right into Barhill Road

Opening
Daily; 10.30am–4.30pm (3.30pm in winter)

Admission
Families free (donations welcome)
Groups please phone for details

Contact
Barhill Road,
Erskine, Renfrewshire PA8 6BX

t 0141 8125335
w lamontcityfarm.co.uk

876 Glasgow

Loch Lomond Shores

3 hrs+   All year

Loch Lomond offers activites for all weathers amidst the breathtaking scenery of Scotland's first national park. There are interactive exhibitions charting the history and wildlife of the area.

* 4-Star attraction
* Canoe & bike hire

Location
Signed from M74, M6, M73 & M8

Opening
Daily; at any reasonable time

Admission
Varies depending on activity
Please phone for details

Contact

Ben Lomond Way,
Balloch,
Dunbartonshire G83 8GL

t 01389 721500
w lochlomondshores.com
e info@lochlomondshores.com

877 Glasgow

Motoring Heritage Centre

1 hr   All year

The display tells the story of Scotland's motoring history with fine cars and unique archive film. Guided tours are available.

* 2-Star attraction

Location
In Alexandria within walking distance of Balloch by Loch Lomond. Follow A82 to Balloch

Opening
Mon, Fri, Sat, 10am–5pm Sun 11am–5pm
Closed Tue-Thu

Admission
Adult £1.50, Child 75p, Concs £1

Contact
Loch Lomond Outlets,
Main Street, Alexandria,
West Dunbartonshire G83 0UG

t 01389 607862
w motoringheritage.co.uk

878 Glasgow

Museum of Scottish Country Life

3 hrs   All year

Set in 170 acres of farmland, with a Georgian farmhouse and steadings, this museum gives an insight into the working lives of the people of Scotland.

* Exhibition building
* Historic farm & demonstrations

Location
Just off A749 or A726 S of Glasgow & W of East Kilbride

Opening
Daily; 10am–5pm

Admission
Adult £4, Child (4–13) Free, Concs £3

Contact
West Kittochside,
East Kilbride G76 9HR

t 01355 224181
w nms.ac.uk

879 Glasgow

Museum of Transport

2 hrs   All year

The museum uses its collections of vehicles and models to tell the story of transport by land and sea, with a unique Glasgow flavour. Here you will find the oldest surviving pedal cycle and the finest collection in the world of Scottish-built cars.

* World famous makes such as Argyll and Albion
* Fully restored Spitfire on display

Location
In the city's West End, opposite Kelvingrove Art Gallery and Museum

Opening
Daily; Mon–Thu & Sat 10am–5pm, Fri & Sun 11am–5pm

Admission
Free

Contact
Kelvin Hall, 1 Bunhouse Road, Glasgow G3 8DP
t 0141 287 2720
w glasgowmuseums.com

880 Glasgow

People's Palace

2 hrs+   All year

The People's Palace is Glasgow's social history museum and a chance to see the story of the people and city of Glasgow from 1760 to the present. You can see paintings, prints and photographs displayed alongside a wealth of historic artefacts, film and computer interactives.

* Discover how a family lived in a typical single end Glasgow tenement

Location
A short walk from the heart of the city

Opening
Daily; Mon–Thu & Sat 10am–5pm Fri & Sun 11am–5pm

Admission
Free

Contact
Glasgow Green G40 1AT
t 0141 271 2951
w glasgowgalleries.co.uk

881 Glasgow

The Piping Centre

2 hrs   All year

The Piping Centre houses the National Museum of Scotland's fine collection of bagpipes, making it the most authoritative display of its kind. The priceless collection is presented in a lively, audio-visual format that is as entertaining as it is enlightening.

* 4-Star museum attraction

Location
In Glasgow, off junction 16 of M8 & along A804 towards the E

Opening
Daily; 9am-9pm
Closed Sun in Winter

Admission
Adult £3, Child £2, Concs £2

Contact
30-34 McPhater Street,
Glasgow G4 0HW

t 0141 3530220
w thepipingcentre.co.uk
e reception@thepipingcentre.co.uk

882 Glasgow

Scotkart

1 hr   All year

Experience the thrill, the speed and the buzz of Scotland's largest and fastest indoor karting centre. This indoor circuit features 200cc race karts. All the equipment, instruction and computer timings are included in the price.

* 200cc race karts

Location
Follow Clydebank signs along the expressway then the Dunbarton road. At Yoker look for the brown tourist signs – Scotkart is 200 yards from Yoker station

Opening
Daily; 12 noon–10pm

Admission
Adult £12 per session (12 mins),
Child £10 per session (12 mins)

Contact
John Knox Street,
Clydebank, Glasgow G81 1NA

t 0141 6410222
w scotkart.co.uk

883 Glasgow

Tall Ship in Glasgow Harbour

1 hr+   All year

Built in 1896, the tall ship *Glenlee* circumnavigated the globe four times. Discover her rich history, depicted on board, and gain a real sense of what it was like to live and work on board in her seafaring days. Special events include pirate crafts and seafaring superstitions.

* Caters for children's birthday parties
* One of only five Clyde-built sailing ships afloat in the world

Location
Off M8 junction 19, follow brown thistle signs

Opening
Daily; Mar–Nov 10am–5pm
Dec–Feb 11am–4pm

Admission
Adult £4.50, Child £2.50, Concs £3.25
(one child free with each paying adult)

Contact
100 Stobe Cross Road, Glasgow G3 8QQ

t 0141 2222513
w thetallship.com
e info@thetallship.com

884 Kenmore

Scottish Crannog Centre

1 hr+   Mar–Nov

Visit Scotland's only authentic recreation of an Iron Age loch-dwelling. Guided tours, exhibits, video and ancient crafts bring the past to life.

* Regular hands-on activities
* Themed special events and re-enactments

Location
Just off A827, 6 miles W of Aberfeldy. Easily reached from Edinburgh & Glasgow

Opening
Daily; Mid Mar–Nov 10am–5.30pm
(4pm closing in Nov); last admission
1 hr before closing

Admission
Adult £4.25, Child £3.25

Contact
Kenmore, Lock Tay,
Perthshire PH15 2HY

t 01887 830583
w crannog.co.uk
e info@crannog.co.uk

885 Kinloch Rannoch

Loch Rannoch Watersports & Quads

4 hrs+   All year

Try your hand at a variety of water-based activities, from canoeing and windsurfing to sailing, motor boating and kayaking.

* Reindeer safaris at Christmas
* Quad-bike & field-sport centre (for ages 14+)

Location
Signed for Kinloch Rannoch off A9 N of Pitlochry

Opening
Daily; in summer 9.30am–9pm;
in winter 10.30am–5pm

Admission
Activities priced individually

Contact
Kinloch Rannoch, Perthshire

t 01882 632242
w goforth.co.uk

886 Kirriemuir

Peel Farm

1 hr+   Mar–Dec

There are many animals and birds at Peel Farm, as well as a walk along a varied and interesting farm trail that includes a gorge and waterfall and red deer park.

* Possible wild otter sightings
* The courtyard exhibits paintings and crafts

Location
20 miles N of Dundee, off B951 from Kirriemuir or B594 from Alyth

Opening
Daily; Apr–Dec 10am–5pm;
Jan–Mar open Sat, Sun 10am–5pm

Admission
Free

Contact
Lintrathen, by Kirriemuir, Angus DD8 5JJ

t 01575 560205
w peelfarm.com
e Frances@peelfarm.com

887 Linlithgow

Linlithgow Palace

 2 hrs   All year

Set in its own park and beside Linlithgow Loch, this is a maginficent ruin of a great royal palace. A favoured residence of Stewart royalty, James V and Mary Queen of Scots were both born here.

* 4-Star Historic Attraction

Location
In Linlithgow off M9

Opening
Daily; 1 Apr–30 Sept 9.30am–6pm;
1 Oct–31 Mar Mon–Sat
9.30am–4.30pm & Sun 2–4.30pm

Admission
Adult £3, Child £1, Concs £2.30

Contact
Kirkgate,
Linlithgow,
West Lothian EH49 7AL

t 01506 842896
w historic-scotland.gov.uk
e hs.historic@scotland.gov.uk

888 New Lanark

New Lanark World Heritage Site

 2 hrs+   All year

This beautifully restored conservation village was once Britain's largest cotton-manufacturing centre and is the birthplace of Robert Owen's reforms. Now a World Heritage Site, New Lanark's award-winning visitor centre features the amazing Millennium Experience.

* World Heritage Site
* Millworkers' house

Location
New Lanark is signed from all major routes (A72/M74/A70) and is less than 1 hour from Glasgow, Edinburgh & Stirling by car

Opening
Daily; 11am–5pm

Admission
Adult £5.95, Child £3.95, Concs £3.95

Contact
New Lanark Mill,
Lanarkshire ML11 9DB

t 01555 661345
w newlanark.org
e visit@newlanark.org

889 Perth

Dewar's Centre

3-4 hrs   All year

Come and brush up on your curling skills, or take the plunge and learn to skate for the first time. Everyone is catered for, including the little ones, with Tiny Tots on Ice.

* 8-rink indoor bowling arena
* Superb catering facilities

Location
Situated in the centre of Perth

Opening
Daily; but please check before visiting as times vary

Admission
£4.70 (Under 5s go free)

Contact
Glover St,
Perth PH2 0TH

t 01738 624188
w curlingscotland.com
e info@curlingscotland.com

890 Perth

Noah's Ark

2 hrs   All year

Noah's Ark is a specially equipped children's soft play barn for under-12s. There are three separate areas to ensure the safety of all the children. Indoor karting is available seasonally.

* 4-Star Visitor Attraction
* Tenpin bowling, ceramic studio and trampolines

Location
On Western Edge of Perth,
½ mile from A9

Opening
Soft play: Daily
Please phone to confirm times

Admission
Adult Free, Under-5s £3.75,
Over-5s £4.25

Karting: £3.50 for 5 mins,
£4 for 5 mins in twin karts

Contact
Old Gallows Road,
Perth PH1 1QE

t 01738 445568
w noahs-ark.co.uk
e info@noahs-ark.co.uk

891 Pitlochry

Atholl Country Life Museum

3 hrs+   Apr–Sep

This lively museum explores the reality of country life and the social history of the Atholl people. It uses detailed facts, 100 historical photographs, and stories set in a wide range of imaginative displays.

* Stuffed highland cow
* Trinofour Post Office

Location
Turn off A9 for Blair Atholl, 7 miles N of Pitlochry

Opening
Daily; Easter & end May to end Sep 1.30pm–5pm; Jul & Aug from 10am on weekdays

Admission
Adult £3 , Child £1

Contact
Blair Atholl, Pitlochry,
Perthshire PH18 5SP

t 01796 481232
e janet.com@virgin.net

892 Pittenweem

Kellie Castle & Garden

2 hrs   All year

This beautiful castle was started in 1360, although much of the present building was built in C16 and early C17. Don't miss the Victorian nursery with its fascinating collection of dolls and toys. Outdoor attractions include Victorian stables, a dovecot and a charming walled garden.

* Fine example of domestic architecture
* Beautiful walled garden

Location
On B9171, 3 miles from Pittenweem

Opening
Castle Daily; Easter & Jun–Sep 1pm–5pm
Garden Daily; 9.30am–sunset

Admission
Castle & grounds Adult £5, Concs £3.75

Garden £2

Contact
Pittenweem, Fife KY10 2RF

t 01333 720271
w nts.org.uk
e info@1001daysout.com

893 Plean

Plean Country Park

3 hrs+   All year

This beautiful Victorian estate offers extensive woodland walks, parkland, a picnic area and orienteering courses.

* Varied events throughout the year

Location
Off M9, M80 & M876, S of Stirling

Opening
Daily; dawn–dusk

Admission
Free

Contact
President Kennedy Drive, Plean, Stirling

t 01786 442541
w stirling.gov.uk/countryside

894 St Andrews

British Golf Museum

½ hr+   All year

Ever wondered where the word golf comes from? Why there are 18 holes on a golf course? Why golfers shout 'fore'? Here you'll learn the answers and many more interesting facts besides. The museum tells the story of British golf from its origins to the present day.

* Based in St Andrews, the home of golf
* Guided walks on the Old Course (summer only)

Location
Signed from town centre

Opening
Daily; Apr–Oct 9.30am–5.30pm
Winter times vary

Admission
Adult £4, Child £2, Concs £3

Contact
Bruce Embankment, St Andrews, Fife KY16 9AB

t 01334 460046
w britishgolfmuseum.co.uk
e alisonwood@randagc.org

895 St Andrews

Scotland's Secret Bunker

1 hr+   Apr–Oct

Hidden beneath a farmhouse is a 24,000 sq ft secret nuclear bunker. Walk down the 150m entrance tunnel and through the 3-ton blast-proof doors to discover 24,000 sq ft of secret accommodation. Up to 300 staff would have lived here for up to 3 months at a time.

* Built in secrecy in the 1950s
* Uniquely designed to withstand a nuclear attack

Location
On B940, between St Andrews & Anstruther

Opening
Daily; Apr–Oct 10am–6pm

Admission
Adult £7.20, Child £4.50, Concs £5.95

Contact
Crown Buildings, Troywood, nr St Andrews, Fife KY16 8QH

t 01333 310301
w secretbunker.co.uk
e mod@secretbunker.co.uk

896 Stirling

Blair Drummond Safari & Adventure Park

4 hrs+   Mar–Oct

A fascinating collection of animals from all over the world, including elephants, giraffes, lions, tigers, and rhinos. You can take a safari to Chimpanzee Island, watch the performing sea lion show or visit the Pet Farm.

* Elephant training course every day
* Three african Rhinos

Location
In Blair Drummond by junction 10 of M9, 4 miles along A84 towards Callander

Opening
Daily; 20 Mar–4 Oct 10am–5.30pm (last admission 4.30pm)

Admission
Adult £9, Child £5, Concs £5.50

Contact
Blair Drummond, Stirling
Stirlingshire FK9 4UR

t 01786 841456
w blairdrummond.com
e enquiries@blairdrummond.com

897 Stirling

Bannockburn Heritage Centre

2 hrs   All year

Situated at the site of the famous battlefield where King Robert the Bruce routed the forces of King Edward II to win freedom for the Scots from English domination, the centre contains an exhibition on the period of the battle and an audio-visual presentation.

* Living history actors

Location
On A872, 2 miles S of Stirling

Opening
Daily; Feb & 1 Nov–24 Dec 10.30am–4pm; 1 Mar–31 Oct 10am–5.30pm; last audio-visual show ½ hour before closing

Admission
Adult £3.50, Child £2.60, Concs £2.60

Contact
Glasgow Road, Stirling,
Stirlingshire

t 01786 812664
w nts.org.uk

898 Stirling

Stirling Castle

3 hrs — All year

Considered by many to be the grandest of Scotland's castles. There is a medieval kitchens display and an exhibition of life in the Royal Palace.

* Re-enactments & performances

WC 🏕 🍴 ♿

Location
At the head of Stirling's historic Old Town, off M9

Opening
Daily; Apr–Sep 9.30am–6pm;
Oct–Mar 9.30am–5pm

Admission
Adult £8, Child £2, Concs £6

Contact
Castle Wynd, Stirling,
Stirlingshire FK8 1EJ

t 01786 450000
w historic-scotland.go.uk

899 Stirling

The MacRobert Centre

2 hrs+ — All year

The MacRobert Centre is a premier children's art venue and Scotland's first dedicated children's theatre. It includes projection facilities for animation and other film work produced by children, and there is a fully supervised crèche involving children in art activities.

* Ideal for children with special needs

WC 🏕 🍴 ♿

Location
Off A9, follow signs to the University of Stirling

Opening
Daily; 10am–Late
Please phone for tickets & information

Admission
Varies, please phone for details

Contact
University of Stirling,
Stirling FK9 4LA

t 01786 466666
w macrobert.org
e macrobert-arts@stir.ac.uk

900 Aberdeen

Aberdeen Maritime Museum

1 hr+ All year

Discover what it is like to live and work on a massive oil platform in the middle of the North Sea. Using models, real equipment and computer displays, the exhibitions bring the maritime experience to life. There are models of fast clipper ships and fishing displays.

* Incorporates Provost Ross's House, built in 1593
* Offers a spectacular viewpoint over the busy harbour

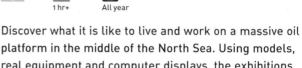

Location	Contact
On the harbour	Shiprow, Aberdeen AB11 5BY
Opening	t 01224 337700
Daily; Mon-Sat 10am-5pm Sun 12pm-3pm	w aagm.gov.uk
	e info@aagm.co.uk
Admission	
Free	

901 Aberdeen

Beach Leisure Centre

4 hrs+ All year

Relax at this leisure centre with pool and flumes, fitness studio, health suite, climbing wall and sports hall. There is also an adjoining ice arena.

* Free crèche
* Refurbished café

Location	Contact
Next to the beach at Aberdeen	Beach Promenade, Aberdeen AB24 5NR
Opening	t 01224 647647
Please phone for details	w aberdeencity.gov.uk
Admission	e info@aberdeencity.gov.uk
Facilities individualy priced	

902 Aberdeen

Codona's Pleasure Fair

3 hrs+   All year

Codona's amusement park is packed with more than 30 sensational rides and attractions for all the family. There are fun children's rides and, for the white knuckle fans, there's the giant Log Flume and 360 degree Looping Star Roller Coaster.

* Haunted house
* Dodgems

WC | Y1 | &

Location
Travelling from the S take A90. Coming from Inverness take A96 Inverness–Aberdeen route. Once in Aberdeen follow the signs to Aberdeen Fun Beach

Opening
Daily; 10am–midnight
Please phone for details

Admission
Rides priced individually

Contact
Beach Boulevard,
Aberdeen, Aberdeenshire AB24 5NS

t 01224 595910
w codonas.com

903 Aberdeen

Gordon Highlanders Museum

2 hrs   Apr–Oct

Relive the compelling and dramatic story of one of the British Army's most famous regiments through the lives of its outstanding personalities and of the kilted soldiers of the north-east Scotland.

* Tartan day, national garden day
* Interactive displays

WC | Y1 | &

Location
Off Queens Road, known as the Highland Tourist Route in & out of Aberdeen

Opening
Apr–Oct Tue–Sun 10.30am–4.30pm & Sun 1.30pm–4.30pm; closed Mon; Nov–Mar open by appointment only

Admission
Adult £2.50 , Child £1.00 , Concs £1.50

Contact
St Luke's, Viewfield Road
Aberdeen AB15 7XH

t 01224 311200
w gordonhighlanders.com
e museum@gordonhighlanders.com

904 Aberdeen

The Old Royal Station, Ballater

3 hrs   All year

This renovated railway station features royalty and railway exhibitions with commentary and audio-visual presentations about Royal Deeside.

* 4-Star Speciality Attraction

WC | Y1 | &

Location
In the centre of the picturesque Deeside village of Ballater, on A93 Aberdeen–Braemar road

Opening
Daily; Jan–May 10am–5pm
Jun–Sep 9am–6pm
Oct–Dec 10am–5pm

Admission
Free

Contact
Station Square, Ballater AB35 5AB

t 01339 755306
e ballater@agtb.org
w aberdeen-grampian.com

905 Aberdeen

Satrosphere

2 hrs   All year

Fun for families and for grown-ups who love to explore, experiment and find out how the world works. Look into infinity, light up a plasma dome, step inside a bubble or make a skeleton ride a bike – it's all possible at Satrosphere.

* Interactive shows
* Workshops

WC | Y1 | &

Location
Off Beach Boulevard & Links Road near the Patio Hotel

Opening
Daily; Mon–Sat 10am–5pm & Sun 11.30am–5pm

Admission
Adult £5.50, Child, Concs £4

Contact
The Tramsheds,
179 Constitution Street,
Aberdeen AB24 5TU

t 01224 640340
w satrosphere.net
e Satrosphere@satrosphere.net

906 Ballaster

Balmoral Castle & Estate

1 hr+   Easter–Aug

See inside one of the Queen's residences, visit the ballroom, the formal and vegetable gardens or enjoy an audio-visual display. Other activities on the estate include pony-trekking, a Land-Rover safari, guided walks, fishing and trailer rides.

* Built 1853-56 for Queen Victoria

Location
Off A93, between Ballater & Braemar

Opening
Daily; Easter–Aug 10am–5pm

Admission
Adult £6, Child £1, Concs £5

Contact
Estates Office, Balmoral Estates, Ballater, Aberdeenshire AB35 5TB
t 013397 42534
w balmoralcastle.com
e info@balmoralcastle.com

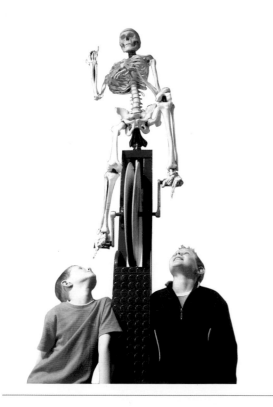

907 Braemar

Braemar Castle

2 hrs   Apr–Oct

Located in the Cairngorms on Royal Deeside, this impressive fortress was built in 1628 by the Earl of Mar. Don't miss the toy room which has many wonderful children's toys including a doll's house, a cradle, a cot and a teddy bears' tea party.

* Home of the world's largest cairngorm (52 lbs)
* Curio room with interesting memorabilia

Location
½ mile NE of Braemar on A93 Aberdeen-to-Perth scenic route

Opening
Apr-Oct, Sat-Thu, 10am-6pm

Admission
Adult £3, Child £2.50, Concs £2.50

Contact
Braemar, Aberdeenshire AB35 5XR
t 013397 41219
w braemarcastle.co.uk
e invercauld@btconnect.com

908 Drumoak

Drum Castle, Garden & Estate

2–4 hrs   Apr–Sep

The late C13 keep, fine adjoining Jacobean mansion and the additions of Victorian lairds make Drum Castle unique. The building is set in spectacular grounds, including a garden of historic roses, woodland trails and a children's playground.

* Old Wood of Drum is Site of Special Scientific Interest

Location
Off A93, 3 miles W of Peterculter, 8 miles E of Banchory & 10 miles W of Aberdeen

Opening
Daily; 1 Apr–31 May & 1–30 Sep 12.30pm–5.30pm; 1 Jun–31 Aug 10am–5.30pm

Admission
Please phone for details

Contact
Drumoak, Banchory, Aberdeen & Grampian AB31 5EY
t 01330 811204
w drum-castle.org.uk
e drum@nts.org.uk

909 Fraserburgh

The Museum of Scottish Lighthouses

2 hrs+   All year

Located in Scotland's oldest lighthouse, the museum tells the history of Scotland's lighthouses. There are multi-screen audio-visual presentations and a guided tour to the top of the fully-restored lighthouse where visitors can enjoy panoramic views of the Buchan Coast.

* Largest collection of lighthouse equipment in UK
* First lighthouse built on top of a fortified castle

Location
In Fraserburgh

Opening
Daily; Apr-Oct Mon-Sat 11am-5pm
Sun 12 noon-5pm; Jul-Aug Mon-Sat
10am-6pm Sun 11am-6pm; Nov-Mar
Mon-Sat 11am-4pm Sun 12 noon-4pm

Admission
Adult £4.75, Child £2, Concs £4

Contact
Kinnaird Head, Stevenson Road,
Fraserburgh AB43 9DU

t 01346 511022
w lighthousemuseum.co.uk
e enquiries@lighthousemuseum.
demon.co.uk

910 Huntly

Leith Hall

3 hrs +   Apr–Sep

The home of the Leith family since 1650, the mansion house contains interesting personal possessions and a military exhibition. The estate has a garden with two ponds, a bird hide, ice house and stables.

* Halloween events
* Easter-egg hunt

Location
On B9002, 1 mile W of Kennethmont &
34 miles NW of Aberdeen. Signed off
A96

Opening
Easter weekend & 1 May-Sep
Fri-Tue 12 noon-5pm
(last admission 4.15pm)

Admission
Varies according to ticket type
Please phone for details

Contact
Kennethmont, Huntly,
Aberdeenshire AB54 4NQ

t 01464 831216
w nts.org.uk

911 Macduff

Macduff Marine Aquarium

1 hr+   All year

This most northerly of Scotland's aquaria has several unique features, including the main tank which is open to the air.

* Estuary & deep-reef exhibits
* Feeding times & dive sessions

Location
A short walk from Macduff town
centre, just E of the harbour. Reached
via A98, A947 or A96

Opening
Daily; 10am-5pm

Admission
Adult £4.50, Child £2, Concs £2.50

Contact
11 High Shore, Macduff
Banffshire AB44 1SL

t 01261 833369
w marine-aquarium.com

912 Maryculter

Storybook Glen

2–4 hrs   All year

This 28-acre family theme park has over 100 life-size models set in beautifully landscaped gardens.

* 20 acres of scenic beauty
* Old Macdonald's farmhouse

Location
In Maryculter, just off South Deeside Road (the B9077), 5 miles W of Aberdeen

Opening
Daily; 1 Mar–31 Oct 10am–6pm (last admission 4pm); 1 Nov–end Feb 10am–4pm

Admission
Adult £4.15, Child £3.10, Concs £3.25

Contact
South Deeside Road, Maryculter, Aberdeen

t 01224 732941
w activitypoint.co.uk

913 Mintlaw

Aberdeenshire Farming Museum

2 hrs   Apr–Oct

Discover 200 years of farming and family life at this museum, set in C19 farm buildings. There is also a working 1950s-style farm.

* Collection of farming artefacts
* Sensory garden

Location
1 mile W of Mintlaw on A950

Opening
Daily; May–Sep 11am–4.30pm; Apr & Oct weekends only 12pm–4.30pm
Park open all year
Please phone for details

Admission
Free

Contact
Aden Country Park, Nr Mintlaw, Aberdeenshire AB42 5FQ

t 01771 622906
w aberdeenshire.gov.uk/heritage

914 New Pitsligo

Northfield Farm Museum

1–2 hrs   May–Sep

Come and enjoy looking at exhibits such as tractors, motorbikes, farm implements, household items and a smiddy engineer's workshop.

* Unique private collection of farm machinery
* 1920s tractors

Location
10 miles SW of Fraserburgh, just off A98

Opening
Daily; May–Sep 11am–5.30pm

Admission
Adult £1.50, Child 75p, Concs 75p

Contact
New Pitsligo,
Nr Fraserburgh,
Aberdeenshire AB43 6PX

t 01771 653504

915 Peterhead

Peterhead Maritime Heritage

1 hr+   Jun–Aug

This heritage centre offers a historic look back at the Peterhead experience of fishing and whaling, and gives a brief insight into the oil industry.

* 3–Star Speciality Attraction

Location
Overlooking Peterhead Bay & beside the beach and marina. Reached via A90 or A950

Opening
Daily; Jun–Aug 10.30am–5pm & Sun 11.30am–5pm

Admission
Please phone for details

Contact
South Road, Peterhead, Aberdeenshire AB42 2YP

t 01779 473000

916 Ardrishaig

Lochfyne Miniature Railway

1 hr   Apr–Sep

This miniature 10½-inch gauge steam railway runs the length of Ardrishaig Front Green from Greenend Station to the John Smith Memorial Garden.

* Fun for all the family
* Regular timetable

Location
2 miles S of Lochgilphead on A83
Campbeltown road, 40 miles S of Oban

Opening
Apr–Sep Sat & Sun from 12.30pm
(weather permitting)

Admission
Rail fare: £1

Contact
The Front Green,
Ardrishaig,
Argyll PA 30

t 01546 602918

917 Aviemore

Cairngorm Reindeer Centre

1 hr   All year

Travel in a cavalcade to see 150 reindeer ranging free in the Cairngorms. Under the watchful eye of a guide, visitors can feed, stroke and photograph the reindeer. Suitable for all ages, even babies in back carriers. Book well in advance for Christmas sleigh-pulling events.

* Britain's only herd of reindeer
* Wall displays tell visitors more about reindeer

Location
6 miles E of Aviemore

Opening
Daily; 10am–5pm
Closed Jan

Admission
Adult £8, Child £4, Concs £4,
Paddocks £2, £1

Contact
Glenmore, Aviemore,
Invernesshire PH22 1QU

t 01479 861228
w reindeer-company.demon.co.uk
e info@reindeer-company.demon.co.uk

918 Aviemore

The Fun House

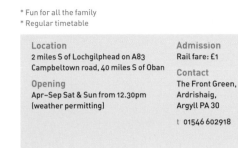

2 hrs   All year

The Fun House is a first choice for family entertainment with mini golf, a tree house, tenpin bowling, air hockey and soft play areas. There is also a crèche for toddlers.

* 3 Star Visitor Attraction

Location
Off B970, on a wooded riverside estate
of 65 acres (on the ski road)

Opening
Daily; 10am–6pm

Admission
Please phone for details

Contact
Hilton Coylumbridge Hotel, Aviemore,
Invernesshire PH22 1QN

t 01479 813081
w aviemorefunhouse.co.uk
e aviemorefunhouse.co.uk

919 Aviemore

Strathspey Steam Railway

2 hrs   Mar–Oct & Dec

This steam railway runs between Aviemore and Boat of Garten and on to Broomhill, near Nethy Bridge. Enjoy your journey through unspoilt countryside with mountainous views.

* 2–Star Visitor Attraction

Location
Boat of Garten is off A95 between
Aviemore & Grantown-on-Spey, or off
B970 between Nethy Bridge &
Inverdruie

Opening
Daily; end Mar–end Oct & selected
days in Dec. Please phone for details

Admission
Adult £9, Child £4.50, under 5's go free

Contact
Aviemore Station,
Dalfaber Road, Aviemore,
Invernessshire PH22 1PY

t 01479 810725
w strathspeyrailway.co.uk

920 Ballindalloch

Ballindalloch Castle

2 hrs+   Easter–Sep

A magnificent C16 Castle set in romantic gardens with rare paintings and Wemyss pottery.

* Ballindalloch herd of Aberdeen Angus cattle
* Golf course

Location
14 miles NE of Grantown-on-Spey on A95

Opening
Easter–30 Sep Sun–Fri 10.30am–5pm

Admission
Please phone for detail

Contact
Ballindalloch, Banffshire AB37 9AX

t 01807 500206
w ballindallochcastle.co.uk
e enquiries@ballindallochcastle.co.uk

921 Balmaha

Loch Lomond National Nature Reserve

3 hrs   All year

Famous the world over for its beauty, the reserve includes five of the loch's islands, each supporting oak woodland, and the mouth of the River Endrick has fen, grassland and swamp woodland. Visit May–June for woodland wildlife and winter-early spring for wildfowl.

* Wonderful camp & picnic site
* Remains of a C13 parish church

Location
Inchailloch is reached by ferry from the Balmaha boatyard.

Opening
Daily; at any reasonable time; wardens present Apr–Sep

Admission
Free

Contact
Loch Lomond & Trossochs National Park, Balmaha Visitor Centre

t 01389 722600

StrathspaySteamRailway©

922 Barcaldine

Scottish Sealife & Marine Sanctuary

2½ hrs   All year

Scotland's leading marine animal rescue centre cares for abandoned seal pups, and also has resident common seals and otters.

* 3-Star Marine Attraction
* New displays added regularly

Location
10 miles N of Oban on A82

Opening
Daily; Feb–Nov 10am–6pm (last admission 5pm); Dec & Jan w/e hols

Admission
Adult £7.95, Child £5.50, Concs £6.50

Contact
Sanctuary, Barcaldine by Oban, Argyll PA37 1SE

t 01631 720386
w sealsanctuary.co.uk
e oban@sealife.fsbusiness.co.uk

923 Birsay

Kirbuster Museum

1 hr+   Apr–Oct

The custodian at this folk museum describes the farming life of the past. The museum has the last traditional peat-burning central hearth and stone neuk bed.

* Putting green
* Livestock in grounds

Location
In Kirbuster, Birsay

Opening
Daily; 1 Apr–end Oct 10am–4pm

Admission
Free

Contact
Kirbuster, Birsay
Orkney KW17 2LR

t 01856 771268
m orkney.gov.uk/heritage
e museum@orkney.gov.uk

924 Carrbridge

Landmark Forest Theme Park

5–6 hrs   All year

Scotland's favourite heritage park, Landmark has a wide range of fun, discovery and adventure activities for all ages in all weather, including wild water coaster, a red squirrel nature trail, steam-powered sawmill and a wildforest maze.

* 4-Star Speciality Attraction
* Treetop trail

Location
7 miles N of Aviemore, 23 miles S of Inverness just off A9 at Carrbridge

Opening
Daily; Nov–Mar 10am–5pm;
April–mid July 10am–6pm;
Mid Jul–mid Aug 10am–7pm; Sep–Oct 10am–5pm

Admission
Adult £8.85, Child £6.40, Under-4s free

Contact
Main Street, Carrbridge, Invernessshire PH23 3AJ

t 01479 841613
w landmark-centre.co.uk
e landmarkcentre@btconnect.com

925 Corrigal

Corrigall Farm Museum

2 hrs   Mar–Oct

This museum interprets the farming and domestic life of the people of Orkney from the C18 to C20. You can also see the North Ronaldsay sheep that feed on seaweed.

* Various livestock
* Peat fires

Location
Signed from the main
Kirkwall–Stromness road

Opening
Mar–Oct Mon–Sat 10.30am–1pm &
2pm–5pm, Sun 2pm–7pm

Admission
Free

Contact
Midhouse, Corrigall,
Harray KW17

t 01856 771411
w orkney.gov.uk/heritage
e museum@orkney.gov.uk

926 Culloden

Culloden

2–4 hrs   All year

This was the site of one of the most infamous battles in Scottish history, when more than 1,500 Jacobites were killed. Today it is a poignant and haunting location. The visitor centre has a fascinating exhibition, including an audio-visual programme.

* Living history presentation in the summer
* Tours taken by guides in full highland dress

Location
On B9006, 5 miles E of Inverness

Opening
Visitor centre: Daily; 1 Feb–31 Mar &
1 Nov–31 Dec 11am–4pm;
1 Apr–31 Oct 9am–6pm

Admission
Adult £5, Child £3.75, Concs £3.75

Contact
Culloden Moor. Inverness,
Highlands IV2 5EU

t 01463 790607
w nts.org.uk
e culloden@nts.org.uk

927 Dornoch

Historylinks Museum

1 hr+   May–Sep

This small museum is packed with 7,000 years of history – the treachery and violence of the Picts and Vikings, feuding clans, and the shameful burning of Scotland's last condemned witch.

* Activities & quizzes
* Dressing up for children

Location
In Dornoch town centre, 2 miles from
A9

Opening
Easter–Oct Mon–Fri 10am–4pm

Admission
Adult £2, Child Free

Contact
The Meadows, Dornoch,
Sutherland IV25 3SF

t 01862 811275
w historylinks.org.uk
e historylinks@connectfree.co.uk

Loch Ness Monster Exhibition Centre

4 hrs   All year

Loch Ness 2000 is the Highlands' most popular visitor attraction, offering a fully automated seven-room walk-through story of Loch Ness.

* 4-Star Speciality Attraction
* Boat trips on Loch Ness in summer

Location
14 miles S of Inverness & 20 miles N of Fort Augustus on A82

Opening
Easter-May 9.30am-5pm, Jun & Sep 9am-6pm, Jul-Aug 9am-8pm, Nov-Easter 10am-3.30pm

Admission
Adults £5.95, Child £4, Seniors £4.50

Contact
Drumnadrochit,
Invernessshire IV63 6TU

t 01456 450573
w loch-ness-scotland.com
e info@loch-ness-scotland.com

Elgin Cathedral

2 hrs   All year

The superb remains of a majestic and beautiful C13 cathedral which was almost destroyed in 1390 by Alexander Stewart, the infamous Wolf of Badenoch. You can also visit the bishop's home at Spynie Palace, two miles north of the town.

* 4-Star Historic Site Attraction

Location
On A96

Opening
Daily; Apr-Sep 9.30am-6.30pm;
Oct-Mar Mon-Wed & Fri-Sat
9.30am-4.30pm & Sun 2pm-4.30pm;
Closed Thurs in winter & 25, 26 Dec

Admission
Adult £3, Child £1, Concs £2.30
Joint ticket available with Spynie Palace

Contact
Historic Scotlandf, Longmore House,
Salisbury Place, Edinburgh EH9 1SH

t 01343 547171
w historic-scotland.gov.uk
e hs.explorer@scotland.gov.uk

Moray Firth Wildlife Centre

2 hrs+   Mar-Dec

A wildlife centre with exhibitions about dolphins, ospreys, otters and wildfowl. Run by the Whale and Dolphin Conservation society with children's activities available throughout the summer

* Nature reserve adjacent
* Wildlife activity holidays

Location
On A96 at the mouth of the Spey, 5 miles N of Fochabers

Opening
Feb-Mar Sat, Sun 10.30am-5pm
Daily; Apr-Oct 10.30am-5pm
Oct-Dec Please phone for details

Admission
Free

Contact
Fochabers,
Moray IV32 7PJ

t 01343 820339
w mfwc.co.uk
e enquiries@mfwc.co.uk

931 Fort William

Vertical Descents

3 hrs+   All year

This adventure centre offers canyoning, white-water rafting, paint-balling, funyakking, adventure holidays, adrenalin sports, adventure travel, mountain-biking, abseiling, and a bridge swing (like a bungee with a swing). No previous experience required.

* All specialised equipment available
* Some activities not suitable for younger children

Location
Off A82, 7 miles S of Fort Willaim

Opening
Daily; from 9am

Admission
£30 (half-day canyoning,
£35 (half-day funyaking)

Contact
Inchree Falls, Inchree, Onich, Fort
William PH33 6SE

t 01855 821593
w activities-scotland.com
e info@activities-scotland.com

932 Fort William

Treasures of the Earth

1 hr   Feb–Dec

One of Europe's finest collections of gemstones, crystals and fossils set in simulated caves, caverns and mining scenes.

* 2–Star Tourist Attraction

Location
In Corpach by Fort William

Opening
In summer 9.30am–7pm; in winter
10am–5pm
Closed Jan

Admission
Adult £3.50, Child £2, Concs £3

Contact
Corpach,
Fort William,
Inverness-shire PH33 7JL

t 01397 772283

933 Glencoe

Glencoe Visitor Centre

1 hr   All year

Built in 2002, this state-of-the-art eco-friendly centre is built from timber, insulated with sheep's wool and heated by burning local wood chips. The exhibition covers the ecology and geology of Glencoe, mountaineering and the history of Glencoe.

* Buildings designed as a clachan or settlement

Location
On A82, between Glasgow & Fort
William

Opening
Daily; Mar 10am–4pm
Apr–Aug 9.30am–5.30pm
Sep–Oct 10am–5pm
Nov–Feb Thu–Sun 10am–4pm

Admission
Adult £4.50, Child £2.95, Concs £2.95

Contact
Ballchulish, Argyil PH39 4HX

t 01855 811307
w nts.org.uk
e sborland@nts.org.uk

934 Inverary

Inverary jail

1 hr+   All year

Sit and listen to trials in the 1820 courtroom. Talk to guides dressed as warders, prisoners and the matron. Visit the two prisons and experience the sounds and smells as they would have been.

* View a Black maria prison transport vehicle
* Try the crank machine, whipping table & hammocks

Location	Admission
Off A82/83 Glasgow–Campbeltown road	Adult £5.75, Child (4–16) £2.80, Concs £3.75
Opening	Contact
Daily; Apr–Oct 9.30am–6pm Nov–Mar 10am–5pm Last admission 1 hr before closing	Church Square, Inveraray Argyll PA32 8TX
	t 01499 302381
	w inverarayjail.co.uk
	e inverarayjail@btclick.com

935 Inverness

Inverness Dolphin Cruises

1 hr+   Mar–Oct

Enjoy a 1½ hour cruise on the *Serenity* out on the Moray Firth, where you will see the most northerly resident colony of dolphins in the world, common and grey seals, porpoise, Minke whales, red kites and ospreys.

* Room for 90 passengers
* Commentary from professional guide

Location	Admission
Boat leaves from Inverness harbour	Adult £10, Child £7.50, Concs £8
Opening	Contact
Daily; Mar–end Oct; cruises at 10.30am, 12 noon, 1.30pm, 3pm, 4.30pm (& 6pm in Jul & Aug)	Shore Street Quay, Shore Street Inverness IV1 1NF
	t 01463 717900
	w inverness-dolphin-cruises.co.uk
	e info@inverness-dolphin cruises.co.uk

936 Inverness

Inverness Terror Tour

1 hr+   All year

Lead by Davy the Ghost, this walking tour of horror and laughter takes you through the streets of Inverness, ending at the haunted tavern, where a free drink is provided.

* Witches, ghosts, torture & murders

Location	Contact
Outside the tourist information centre on Bridge Street	Tourist Information, Bridge Street, Inverness IV2 3BJ
Opening	t 07730 831069
Daily; 7pm	e davytheghost@btinternet.com
Admission	
Adult £6, Child £4, Concs £5.50	

937 Isle of Barra

Kisimul Castle

1 hr+   Apr–Sep

The historic restored seat of the MacNeils of Barra, chiefs of the Clan MacNeil. Located on an island, it is reached by a small boat from the village of Castlebay.

* Real & living castle
* Fabulous views of Castlebay

Location	Contact
In Castlebay, Isle of Barra, reached by a small boat	Castlebay, Isle of Barra, Western Isles HS9 5XD
Opening	t 01871 810313
Daily; Apr–Sep 9.30am–6.30pm	w historic-scotland.gov.uk
Admission	e hs.explorer@scotland.gsi.gov.uk
Adult £3.30, Child £1, Concs £2.50	

ArnolBlackhouse©

938 Isle of Lewis

The Blackhouse, Arnol

2 hrs   All year

Visit a traditional Isle of Lewis thatched house museum and visitor centre, fully furnished, complete with attached barn, byre, stackyard and peat fire.

* Guided tours all day
* Interactive displays

WC ♿

Location
In Arnol village, Isle of Lewis

Opening
Apr–Sep Mon–Sat 9.30am–6.30pm;
Oct–Mar Mon–Sat 9.30am–4.30pm

Admission
Adult £3, Child £1, Concs £2.30

Contact
Arnol, Isle of Lewis,
Western Isles HS2 9DB

t 01851 710395
w historic-scotland.gov.uk
e hs.explorer@scotland.gsi.gov.uk

939 Isle of Raasay

Raasay Outdoor Centre

4 hrs+   Apr–Oct

Raasay Outdoor Centre is situated in the historic mansion of Raasay House. Try your hand at sailing around the seas of Skye, kayaking around Raasay's sheltered bays or rock climbing and abseiling in some of the island's most beautiful locations.

* Whole range of outdoor activities
* Café & fine restaurant

WC ⛟ 🍴

Location
Isle of Raasay is a 15 minute ferry journey from the Isle of Skye. There is a direct bus route from Inverness & Glasgow

Opening
Daily; Apr–Oct 8am–11pm or fully residential

Admission
Free (activities range from £22.50)

Contact
Rassay House,
Isle of Raasay, by Kyle IV408 8PB

t 01478 660266
w raasayoutdoorcentre.co.uk

940 Isle of Skye

Bella Jane Boat Trips

3 hrs+   Mar–Oct

Bella Jane Boat Trips take you to the world-famous Loch Coruisk and the seal colony at the heart of the Cuillin on the Isle of Skye. During the journey you will see a wealth of sea life and enjoy breathtaking scenery.

* 5–Star Visitor Attraction
* Excursions to Canna & Rum

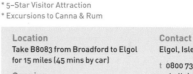

Location
Take B8083 from Broadford to Elgol for 15 miles (45 mins by car)

Opening
Daily; Mar–Oct

Admission
£10–£20
Please book in advance

Contact
Elgol, Isle of Skye, IV49 9BJ

t 0800 731 3089 (7.30am–10am)
w bellajane.co.uk
e bella@bellajane.co.uk

941 Isle of Skye

Family's Pride II Glassbottom Boat Trips

1 hr   Mar–Oct

Cruise in the spectacular Bay of Islands in a glass-bottomed boat. See seals, birds and porpoises above deck, then step below and see the amazing sights of the underwater world.

* Frequent daily sailings
* Stunning coastal scenery

Location
In Broadford, Isle of Skye, 8 miles from the Skye Bridge. There is a free minibus collection at the Information Centre if required

Opening
Daily; Mar–Oct 10.30am–4.45pm

Admission
Adult £9.50, Under-12s £4.75

Contact
5 Scullamus, Breakish, Isle of Skye IV42 8QB

t 0800 783 2175
w glassbottomboat.co.uk

942 Isle of Skye

The Bright Water Visitor Centre

2 hrs   Apr–Oct

A unique child-friendly, interactive experience that unfolds the area's dramatic history and celebrates the wealth of local wildlife and the memory of Gavin Maxwell.

* 3–Star Speciality Attraction
* Visit Stevenson Lighthouse

Location
Take the Kyleakin exit at the Skye roundabout (at the end of the Skye Bridge)

Opening
Apr–Oct Mon–Fri 10am–4pm

Admission
Free (donations requested)

Contact
The Pier, Kyleakin, Isle of Skye IV41 8PL

t 01599 530040
w eileanban.com
e enquiries@eileanban.com

HighlandFolk©

Kincraig

Working Sheepdogs

2 hrs   All year

Participate in the working day of a Highland shepherd and his dogs. Help to shear a sheep and bottle-feed orphan lambs. Meet the friendly pups.

* 2–Star Wildlife and Nature Attraction
* Live performances

Location
On a working farm, 5 miles S of Aviemore & 5 miles N of Kingussie on B9152

Opening
Daily; demonstrations at 12 noon & 4pm;
Private bookings available

Admission
Please phone for details

Contact
Leault Farm,
Kincraig,
Invernessshire PH21 1LZ

t 01540 651310

---

944 Kingussie

Highland Folk Museum, Newtonmore

3 hrs   All year

A fascinating glimpse into 300 years of Highland life at this recreation of a thriving C18 farming township with clockmaker's workshop and working croft.

* 4–Star Visitor Attraction
* Vintage buses on site

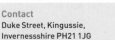

Location
On A86, ¼ mile north of Newtonmore

Opening
Please phone for details

Admission
Please phone for details

Contact
Duke Street, Kingussie,
Invernessshire PH21 1JG

t 01540 661307
w highlandfolk.com
e highlandfolk@highland.gov.uk

---

945 Kingussie

Highland Wildlife Park

3 hrs+   All year

Enjoy a wild day out in the Cairngorm National Park. Drive through a scenic main reserve and explore the rest of the park on foot. There are wolves, otters, reindeer, lynx, pine martens, capercaillie and more.

* 4–Star Visitor Attraction
* Educational tours & talks

Location
Off A9, 7 miles S of Aviemore, 2½ hrs from Edinburgh

Opening
Daily; Apr–Oct 10am–6pm; Jun–Aug 10am–7pm; Nov–Mar 10am–4pm; last entry 2 hrs before closing; if heavy ice or snow please phone before visit

Admission
Please phone for details

Contact
Kincraig, Kingussie,
Invernessshire PH21 1NL

t 01540 651270
w highlandwildlifepark.org
e info@highlandwildlifepark.org

946 Kirkwall

Scapa Flow Visitor Centre & Museum

2 hrs+   May–Oct

A British Navy base in the First and Second World War, Scapa Flow is now a museum with many interesting relics from the war days. Advance booking is required for ferry from Houton to Liness.

* Artefacts from HMS *Hampshire*
* Display on HMS *Royal Oak*

Location	Contact
Near Lyness Pier, on the island of Hoy	Lyness, Hoy, Kirkwell, Orkney KW16 3NU
Opening	t 01856 791300
Daily; May–Oct Mon–Fri 9am–4.30pm & Sat–Sun 9.30am–6pm	w orkney.gov.uk/heritage
	e museum@orkney.gov.uk
Admission	
Free	

947 Kirkwall

The Orkney Museum

3 hrs   Apr–Oct

Discover the story of Orkney, from prehistory to C21, at this museum with four floors of exhibits.

* C16 Scottish vernacular architecture
* Archaeological and social history collections

Location	Contact
Kirkwall, Orkney, opposite St Magnus Cathedral	Tankerness House, Broad Street, Kirkwall, Orkney KW15 1DH
Opening	t 01856 873191
Apr–Oct Mon–Sat 10.30am–12.30pm & 1.30pm–5pm	w orkney.gov.uk/heritage
	e museum@orkney.gov.uk
Admission	
Free	

948 Kyle of Lochalsh

Seaprobe *Atlantis*

1–2 hrs   Apr–Oct

In this fabulous semi-submersible, glass-bottomed boat, you can enjoy views of a Second World War shipwreck, kelp forests, fish, jellyfish, sea urchins, starfish and occasional dolphins and whales. Visit seal and bird colonies, and look out for otters.

* 4-Star Visitor Attraction

Location	Admission
Off A87 at Kyle of Lochalsh; the boat departs from below the Lochalsh Hotel (follow the brown tourist signs)	*For 1 hr trip:* Adult £12, Child (3–12) £6
Opening	**Contact**
Daily; Easter–Oct 10am–evening	Old Ferry Slipway, Kyle of Lochalsh, Ross-shire
	t 0800 9804846
	w seaprobeatlantis.com

949 Lairg

Ferrycroft Countryside Centre

2 hrs   Apr–Oct

A hands-on family-oriented visitor centre displaying the natural and archaeological history of an area rich in beauty and wildlife.

* Indoor & outdoor play areas
* Countryside ranger

Location	Contact
Central Sutherland, on the shore of Loch Shin	Lairg, Sutherland IV27 4TP
Opening	t 01549 402160
Daily; Apr, May, Sep & Oct 10am–4pm Jun–Aug 9.30am–5pm	w lairghighlands.org.uk
Admission	
Free	

TombEagles©

950 Lewis

Lewis Karting Centre

Varies All year

Arrive and drive at this outdoor karting centre. There are karts for hire for children aged 8 upwards and a Kiddie Kart section for the younger driver on a safe inflatable circuit.

* Sessions include briefing, kit & 12 minutes on the track

Location
4 miles S of Stornoway on A859

Opening
Thu, Fri 3pm–8pm & Sat 12pm–8pm
Wed–Thu 2pm–10pm by arrangement only

Admission
Per session (12 mins): **Adult £5**
Child (13–16) £6 Child (8–12) £5

Contact
Creed Enterprise Park, Lochs Rd, Stornoway, Isle of Lewis HS2 9JN

t 01851 700222
w lewiscarclub.co.uk

951 Liddle

Tomb of The Eagles

1–2 hrs All year

A visit to the Tomb of the Eagles gives a valuable insight into the life of our neolithic ancestors. Visitors are given the opportunity to handle some of the original artefacts.

* Guided tour of Bronze Age house
* Children's indoor play area

Location
South Ronaldsay, Orkney. Overlooking the Pentland Firth, mainland Orkney

Opening
Daily; Apr–Oct 9.30am–6pm; Nov–Mar 10am–12pm (or by arrangement)

Admission
Please phone for details

Contact
Liddle , South Ronaldsay, Orkney KW17 2RW

t 01856 831339
w tomboftheeagles.co.uk
e info@tomboftheeagles.co.uk

952 Mallaig

Mallaig Marine World

3 hrs **All year**

A highly original marine aquarium and exhibition featuring the sea life of the west coast of Scotland. Models, photographs and a unique video (filmed locally) bring the story of Mallaig's fishing fleet to life.

* Guided tours for groups available on request
* Video presentations

WC

Location
40 miles W of Fort William, in NW Highlands, or a short ferry trip from Armadale on Skye

Opening
Please phone for details

Admission
Please phone for details

Contact
The Harbour , Mallaig, Invernessshire PH41 4PX

t 01687 462292
w road-to-the-isles.org.uk/marine-world

953 Shapinsay

Balfour Castle

2 hrs **May–Sep**

A Victorian castle surrounded by landscaped grounds and a plantation of trees. Orkney afternoon tea included.

* Victorian walled gardens
* Ferry trip included

WC

Location
2 minutes from Shapinsay Harbour, reached by car ferry from Kirkwall on Orkney mainland, a 25-minute journey

Opening
May–Sep for guided tours every Sun; Other times by prior arrangement only

Admission
Adult £17, Child £8.50 includes ferry charge

Contact
Shapinsay, Orkney KW17 2DY

t 01856 711282
w balfourcastle.co.uk
e enquiries@balfourcastle.com

954 Spean Bridge

Monster Activities

2 hrs **All year**

Go rafting in a beautiful Highland river with large grade-3 rapids guaranteed. A host of other activities includes canoeing, kayaking, sailing, waterskiing, mountain-biking, abseiling, and archery. A range of accredited courses available for all ages and abilities.

* Equipment for hire
* Qualified instructors and full safety licence (AALA)

WC

Location
On A82, between Fort William & Inverness

Opening
Daily; 9.30am-5.30pm

Admission
Depends on activity, please phone for details

Contact
Great Glen Water Park, South Laggan, Spean Bridge, Invernessshire

t 01809 501340
w monsteractivities.com
e info@monsteractivities.com

955 Westray

Westray Heritage Centre

2 hrs+ **May-Sep**

A uniquely artistic, permanent natural history display, with annual historic exhibitions, hands-on children's models, family history displays and crafts.

* 4-Star Visitor Attraction

WC

Location
Located on the island of Westray

Opening
May–Sep;
Other times by arrangement. Please phone for details

Admission
Adult £2, Child 50p, Concs£1.50

Contact
9 Gill Pier, Westray, Orkney KW17 2DL

t 01857 677231

956 Ancrum

Harestanes Countryside Visitor Centre

2 hrs+   Apr–Oct

This visitor centre has lots of events, exhibitions and walks for all the family and the biggest play park in the Borders.

* Play park
* Exhibitions, events & activities

Location
3 miles N of Jedburgh. Well signed from A68, A698 & B6400

Opening
Daily; Easter–31 Oct 10am–5pm

Admission
Free

Contact
c/o Scottish Borders Council, Ancrum, Jedburgh TD8 6UQ

t 01835 830306
e harestanes@scotborders.gov.uk

957 Ayr

Tam O'Shanter Experience

2 hrs   All year

Laser– disk technology and theatrical effects brings Robbie Burns' best–loved tale to life in a special audio–visual presentation.

* 3–Star Speciality Attraction
* Perfect base to explore Burns' rich heritage

Location
In the village of Alloway 5 miles S of Ayr town centre

Opening
Daily; Apr–Sep 10am–5.30pm; Oct–Mar 10am–5pm

Admission
Adult £5, Child £3, Concs £3

Contact
Murdochs Lone Alloway , Ayr, Ayrshire KA7 4PQ

t 01292 443700
w burnsheritagepark.com
e info@burnsheritagepark.com

958 Berwick-upon-Tweed

Fishwick Mains Amazing Maize Maze

2–3 hrs   Jul–Sep

Visitors to this maize maze are provided with a booklet of clues, riddles and puzzles to help you find your way through the intricate labyrinth.

* New maze design each year
* Over 3 miles of paths

Location
Off B6461, 5 miles W of the Berwick-upon-Tweed bypass on the N side of the River Tweed

Opening
Daily; mid Jul–mid Sep 11am–6pm; last admission 4pm

Admission
Adult £4, Child £3

Contact
Nr Paxton, Berwick-upon-Tweed, Berwickshire TD15 1XQ

t 01289 386111
w fishwickmaze.com

959 Berwick-upon-Tweed

Paxton House & Country Park

2 hrs   Apr–Oct

This beautiful C18 Palladian country house has lots of activities for young people. Younger children can follow the Paxton ted house trail and for older children there's an activity guide. Outside there is a nature detective trail and an adventure playground.

* Winner of a BT Environment Week Challenge award
* Children's summer activity club

Location
On B6461, 3 miles from A1 Berwick-upon-Tweed bypass

Opening
House Daily; Apr–Oct 11am–5pm
Garden Daily; Apr–Oct 10am–sunset

Admission
House & garden Adult £6, Child £3
Garden only Adult £3, Child £1.50

Contact
Berwick-upon-Tweed TD15 1SZ

t 01289 386291
w paxtonhouse.com
e info@paxtonhouse.com

Threave©

960 Caerlaverock

WWT Caerlaverock Wetlands Centre

4 hrs+   All year

Caerlaverock has a 1,400-acre wild nature reserve with modern hides and observation towers linked by a network of screened approaches. In winter see thousands of barnacle geese and watch twice-daily feeds of wild swan.

* Self-catering accommodation available
* Badger-watching & summer nature trail

Location
Located 9 miles SE of Dumfries along the Solway Coast Heritage Trail

Opening
Daily; 10am–5pm;

Admission
Adult £4.40, Child £2.70, Concs £3.60

Contact
Eastpark Farm, Caerlaverock, Dumfriesshire DG1 4RS

t 01387 770200
w wwt.org.uk
e info.caerlaverock@wwt.org.uk

961 Castle Douglas

Cream O'Galloway

3 hrs   All year

A natural experience for the whole family, in which you can enjoy the adventure playground, nature trails, dog walk and beautiful scenery.

* 4–Star Visitor Attraction
* Ice cream factory with viewing gallery

Location
In the SW of Scotland. From A75 near Gatehouse-of-Fleet, take the road to Sandgreen. Turn left after 1½ miles

Opening
Please phone for details

Admission
£1.50 per person, under-5s & over-60s free

Contact
Rainton, Gatehouse-of-Fleet, Castle Douglas DG7 2DR

t 01557 814040
w creamogalloway.co.uk
e info@creamogalloway.co.uk

962 Castle Douglas

Threave Garden, House & Estate

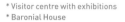

3 hrs   All year

A garden for all seasons, best known for its springtime display of daffodils. Herbaceous beds are colourful in summer and the trees and heather striking in autumn.

* Visitor centre with exhibitions
* Baronial House

Location
Off A75 near Castle Douglas

Opening
House: 1 Apr–31 Oct Wed–Fri & Sun (guided tours)
Garden: Daily; 9.30am–sunset

Admission
Please phone for details

Contact
Castle Douglas,
Dumfries & Galloway

t 01556 502575
w nts.org.uk

963 Coldingham

St Abb's Head Nature Reserve

2-4 hrs   All year

This National Nature Reserve is an important site for cliff-nesting seabirds in summer. Visitors can watch them wheeling and diving below the high cliffs and take guided walks with a ranger.

* Formed by extinct volcano
* National Nature Reserve

Location
Off A1107, 2 miles N of Coldingham

Opening
Daily; at any reasonable time

Admission
Free

Contact
Ranger's Cottage,
Northfield, St Abb's,
Eyemouth, Borders TD14 5QF

t 018907 71443
w nts.org.uk

964 Creetown

Creetown Heritage Museum

1 hr   Apr–Oct

An exhibition of Creetown past and present, shown through a large collection of historical photographs, artefacts, audio and video presentations and hands-on activities.

* 3-Star Speciality Museum
* Wigtown Bay nature reserve

Location
500 yards off A75 between Gatehouse-of-Fleet & Newton Stewart

Opening
Apr–Oct Sun–Tue & Thu–Fri 11am–4pm; Easter week open daily; Jun–Aug also open Wed

Admission
Adult £1.50, Child 75p, Concs 75p

Contact
91 St John Street, Creetown,
Newton Stewart DG8 7JE

t 01671 820471
w creetown-heritage-museum.org

965 Dalbeattie

Dalbeattie Museum

1 hr   Apr–Sep

This museum gives an insight into what we used in the past. Visitors can view and handle household utensils and children's games, as well as agricultural, quarrying and bobbin-making tools. There is also a model of the *Titanic* and an exhibition on the disaster.

* True story of First Officer Murdoch of *Titanic* fame

Location
On the corner of Southwick Road & High Street in the town centre

Opening
Daily; Apr–Sep Mon–Sat 10am–4pm & Sun 2pm–4pm

Admission
Adult £1, Accompanied child free,
Concs 50p

Contact
1 Southwick Road,
Dalbeattie DG5 4BS

t 01556 610437
w dumfriesmuseum.demon.co.uk

966 Dumfries

Caerlaverock Castle

1 hr+   All year

With its moat, twin-towered gatehouse, and imposing battlements, Caerlaverock Castle is the epitome of the medieval stronghold. The castle's turbulent history owes much to its proximity to England which brought it into border conflicts.

* Children's adventure park & a nature trail.
*Video presentation available

Location	Contact
8 m SE of Dumfries on the B725	Caerlaverock, Dumfries, Dumfriesshire DG1 4RU
Opening	
Daily; Apr–Sept 9.30am–6.30pm , Oct–Mar 9.30am–4.30pm	t 01387 770244
	w aboutbritain.com/ CaerlaverockCastle
Admission	
Adult £4.00, Child 1.60, Concs £3.00	

967 Dumfries

Dumfries Museum & Camera Obscura

1-2 hrs   All year

Set in its own gardens, Dumfries Museum & Camera Obscura is situated in a converted windmill. From the camera you can see a panoramic view of Dumfries. The museum is a treasure house of history in Dumfries & Galloway.

* Museum trail & talking toys tour
* Children's worksheets available

Location	Admission
On the Maxwelltown bank of the River Nith overlooking the hilltop between Old Bridge & St Michael's Bridge	Museum: Free, Camera Obscura: £1.55 per person Concs 80p
Opening	**Contact**
Daily; Apr–Sep Mon–Sat 10am–5pm & Sun 2pm–5pm; Oct–Apr Tue–Sat 10am–1pm & 2pm–5pm	The Observatory, Dumfries DG2 7SM
	t 01387 253374
	w dumgal.gov.uk/museum
	e dumfriesmuseum@dumgal.gov.uk

968 Dumfries

Neverland Adventure Play Centre

1 hr   All year

Neverland is an indoor adventure play centre for children up to age 10. Themed on J. M. Barrie's story of *Peter Pan*, children can meet all their favourite characters.

* Suitable for children 1–10 years old
* Set in original site of novel

Location	Contact
In Dumfries town centre, reached via A75, A76, A701 or A74(M)	Park Lane, Dumfries, Dumfriesshire DG1 2AX
Opening	
Daily; 10am–5pm	t 01387 249100
	e Never.land@btclick.com
Admission	
£2.50 per child	

969 Dumfries

Old Bridge House Museum

1 hr+   Apr–Sep

Visit Dumfries' oldest house, now a museum of everyday life. You can see the family kitchen, nursery and bedroom of a Victorian home and pay a visit to an early dentist's surgery.

* 3-Star Visitor Award
* Worksheets for children

Location
At the end of the Old Bridge on the Maxwelltown bank of the River Nith

Opening
Daily; Apr–Sep Mon–Sat 10am–5pm & Sun 2pm–5pm

Admission
Free

Contact
Mill Road, Dumfries DG2 7BE

t 01387 256904
w dumgal.gov.uk/museum
e dumfriesmuseum@dumgal.gov.uk

970 Dumfries

Robert Burns Centre

1 hr   All year

Situated in an old mill building, this museum is dedicated to the history and literature of the poet Robert Burns.

* 4-Star Visitor Award
* Film theatre

Location
On Mill Road by the River Nith at the Old Wear on Maxwelltown Bank

Opening
Daily; Apr–Sep Mon–Sat 10am–8pm & Sun 2pm–5pm; Oct–Mar Tue–Sat 10am–1pm & 2pm–5pm

Admission
Free

Contact
Mill Road, Dumfries DG2 7BE

t 01387 264808
w dumgal.gov.uk/museum
e dumfriesmuseum@dumgal.gov.uk

RobertBurnsCenter©

971 Dumfries

Robert Burns House

1 hr   All year

This is the house in which the famous poet Robert Burns died. It has been preserved in its original condition and contains many original artefacts and manuscripts.

* Children's worksheets available

Location
Burns Street, off Shakespeare Street, next to Brooms Road car park

Opening
Daily; in summer Mon–Sat 10am–5pm & Sun 2pm–5pm; in winter Tue–Sat 10am–1pm, 2pm–5pm

Admission
Free

Contact
Burns Street, Dumfries DG1 2PS
t 01387 255297

972 Dumfries

Shambellie House Museum of Costume

1 hr+   Apr–Oct

Step back in time and experience Victorian and Edwardian elegance in this museum showing original costumes in appropriate room settings.

* Free croquet hire
* Regular events for families

Location
7 miles S of Dumfries on A710, Solway Coast Road

Opening
Daily; Apr–Oct 10am–5pm

Admission
Adult £3, Under-13s Free, Concs £2

Contact
New Abbey, Dumfries Dumfriesshire DG2 8HQ
t 01387 850375
w nms.ac.uk

973 Dundonald

Dundonald Castle

½–1 hr   Apr–Oct

The castle's association with the Stewarts gives Dundonald its special importance. It was built by Robert Stewart in 1371 to mark his succession to the throne of Scotland.

* 4–Star Historic Attraction
* Available for wedding ceremonies

Location
In the village of Dundonald on A759, 6 miles from Ayr & 3 miles from Kilmarnock

Opening
Daily; Apr–Oct 10am–5pm

Admission
Adult £2.50, Child £1.25, Concs £1.25

Contact
Winehouse Yett, Dundonald, Ayrshire
t 01563 851489
w historic-scotland.gov.uk
e hs.historic@scotland.gov.uk

974 Eyemouth

Eyemouth Museum

1 hr   Apr–Oct

This museum has exhibitions on fishing, farming, milling, wheelwrighting, and blacksmithing. One of the highlights is a large tapestry which commemorates the great east-coast fishing disaster of 1881 in which 189 local fishermen were drowned.

* Visit Scotland 3-Star attraction

Location
In the centre of Eyemouth

Opening
Daily; Apr–Jun & Sep, Mon–Sat, 10am–5pm, Sun 12 noon–2pm; Jul–Aug, Mon–Sat, 10am–5.30pm, Sun 12 noon–2pm; Oct, Mon–Sat, 10am–4pm

Admission
Adult £3, Child free, Concs £1.50

Contact
Auld Kirk, Manse Road, Eyemouth
t 018907 50678

975 Fairlie

Kelburn Castle & Country Centre

4 hrs+   All year

Kelburn is a historic country park with a castle, gardens, waterfalls and exhibitions to visit, as well as outdoor pursuits such as horse-riding.

* Falconry centre
* Secret Forest

Location
On the A78 between Ayr & Greenock

Opening
Daily; Easter–Oct fully 10am–6pm;
Nov–Easter (grounds & riding centre only) daily 11am–5pm

Admission
Adult £5, Child £3.50, Concs £3.50

Contact
South Offices, Fairlie,
Ayrshire KA29 0BE

t 01475 568685
w kelburncountrycentre.com
e admin@kelburncountrycentre.com

976 Fenwick

Rowallan Activity Centre

2-4 hrs   All year

Whether you want to play football, learn to ride or discover the thrill of paintballing, this multi-functional indoor and outdoor centre has something for everyone.

* Soft play area
* New health club, climbing wall, swimming and more

Location
From A77 Glasgow–
Kilmarnock road (nr Fenwick) turn
(at the Fenwick Hotel) onto B751
towards Kilmaurs. The centre is 1 mile
on the left

Opening
Daily; 8am–late;

Admission
Free

Contact
Melklemosside, Fenwick,
Ayrshire KA3 6AY

t 01560 600769

977 Galston

Loudoun Castle Family Theme Park

4 hrs+   Apr–Sep

A great day out for all the family with rides and entertainment to suit all ages, in a historic setting.

* Twist & Shout roller-coaster
* New Dougall McDougal's farm

Location	**Contact**
On A719 on the edge of Galston	Galston, Ayrshire KA4 8PE
Opening	
Daily; Mid May–Aug 10am–5pm Open some days in Apr & Sep (please phone for details)	t 01563 822296 e loudouncastle@btinternet.com
Admission	
Please phone for details	

978   Dumfries

Gretna Green World Famous Blacksmith's Shop

1 hr+   All year

Visit the blacksmith's shop where many 16-year-olds got married after running away from England. The centre also has an exhibition about the history of Gretna Green, a coach museum with horse-drawn carriages, a native breeds' park with Highland cattle, and a play park.

* One of Scotland's earliest visitor attractions
* Site of thousands of weddings since C18

Location
On A74, just N of the border

Opening
Daily; Apr–Sep 9am– early evening
Oct–Mar 9am–5pm

Admission
Exhibition Adult £2.50, Child £2

Contact
Gretna Green Group Ltd,
Headless Cross, Gretna Green,
Dumfriesshire DG16 5EA

t 01461 338441
w gretnagreen.com
e info@gretnagreen.com

979   Hawick

Drumlanrig's Tower

1½ hrs   Apr–Oct

Drumlanrig's Tower interprets Hawick's turbulent history from medieval times, using the latest audio-visual technology. The exhibition is housed in a beautifully restored period building.

* Steve Hislop commemorative exhibition
* 4–Star Museum

Location
In the centre of Hawick, S of Selkirk on the A7 & W of Jedburgh on A698

Opening
Daily; Apr–Sep Mon–Sat 10am–5pm (5.30pm closing in Jul & Aug) & Sun 1pm–4pm

Admission
Adult £2.50, Concs £1.50,
Accompanied under-16s free
Scottish Border residents Free

Contact
Tower Knowe, Hawick,
Roxburgh TD9 9EN

t 01450 377615

980   Heathhall

Dumfries & Galloway Aviation Museum

3 hrs   All year

A fascinating collection of aircraft and memorabilia reaching back to the golden era of flight.

* 3–Star Award
* Huge collection of artefacts

Location
On the Heathhall Industrial Estate, easily accessed from A75 Dumfries bypass. From the town centre follow the A701 Edinburgh road

Opening
Easter–Oct Sat–Sun 10am–5pm;
Jul–Aug also Wed–Fri 11am–4pm;
Oct–Easter Sun only 11am–4pm

Admission
Adult £2.50, Child £1.50, Concs £1.50

Contact
Heathhall Industrial Estate
Heathhall, Dumfries DG13PH

t 01387 251623
w dumfriesaviationmuseum.com
e alammin@hotmail.com

981   Hirsel

Coldstream

4 hrs+   All year

The seat of the Home family, Coldstream has interesting grounds with a museum and craft centre, plus nature trails along a lake and into woodland.

* Birthplace of the Coldsteam Guards
* Once a rival to Gretna Green

Location
15 miles from Berwick-upon-Tweed on A698

Opening
Garden & Grounds: Daily; dawn–dusk
Museum: Daily; 9am–5pm

Admission
Admission Free, Car park £2

Contact
Douglas & Angus Estates,
Hirsel Country Park,
Hirsel TD12 4LP

t 01890 882834
w hirselcountrypark.co.uk

982 Innerleithen

Robert Smail's Printing Works

1-2 hrs   Jun–Sep

At this restored printing works, visitors will discover how the industry worked at the beginning of the C20. See the printing presses in action and try your hand at old-fashioned typesetting.

* Secrets of the printing works
* Shop

WC

RobertSmailPrintingWorks©

Location
6 miles E of Pebbles

Opening
1 Jun–30 Sep Thu–Mon 12pm–5pm
(1pm opening Sun); also open Good
Fri–Easter Mon

Admission
Adult £3.50, Concs £2.60

Contact
High Street,
Innerleithen, Borders

t 01896 830206
w nts.org.uk
e smail@nts.org.uk

983 Isle of Arran

Balmichael Visitor Centre

4 hrs+   All year

This centre occupies a restored farm. It has quad-bike tracks, an adventure playground, a putting green and a heritage area.

*4–Star Visitor Attraction
* Quad circuits & hill treks

Location
7 miles from Brodick over the hill via
the String Road, 3 miles from
Blackwaterfoot

Opening
Daily; in summer Mon–Sat 10am–5pm
& Sun 12pm–5pm; in winter closed
Mon & Tue

Admission
Please phone for details

Contact
Shiskine,
Isle Of Arran KA27 8DT

t 01770 860430
w thebalmichaelcentre.co.uk
e bvcltd@yahoo.com

984   Isle of Arran

Brodick Castle, Garden & Country Park

4 hrs+   Apr–Oct

With a history dating back to the Vikings, Brodick Castle offers a wonderful day out of heritage, nature and relaxation. The castle boasts an impressive collection of sporting pictures and trophies, while the gardens and park offer delightful trails.

* Waymarked trails & Wildlife garden
* Various events held throughout the year

Location
Take the ferry from Ardrossan to Brodick for the connecting bus to the castle

Opening
Castle: **Daily; 1 Apr–31 Oct**
11am–4.30pm (3.30pm closing in Oct)
Country park: **Daily; 9.30am–sunset**

Admission
Please phone for details

Contact
Isle of Arran

t **01770 302202**

---

985   Jedburgh

Jedburgh Castle Jail & Museum

1 hr+   Mar–Oct

A C19 reform prison with displays interpreting the history of Jedburgh.

* 3-Star Museum Attraction
* Outdoor play area

Location
Off A68, SE of Selkirk

Opening
Daily; Mar– Oct = Mon–Sat
10am–4.30pm & Sun 1pm–4pm

Admission
Adult £2,Concs £1.50,
Accompanied under-16s &
Scottish Border residents Free

Contact
Castlegate,
Jedburgh TD8 6QD

t **01835 864750**

---

986   Jedburgh

Jedforest Deer & Farm Park

3 hrs+   May–Oct

At this modern working farm you can see deer herds and rare breeds as well as your favourite farm animals.

* Birds of prey displays & tuition
* Feeding the animals

Location
5 miles S of Jedburgh on A68

Opening
Daily; May-Aug 10am–5.30pm;
Sep-Oct 11am–4.30pm

Admission
Please phone for details

Contact
Mervinslaw Estate,
Jedburgh,
Roxburghshire TD8 8PL

t **01835 840364**
w aboutscotland.com/jedforest/
e mervinslaw@ecosse.net

987 Jedburgh

Mary Queen of Scots Visitor Centre

1 hr   Mar–Nov

A fine C16 fortified house with period rooms set in formal gardens. The visitor centre tells
the story of the life of the tragic queen, who visited Jedburgh in 1566.

* One of Scotland's top visitor attractions
* See some of Mary's possessions

Location
On A68 in the centre of Jedburgh, SE of Selkirk

Opening
Daily; Early Mar–Nov Mon–Sat 10am–4.30pm & Sun 11am–4.30pm

Admission
Adult £3, Concs £2, Accommpanied under-16s & Scottish Borders residents Free

Contact
Queen Street, Jedburgh TD8 6EN

t 01835 863331

988 Kelso

Floors' Castle

2 hrs   Apr–Oct

This fairy-tale castle is set in parkland which abounds with fauna and wildlife. Look out for oyster catchers, herons, tawny owls and red squirrels or have fun in the adventure playground which has a flying fox, swings, a slippery dip and other fun games.

* Gallery room with the family's costume collection
* Works by well-known artists, including Matisse

Location
On the edge of Kelso

Opening
Daily; Apr–Oct 10am–4.30pm

Admission
Adult £5.75, Child £3.25, Concs £4.75

Contact
Kelso, Roxburghshire TD5 7SF

t 01573 223333
w floorscastle.com
e marketing@floorscastle.com

989 Kilmarnock

Galleon Centre

2 hrs+   All year

This leisure facility has a swimming pool and ice rink, as well as a games hall which is suitable for badminton, football, basketball and table tennis.

* Trampolining clubs
* Swimming & skating lessons

Location
Kilmarnock town centre (follow the signs)

Opening
Daily; Mon–Fri 7am–11pm, Sat 8am–6pm & Sun 9am–11pm

Admission
Adult £1, Child 80p, Concs 75p
Various activities priced separately

Contact
99 Titchfield Street, Kilmarnock KA1 1QY

t 01563 524014

990 Kilmarnock

The Garage

2 hrs+   All year

The Garage offers entertainment and fun for all the family. There is indoor karting and 12 lanes of bowling, plus a soft play area with ball pools, swings, slides and chutes.

* Helmets & safety suits provided
* Viewing gallery

Location
Off A77

Opening
Daily; 10am–12 midnight

Admission
Free (activities priced individually)

Contact
36–40 Grange Street, Kilmarnock

t 01563 573355
w www.garageleisure.co.uk
e thegarage@
  kilmarnock10freestyle.co.uk

991 Kilmarnock

Scottish Maritime Museum

 1 hr+ All year

Irvine Harbour was once one of Glasgow's main trading ports. There are many facilities from the Magnum Leisure Centre to bird watching on the river estuary. There are fine walks and rides with magnificent views of the Firth of Clyde on the beach.

* Guided tours throughout the day

Location
W of Kilmarnock on the A71.
10 min walk from Irvine train station

Opening
Daily; 10am–5pm

Admission
Adult £2.50, Concs £1.75

Contact
Harbourside, Irvine,
Ayrshire KA12 8QE

t 01294 278283
w scottishmaritimemuseum.org/irvine

992 Kilwinning

Dalgarven Mill Museum

 1 hr+ All year

A country-life museum and costume collection housed in a C16 restored grain mill.

* 3-Star Visitor Attraction
* River beach & wildflower meadows

Location
On A737 between Kilwinning & Dalry

Opening
Easter–Oct Tue–Sun 10am–5pm;
Nov–Easter Tue–Fri 10am–4pm &
Sat–Sun 10am–5pm

Admission
Please phone for details

Contact
Dalgarven Mill , Dalry Road,
Kilwinning, Ayrshire KA13 6PL

t 01294 552448
w dalgarvenmill.org.uk
e admin@dalgarvenmill.org.uk

993 Kirkcudbright

Galloway Wildlife Conservation Park

 2–3 hrs All year

This wildlife park has plenty to entertain all the family, including new South America exhibits, a play area, pets corner and free snake encounters depending on the weather.

* 27-acre site
* Over 200 animals

Location
1 mile from Kirkcudbright on B727,
turn up the hill at the Royal Hotel;
signed from A75

Opening
Daily; Mar–Oct 10am–5pm;
Nov–Feb Fri–Sun 10am–4pm

Admission
Adult £4.95, Child (4–15) £3.50,
Concs £4.50

Contact
Lochfergus Plantation, Kirkcudbright,
Dumfries & Galloway DG6 4XX

t 01557 331645
w gallowaywildlife.co.uk
e info@gallowaywildlife.co.uk

994 Kirkpatrick Fleming

Robert the Bruce's Cave

 1 hr+ Mar–Nov

This world-famous ancient monument marks the site where Robert the Bruce hid in a cave during the wars of independence.

* Fishing
* Cycling

Location
Follow the brown tourist signs
from Gretna

Opening
Daily; Mar–1 Nov 9.30am–9pm
(closing times may vary)

Admission
Adult 50p, Child 35p, Concs 35p

Contact
Cove Farm,
Kirkpatrick Fleming,
Dumfries & Galloway DG11 3AT

t 01461 800285
w brucescave.co.uk
e enquiries@brucescave.com

995 Largs

The Viking Experience

 1 hr · All year

Travel back in time to 825AD and experience the sounds and smells of a homestead beside a Norwegian fjord. Meet resident Vikings who will tell sagas associated with Viking life and culture. Visit the longhouse with views over the fjord and see longships moored outside.

* Shows begin regularly
* Viking myths and legends

Location
On the Largs seafront

Opening
Daily; Apr-Sep 10.30am-5.30pm
Oct & Mar 10.30am-3.30pm;
Nov & Feb Sat 12.30pm-3.30pm
Sun 10.30am-3.30pm

Admission
Adult £4, Child £3, Concs £3

Contact
Vikingar, Greenock Road, Largs,
Ayrshire KA30 8QL

t 01475 689777
w vikingar.co.uk
e info@vikingar.co.uk

996 Lauder

Thirlestane Castle

1 hr+ · Mar-Oct

Thirlestane is Scotland's fairy-tale castle. Family home of the Maitlands, it has fine furnishings, family treasures, historic toys and an exhibition on country life.

* Adventure play area & woodland walks
* 4-Star Visitor Attraction

Location
Follow castle signs from A68

Opening
May, Jun & Sep Sun & Wed- Fri 10am-
2.30pm Jul & Aug Sun-Fri
10am-2.30pm

Admission
Adult £5.50, Child £3, Concs £5

Contact
Lauder TD2 6RU

t 01578 722430
w thirlestanecastle.co.uk
e admin@thirlestanecastle.co.uk

997 Melrose

The Three Hills Roman Heritage Centre

1 hr · Apr-Oct

A modern exhibition of life on the Scottish Roman frontier. There are artefacts, gems, models, replicas, an audioguide, an amphitheatre and guided site walks.

* 2-Star Historic Attraction
* Take the Trimontium Walk (Thursdays)

Location
Off A6091 Melrose bypass, linking A1 & A68

Opening
Heritage Centre: Daily; 17 Mar-31 Oct
10.30am- 4.30pm (closed 1-2pm at weekends); 1 Nov-31 Mar on request
Walk: Apr-Oct Thu 1.30pm
(also Tue in Jul & Aug)

Admission
Adult £1.50, Child £1

Contact
The Ormiston, Market Square,
Melrose TD6 9NP

t 01896 822651
w trimontium.net

998 New Galloway

Galloway Red Deer Range

1-2 hrs · All year

Visitors can walk amongst and handle the red deer, as well as taking close-up photographs.

* Part of largest forest park in Britain
* Forested hills, wild & rugged moorland

Location
On A712, halfway between New Galloway & Newton Stewart; follow signs to car park

Opening
Please phone for details

Admission
Please phone for details

Contact
Laggan O Dee
New Galloway,
Dumfries & Galloway DG7 3SQ

t 07771 748401

999 Saltcoats

North Ayrshire Museum

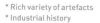

1 hr   **All year**

Visit the newly refurbished North Ayrshire Museum and discover the history of this region from prehistoric times to the present day.

* Rich variety of artefacts
* Industrial history

Location
Just off A78 & A738

Opening
Mon–Tue & Thu–Sat 10am–1pm & 2pm–5pm

Admission
Free

Contact
Manse Street,
Saltcoats,
Ayrshire KA21 5AA

t 01294 464174
e namuseum@north-ayrshyire.gov.uk
w north-ayrshire.gov.uk/museums

1000 St Sanquhar

Sanquhar Tolbooth Museum

 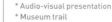

1 hr   **Apr–Sep**

Housed in a fine C18 tolbooth, this museum charts the life of ordinary Upper Nithsdale people. Exhibits recreate life in a local jail and tell the story of the mines and the local knitting tradition.

* Audio-visual presentation
* Museum trail

Location
At the end of the High Street in St Sanquhar town centre

Opening
Apr–Sep Tue–Sat 10am–1pm & 2pm–5pm, & Sun 2pm–5pm

Admission
Free

Contact
High Street
St Sanquhar DG4 6BN

t 01659 50186
w dumgal.gov.uk/museums
e dumfriesmuseum@dumgal.gov.uk

1001 Selkirk

Halliwell's House Museum

1-2 hrs   **Apr–Oct**

Step back in time in Halliwell's House and discover the building's former use as a home and ironmonger's shop.

* Guided tours (by arrangement)
* Children's play area

Location
Situated just off Market Place in the heart of Selkirk. Selkirk can be reached by A7 from Galashiels

Opening
DailyApr–Sep Mon–Sat 10am–5pm (5.30pm in Jul & Aug) & Sun 10am–12pm; Oct Mon–Sat 10am–4pm

Admission
Free

Contact
Halliwell's Close,
Market Place,
Selkirk TD7 4BL

t 01750 720096
e museums@scotborders.gov.uk

Halliwell'sHouse©

Index

Acknowledgements & Picture Credits

The Publishers would like to acknowledge the important contribution the British Tourist Authority made to this publication through the use of images from its website, *www.britainonview.com*

The publishers would like to thank The National Trust, The National Trust for Scotland and English Heritage who kindly supplied photographs for use with their entries.

The publishers would also like to thank all contributors who provided information, and particularly all those who kindly supplied photographs.

Compiled, edited and designed by Butler and Tanner. Edited by Helen Burge, Julian Flanders and Dara O'Hare. Design and layout by Lyn Davies and Carole McDonald. Special thanks to Carl Luke, Arran Macdonald and Jennie Golding.